THE NELSON A. ROCKEFELLER SERIES

*in Social Science and Public Policy*

*Brian J. L. Berry, 1992*
America's Utopian Experiments: Communal
Havens from Long-Wave Crises

*Giulietto Chiesa, with Douglas Taylor Northrop*
Transition to Democracy: Political Change
in the Soviet Union, 1987–1991

GIULIETTO CHIESA

WITH DOUGLAS TAYLOR NORTHROP

# Transition to Democracy

## POLITICAL CHANGE IN THE

## SOVIET UNION, 1987-1991

DARTMOUTH COLLEGE

Published by University Press of New England / Hanover and London

Dartmouth College
Published by University Press of New England, Hanover, NH 03755
© 1993 by Giulietto Chiesa
Printed in the United States of America  5  4  3  2  1
CIP data appear at the end of the book

TO FIAMMETTA

"Я не верю в прежние революционные пути и стараюсь понять шаг людской в былом и настоящем, для того, чтоб знать как идти с ним в ногу."

А. И. Герцен
*Собр. Соч. в 30 томах*
(Москва, 1960), Том XX, 586.

"I do not believe in the old revolutionary ways, but try to understand the march of mankind in the past and present so that I might know how to keep in step with it."

A. I. Herzen (Gertsen)
*Sobr. Soch. v 30 tomakh* (Moscow, 1960), 20:586.

# CONTENTS

In the last decade of the twentieth century, as the global community faces a growing array of complex and interrelated social problems, public policymakers increasingly will turn to scholars and practitioners for guidance. To chronicle and disseminate the substance of the compelling discussions that will result, the Nelson A. Rockefeller Center for the Social Sciences at Dartmouth College, in collaboration with University Press of New England, has inaugurated this series of books.

Rockefeller Series books will be disparate in content but united in a common approach: presenting ways in which social scientific expertise is brought to bear on public policy issues of current or historic importance. The specific topics addressed will be as diverse as were the interests and work of U.S. Vice-President Nelson A. Rockefeller, which included state and local government, the environment, Third World economic development, publicly funded art, racism and intergroup conflict, and the functioning of communities. Authors will assess historical or existing policies, as well as the need for new or adjusted policies, in a search for viable solutions to pressing social, political, and economic problems.

The Rockefeller Series draws upon two sources for its books, the annual Nelson A. Rockefeller Monograph Competition, and works generated from Rockefeller Center research programs or Center-sponsored conferences. Included in the latter are scholarly works originating in one or more of the eight social science departments associated with the Center.

The overriding goal of the Nelson A. Rockefeller Series is to stimulate academics, policymakers, practitioners, and the public to think about and understand societal processes and the public policy implications associated with them. It is our fondest hope that these volumes will promulgate innovative and useful ideas, for as P. W. Bridgman notes, "There is no adequate defense, except stupidity, against the impact of a new idea."

George J. Demko, Director of the Rockefeller Center

# PREFACE

This book could not have been completed without the help of the Kennan Institute for Advanced Russian Studies, a division of the Woodrow Wilson International Center for Scholars in Washington, D.C. As a Fellow of the Wilson Center from September 1989 until August 1990, I was fortunate enough to spend a sabbatical year studying the emergence of the first democratic legislature within the Soviet Union. Part of the resulting work has already been published in Italy (*Transizione alla Democrazia*, Rome: Lucarini Editore, 1990).

I am deeply grateful to the patrons of my Fellowship: Giuseppe Boffa, Robert Daniels, Moshe Lewin, Roy Medvedev, and Michal Reiman. Likewise I am grateful to the Kennan Institute, to its director Blair Ruble and to his staff for the assistance provided to me. Such a multiplicity of contacts, discussions, and interdisciplinary approaches as exist at the Institute could not but enrich my own work. I also prize the discussions I have had in Moscow with Soviet researchers Leonid Gordon, Alla Nazimova, Viktor Sheinits, and Valerii Tishkov, all of whom were kind enough to allow me to examine their "works in progress."

This book itself might best be described as a "work in progress," as it was completed while the events it describes continued to evolve. Many times it seemed to me as though my subject was melting before my eyes. No doubt the final composition of the resulting "alloy" will differ from that predicted by contemporary observers, myself included. Nevertheless, I can only hope that my prediction is a reasonably good one.

Finally, I must warmly thank Arthur Burris, whose diligence and intelligent cooperation as my research assistant greatly aided the preparation of the Italian version of this book, and Rodolfo Brancoli, to whom I am indebted for many suggestions about the final Italian version. Particular gratitude is due to Harvey Fergusson II for his brilliant translations of several of the later chapters of this book. Doug Northrop and I both also wish to thank James Felley and David Dance of the Smithsonian Institution's Office of Information Resource Management for their technical assistance, and Patrick Gilmartin for rendering tables 11 and 12.

G.C.

*Moscow*
*May 1992*

# NOTE ON THE EXPANDED EDITION

Since publishing the original version of this book in Italian I have expanded significantly both its scope and its depth of analysis. Most of the new material is located subsequent to chapter 13 and concerns the Second and Third Congresses of People's Deputies. These chapters are the product of my collaboration with Douglas Northrop, a graduate student in Soviet history at Stanford University. These sections of the book represent a qualitative improvement over anything offered in the Italian edition, breaking new methodological ground in their extensive use of statistical analysis. Although I am responsible for the overall structure of the book, for the basic ideas contained in it, and for assigning the (unavoidably subjective) political values to speeches and roll-call votes in the Congress of People's Deputies, credit for the technical, graphical, mathematical, and analytic aspects of this additional work goes almost exclusively to Doug. Its methodological basis, presentation in written form, and integration into the existing text represent a joint effort. Our collaboration on this expanded edition has, I believe, in the end produced a book that meaningfully confirms and significantly extends my earlier arguments regarding the nascent Soviet democracy. Doug has also undertaken the daunting task of rewriting virtually all of the book to yield the most lucid English prose possible under tight time constraints. For his efforts on all of these levels, I thank him.

G.C.

# TRANSITION TO DEMOCRACY

CHAPTER ONE

# Two Hundred Years Later

"The script for the events awaiting us was already written 200 years ago, at the time of the French Revolution."[1] Economist Nikolai Shmelev made this assertion early in his speech to the Soviet Congress of People's Deputies on 8 June 1989. Almost exactly two hundred years earlier world history had reached a turning point in Louis XVI's France, a turning point which strongly influenced nearly all subsequent global historical development. Most Europeans in 1789, however, did not realize or understand the significance of the events in Paris and Versailles. Most of the world had not yet left its "prehistory." Marx had not even been born. Why had Shmelev chosen such a retrospective prophecy to forecast the Soviet future?

Despite belonging to another historical era, the France of 1789 served Shmelev's purposes well by allowing his "script" to teem with dark implications for the future of Soviet *perestroika*, implications that he soon made explicit. "A system of general rationing awaits us," he warned, "an abrupt devaluation of the ruble, an explosion of the black market and underground economy, a collapse of the consumer market, and a forced return—I repeat, forced— . . . to the rigid discipline of administrative economic command."[2] Recent events have shown the basic accuracy of Shmelev's dark predictions, and there is little doubt that he was well justified in at least one sense when he chose revolutionary France for his historical analogy. The ongoing process of change in the former Soviet Union is fully as epoch-making, and as likely to influence future development, as was that in France two centuries ago. This reform is, in essence,

1. *Izvestiia*, 9 June 1990. Transliterations from the Russian in this book will follow the Library of Congress system. The only exceptions follow recognized spellings and omit diacriticals. ("Yeltsin," that is, rather than "El'tsin."). These exceptions are maintained except in the List of Deputies following the text.
2. *Izvestiia*, 9 June 1990.

creating a completely new historical situation that will affect the entire world, deeply and permanently. The Soviet Union itself ceased to exist at the end of 1991; change during the preceding three years permitted the upending of the post-1945 European order and forced the rethinking of long-static military, economic, and political doctrines. Furthermore, it both necessitated revamping the cultural, social, and political philosophies underlying these doctrines and implied the need fundamentally to restructure the global system of international relations.

The rapidity of events in the Soviet Union and Eastern Europe during 1989 stunned nearly all international observers and startled most of the main protagonists. This chapter will first explain why these developments, and their speed, surprised the world, and will then sketch their historical roots. Doing so will allow us both to appreciate the ebb and flow of history and to draw out lessons that might help us to predict possible future developments in that part of the world now known, at least for the time being, as the Commonwealth of Independent States.

Underestimating the vast scope of Gorbachev's revolution—or failing to realize this scope soon enough—has already gravely delayed attempts to understand how *perestroika* will affect the world as a whole. Gorbachev's actions triggered change that will potentially define an epoch by altering radically the socioeconomic system of one of the world's two largest powers. Clearly, such change is fraught with dangers (as well as opportunities) for other nations. The Soviet leader himself was among those most aware of the broader significance of Soviet reform, warning the international community that his "new way of thinking" ("*novoe myshlenie*") would mean a "*perestroika* for the USSR, and [also] for the whole world."[3]

If we compare *perestroika* with an earthquake, we could say that its shock waves have spread to other countries. A series of aftershocks—or perhaps new quakes—continues, jarring the conventional wisdom and forcing policy-makers to think along new lines. Extending the metaphor, *perestroika*'s epicenter is in Moscow, until recently the power center of traditional Communism, but its tremors have expanded outward, causing basic assumptions to be questioned in both Communist and non-Communist systems. The metaphor essentially stresses the importance of modern global interconnectedness, and makes clear that events and changes—particularly those taking place in a superpower—affect other nations. Chernobyl, for example, alarmed millions both inside and out of the Soviet Union. Eastern Europe was not the only area affected by the upending of the post-Yalta European order. And the end of the Cold War

3. Mikhail S. Gorbachev, *Perestroika: New Thinking for Our Country and the World* (New York: Harper & Row, 1987). In particular, see chap. 3, 151.

will in the long term change not only East-West, but also North-South, relations.[4] Industrial, financial, and economic development policies of the world's economic powers—the United States, Japan, and the European Economic Community—will change, and the Third World will demand more attention.

This book can suggest such issues, but obviously cannot treat them all in detail. Its scope is decidedly more modest, seeking only to describe the salient features of the political revolution that took place in the last years of the Soviet Union's existence. In doing so, we will try to portray the embryonic stages of Soviet democracy, and to offer a preliminary evaluation of its vitality. Even with such a limited scope, however, we will need to overcome many of the psychological and ideological prejudices that for decades have obstructed accurate analysis of ongoing processes in the Soviet Union if we are to see how these processes helped to form the terrain in which Gorbachev's *perestroika* flourished.

Here, indeed, we may already have a key to interpreting the delays in the West's appreciation of the scope of Gorbachev's reforms. In its seventy-year lifespan, the Soviet Union proved a difficult, elusive country to study. Not only was it enormously large and complex, but it also was the site of an unprecedented historical experiment. The October Revolution of 1917 set out—at least in theory—to construct an entirely "organic" social system, one radically different from its predecessors. Although carried out in Marx's name, this experiment took place in conditions that Marx would have deemed unsuitable.[5] Furthermore, it took place at the Eurasian crossroads, the precise place at which previous "enlightened" efforts to Westernize, or Europeanize, had failed.

Economic and cultural backwardness, an "Asiatic system of production," and the imperial dimension all weighed heavily on Soviet leaders during the decades that followed 1917. The very fact that the experiment had started, though—that a self-professed Marxist regime had by 1921 succeeded in asserting its control over such a large, important country— helped to distort and impede analysis of the new Soviet society. Moreover, the revolution kindled hopes that spread throughout Western working classes and, particularly, among millions of workers in the colonial world. The anomaly of the experiment's location in the backward Russian Empire combined with its "Asiatic diversity" and the Stalinist terror to add an element of righteous, if fearful, detached condemnation to Western

4. Indeed, the Persian Gulf crisis that began in August 1990 revealed the first such short-term changes, simultaneously affecting East-West and North-South relations.

5. Antonio Gramsci clearly understood this problem when, in a commentary of 24 December 1917 in *l'Avanti!*, he defined the Leninist choice as being a "Revolution against *Capital*.'"

views. From the other side, forced rigid adherence to a Marxist-Leninist concept of class conflict and the prevalence of "ideological,"[6] conflicting approaches burdened with ideological value judgments any internal attempts at an objective analysis of Soviet society.

The Soviet Union remained a difficult place to study throughout the Cold War. Creators of Soviet propaganda, partly from fear of capitalist encirclement, hid Soviet weaknesses and portrayed Western flaws as mileposts along the historically inevitable road leading to a Communist triumph. Many in the West, in turn, perhaps partly because they feared this Soviet prediction, trumpeted the failures of Soviet communism while minimizing the importance of weaknesses in capitalist society. In the Soviet case, however, the growing disparity between reality and official statements took on an internal political significance.

Under Stalin, the Soviet government used brutal "administrative methods" to assert its control over society. The Stalinist regime that evolved— socialist in trappings and authoritarian in substance—had to create an ideology to legitimize itself. This ideology reconciled *de facto* social inequality and hierarchies of privilege with egalitarian rhetoric. All-too-obvious poverty was explained in terms of promised, "inevitable" future socialist achievements. The new ideology adduced the presence of alleged enemies, both internal and external, and the low level of popular political development to justify widespread repression and the lack of personal liberties.

Generations of Soviet citizens learned to tailor their behavior to an official system of "double truth," which, according to a popular anecdote, amounted to saying one thing, doing another, and thinking yet another. The long-term effects of this system were disastrous. Applied widely throughout state and Party, it led to a near-total substitution of optical and verbal illusions for truthful information in official communications and statistics. Trapped in this web of doublespeak, the Soviet leadership found itself gradually deprived of meaningful information about the country it ostensibly led. The political system lacked feedback from below almost completely, functioning only—and increasingly ineffectively—to channel orders and campaigns from leaders to the rank and file. The Party controlled the Soviets (government councils); elections to governmental posts, appropriately for a land of "double truth," served only as periodic farces. Hence, the government was no more capable than the Party of supplying leaders with reliable information about popular feelings or conditions on the street. Although many Westerners perceive the KGB as omniscient and dedicated simply to Stalinist repression, it was then-KGB

6. In the Marxian sense of "false consciousness."

director Iurii Andropov who in 1983 first admitted that Soviet leaders and scientists lacked even the most basic information about their own country.[7]

For all of these reasons, outside observers found it difficult to paint a detailed picture of Soviet society even before the upheavals of 1989 began.[8] With the starting point so unclear and Soviet society already changing rapidly, appreciating the scope of change implied by Gorbachev's reforms thus became virtually impossible. As Moshe Lewin has since demonstrated convincingly,[9] Soviet society in 1980 had already changed radically since Stalin's death and the turning points of the Twentieth and Twenty-second Party Congresses, which had marked the beginning of de-Stalinization. By this time, too, the USSR had already entered a deep socioeconomic crisis. Like Andropov before him, Gorbachev came to power clearly aware of the need for rapid, substantial change, realizing that the amount of time left to "salvage the salvageable" was small. Under the blunt slogan "There is no other way," Gorbachev in March 1985 won election as Party general secretary. He expressed his sense of alarm so strongly that he induced even many conservative, recalcitrant Party members to vote for him, in essence throwing in their lots with reformers.

By his own admission, however, we now know that even Gorbachev did not fully realize the seriousness of the social and economic crisis facing the Soviet Union in March 1985. Hence, he did not at first know how, or how quickly, to begin what would soon become an attempt to overhaul the entire Soviet system. Probably for this reason, *perestroika* in its first stage began as a series of isolated economic reforms. Indeed, in many ways it simply resumed the Krushchev economic reforms of the 1960s that had been derailed during the Brezhnev-era stagnation. "Acceleration" (*"uskorenie"*) and "passage to the intensive [economic] phase" were Gorbachev's first catchwords, and for roughly eighteen months after March 1985 Gor-

7. In an essay marking the centennial of Marx's death, Andropov opined: "It is impossible not to realize that [in our information base] we lag behind that required by the present level of material, technical, social and cultural development in Soviet society" (*Kommunist* 3 [1983]).

8. A curious tendency of many external observers (including those most critical of Soviet society), however, implicitly to accept tenets of conservative Soviet ideology extended into this period. The idea of an essentially monolithic Soviet society, devoid of internal conflicts or contradictions and devoted to egalitarian ideals, for instance, was shared by Stalinist conservatives and Western Cold Warriors. They also shared other ideas, such as the (equally false) understanding of Soviet dissent as a phenomenon that was, albeit notable, confined to small groups of intellectuals located mostly in large cities.

9. See M. Lewin, *The Gorbachev Phenomenon* (Berkeley: University of California Press, 1988), particularly pt. I, "From Village to Megacity—A Country in a Hurry."

bachev's programs could be portrayed as nothing more than earlier efforts warmed over. In early 1987, however, he broke new ground. Gorbachev radically shifted course, auguring potentially fundamental changes in the Soviet system. Our story begins at this point.

In his report to the Party plenum of January 1987 Gorbachev explicitly called for "political reform," a call soon echoed by other reform-minded Soviet officials.[10] This shift from the economic to the political was crucial. To summarize Gorbachev's position briefly, the reformist nucleus of the Soviet leadership understood that real economic reform was impossible without changes in the country's political structures. Gorbachev concluded that blame for the economic and social crisis—the crisis that by 1982 had reduced Soviet economic growth to zero—did not belong entirely to Brezhnev.[11] The roots of the crisis were deeper, he argued, extending back into the 1920s. The real blame lay with the "deformation" of socialism produced by Stalin when he eliminated democracy from the Soviet system. The system of "administrative command" could not be seen simply as an economic mechanism, he continued. In Marxist terms, it was not a part of the structural base, but was rather an integral part of the political-institutional superstructure. Similarly, the command-administrative system was not just one style among many of state planning, or of "production relations," but rather infiltrated and influenced the entire system of social and political relations.

The complete nationalization of the means of production, Gorbachev contended, had become the *de facto* nationalization of society as a whole. The state had absorbed individuals' material and intellectual productivity and subordinated their rights and aspirations to itself. As a result, civil society was prevented from developing and, indeed, the state depended on its not developing. From this perspective, Gorbachev's reformist conclusion became clear: not only was it impossible to reform the Soviet system economically without changing its political institutions, but economic reform *was* political reform. *Perestroika*, then, was needed to save the country. *Perestroika* divorced from a wide-ranging democratization, however, was impossible.

Were Gorbachev's conclusions correct? Did the social and economic crisis gripping the Soviet Union in the late 1980s begin with Stalin in the 1920s? Or is it necessary to look farther back in time to find the roots

10. High drama characterized this plenum, which was thrice rescheduled before opening at all. The first split among the forces that had backed Gorbachev's accession appeared at this time. For more information, see Roy Medvedev and Giulietto Chiesa, *Time of Change* (New York: Pantheon Books, 1990), chap. 4.

11. *Pravda*, 28 January 1987.

of the crisis? These questions have been widely debated in the former Soviet Union, and Gorbachev's thesis has come under increasing fire.[12] A sizable number of ex-Soviet citizens do share Gorbachev's view that Stalin is culpable, but many others feel that the real root lies even farther back in time. They trace the concepts and practices that created the one-party system to 1917, to Lenin and the October Revolution. This debate is unlikely to be settled anytime soon, and indeed had hardly begun in the Soviet Union by the time Gorbachev himself resigned as Soviet president, and the USSR ceased to exist, in late 1991. Its mere presence, however, serves our purposes, for the rise of this debate signifies a conceptual and practical turning point in Soviet political life. This turning point, reached by Gorbachev in early 1987, spawned the impressive series of political changes that is the subject of this book.

Our aim is not only to analyze the main features of the beginnings of a "transition to democracy," but also to describe the political, institutional, and psychological foundations on which this process has been based. For this reason, our focus will be largely on internal affairs, rather than on the effects of international events in Eastern Europe and elsewhere. Plainly, it is impossible to attempt to explain the turning point of the elections of 26 May (chapter 4) without considering both the ideas dominating the Soviet leadership at that time (chapters 3 and 4) and the main political features of the Congress produced by these elections (chapters 5, 9, 10, and 12). Subsequent events have proved complex and contradictory. We shall describe them by considering a variety of paths to political pluralism (chapter 6), taking a "snapshot" of the First Congress' political geography (chapter 7), and elaborating a methodological approach of "three-dimensional analysis" (chapter 8). Chapters 11 and 12 describe emerging political forces and attempt to predict possible future political and social alliances. Subsequent chapters, centered on a detailed statistical analysis, trace the evolution of this political geography during the Congress of People's Deputies' first year as a democratic Soviet legislature.[13]

12. A vast literature appeared on this theme in 1988 and 1989. A famous and illustrative example is Tsipko's article on "The Origins of Stalinism." See Aleksandr Tsipko, "*Istoki Stalinizma*," *Nauka i Zhizn* 11–12 (1988) and 1–2, (1989).

13. Since the appearance of this book's first edition the complete records to the First Congress of People's Deputies have been published in English. See Rolf H. W. Theen, ed., *The U.S.S.R. First Congress of People's Deputies: complete documents and records, 25 May 1989–1 June 1989* (New York: Paragon House, 1991), 4 vols.

# Soviet Democracy's First Model

Gorbachev outlined the broad contours of his vision for Soviet democratization in early 1987. The first clearly discernible hint of political reform, in the form of a call to "increase the role of the Soviets," had appeared in Gorbachev's speech at the opening of the Twenty-seventh Party Congress in late February 1986. Such a formulation, however, could be interpreted in various ways. Indeed, it seemed to continue a tradition of vague entreaties for systemic improvement made by previous Soviet leaders—even by Brezhnev. Gorbachev's first, more explicit break with the past, clearly differentiating Party and state roles, can be found in the modifications to the Party Charter approved by the Twenty-seventh Congress.[1] We need, then, to reconsider Gorbachev's first model for Soviet democratization. Such a reexamination is not an empty historical exercise. Rather, it will allow us both to measure the progress made since 1987 in transforming the Soviet political system and to assess the personalities and intellectual capacities of the Soviet leader and his team.

The preservation of the one-party system was an integral part of Gorbachev's first model. He justified his position on political (rather than ideological) grounds, and stressed that the Soviet one-party system was the result of certain specific historical processes. Thus, it could not be considered illustrative of any universal principle of political and social development. In employing such a relativistic, historicist approach, Gorbachev's reasoning differed dramatically from that of earlier Soviet leaders. Nevertheless, his ultimate support of the one-party system seemed unshakable, and he showed no signs of changing his mind on this issue through 1989.

Whatever the burden of his individual experience and of the ideo-

---

1. *Pravda*, 26 February 1986.

logical tradition to which he subscribed, Gorbachev plainly was aware of the existence of large, deeply conservative strongholds within both the Party apparatus and society at large. Even leaving aside the Soviet leader's personal convictions—the exact nature of which remains uncertain—no reasonable person could have expected Gorbachev preemptively to renounce the CPSU's "leading role."[2] Several times after 1987, indeed, Gorbachev offered a straightforwardly *political* reason for retaining the Party's leading role, a reason that followed logically from his projection of current trends into the future. *Perestroika*, he argued, would inevitably produce growing social and territorial differentiation in a country that was both heterogeneous and lacking a mature, organized civil society. From this perspective, the need for a socially unifying force would not diminish, but only increase in the short and medium term. Such a force would be needed to guide accelerating social mobilization and to mediate between conflicting interests during the crisis of traditional egalitarian values. The only force potentially able to fulfill this role, Gorbachev felt, was the Communist Party.

He entrusted the duty of representing new social interests to various "social organizations," many preexisting and others to be created from above, essentially by *diktat*.[3] These organizations would be responsible for promoting (and controlling) these interests, and also for negotiating among them when conflict arose. This plan, although logical, rested on two presumptions of change: rapid democratization of the Party and significant restructuring of the social organizations, which for decades had been empty, ineffective bureaucratic shells, deprived of prestige and incapable of meaningfully representing real social interests.[4] Did Gorbachev genuinely believe that his proposed model would work? The question is legitimate: the Soviet leader showed more than once his ability to hold ambitious projects in abeyance while publicly arguing for a more moderate approach. Nonetheless, it seems likely that Gorbachev thought it possible to democratize Soviet society *under the guidance of* traditional organizations, at least once their structures and ruling cadres had been thoroughly revamped.

Still, we cannot overlook the fact that this model was formulated by a

2. We cannot, then, consider many Western Sovietologists "reasonable people." Such Western scholars expressed skepticism and misgivings about Soviet democratization because Gorbachev's model did not call explicitly for the introduction of a multiparty system and accept unconditionally the Western parliamentary ideal.

3. Three such organizations created in 1987 were the "Union of Soviet War and Labor Veterans," the "Committee of Soviet Women," and the "Foundation for Culture."

4. Speaking at the Congress of Unions and of the Komsomol, Gorbachev strongly criticized the leaders of these organizations for their ultraconservatism and reluctance to advance *perestroika*.

leadership that was, although internally divided and uncertain, in many ways conservative.[5] Both conservatives and reformers in the Politburo and Central Committee were well aware that "democratizing the Party" meant subjecting that Party's apparatus to an extremely, perhaps fatally, difficult trial. Political and economic reforms did not only require that the apparatus be reorganized and reduced in size. They also implied a far-reaching reduction of the *apparat*'s economic and political decisionmaking power, radically changing both its function and its style of operation.

Hundreds of thousands of cadres would be forced to "restructure" themselves, both politically and psychologically. This task would be overwhelming for most such cadres, particularly for those who had entered the *apparat* under Brezhnev. Not illogically, there developed within the Soviet leadership a group of "defense attorneys" to protect the entrenched interests that were endangered by reforms.[6] When "democratization" was defined to include controls on the *apparat*, ministries, and the Party itself, it inevitably meant that misconduct, both recent and in the distant past, would be uncovered. The legacy of the Party's power monopoly—extended networks of privilege and corruption, illegal practices, and blatant abuses of state power—would be exposed to public view. Many members of the national, republican, and regional Party and governmental leaderships could only fear such developments.

Consequently, Gorbachev and his reformist allies initially moved tentatively and cautiously. The strength and breadth of the conservative resistance dictated such prudence. The reformists realized that the Soviet transition to democracy had to begin almost from scratch, since virtually all power was held by those who would in the end have to relinquish it. To borrow an expression of Antonio Gramsci's, Gorbachev's high-wire act aimed to create a "system of social and political alliances." This system, however, would have to be built in the political environment of Soviet society in the mid-1980s, an environment in which *apparatchiki* controlled politics and most social forces remained either politically unaware or lacking the means to express themselves politically.

The reformers in the Party therefore started from a position where both

5. By way of illustration, we need only consider Anatolii Lukianov's article of 25 April 1986 in *Pravda*. Lukianov, then head of a Central Committee department, reiterated old formulas in his theoretical discussion of "Socialist People's Self-Management." Lukianov, almost ignoring Gorbachev's entreaties at the Party Congress, praised the "people that is united with its state through the deputies' Soviets, mass organs of state power, in whose election practically the whole adult population of the country participates."

6. According to Soviet experts, at least 16 million people—members of the *apparat upravleniia* and their families—were threatened by political and economic reform. The state treasury spent about 30 billion rubles a year to support these people.

the subjects and the objects of change—that is, the Party and society—
were, for different reasons, unprepared. The former remained, for the
most part, hostile; the latter, although already potentially mature, had
not yet sufficiently organized itself. Mainly for this reason, Soviet reform
at first was compelled to be *gradual* and *prudent*. This necessity produced
the idea of attempting *progressively* to transfer Party power to the state
without destroying existing institutional frameworks. Drastic changes in
the governmental structure (central and peripheral, republican and local)
were also needed, since the Soviets and the empty ritual of their elections had become a meaningless formality incapable of representing the
popular will or even of legitimating Party control. Gorbachev realized the
importance of this reform, denouncing the "serious defects in the functioning of the institutions of socialist democracy" to the Party plenum of
January 1987 and calling for radical changes in these institutions.[7] In this
first phase, however, Gorbachev remained unable to detail the changes
he had in mind, and could produce no more than a preliminary sketch.
Democratization of the Party was perceived to be more important than
that of the government. Hence, the most radical, detailed, and innovative
suggestions concerned Party reform directly. Such ideas included using
multi-candidate, secret ballots to elect all levels of the Party leadership,
and requiring the Party to install more "nonparty [*bezpartiinye*] people" in
state posts.

Gorbachev had reintroduced "*glasnost*" ("openness") as a catchword
in 1985. It became the main instrument of this first phase of democratization. "Openness" in fact served two interconnected purposes in the
political struggle during the months that followed. First, the reformers
in the Party were aware of deep, unvoiced dissatisfaction among many
groups in society. Consequently, they searched for ways to give these
groups the means of expression and the capability of developing organizational structures. These reformers perceived an urgent need to build
a system of progressive *social* alliances and to enroll an ever-increasing
number of people on the reformist lists in the battle for democratization.
The "creative intelligentsia," the main natural ally of these reformers, was
undoubtedly mostly progressive but, alone, it lacked sufficient power to
decide the struggle. The reformers therefore understood that the "diffuse
intelligentsia"—defined by Aleksandr Zinovev as "Moscovia," the product of the massive social changes that had occurred in the Soviet Union
since the 1950s—would be needed as well.[8] *Glasnost* secondly served to

---

7. *Pravda*, 28 January 1987.
8. For definitions of "creative" and "diffuse" intelligentsia, see the discussion of
social and professional groups in chap. 5, below.
The reformist group was not a prisoner to the idea of an immobile Soviet society.

weaken the *apparat's* absolute power. By exposing networks of privilege to the public, it forced the *apparat* to justify itself.

*Glasnost* also helped create a system of alliances within the Party. By definition, the directors of prominent newspapers, political-literary magazines, and radio and television organizations belonged to the *nomenklatura*.[9] Gorbachev's public policy gradually but explicitly granted them powers of autonomous expression. Again borrowing a Gramscian idea, we can say that newspapers and magazines functioned as rudimentary political parties. Each publication helped preliminarily to organize a different sector of the public, and to encourage political expression in the Party and society at large. This process could only partially be controlled, and expanded rapidly throughout society. Whereas between 1985 and 1987 *glasnost* had only allowed political diversification within the Party, it now justified a far broader expansion of the political arena. New groups coalesced and started to demand a role in policy-making, thus ending the *apparat's* stranglehold on political debate.

---

Political stagnation had only masked deep social changes that produced a variety of psychological changes, particularly among the educated and urban populations:

> On the whole, in 1980 about 272 Soviet cities have more than 100,000 inhabitants (there were only 89 in 1939), and these cities by now contain almost half the urban population, and about one third of that of the whole country. . . . It is this large picture of changes, determined by the diffusion and growth of the cities, particularly of the larger ones, that sets the tone for the rest of the country, and, in many respects, defines the country in its contemporary reality. Certainly other countries have had analogous experiences, but not on such a vast scale, and not so powerfully concentrated in a short period of time. And this in a country that was already a superpower even before the advent of urbanization. For Russia, for the Soviet system, in any case, this is all new and unprecedented (M. Lewin, *The Gorbachev Phenomenon* [Berkeley: University of California Press, 1988], 32, 42).

In a slightly different form, two Soviet scholars have expressed the same idea:

> Our situation today is defined by the changes that took place in the '50s, '60s, and '70s. Strictly speaking, the notion of 'stagnation' ultimately reflects changes that have occurred during the past quarter-century. But it would not be correct to take the term literally, as characterizing the entire period. In the USSR [during that period] considerable changes took place, even if they were unfortunately unbalanced and internally contradictory (Leonid Gordon and Alla Nazimova, *"Perestroika: Vozmozhnye Varianty?" Kommunist* 13 [1989]).

9. The term *nomenklatura* is used here in the strict sense of Mikhail Vozlenskii, the author of a famous book of the same title. It includes those men and women included in the lists of the most important Party and state positions, positions under the direct authority of the Politburo and Secretariat of the CPSU Central Committee.

Observers still argue about Gorbachev's intentions at this point. Skeptical Western analysts stress the instrumental character of *glasnost*, seeing Gorbachev's tactics in almost Machiavellian terms. By emphasizing that Gorbachev had *chosen* to use *glasnost* as a political weapon, these analysts cannot appreciate how quickly this weapon escaped Gorbachev's control, creating an independent public opinion and reducing popular fear of speaking out. Such analysts are also ill-equipped to perceive how deeply Gorbachev's weapon of choice disrupted Soviet social equilibria. Gorbachev, by contrast, seemed completely aware of, and unapologetic for, what he had done. The Nineteenth Party Organizational Conference resolved in mid-1988 that the Soviet Union had to become a socialist "rule-of-law" state, with state and Party clearly separated and with the Party subordinated to state laws. Speaking in Krasnoiarsk in September 1988, Gorbachev claimed that *perestroika*'s great achievement was "giving politics back" to Soviet citizens.[10]

The protagonists of these battles almost certainly did not foresee with any clarity the results of their actions. Nor, of course, can we be sure of their motivations. Nevertheless, Gorbachev fought resolutely to convene the Nineteenth Party Conference, confronting and defeating opposition within the Central Committee to do so.[11] At this conference he pressed for major reforms, succeeding on such issues as the "rule-of-law" resolution cited above. At stake, the reformists thought, was the end of revolution from above as an instrument of change. These reformists wanted to shift responsibility for *perestroika* onto the populace, creating a revolution from below. Conservatives—with good reason—feared the risks of permitting such massive popular participation to determine the pace and content of reform. Gorbachev, however, had decided that *perestroika* could not defeat the social and political resistance facing it without popular involvement. The choice to cede power by inviting the people into politics was risky, even for Gorbachev. Nevertheless, after carefully weighing the options, he realized that he had no real alternatives. His choice was conscious, and when he had made it, Soviet democratization had begun.

10 *Pravda*, 17 September 1988. For another example of the Soviet leader's thoughts on democratization, see his report to the Nineteenth Party Conference in the summer of 1988.

11. *Pravda*, 28 January 1987. The proposal to convene the conference, listed as a "hypothesis" in the plenum's report of January 1987, did not receive sufficient support to appear among the plenum's final decisions. Only in June did Gorbachev succeed in gaining Party approval for convening the conference. Strong opposition in the Central Committee, however—and probably in the Politburo itself—stymied Gorbachev's original hope to have the conference perform the role of a "half-term Congress" with the power to change the Central Committee.

# Compromise, Constitutional Change, and New Electoral Law

Social and political tensions surrounded the preparations for the Nineteenth Party Conference. Conflict had erupted between Armenia and Azerbaijan over Nagorno-Karabakh in early 1988, and a pogrom at Sumgait gave tragic notice that the Soviet road to democratic civil society would be hard. The experience of the past four hundred years in Europe and elsewhere could not simply be replicated in the USSR. The historical and political legacy of the backward tsarist Russian Empire remained, with the effects of the October Revolution and Stalinism overlaid upon it; the combination created unique problems. Levels of political awareness remained low, and the concept of national identity—the only group loyalty felt by many Soviet citizens—had more potential to divide than to unify.

The failure of attempts in the 1970s and earlier to create a nonethnic, "Soviet" national consciousness meant that ethnically-based calls for national unity in the 1980s could only undercut the Soviet state. National feelings in the USSR, however, varied widely among ethnic groups. In the politically well-developed Baltic republics, nationalism quickly aimed at political independence. Such calls, expressed forcefully but in an orderly manner, appealed to the memory of these republics' interwar period of independent statehood. Slavic nationalism at first became only fitfully active, at least partly because many Slavs felt that the Slavic numerical advantage in central decision-making bodies sufficiently safeguarded their interests. Nevertheless, as non-Slavic national movements gained in strength, the slumbering giant of Slavic nationalism began to come to life in reaction. In the Caucasian and Central Asian republics, economic, social, and cultural backwardness combined with bitter religious issues to complicate the picture. The demise of authoritarian controls in these areas led to near-anarchy. After uniting to destroy the power of central state and Party bureaucracies, ethnic groups found themselves free to express their own grievances. Since hated bureaucracies had often been perceived as serving the interests of ethnic Russians, hostility towards Moscow and the *apparat* easily could degenerate into an anti-Russian crusade and, in many cases, Russians perceived events in exactly this way.

For their part, conservative members of the central apparatus struggled desperately to organize a counteroffensive against the twin dangers of *glasnost* and *perestroika*. The appearance of the "Anti-*Perestroika* Platform" of Nina Andreeva, a reactionary Leningrad schoolteacher, showed that conservatives hoped to use the upcoming Party conference to block reformist plans to democratize Soviet society.[1] A battle broke out over the election of delegates to the conference; when the dust settled, conservatives seemed to have won a crushing victory. Gorbachev faced a hostile majority, comprised largely of *apparatchiki* who opposed his reformist vision and remained protective of their privileges. As the conference progressed, however, reformist forces proved stronger than expected. This surprising resurgence, combined with Gorbachev's masterly technique, enabled reformists to secure approval of all essential points contained in their preconference platform. It did not, however, equal some of Gorbachev's earlier victories, and could not be described as a total success. Careful compromises between opposing views emerged in the conference's final resolutions.[2]

As already mentioned, the conference's final resolution called for the creation of a socialist "rule-of-law" state in the Soviet Union. The crux of this resolution, which was enacted into law almost in its entirety by the Supreme Soviet in late 1988, was the declared transfer to the Soviets of "all questions specifically concerned with the governmental, economic, social, and cultural life of the country." The Party's role would remain undiminished, the resolution continued, but its style of operation would change radically, forsaking direct control of social and economic life in favor of purely ideological activities. For the first time in Soviet history a limit on leadership tenure was decreed: no public office, either state or Party, could be held for more than two consecutive five-year terms. The Party officially called for multi-candidate, secret elections to all Soviets.

1. *Sovetskaia Rossiia*, 13 March 1988. The Nineteenth Party Organizational Conference had been called in June 1987 under strong pressure from Gorbachev to accelerate *perestroika*. Party conferences had had different functions and powers at different times during the history of the CPSU. The last such conference, the Eighteenth, had been held by Stalin in the 1940s to change the Central Committee dramatically. Most likely Gorbachev wished to use the Nineteenth Conference to expel from this leading body many who opposed his policies. He was, however, unsuccessful in doing so.

2. For a detailed analysis of the Nineteenth Conference, see Roy Medvedev and Giulietto Chiesa, *Time of Change* (New York: Pantheon Books, 1990), chap. 8, 217–37.

The role of Soviets would be "radically increased," and elective assemblies would meet for a duration appropriate to their functions. As a result, the practice of holding only two brief, formal meetings each year to ratify decisions of executive bodies (which in reality answered to the corresponding Party committees) would end.

Despite the dramatic changes, the conference left many details unresolved. It realized that a dramatic rise in legislative output would be needed, and declared its support for constitutional amendments to delineate more precisely the relative functions of both houses of the Supreme Soviet. In a surprise to both delegates and outside observers, the conference also considered and approved a proposal not even contained in the preconference theses. This proposal created a two-tiered parliament, with the bottom level—a 2,250-member Congress of People's Deputies— to be elected directly by the Soviet people. This Congress would in turn select the 542 members of the Supreme Soviet from its own ranks. The Supreme Soviet was still to be divided into two 271-member chambers— a Soviet of Nationalities and a Soviet of the Union—but suddenly it was expected to function as a permanent legislature, holding annual sessions to last several months at a time. The lower Congress would meet "once a year," presumably briefly.[3]

We have already considered the political climate in which these proposals originated, but another layer of analysis is necessary in order to understand more fully the dynamics of the conference. The conference's products—both its theses and Gorbachev's report—resulted from a protracted, complex process of political mediation amongst differing, even diametrically opposed, factions. Full responsibility for the plan that emerged, therefore, cannot be assigned to any one figure, even one as powerful as Gorbachev. Subsequent events, indeed, become much more difficult to understand if the plan's paternity is ascribed only to Gorbachev.

Clearly delineating the precise contributions of these different groups to the final resolutions of the conference is difficult, since nearly all present defended the final compromise and refused to air their disputes in public. Analysis of the debate in the central press, though, both before and after the conference, can help sketch the broad outlines of disagreement. Some reformers, both in and out of the Party leadership, favored a presidential solution and the direct popular election of a head of state. Despite the legal arguments they proffered, their reasoning was clearly political;

3. At the start of the conference's first session, Gorbachev made it clear that he remained open to allowing this lower Congress to meet for two, rather than one, sessions each year.

they wished to reduce the power of the Politburo and the Central Committee by limiting these bodies' influence in selecting a president of the Supreme Soviet.[4] On this issue, conservatives prevailed; the conference did not adopt the radical position.

Conservatives did not succeed in every case, however. Fiery debate broke out over a proposal to combine Party and state offices, a proposal that flew in the face of the conference's affirmation of the need for Party-state separation. A hailstorm of criticism, both legal and political, greeted the proposal from the radical intelligentsia. From one perspective, of course, such a suggestion represented a reasonable, defensive reaction of the Party *apparat*, which wished to protect its power over the Soviets, particularly at a time when more administrative and political power was to be devolved to the Soviets. Gorbachev, however, enthusiastically supported the *apparat* on this measure. To explain the apparent contradiction with his reformist aims, we need to remember that at this time Gorbachev himself was preparing to assume the position of president of the Supreme Soviet, while remaining Party general secretary.

By supporting the radicals, therefore, Gorbachev would be caught in a contradiction, and might—he thought—be forced to choose between his leadership positions. In choosing, he feared losing power and perhaps even control of the country. The powers of the president remained undefined; if Gorbachev abandoned his Party post, a new general secretary could obstruct reform. On the other hand, if he remained only general secretary, he would both be unable to direct the new parliament through the most delicate phases of the power transfer and be basing his political future on an organization that he had decided to weaken. Following the tradition of Brezhnev, Andropov, and Chernenko by unifying the two supreme positions seemed the path of most promise and least resistance.

4. In a long article, Fedor Burlatskii—clearly well-informed about ongoing discussions within the leadership—outlined some of the options open to progressive reformers. Besides the direct popular election of the president, Burlatskii proposed the election of the CPSU general secretary by the Party Congress rather than by the Central Committee. This proposal aimed to remove control of the Party's top leadership from the apparatus and simultaneously hoped to reduce Party control over state legislative bodies. Burlatskii also sought to prevent a sudden conservative *coup de main* by granting the president (who, it was assumed, would be Gorbachev) a long term in office with no means of his removal controlled by the apparatus. (See F. Burlatskii, "O Sovetskom Parlamentarizme," *Literaturnaia Gazeta*, 15 June 1988.) Eighteen months later, in March 1990, facing another conservative attack and the danger of state disintegration, Gorbachev hurriedly adopted a proposal very similar to Burlatskii's. The element of direct popular election, however, was delayed for five years. Gorbachev was elected president of the Soviet Union by the Congress of People's Deputies, which also approved a series of major constitutional amendments expanding his executive powers and virtually eliminating the possibility of his being removed from office by the CPSU Central Committee.

Conservatives, while accepting the unification of the two top positions, demanded the extension of this principle throughout the hierarchies of state and Party. Even discounting the legal arguments of radicals, the political difficulties of such an extension were significant, surfacing a year later during the new elections.[5] Nevertheless, many Party leaders still felt that they would be able yet again to manipulate nomination and election procedures sufficiently to safeguard their own power. They thought it likely that elections to renew the Soviets would almost automatically confirm Party leaders.

If the unthinkable happened, however, and high Party leaders were rejected by the populace, it would imply a lack of faith in them and in the Party, ostensibly the "leading force" in society. As a result, their positions would become legally and practically untenable. In retrospect, it is clear that combining state and Party offices potentially allowed the Soviet populace unprecedented opportunity to judge the *apparat*. Hence, the compromise could—and did—trap many conservatives. Far from being a simple, minor concession to conservative forces, it effectively ensured the fates of many members of the central and republican *nomenklatura*. The most prominent victim was Iurii Solovev, first secretary of the Leningrad Party and candidate member of the Politburo. The sole candidate from his district, he was rejected by a majority of electors and soon vacated all his posts.

The overall compromise was patched together with difficulty during the autumn of 1988. Highly refined in some areas, it remained only rough and ambiguous in others. Its uneven form revealed the extent of the changes being debated, the struggle over how far these changes would be allowed to permeate society, and the few points on which reformers and conservatives could temporarily agree. The entire process was political, depending heavily on shifting balances of forces, and it must be understood as such. Conservatives, although underestimating the dangers of the reformist program, understood the risks posed by completely free elections and hence sought procedures to select and co-opt docile, controllable candidates. Gorbachev, in the center, shared some conservative worries, albeit for a different reason. Once begun, he realized, the pro-

---

5. The call to unify Party and state posts at every level rested on the implicit assumption that, if the holders of these posts were to be elected from below, the will of the Soviet people at large would always coincide with the will of the restricted electorate represented by Party members. While plainly absurd, this contradiction pointed out vividly the nature of previous electoral mechanisms. No prior contradiction had existed in the elections to state and Party because the Party determined the results of both. And since posts were often filled by appointments from above instead of through elections from below, the essence of democratic control was lacking. Both parts of the assumption therefore remained meaningless.

cess of democratically-based reform could acquire momentum of its own, escaping the gradualism and central control that he thought necessary. Hence, in an effort to inject stability, control, and political moderation into the new democratic institutions, Gorbachev and conservatives agreed to reserve to representatives of the social organizations the power to name one-third of the deputies in the Congress of People's Deputies.

In late 1988 the old Supreme Soviet approved a new electoral law and the constitutional alterations that had been proposed at the Nineteenth Party Conference. These laws combined with the agreement over the social organizations' representation in the Congress of People's Deputies to form the initial compromise between progressives and conservatives over Soviet reform. On both the constitutional and electoral questions, elements of caution and reformism were equally apparent at every stage of the legislative process and in every article of the finished texts. The interlacing of both positions is enlightening, and as a suggestive example we will outline the electoral law's provisions for the structure of the Congress of People's Deputies.

The electoral law assigned specific numbers of deputies to specific organizations, allocating 525 deputies in this manner.[6] The law then partitioned the remaining 225 social-organization deputies into three groups, with 75 deputies each being split among scientific organizations, creative unions, and "other all-Soviet organizations." A Central Electoral Commission (CEC) was created and charged with the responsibility for distributing seats within these three categories, and also for considering requests for representation from other organizations. Such requests, however, could only emanate from organizations "instituted in accordance with legal procedures and associated with leading pan-Soviet or republican organs," preventing tens of thousands of informal organizations from making application for seats in the Congress.[7] In the end only 39 social organizations qualified for representation.[8]

It is worth pausing a moment to consider one of these 39 organizations. The CPSU, the "leading" (and only) political party, chose to include

6. Article 18, "*Zakon Soiuza Sotsialisticheskikh Respublik o Vyborakh Narodnykh Deputatov SSSR*," as printed in *Pravda*, 4 December 1988. The CPSU was allocated 100 deputies, as were both the Central Council of Syndicates (trade unions) and the Cooperative Organizations. The Komsomol, the Women's Unions, and the War and Labor Veterans each received 75 deputies.

7. Invoking Article 18, for instance, the CEC refused to grant deputies to the Interregional Association of Cooperatives, even though this group had a large membership throughout the RSFSR and Ukraine and numbered more than 300 cooperatives. The *Memorial* organization, founded by intellectuals under the leadership of Andrei Sakharov, also did not have time to satisfy the procedural requirements for registration as an "all-Soviet organization," and thus was excluded.

8. For a complete list, see table 2.

itself among the social organizations. This decision carried important, if politically and legally contradictory, implications. In one sense, the Party placed itself on the same level as other political forces, forces subordinate to it both constitutionally and practically. Apparently so lowering itself, however, served an important purpose: it enabled the entire Politburo, and many other high-level Party leaders, to avoid electoral competition and to be guaranteed seats in the Congress.[9] It also prevented any public determination of the comparative levels of popular support enjoyed by various Party leaders, thereby not upsetting the internal balance of forces. Gorbachev himself would have had little difficulty in securing reelection, but, whether as an unopposed candidate or as the victor over an unknown opponent, could only have secured a victory without prestige. Meaningful victory could only come against a strong opponent, who would receive many votes—and, in a double bind, Gorbachev would then lose political capital by not trouncing his opponent.

These political reasons, more than any rational or legal considerations, impelled Gorbachev to allow 750 seats to be reserved for the social organizations. To avoid real political hazards, the Party leadership—including its democratic, reformist members—created this institutional aberration, even though it undercut the notion of democratic equality. The principle of "one person, one vote" had from the very start been violated.[10] "Big" voters, those belonging to the plenums of represented social organizations, cast votes that equalled in influence those of tens of thousands of Soviet citizens.[11] The obvious contradictions with democratic principles did not escape sharp criticism during the public debate over the electoral law and the constitutional changes, but Gorbachev and the Supreme Soviet held their ground.

The remaining 1,500 deputies of the Congress were divided evenly

9. To be precise, it guaranteed the presence in the Congress of most Politburo members who did not also occupy government posts. With the exception of the presidents of the Supreme Soviet and of the Council of Ministers, the electoral law decreed the incompatibility of parliamentary and ministerial offices. As a result, the ministers of foreign affairs (Shevardnadze) and defense (Iazov) and the vice president of the Council of Ministers (Biriukova) did not become candidates for the Congress.

10. Members of the plenums of social organizations enjoyed the right to vote at least twice, once for a territorial deputy (actually twice; see n. 13 below) and once for the social organization's representative. It was also possible for some to vote three times or even more, since a Central Committee member could easily be a member of the ruling body of one or more other social organizations.

11. As an illustration, consider the CPSU, where 641 members of the party plenum (an enlarged version of the Central Committee) elected 100 deputies. Since the electoral law specified that each territorial seat represented 257,300 voters, we may conclude that each member of the CPSU plenum wielded influence roughly equivalent to 40,000 popular votes.

between those elected "territorially"[12] and those elected "national-territorially."[13] Even here, however, the law provided filters that could be used to restrict and moderate possible popular radicalism. Candidates could be nominated by a majority vote in grass-roots assemblies called by either workplace or territorial organizations.[14] Territorial assemblies needed at least 500 participants and had to be certified by a district electoral commission, which in turn was controlled by the Party. Workplace assemblies, on the other hand, were valid regardless of size. Conservatives hoped that this structure of the nomination process would force most candidacies to emanate from factories, farms, and companies.[15] These smaller units, closed to outside interference and participation, were presumed to be more easily controllable by Party organizations, company boards, and trade union committees. Conservatives hoped in this way to prevent as many radicals as possible from establishing candidacies.

A last, and expected to be decisive, obstacle to radical candidates was the final certification required of all nominees by a preelectoral district assembly (*predvybornoe okruzhnoe sobranie*, or POS). The POSs, established and summoned by district electoral commissions, consisted of representatives of all registered organizations and assemblies nominating candidates. Each POS ultimately decided how many and which candidates would be considered by the public. This mechanism proved extremely effective in filtering out candidates: of the original 9,505 nominees, only 5,074 succeeded in having their names reach the final, printed ballots.[16]

As we shall see in chapter 4, analysis of the electoral campaign and of the available numerical data suggests that local Party organizations in hun-

12. That is, in voting districts (*okrugi*) of 257,300 voters each.

13. National-territorial seats were apportioned as follows: 32 to every republic, 11 to every autonomous republic, 5 to every autonomous region, and 1 to every autonomous district, in each case regardless of the number of people living in each area. This approach confirmed that already in existence for elections to the Soviet of Nationalities. Each Soviet citizen voted both for a territorial and for a national-territorial deputy. Therefore, the system for the 1,500 deputies who were elected directly and popularly might be described as "one person, two votes." In the end, the Congress had less than 2,250 deputies (2,245 in both the Second and Third Congresses) because some had not yet been elected and others had died after being elected.

14. Article 9, electoral law cited above.

15. This conservative expectation proved to be accurate. According to Jeffrey Hahn, in a study presented to the annual meeting of the American Association for the Advancement of Slavic Studies, Chicago, 2–6 November 1989, only 282 of the 9,505 candidates registered during the campaign's first phase were selected by territorial assemblies. Hahn stressed that the article 45 of the electoral law imposed a further limitation with the requirement that candidates' electoral platforms "cannot conflict with the Constitution of the USSR and with Soviet legislation."

16. *Pravda*, 6 October 1989. See also table 1.

dreds of electoral districts used all means at their disposal, both legal and illegal, to exclude "undesirable" candidates from the final ballot. Often, public opinion remained quiescent in the face of such electoral manipulation; many Soviets, as we have seen, remained passive and politically unaware, while oppositionists were disorganized and unprepared. In a few cases, however, abuses of power by local officials sparked sufficient public outcry to force the same officials to retreat. Echoes of such outcry reached the Congress itself, where Boris Gidaspov, president of the Mandate Commission, reported that the CEC had received more than eight thousand letters protesting violations of the electoral code by Party officials. Gidaspov specifically mentioned the problems of "pressures being brought to bear on voters" and of "unjustified refusals to register candidates." [17]

The constitutional amendments proposed by the Nineteenth Party Organizational Conference and enacted into law by the Supreme Soviet complemented the electoral law and provided the finishing touches for Gorbachev's vision of carefully controlled reform.[18] Under these constitutional changes, the old Supreme Soviet disappeared. The Congress of People's Deputies grew by one-third, from 1,500 to 2,250, to accomodate the representatives of social organizations, but 1,500 deputies were to be elected directly and secretly, by universal adult suffrage. The new Supreme Soviet, comprised of 542 deputies elected by and from the Congress, assumed the functions and aspect of a permanent, semiprofessional parliament.

This body, the primary seat of legislative production in the new socialist "rule-of-law" state, was thereby to be elected in large part popularly, if still indirectly. Furthermore, it boasted another innovation: the composition of the Supreme Soviet would not remain static for its five-year tenure, but 20 percent of its deputies would be "rotated" every year.[19] The official reason for this rotation was to place all deputies of the Congress on an equal footing with those who also served as members of the Supreme Soviet. In fact, the rotation could be interpreted as another form of conservative control, allowing the Party *apparat*, as long as it controlled a Congress and Supreme Soviet majority, to purge the Supreme Soviet of

17. *Izvestiia*, 26 May 1989. The author personally witnessed repeated attempts in Moscow to exclude candidates illegally. This situation existed in the capital, where public opinion exerted great influence and where, in the end, at least two candidates succeeded in registering in every electoral district. In the countryside—both in the RSFSR and other areas, such as Armenia, Georgia, and Central Asia—frequent abuses were reported, and some have been documented by the central news media.

18. "*Zakon Soiuza Sotsialisticheskikh Respublik ob Izmeneniakh i Dopolneniakh Konstitutsii (Osnovnogo Zakona)*," as printed in *Pravda*, 3 December 1988.

19. Article 111, *Pravda*, 3 December 1988.

deputies who proved too radical. In any case, such annual rotation clearly could impede the development of a competent, professional, and well-organized parliament. Each year, the Supreme Soviet would lose many experienced members, replaced by hundreds of "milkers" and "vanguard workers" proposed by the *apparat* and not offering real solutions to the country's problems.[20]

The constitutional modifications reserved enormous powers for the president of the Supreme Soviet—that is, as all expected, for Mikhail Gorbachev—in all matters concerning the formation and functioning of the Congress and the Supreme Soviet.[21] In particular, the president was to enjoy wide discretion in the selection of men and women to fill top-level state positions. Although the Congress as a whole could confirm or reject his nominations, it could not propose alternative candidates.[22]

Despite the wide array of measures designed to protect the power of the *apparat* and the president, the constitutional modifications and the new electoral law represented a quantum leap in the development of Soviet democracy, laying the foundations for radical political reform and establishing new (and unprecedentedly powerful) instruments of popular participation. First, for example, it was proclaimed that ". . . the most important all-Soviet, republican, and local questions will be decided in the meetings of the Congress of People's Deputies, the sessions of the Supreme Soviet, and the sessions of local Soviets of People's Deputies, or will be subjected to a referendum by these bodies."[23] And as we shall see, the new Supreme Soviet transformed itself from a Party rubber stamp into a parliament that in some respects resembled those of Western representative democracies. It now met twice a year, for three to four months at a

20. "Milkers" were referred to, ironically, as the equally manipulable countryside counterparts of "vanguard workers"—that is, those men and women removed from their factories and placed in positions of authority by the *apparat*. Article 111 did not provide that *all* of the 2,250 deputies would eventually rotate onto the Supreme Soviet. In fact, no more than 974 deputies could have this opportunity. Andrei Sakharov was the first to reach this conclusion, during the First Congress. When he announced his figures to his fellow deputies, many were surprised, since most commentators—ignoring the fine points of the law's language—had simply assumed that a 20 percent rotation over five years would offer at least the potential for all Congress deputies to serve on the Supreme Soviet. Nonetheless, the positive side of Article 111 became apparent when the conservative majority at the First Congress succeeded in excluding nearly all of *perestroika*'s most vocal advocates from the Supreme Soviet. Without this article, it would have been impossible to modify the composition of the Supreme Soviet for five full years.

21. One significant detail was the modification of the title of "President of the Presidium of the Supreme Soviet" to "President of the Supreme Soviet," apparently to lend greater weight to the personal role of the leader.

22. Article 121, *Pravda*, 3 December 1988. This rule would prove crucial in a variety of situations during the first session of the Congress.

23. Article 91, *Pravda*, 3 December 1988.

time, and its permanent commissions and committees worked throughout the year. Such changes in the Supreme Soviet altered the character and power of a typical deputy, who started to evolve into a professional politician.[24]

Rules that Stalinist and Brezhnevite legislators had held to be "useless" now found themselves established as constitutional principles. The president of any Soviet—including the Supreme Soviet—could be "recalled at any time by a secret vote of the Congress" or of the corresponding assembly that had elected him or her.[25] Among other changes in the nature of Soviet politics was the sudden incompatibility of executive state positions with legislative powers. Ministers, judges, and state arbiters could no longer simultaneously serve in parliament.[26] This rule extended to all levels of the governmental hierarchy, even excluding members of local Soviet executive committees from local elective assemblies. Furthermore, for the first time ever a rule established that "a citizen of the USSR cannot simultaneously be a people's deputy in more than two Soviets."[27]

In contrast with the concepts of representation at work in Western democracies, the constitutional changes preserved, albeit in a slightly modified form, the power of an electoral college to revoke an individual's parliamentary mandate during his or her term in office.[28] Admittedly, Soviet history offers few examples of a parliamentary mandate being revoked from below, and the Supreme Soviet never clarified how such an action was to be taken. Nevertheless, in conditions of increased popular participation and activism, the threat of such revocation became a potentially powerful weapon.[29]

The greatest innovation introduced in the constitutional amendments

24. Articles 104 and 124 of the constitutional reform allowed Supreme Soviet deputies to hold other offices, either in government or elsewhere (for example, as a factory director). Such a policy allowed party leaders to avoid holding a single, full-time position. This rule permitted Gorbachev simultaneously to occupy the posts of president of the Supreme Soviet and general secretary of the CPSU, but also enabled hundreds of regional first secretaries to sit in parliament. A bitter argument erupted over this issue in Congress, and was resolved by a conservative majority vote prohibiting the holding of additional public offices by Supreme Soviet members "as a rule." The formula adopted, however, permitted many exceptions.

25. Article 120, law cited above.

26. Article 98, law cited above.

27. Article 95, law cited above.

28. See Article 107, law cited above. "Any deputy who proves not worthy of the voters' trust or of that of [his or her] social organization may be recalled at any time by a majority decision of the voters, or of the social organization that elected him [or her], following the procedures established by law."

29. After the First Congress, many citizen assemblies—dissatisfied with the conduct of their representatives—petitioned the Supreme Soviet urgently seeking approval of a law to regulate the revocation of a parliamentary mandate.

of 1988, however, was the creation of a Constitutional Control Committee.[30] Comprised of twenty-three legal experts and elected by the Congress for a ten-year term, this committee represented the first real step towards a division of powers within the Soviet Union. Legislative production of the Supreme Soviet, republican Soviets, the Council of Ministers, and all other state bodies potentially became subject to review by this independent body. The degree of real independence that would be permitted to the committee remained in practical terms a decision to be made by the Congress, but the implied acceptance of the principle of the separation of governmental powers was unprecedented.

The electoral law, too, despite its elements of conservative control, contributed to the expansion of a public space in Soviet politics by establishing a broad series of new rights for the public, for candidates for office, and for elected deputies. This new spirit and intent of the law helped transform the electoral campaign into a truly public event. For the first time, self-nominations were possible,[31] eliminating at least a few of the old bureaucratic hassles that obstructed outsiders from entering politics. Candidates received the right to publicize their platforms in newspapers and on radio and television. Any candidates successfully registering with district electoral commissions could choose "trustworthy representatives" ("*doverennye litsa*") to propagandize on their behalf. Mass media representatives enjoyed access to all phases of the electoral campaign, up to and including ballot-counting. Candidates themselves enjoyed certain powers at this stage: their representatives could check on and verify the honesty of all phases of the voting. Real competition between candidates was established as a principle, and the entire process was placed under the protection of the official *glasnost* campaign.

Abuses of power, of course, did occur during the electoral campaign that followed. Nevertheless, these reforms almost certainly reduced the magnitude and frequency of electoral fraud, particularly in those areas where the electorate had organized itself sufficiently to defend its chosen candidates against the *apparat*. The end result was, in the spring of 1989, a departure from the farcical votes of the past and the first real, honest elections in the Soviet Union in more than seventy years. A system of representative democracy was forming. The static power balance of old among workers, peasants, *intelligenty*, and Party functionaries became obsolete, replaced with dynamism, political spontaneity, and battles among a variety of bitterly opposed political groups. The situation varied widely in different areas and republics, but the Congress elected on

30. Article 125, law cited above.
31. Article 100, law cited above, in *Pravda*, 3 December 1988.

26 March 1989 was unrecognizable in terms of the old system. Elements of conservatism in the compromises of 1988 succeeded in preventing a total seizure of power by radicals, but the changes allowed by the constitutional revisions and the new electoral law were remarkable. Hundreds of deputies—a minority of the Congress, to be sure, but a vocal, pugnacious minority—were "new men" (and "new women"), heterogeneous, independent-minded, uncontrolled by and not beholden to the Party apparatus.

# The Electoral Campaign

The electoral campaign of early 1989 defied all expectations, quickly obsoleting the compromises reached by Gorbachev and conservatives in 1988. In attempting to contain and control the process of democratization, the "Soviet socialist conservatives"[1] badly miscalculated. But the radical intelligentsia erred, too, ironically also underestimating the rate and depth of the political awakening sweeping many sections of Soviet society. Gorbachev's confidence that the pace of events in the USSR could be controlled proved unfounded. Procedural traps designed to slow or restrict popular political expression often did not spring, and when they did, they (unexpectedly) most often caught members of the *apparat* as their victims. In the elections of 1989 the *apparat*'s candidates went down to defeat in hundreds of districts. Not even the buffer of social organizations completely withstood the pressure from below. Although most deputies appointed by social organizations did prove to be conservative or at most moderate, a startling number turned out to be progressive and even radical.

As we have already seen, the electoral law in many places breached the protective wall erected by the *apparat*. Article 37 contained one of the most important of these breaches, stating that "in the [preliminary] meetings, an unlimited number of candidacies may be proposed."[2] Article 38, however, established the discretionary power of district-level electoral commissions to "summon [a] preelectoral district assembly" (POS) to rule on the final registration of these candidacies on the ballot. This authority, meant only to serve as one option among many for district

---

1. The phrase is Gavriil Popov's. See Medvedev and Chiesa, *Time of Change* (New York: Pantheon Books, 1990), 181.
2. *Pravda*, 3 December 1988, previously cited law.

leaders in protecting their position, became the *apparat*'s weapon of choice in eliminating radical candidates.

Article 37's use of the word "unlimited" precluded establishing a ceiling on the maximum number of candidates permitted. At the same time, though, it did not specify any required minimum number of candidates, and thus did not proscribe one-candidate elections. Conservatives fully exploited this weakness of Article 37 in tandem with their powers under article 38. The resulting figures speak eloquently. Fully 9,505 candidates emerged during the first, preliminary phase of nominations, representing 4.2 candidates for each seat in Congress. Only 5,074 of these candidates, however—somewhat more than half of those nominated, and only 2.3 per seat—managed to secure registration with their POS. Most POSs functioned as filters, just as conservative legislators had hoped they would.[3] Not surprisingly, the social organizations most effectively avoided multi-candidate elections, allowing only 912 men and women to compete for 750 seats (a ratio of 1.2 to 1). The degree to which these organizations controlled their nominees in many cases made the final balloting almost meaningless.[4]

## The Social Organizations

We have already seen how the social organizations' seats were apportioned, but a few surprises marked the actual voting. On the one hand, the seat-distribution mechanism, the controls on candidate nomination, and the election by small groups in the organizations' plenums often combined to produce the result expected by conservatives, namely the election of moderate *intelligenty* and conservative bureaucrats to most of the 750 seats. On the other hand, however, fierce struggles broke out in the plenums of certain organizations over the elections. Roughly fifty radical reformers, who would have faced difficulties in surmounting the obstacles placed before territorially-elected delegates, emerged from the social organization elections as people's deputies.

Political divisions, then, cut across all sectors of Soviet society, even across those assumed to be the most conservative. No social group stood homogeneously for or against *perestroika* and political reform. Indeed, the possibility of placing a few extra radicals in the Congress through the social organizations may even have helped persuade Gorbachev and his reformist allies to defend the odd mechanism of allocating seats to the social organizations. In some cases, social organizations even produced a

3. See table 1.
4. See table 2.

more accurate cross-section of society in their delegations to the Congress than did territorial elections. Even the CPSU could be taken as a case in point, with intellectuals of all ideological stripes—including well-known reformers—taking their places in the Party delegation.

The election of deputies at the Academy of Sciences most effectively demonstrates the complex nature of the social organizations' elections. An informal coalition of institute leaders and academy bureaucrats first suceeded in excluding progressive candidates from consideration. When vigorous protests swept the scientific community, however, and Central Committee reformers brought pressure to bear, the academy's Party organization was forced to intervene and reinstate the progressive nominees. When the Academy's 1,278 members met to consider 23 nominees for 20 seats, nearly 500 ballots rejected all 23.[5] Only 8 nominees won the required majority approval, and the procedure was repeated to fill the 12 seats still vacant. Twenty-five new, and for the most part progressive, candidates were considered on 21 April. Many well-known reformers— including Andrei Sakharov, Nikolai Shmelev, Iurii Kariakin, Pavel Bunich, Roald Sagdeev, Gennadi Lisichkin, Vitalii Ginzburg, and Georgii Arbatov—thus won election to the Congress.[6] Sakharov could certainly have won election in virtually any territorial district, and in fact was nominated by several assemblies. The other reformist scientists, however, did not enjoy the same public renown, and likely would not have been elected without a franchise restricted to the academy.

Similar situations arose in a number of other social organizations. The Union of Engineering Societies elected Gavriil Popov, editor of the journal *Voprosy Ekonomiki* and later mayor of Moscow; the Foundation for Peace selected Fedor Burlatskii, political commentator for *Literaturnaia Gazeta*. The Scientific Societies elected sociologist Tatiana Zaslavskaia, the Academy of Agricultural Sciences chose radical economist Vladimir Tikhonov, the Foundation for Culture tapped academician Dmitrii Likhachev, and the Cinema Union selected Egor Iakovlev, editor of the radical newspaper *Moskovskie Novosti*. Other artistic and media unions compromised, choosing deputies of widely varying political persuasions. The Writers' Union, for example, elected both the progressives S. Zalygin and A. Gonchar and the conservative "Russophiles" Viktor Astafev and Valentin Rasputin.

Of the candidates favoring a radical acceleration of *perestroika*, in fact, relatively few were prevented outright from entering the Congress by

5. *Sovetskaia Kultura*, 25 March 1989.
6. Arbatov had previously been defeated in elections for the delegation of the Soviet Committee for the Defense of Peace, another social organization.

the social organizations' conservative elements. The Journalists' Union refused to select Aleksandr Bovin or Otto Lazis, but did elect Mikhail Poltoranin, a chief aide of Boris Yeltsin, after Poltoranin had been rejected by *Moskovskaia Pravda*. The Union of Theater Workers refused to approve Mikhail Shatrov,[7] but other prominent intellectuals, once spurned by social organizations, became territorial candidates. Such tenacious tactics eventually gained many reformers a seat in Congress.[8]

The notable reformist exceptions, however, should not cloud the overall picture. The electoral mechanisms and safeguards did in the main ensure the quiet election of controllable deputies to represent most social organizations. As we shall see, very few of the 750 social-organization deputies turned out to be progressive. Particularly among the 325 deputies representing the trade unions, *kolkhozy*, Veterans' Union, and Womens' Unions, reformists remained pitifully few in number.[9] The most contradictory, surprising—and apparently antidemocratic—situation arose in the elections for the 100-member CPSU delegation. The Party, which at the Nineteenth Conference had issued its clarion call for democratic reform, anticipated other social organizations by calling its expanded plenum[10] and then proposing 100 candidates for 100 seats. Even more surprising, Gorbachev himself, the proponent of electoral competition, proposed and lent strong support to such an approach.

During a break in the proceedings of the expanded Party plenum, a prominent intellectual reportedly pointed out to Gorbachev the bad example that would be set at the start of the electoral campaign by not allowing a multi-candidate election for the CPSU delegation. Gorbachev, it is said, replied: "Do you really think that even we [in the Party] have to play along with this comedy?" His alleged remark became well-known in

7. Shatrov tried again to gain a territorial seat in a Moscow district, but was again defeated.

8. Evgenii Evtushenko and Vitalii Korotich, both repeatedly defeated in various social organizations' plenums and in Moscow territorial districts, eventually succeeded in securing election from two territorial districts in the Ukraine.

9. Defeats of conservatives were rare. The Trade Union plenum, for example, rejected the Ukrainian first secretary Vitalii Sologub and the deputy president of the Central Council Vladimir Lomonosov (see *Trud*, 25 March 1989). The accurate analysis of FBIS (Foreign Broadcast Information Service), "Parliamentary Elections in the USSR: Voters Stun Soviet Officialdom," 16 June 1989, pointed out that Pavel Fedirko, president of the Union of Consumer Cooperatives, was elected with 309 of 1,503 votes opposed (see *Selskaia Zhizn*, 25 March 1989). In an analogous situation, Tikhon Khrennikov won election to the last seat available (see *Sovetskaia Kultura*, 21 March 1989).

10. This plenum had 641 members, including 302 full members of the Central Committee, 157 candidate members of the Central Committee, 82 members of the Auditing Commission, all other first and second Party secretaries of the republics, the presidents of the Supreme Soviet and of the Council of Ministers, regional Party first secretaries, ministers of the all-Union government, and the chiefs of military regions.

Moscow, arousing public indignation. Even if he did not actually say it, the cynical sentiment remains apt. It illustrates neatly some of the paradoxes of Soviet democratization, where the strongest boosters of democratic reform often felt that such reform was still an empty exercise and so should not affect them. Conditions for the Soviet transition to democracy clearly remained anomalous.

We have already suggested the probable reasons for Gorbachev's failure to submit himself to a public vote of confidence. He doubtless needed to generate growing pressure from below in order to dislodge *apparatchiki* from positions of power, but at the same time refused to allow internal political equilibria to be upset beyond a certain point. In essence, Gorbachev's initial vision for Soviet democracy included the preservation of certain important aspects of the existing order. He refused at first to allow the principle of public political participation to extend into the Kremlin itself. The list of 100 nominees for the CPSU delegation hence showed all the contradictions of Gorbachev's initial push to create a system that was simultaneously Soviet and democratic in a state that would be simultaneously socialist and governed by the rule of law.

The Party plenum approved the list of 100 nominees, and all entered the Congress. The vote itself, however, revealed the dangers facing the high Party leadership. If only 110 nominees had competed for the 100 CPSU seats, six of the nominated Politburo members would have failed to enter Congress. If 120 had been nominated, all nine of the Politburo members who stood for election—Gorbachev included—would have been rejected.[11] By arranging for a closed list, Gorbachev and his reformist allies ensured the presence of many progressives in the Congress, such as the surgeon S. Fedorov, the writers Chingiz Aitmatov, B. Oleinik, and D. Granin, and the economist Leonid Abalkin. Proponents of democracy could survive only by resorting to undemocratic tactics.

## The Territorial and National-Territorial Districts

Elections for the 1,500 seats of popularly elected deputies were scheduled to take place on 26 March 1989. On the eve of the voting, the situation could be summarized by a few simple numbers. In 952 districts two candidates fought for a seat; in 149 districts more than two candidates faced off; and in fully 399 districts (that is, 27 percent of races) candidates ran unopposed. The filtering systems described above, loopholes and ambiguities in the electoral law, and maneuvering by members of the *apparat*

11. See table 3. This presumes that the additional nominees would be comparative unknowns who would attract only a few cancellations.

succeeded in eliminating or reducing the danger presented by opposition candidates.

The lack of true multi-candidate elections, however, also revealed the unpreparedness and disorganization of political reformers in many areas and their near-total absence in others. No popular organizations had been developed that could oppose the electoral machinations of republican and district-level Party officials effectively. The importance of opposition organization quickly became apparent. The POSs succeeded almost everywhere in reducing the number of candidates to reach the final ballot, even though the power of these assemblies to "evaluate" candidates did not legally require them to eliminate any.[12] In those few places where political opposition to the local apparatus had become highly developed, however, progressives managed to reduce electoral manipulation and fraud significantly.

Important changes, in any case, had occurred. The days of single-candidate elections, with the candidates being selected by local *apparatchiki*, had ended in most of the country. Electors in 73 percent of the USSR's electoral districts received a ballot with at least two names on it. The extension to the public of a measure of real political power produced strong reactions. In more than half (seventy-six) of the 149 districts with more than two candidates, no candidate received a majority, requiring a run-off election between the two leading vote-getters. Carrying even greater political significance, a majority of voters in 195 of the 1,351 districts with either one or two candidates cancelled all names on the ballot.[13] This action required a complete reopening of the nomination and election process in these districts (representing 14 percent of races), and signified a major vote of no-confidence in the conservative candidates put forward by the *apparat*. Politics had awakened public interest, and enough people familiarized themselves with the complexities of electoral law to realize that they could oppose conservative candidates meaningfully. Even in those districts where filtering mechanisms worked perfectly, conservative bureaucrats could not be assured of victory.

On the second ballot, fully 1,216 candidates competed for 198 electoral districts—that is, an average of 6.1 candidates per district. Very few POSs were convened, effectively limiting the *apparat*'s ability to influence candidate selection. Within a month, the results were dramatic. In Zagorsk district #31, voters found 22 names on the ballot;[14] three districts in Lenin-

12. Only in the three Baltic republics—following decisions by the republican Party organizations—were the POSs simply abolished, thereby ensuring the automatic registration of all candidates.

13. To these 195 districts we must add three Armenian districts, where elections had to be repeated because less than 50 percent of the registered voters took part.

14. *Moskovskie Novosti* 18, 30 April 1989.

grad featured 18, 21, and 28 candidates, respectively;[15] and one district in Kiev may have set an all-Union record with a list of 33 candidates.[16]

## Republican Results

No full analysis of the electoral results by republics has yet been published. The figures and (incomplete) comparative analysis that follow are the result of long research utilizing both central and peripheral media publications. The difficulties that hinder any such effort are only increased by the fragmentary character of the data provided; many lacunae result from Soviet journalists' shortcomings as well as the failure of central and peripheral electoral commissions to gather and publish final results. This latter failure no doubt owes much to the reflexes of the past, whereby many officials, conditioned to the necessity of secrecy, thought it safest not publicly to divulge information at their disposal. Moreover, news coverage of the electoral campaign was spotty, showing the greatest gaps where vote manipulation seemed likely to be the most flagrant. As will be shown below, both *political* and *technical* fraud are most easily discerned in areas with large gaps in the official record.[17]

Although this theme will be treated in detail later, a few examples will suffice to demonstrate the point.[18] Newspapers in Moscow, Leningrad, Lithuania, Latvia, and Moldavia published complete election results for both winners and losers. In five other republics—Kazakhstan, Tadzhikistan, Kirghizia, Turkmenia, and Uzbekistan—local papers limited themselves to printing lists of winners with no further information. In these republics coverage of the candidate nomination process was also poor. This was no coincidence, as these republics also showed a significantly higher-than-average proportion of single-candidate districts. Armenian, Azerbaijani, and Georgian data featured similar gaps, as did that of many regions and autonomous republics of the Russian Federation. The daily paper *Sovetskaia Rossiia*, organ of the RSFSR's Supreme Soviet, was among the most sparing in providing its readers hard information; *Pravda* also distinguished itself by informational parsimony. Somewhat more information may have appeared in local papers throughout the Union, but most republican organs systematically avoided the publication of final, complete lists. The only major exception to this rule was *Izvestiia*, which

15. *Leningradskaia Pravda*, 21–23 April 1989.
16. *Trud*, 16 May 1989.
17. *Political* fraud is here defined as the use of law to swindle the electorate out of its declared rights. *Technical* fraud, which carries legal penalties even under Soviet judicial codes, is by contrast open falsification of ballots or electoral results.
18. These examples rely in large part on the analysis in FBIS, 16 June 1989, "Parliamentary Elections in the USSR: Voters Stun Soviet Officialdom."

printed significantly more information than its competitors; *Sovetskaia Kultura* also supplied almost complete accounts of the voting within various social organizations.

In this context official data regarding voter participation must be seen as dubious.[19] The highest percentages of voter turnout were reported in those areas where postelection information was the most sparse and where, by most criteria of measurement, old manipulative techniques strongly influenced the result.[20] The skeptical observer cannot but raise an eyebrow at reports of 98.5 percent turnout in Azerbaijan, or of 97 percent turnout in Kirghizia and Georgia. Five republics, including Turkmenia and Uzbekistan, reported figures close to the Brezhnev-era standard of 99.9 percent. All of these republics, therefore, reported suspect participation rates at least 10 percent higher than the Russian Federation, which averaged 87 percent. We must take into account the low levels of Central Asian political integration, socialization, and participation that have already been noted, combined with the high numbers of one-candidate districts and *nomenklatura*-dominated elections. As will be shown below, deputies elected from these republics showed significantly less political independence and initiative, and significantly more conservative positions on many issues, than their counterparts from other republics. The official data, therefore, clearly seem not to reflect reality. Consequently, we might propose a general law: *the reported level of participation in the republican elections of spring 1989 is inversely proportional to the actual democratic nature of those elections.*[21]

The participation figures in Moscow, Leningrad, the Baltic republics, and many parts of the Russian Federation, Belorussia, and the Ukraine

19. *Izvestiia*, 5 April 1989, published the communique of the Central Electoral Commission.

20. See table 4, first column.

21. The only exception, which may confirm the rule, was Armenia, with the lowest reported participation rate of 71.9 percent, fully 17.9 percent below the all-Soviet average of 89.8 percent. This result is explicable largely in terms of the state of the republic following the ruinous earthquake of December 1988. Other factors, however, also played a part. The electoral campaign proceeded during the conflict with Azerbaijan, and mass nonparticipation served for many as a form of protest against the "anti-Armenian" character of the solution proposed for the Nagorno-Karabakh crisis. Voting had to be repeated in three districts where participation fell below the legally required minimum of 50 percent, the only places in the Soviet Union where this measure was required. The official figure of 71.9 percent participation may in any case be artificially inflated, as our general law predicts. The author has heard numerous testimonies of vote falsification in Erevan. And although the Mandate Commission of the Congress confirmed all elected deputies, suspicions of irregularities remained. For example, certain top-ranking Armenian Party officials, none notably popular, won unopposed elections with fantastically high levels of support: the Armenian Party first secretary won with 94 percent support; the second secretary, with 97 percent; the chief of the republican KGB, with 96 percent; and a Central Committee secretary, Galoian, with 99 percent.

accurately reflected the presence of an already high level of political consciousness and civic organization, and this fact alone might seem surprising in a country lacking traditions of meaningful electoral competition. The *leitmotif* of the struggles that resulted was a clash of growing mass politicization with the stubborn refusal of the *nomenklatura* to surrender its commanding position. Many observers portrayed the outcome as a severe loss for the Party, and such a portrayal is not without truth. It is also true, however, that 87.6 percent of elected deputies belonged to the CPSU. Perhaps a more accurate assessment, then, would be that members of the *apparat* and the top level of the *nomenklatura* lost badly. The elections demonstrated a clear division between the *apparat* and the Party rank and file membership as well as marked diversity of political opinions at all levels of the Party hierarchy. In what follows, we will try to measure as precisely as possible the dimensions of this defeat of the *apparat*, but the overall pattern is clear. Where a real struggle occurred, the *apparat* lost almost universally. The contrapositive is equally important: in most districts, no real struggle took place.[22]

In total, 117 first regional Party secretaries won election as people's deputies. Adding republican first and second Party secretaries, leaders of republican governments, and presidents of republican Supreme Soviets, this figure reaches 172. At this topmost level, only 35 officials were defeated. Even so, these 35 defeats were significant: in these districts, millions of voters rejected the highest Party and state authorities, men and women once considered to be omnipotent. Widening our analysis to an all-Soviet perspective, it becomes apparent that top-level losers were in fact more numerous than these data suggest. First, it remains unclear how many top-level officials established candidacies in the initial phase of the electoral campaign; only lists of winners and fragmentary information on losers are available. As has already been noted, too, many of these officials bypassed the electoral campaign entirely, instead securing the approval of the CPSU Central Committee expanded plenum. Furthermore, certain high-level officials, particularly in the Baltic republics, won election by soliciting the endorsement of republican popular front organizations.[23]

Finally, top officials on the next rung of the Party and state hierarchy—leaders in republican capitals and large cities—sustained heavy losses in the elections. This result suggests provisional confirmation for another of

22. For evidence supporting the analysis that follows, see tables 4 and 5.
23. The entire top level of the Latvian Party won election in this manner, as did much of the Estonian and Lithuanian Party. See table 5. The analysis in FBIS is correct, and is largely confirmed by checking the converse: Party and state officials in these areas without Popular Front support either went down to defeat or survived by the thinnest of margins.

our generalizations, namely that large and medium-sized urban centers were characterized by higher levels of political awareness than the provinces, smaller cities, and countryside. This variation derived from several causes, including a higher level of cultural organization, stronger and more direct contact with *glasnost*, and more widespread social networks, which themselves aided the growth of political groups and informal organizations. To take one example of urban political independence, Boris Yeltsin won 89.44 percent of votes cast in the Moscow national-territorial district,[24] handily defeating an automotive factory director, Evgenii Brakov, despite the active support given Brakov by virtually every important Party organization in the city.

Vitalii Vorotnikov, the president of the Russian Federation's Supreme Soviet, originally entered his name as a candidate in this district but quietly withdrew rather than face near-certain defeat in a showdown with Yeltsin. He eventually won election as an unopposed candidate in Voronezh, his old political base. Those high-level officials in Moscow who did not share Vorotnikov's wisdom in entering a race elsewhere,[25] however, lost without exception. Two obvious losers were Valerii Saikin, the leader of the Moscow City Council, and Iurii Prokofev, the Moscow Party second secretary, as well as two *raikom* (regional) Party first secretaries.

The *apparat* met even bleaker results in Leningrad, as no city leader won election as a people's deputy. The list of the defeated included: first regional secretary and candidate member of the Politburo Iurii Solovev, who ran unopposed; the city first secretary, Gerasimov; the second regional secretary, Fateev; the president of the executive regional committee, Popov; the mayor, Khodyrev; and the deputy mayor, Bolshakov, who also ran unopposed. Voters in Kiev rejected the city Party first secretary, Masik, and the mayor, Zgurskii. The first secretaries of Lvov and of several republican capitals—Minsk, Alma-Ata, Frunze, Dushanbe, and Kishinev—also lost their races.[26] A brief review of republican results, grouped geographically, allows us to evaluate the extent of the defeat suffered by the *apparat*.[27]

*Transcaucasia*

Official Armenian data have already been shown to be suspect. Almost half of territorial and national-territorial districts in that republic (19 of

24. This district was the largest national-territorial district in the Union, containing 6,857,000 voters.
25. The first secretary of the Moscow Party and member of the Politburo, Lev Zaikov, went even farther than Vorotnikov, avoiding risk altogether by running as one of the 100 candidates elected by the CPSU.
26. See FBIS, "Parliamentary Elections." The first secretaries of Dushanbe and Kishinev won election in the second round of balloting in May.
27. See table 4.

40) featured only one candidate. No information has been made available regarding the number of single-candidate districts in Azerbaijan and Georgia, but the only top-level official defeated in either republic was the president of the Azerbaijani Supreme Soviet. Three first regional secretaries won election in Georgia, as compared with only one in Azerbaijan.[28]

### The Baltic republics

A large majority of the 118 deputies from Estonia, Latvia, and Lithuania competed in multi-candidate elections. Only 3 of 36 districts in Estonia, and 7 of 40 in Latvia, were single-candidate. In Latvia the top Party and state leaders were forced to compete with at least one other candidate. In Lithuania, the *Sajudis* Popular Front won 36 of 42 seats outright[29] and additionally supported, either directly or indirectly, the Lithuanian Party first secretary Brazauskas and second secretary Berezov.[30] By contrast, two officials opposed by *Sajudis*—the president of the Lithuanian Supreme Soviet, Astrauskas, and the president of the Lithuanian Council of Ministers—both suffered heavy defeats.[31] In Estonia, the picture was similar if not quite so one-sided, with the Popular Front winning 16 of 36 seats outright and lending its support to Estonian first secretary Vialias, prime minister Toome, and Supreme Soviet president Riuitel.[32] The Latvian Popular Front also supported certain Party leaders by withdrawing its own candidates, although the resulting votes were not as lopsided as in Lithuania or Estonia. The president of the Latvian Supreme Soviet, Gorbunov, for instance, won 82 percent support, but Party first secretary Vagris won only a bare victory at 51 percent, and Party second secretary Sobolev did only slightly better, at 55 percent. The Latvian Popular Front also had less success than its other Baltic counterparts in gaining outright victories, taking 11 of 40 seats.

### Central Asia

The picture changes substantially when we turn our attention to the 280 territorial and national-territorial deputies elected in Central Asia.[33] In Uzbekistan, a total of 81 deputies included 22 high-level Party and

28. According to the data available, only three Party regional first secretaries were candidates in Georgia, and only one in Azerbaijan. That is, in neither republic was an official at this level defeated in an election. See table 5.

29. *Sajudis* won 31 seats in the first round of voting on 26 March, and added 5 more in the supplementary ballot of 9 April.

30. Brazauskas won 73.5 percent of votes cast; Berezov received 82.6 percent. *Sajudis* could lend indirect support by withdrawing its own candidates in certain districts.

31. Astrauskas, for example, won only 26.5 percent support.

32. Vialias won with 92.8 percent of votes cast; Toome received 91 percent support; and Riuitel won 90 percent support.

33. See tables 4 and 5.

state officials and army officers. Fully 11 of these 22 were regional first secretaries. All four of the topmost Uzbek republican officials—the first and second Party secretaries, the prime minister, and the president of the Supreme Soviet—won election to the Congress. No information was made public regarding the number or proportion of single-candidate districts. Somewhat in contrast, only 3 of 39 districts in Turkmenia were single-candidate. Nevertheless, top-level republican leaders won election handily, along with the three first regional secretaries who entered their candidacies. Tadzhikistan had only one single-candidate district out of 46, but the republic's top four leaders, along with three regional Party first secretaries, easily won seats in the Congress. The paucity of information regarding Kirghizia is almost complete, with no data available on single-candidate districts or defeats of top-level *apparatchiki*. The top four Kirghiz republican leaders won seats in the Congress as well, however. Finally, 35 out of 73 districts in Kazakhstan featured only one candidate. All first secretaries who put their names forward ran without opposition, as did top-level republican Party and state leaders.

### Ukraine

At least 40 of the 175 Ukrainian territorial and national-territorial deputies belonged to the *nomenklatura*, and 27 won election without competition. Vladimir Shcherbitskii, the republican Party first secretary and member of the CPSU Politburo, ran unopposed, as did 19 of 21 first regional secretaries. Of the 4 who lost their elections,[34] 3 ran against at least 1 competitor; taken as a whole, only 2 members of the republican *nomenklatura* won election when forced to compete with another candidate.

### Belorussia

No information is available on the number of single-candidate districts among Belorussia's 60 territorial and national-territorial districts. Seventeen people's deputies, though, were top-level Party, state, or military officials. The republic's top 4 leaders won election, along with 4 regional first secretaries. Two first regional secretaries, however, went down to defeat.

### Moldavia

Out of 43 territorial and national-territorial districts, 15 had only one candidate. Nearly all of the republican Party leadership entered the Congress.

34. See table 5.

*Russian Federation*

No overall data about single-candidate districts are available. In Moscow, all districts featured competition amongst at least two candidates, although 5 of Leningrad's 21 districts had only one candidate. The president of the Supreme Soviet, Vorotnikov, won election without opposition in a district in Voronezh; the premier and candidate member of the Politburo Alexander Vlasov also won with no competition. Out of the 76 first secretaries who established candidacies, 24 were defeated. Of this latter group, 14 came from the Urals, West Siberia and the Far East, implying that political tension was not limited to the largest cities but had reached some peripheral areas of the RSFSR as well. For example, a nonparty candidate won election from the coal-mining region of Kuzbass, while in the Far East the first secretaries of Khabarovsk, Kamchatka, Magadan, Sakhalin, and the autonomous Jewish republic were defeated.[35]

## Electoral Campaign in the Army

According to the data available, 118 candidates for the Congress of People's Deputies were in military service.[36] Of the 25 proposed by social organizations,[37] 22 won seats in the Congress. Of the 93 candidates in territorial and national-territorial districts, however—62 of whom ran without opposition—37 were defeated.[38] The group of defeated soldiers included representatives of the high commands of several regions, such as M. Burlakov, commander of the Southern Group, and M. Khronopulo, commander of the Black Sea Fleet, both based in the Ukraine. The commander of the Pacific Fleet, G. Khvatov, and of the Northern Fleet, F. Gromov, also went down to defeat, as did V. Tsarkov, the commander of Moscow's antiaircraft defense, V. Ermakov, commander of the Leningrad military district, V. Novozhilov, Far East commander, and B. Snetkov, commander of Soviet forces in East Germany. The results clearly represented a major setback for the military high command, and made plain a dramatic loss in military prestige within Soviet society.

35. *Sovetskaia Rossiia*, 18 April 1989.
36. See FBIS, 8–9.
37. These organizations included the CPSU, DOSAAF (Voluntary Association of Cooperation with the Army, Aviation, and Marines), and the Association of War and Labor Veterans.
38. These details are taken from two interviews given by V. Nechaev, deputy chairman of Political Military Direction. The first was printed in *Krasnaia Zvezda*, 9 April 1989, and the second in the Bulgarian daily paper *Narodna Armia*, 11 April 1989.

# A Political Geography of the First Congress

The Congress first met in the Kremlin on 25 May 1989. Socially, politically, and professionally, it differed radically from its predecessor, which had been elected by the Supreme Soviet in 1984, during Konstantin Chernenko's brief tenure as Party leader. Even though the various conservative "filters" and obstacles meant that most deputies remained controllable, the new Congress of 1989 clearly reflected changes in Soviet society and public opinion. An assembly to represent accurately all social and national groups had not yet been realized, but even this imperfect Congress represented a quantum leap over its predecessors. Deputies wielded their power independently, as befitted a truly sovereign body, and expressed opinions that differed dramatically. Antagonism developed between proponents of different legislative strategies. Factions represented many, albeit not all, groups present in Soviet society.

The political struggle allowed by the new electoral law swept away the old quotas for certain social groups, by which percentages of seats had been reserved for workers, for farmers, and for intellectuals, in accordance with primitive Party sociology. It also overturned the hypocritical division between Party members and nonparty members, wherein the Central Committee set aside an artificially high number of seats to be held by (carefully controlled) non-Communists. Fully 87.6 percent of deputies to the Congress held CPSU cards in 1989, up from only 71.5 percent of the Congress elected in 1984. Pointing to this result, many Party *apparatchiki* argued that the elections had confirmed popular trust in the Communist Party. The real story, however, was more complex. Nonparty candidates could not compete with the Communist Party's organizational base, and many Soviet citizens started the political struggle by concentrating on the place where policy was made, that is, on the Party. As we shall see, many of the approximately two thousand Communist deputies differed from the "yes-men" of the past, particularly of the post-Stalin past, in possessing independent power bases. It surprised nearly everyone when the small group of radical intellectuals in the Congress, which had expected to find perhaps a few dozen sympathizers, enjoyed the support of hundreds of deputies. Even some deputies from remote areas, where *perestroika* and *glasnost* seemed to have faltered, voted with the radicals. Reformism's roots had grown deeper than most people suspected.

The Congress that met in Khrushchev's Palace of Congresses included many new faces. Although the numerical strength of the *apparat* remained relatively constant,[1] three other groups' sizes changed noticeably. "Technocrats," or economic leaders and managers, increased their representation from a paltry 6.6 percent to 25.3 percent, and the intelligentsia also increased its proportion of seats.[2] The lower strata of the productive and service spheres declined sharply, from 45.9 percent of the seats in 1984 to 22.1 percent in 1989. Reality had encroached on the *apparat*'s abstract sociological quotas, replacing them with a new system of power apportionment. This new system did not represent every social group proportionately—technocrats comprised far less than 25 percent of the Soviet population—but it did allow new, dynamic social forces to compete with old, entrenched groups. In other words, we can here perceive the beginnings of a political "free market." Reacting to these changes, Party conservatives lashed out bitterly and portrayed themselves as defenders of the working class against a usurpation of power by intellectuals.[3] As we shall see, this represented the first sally of a long-term conservative offensive purporting to express the grievances of dissatisfied groups and hoping to divide the reformist alliance of workers and intellectuals. At this stage, however, the working class was radicalized almost as thoroughly as was the intelligentsia. Many Muscovite workers, for instance, reacted violently against a Central Committee attempt to fashion a "workers'" denunciation of Boris Yeltsin at the March plenum. Conservatives' ability convincingly to portray themselves as defenders of the working class remained limited.[4]

1. See table 6. The group of central and republican *nomenklatura* in the Congress decreased from 41.5 percent to 40.5 percent between 1984 and 1989.

2. See table 6. These figures, however, do not reflect the actual situation well because some intellectuals were subsumed into the *nomenklatura* group. We will later employ different, and more revealing, analytic categories.

3. During the April plenum conservatives made this contention repeatedly. In particular, see the speeches of Bobovikov, the Party leader in Vladimir, and of Melnikov, the first secretary in Komi, in *Pravda*, 27 April 1989.

4. Tikhomirov, one of the five workers to request a Central Committee investigation of Yeltsin, came under strong attack at a Communist Party meeting at his Likhachev factory. Some even demanded his expulsion from the Party, although this motion was narrowly defeated. Tikhomirov's position was saved only by appeal to higher authority. His defenders argued that he sat in the Central Committee and that therefore he could only be expelled from the Party by that body or by the Party at large. Yeltsin's popularity continued to rise.

The radicalism of the working classes, however, differed in important ways from that of the intellectuals. Workers often allied with corporate interests to preserve those small privileges enjoyed by "working aristocracies," such as the special systems of food and consumer-goods distribution organized by large industrial enterprises. A diffuse anti-intellectualism traceable to Stalin's day also undercut any worker-intellectual alliance. Additionally, the sleeping giant of Russian nationalism showed the first signs of awakening, with ominous consequences to be addressed later. For now, though, we will confine the discussion to a description of the new Congress's most salient features. This description will lay the groundwork for the political analysis to follow in succeeding chapters.

*Pravda* published incomplete data on the professional composition of the new Congress in October.[5] Although the criteria by which deputies were categorized differed from those used by *Moskovskie Novosti*,[6] *Pravda*'s data yielded interesting information about the representation of certain low-status groups in the Congress. We will here introduce a third, different system of social and professional classification, a system based on *functional* criteria. Our goal in so doing is not mere description: we do not want simply to take a "snapshot" of the pre-Congress situation. Rather, we want to appreciate the medium- and long-term consequences of political changes. From the start we have argued that, by making possible a new phase of political dynamism, the opening of the First Congress signified a radical change in the Soviet political arena. The new parliamentary structures in fact only rode the crest of a powerful wave—a wave that grew with civil society and with the ever-increasing socialization of Soviet citizens into democratic norms of political behavior. For the first time since January 1918, albeit still imperfectly, a Soviet parliament reflected social and national trends. For the first time, too, real feedback between society and its political representatives, as seen in the formation of self-directed, independent institutions that responded to social pressures, began to exist.

These new, embryonic political forces, however, were still divided. Furthermore, many deputies lacked knowledge of, or experience in, practical political techniques and legislative procedures. Moreover, they had to act immediately, under intense public scrutiny, and felt unprecedently strong pressure from their constituents on a variety of issues. The March elections had ended popular fear of Party reprisals. The Party, indeed, had ceded many of its traditional restrictive powers to new institutions, institutions still too weak to provide strong leadership. The economic,

5. See table 7.
6. See table 6.

social, and political crisis, however, continued to worsen, and hence individual deputies' political positions changed overnight throughout the Congress' ten-day session. Partly as a result, the "political geography" of the First Congress differed from that of the Second, and particularly the Third, Congress. Within a year the political landscape had changed unrecognizably. We cannot employ the sociological and analytic approaches traditionally used in the past to explain Party behavior, since they do not help in understanding the Congress' dynamics. Hence, we shall attempt in other ways to discern the patterns of political evolution that emerged from this chaotic, near-anarchic situation.

## Social and Professional Groups

Several assumptions underlie our approach. First, we take the loss in Party discipline and compactness for granted, although to demonstrate it fully would require more space than is available. Here we need only recall that divisions within the Party emerged more clearly in the last few years than they had for decades, and incontrovertible evidence of dissension and debate at every level of the Party hierarchy exploded myths of a monolithic CPSU. Second, divisions within the Party can be seen as both vertical and horizontal, cutting across layers of the Party hierarchy as well as dividing each layer from others. Consider the upper echelons of Party leaders, members of the superior, mostly central, *nomenklatura*. We will distinguish this group from lower-level Party officials, the peripheral and inferior *nomenklatura*, because it enjoys greater power and has a different, more distant relationship with society. Differences of political culture, psychology, and technology also separate these upper-level leaders (*verkhi*) from their lower-level counterparts. The differences are not unlike those dividing infantry fighting in the trenches from generals mapping grand strategy in the comparative safety of headquarters. The military analogy breaks down, however, since the overall battle and its outcome should (at least in theory) be clearer at headquarters—but the superior *nomenklatura* knew far less than lower-level leaders about the strength of Soviet reformism.

Our approach to outlining the development of new political forces here is strictly *functional*. We hence require a system of sociological classification that differs from those employed by other researchers. Many members of the intelligentsia, for example, clearly belonged to the superior and inferior *nomenklatura*. The intelligentsia, however, occupied a special position in Soviet society, and although its members gained independence and power during the period of *perestroika*, they are readily distinguishable from those of the *nomenklatura* proper. That is, although they enjoyed political influence and material privilege, these men and women were not politicians. Historically and practically they enjoyed far less power and freedom than the rest of the *nomenklatura*: the *nomenklatura* proper could appoint the intelligentsia, rather than the reverse.[7] Hence, we will distinguish between groups based on their *social function*, rather than their *social title*. To take another example, the most senior military officers, both central and peripheral, also belonged to the *nomenklatura*. They have been considered separately here, however, allowing us to investigate whether they as a group were politically homogeneous. Even top-level economic managers traditionally belonged to the central and republican *nomenklatura*, although new laws regulating government enterprises—specifically guaranteeing workers' collectives the right to elect their own managers—did partially alter their status. Additionally, managers' autonomy increased during the debate over economic reform despite the strong resistance of central planning bodies. The managerial group's political and social role—and its projected expansion in size and power—thus placed it squarely at the center of attention. Another group, the Congress' largest, was that of agricultural, industrial, and transportation workers. Finally, the definition of the last main group, the "diffuse intelligentsia," is somewhat more complex. It includes men and women in technical professions, who worked at middle- and lower-level jobs in the productive and governmental structures, but whose jobs could be characterized as "intellectual." To summarize our methodology:[8]

1. *Superior nomenclature* (*nomenklatura*) includes high Party, government, and republican leaders, along with regional Party first secretaries who were not only an integral part of the classical *nomenklatura* but who had immediate access, at least potentially, to the Party's highest leaders; first secretaries of regional capitals; and presidents of *ispolkomy*[9] of regions and major cities. Excluding the military figures mentioned below, the group of "big voters" electing the CPSU delegation to the Congress was drawn completely from this group.

2. *Inferior nomenclature* (*cadres*) comprises the remainder of republican and regional nomenclatures, including government and Party leaders at the *raikom*[10] and lower levels, secretaries of Party organizations, local Kom-

---

7. For example, the chancellor of a major university would be appointed by the central *nomenklatura*, as would the director of an all-Soviet research institute, or the chief editor of a daily paper or a national magazine.

8. See table 8. We will here use the simplified titles.

9. The *ispolnitelnye komitety*, or executive committees, are the managerial bodies of regional Soviets.

10. *Raionnye komitety*, or district committees, are the Party committees at the level of *ispolkomy* in the Soviet state hierarchy.

somol officials, and leaders of trade unions and other social organizations.

3. *Military* includes all deputies in uniform, from whatever social group.

4. *Business executives (managers)* would be called "technocrats" in the West. They include company executives from both state-run and cooperative enterprises, directors of *sovkhozy* (state farms) and presidents of *kolkhozy* (collective farms), and certain ministerial figures whose function changed to make them, in effect, business executives.

5. *Intelligentsia* includes "creative" intellectuals: writers, artists, actors, academicians, professors, university researchers, and some religious figures. Spokesmen for central and peripheral mass media organizations, as well as media editors, also are counted as *intelligenty* because of the unifying role of *glasnost* and the homogeneity of lower-level media employees.

6. *Diffuse intelligentsia (technicians)* represents the most heterogeneous group, including engineers, teachers, technicians, doctors, magistrates, procurators, and lawyers. This group consists of highly qualified professionals, whether participating in the productive process or not.

7. *Material producers (workers)* includes all men and women employed in the actual production of goods and services at the lower levels of professional qualification.

8. *Others* includes pensioners and any others not mentioned above.[11]

## Ethnic Composition

The features and political development of the Congress were closely related to its ethnic composition. The "national question" influenced the entire debate of the Congress, representing a modern politico-theoretico-institutional version of the Gordian knot. Reform could not be carried out without cutting this knot. The architects of Gorbachev's constitutional changes and of the new electoral law, though, worked within the existing institutional structure, which itself was a Stalinist creation. The subdivision of the USSR into fifteen Union republics, with three lower levels of state institutions (autonomous republics, regions, and districts) had originally been arbitrary, aiming to "divide and conquer" by splitting ethnic groups among different territorial units. When Gorbachev chose to begin his reforms by working within the existing institutional frame-

11. For each deputy, the social position held at election has been used for categorization purposes in the First Congress. In some cases, deputies shifted position between Congresses, and therefore are counted in their new groups in the analyses of the Second and Third Congresses.

work, problems inevitably resulted, since the Stalinist institutions harbored decades-old contradictions and conflicts. No other starting point existed, however, in the fall of 1988. Serious discussion of institutional reform had only just begun, and although such reforms might best have preceded the elections, political urgency dictated otherwise. Gorbachev, in turn, himself underestimating the dangers of suddenly releasing pent-up national passions, decided to use the electoral campaign decisively to attack conservative resistance to political and institutional reform.

It soon became clear, unfortunately, that the Party leadership as a whole was paralyzed by the fear of starting a chain reaction by over-hasty action on the explosive issues of Nagorno-Karabakh and Baltic demands for independence. Careful examination of the behavior of Soviet leaders—Gorbachev included—reveals striking cultural, political, and tactical unpreparedness. With rare exceptions, even the Russian intelligentsia's most radical and liberal members showed serious deficiencies in realizing the importance of the national issue. Bureaucratic restrictions for years had prevented sociologists, ethnologists, and political scientists from studying ethnic and national conflicts too deeply. Such restrictions, though, started to boomerang against the Party in 1988, impeding the Party's knowledge of the problem and its ability to mediate conflicts. Significantly, a Party plenum on nationalities issues[12] was postponed repeatedly until the fall of 1989—and even then failed to do more than mouth empty platitudes.

Very likely the institutional framework that had been built under and perfected by Stalin could only function in an atmosphere of fear. When this fear began to fade, and when the central government showed even hints of weakness, the entire system of state institutional relations began to collapse. To make this clear, we must now describe the structure of the Congress elected in 1989. As already mentioned, two-thirds of its deputies were elected from either territorial or national-territorial districts. Territorial districts received deputies according to their populations, and national-territorial districts received predetermined numbers of deputies according to their position in the hierarchy of "national-state" levels decreed by the Soviet constitution of 1936.[13] The intent was to guarantee some smaller nationalities—those which had won territorial recognition at one of the four Soviet levels—at least a minimum threshold of representation in the central parliament, taking into account the fact that elections

12. Gorbachev initially proposed holding such a plenum in early 1988, a few weeks before the Nagorno-Karabakh crisis worsened dramatically.

13. Each of the 15 republics received 32 deputies; the 20 autonomous republics each received 11 deputies; 5 deputies were granted to each of the 8 autonomous regions; and each of the 10 autonomous districts elected 1 deputy.

in territorial districts could not be expected to replicate fully the ethnic distribution of the populace at large.[14] No guarantee of representation was made, however, to those ethnic and national groups that were not recognized at one of the four levels of recognition in the official territorial hierarchy and that consequently lacked any organs of self-government. Moreover, since the entire system of territorial subdivision, as we have seen, was more the result of Stalin-era divide-and-rule tactics than of genuine acknowledgment of national autonomy, many smaller, unrepresented groups remained unsatisfied, as did those larger groups divided territorially.

Herein lies the root of many of the Soviet Union's bitterly divisive ethnic feuds. The lines along which ethnic groups were structured originated in an arbitrary attempt to legislate the "nationalities problem" out of existence by redrawing boundaries. Massive (often forced) migrations of ethnic groups occurred during the Stalin era, and rapid industrialization produced high levels of population mobility in the RSFSR, Kazakhstan, and the European republics. Muted by the generous application of terror and drowned out by endless paeans to the "friendship of nationalities" and by the rhetoric of "internationalism," intransigent ethnic and national problems only festered. By the 1980s the indigenous ethnic population of some republics (and regions and autonomous districts) no longer formed a majority.[15] As decades passed and abuses accumulated, hatreds between and among "minor" and "major" nationalities solidified and became permanent. Democratic reform permitted these tensions to be expressed in purified form.

In the light of these remarks, even the partial and distorted functionality of the already-described electoral mechanisms seems to disappear almost completely. Until the election of 1989, however, the inconsistencies remained hidden by the control from above of the Supreme Soviet's composition. In consultation with republican leaders, the *apparat* had always decided on a detailed system of distribution of seats among nationalities and ethnic groups. *Pro forma* one-candidate elections to republican and central Soviets produced bodies that simply confirmed and reproduced this system. The election of 1989 ended this bureaucratic distribution of

14. Deputies elected to the old Supreme Soviet from national-territorial districts alone comprised the Soviet of Nationalities, one of the two chambers of the Supreme Soviet. In the new Supreme Soviet, now elected by the Congress, the Soviet of Nationalities included deputies from social organizations.

15. Kazakhstan, Iakutiia, and Abkhaziia were three examples. In other republics the indigenous population only barely formed a majority. See table 10 for the varying levels of diaspora among different Soviet peoples according to the census of 1979.

seats, but also underscored distortions within the new institutional structures. Growing popular activism and multi-candidate elections sometimes
combined with the numerical superiority of other ethnic groups to reduce the representation of the smaller nationalities at the national level.[16]
This situation resulted partly from the choices made by voters and partly
from the small sizes of ethnic populations not granted any of the four
levels of state recognition. As a result, dozens of national-ethnic groups
were not represented in the Congress,[17] and even more were excluded
from the Supreme Soviet.[18] In addition to these perhaps involuntary ex-
clusions, in some cases republican or regional majorities consciously attempted to reduce the representation of minorities. Many deputies, for
example, denounced the way in which Latvian local authorities allegedly
gerrymandered electoral districts to favor Latvian candidates over ethnic
Russians.[19]

The imbalances and anomalies, of course, although numerous, varied
widely in severity and effect. A few republics and nationalities were overrepresented. Georgia's proportion of the Congress' deputies, for example,
was more than double its proportion of the Soviet populace.[20] Lithuanians also found themselves favored (with 2.2 percent of seats for only 1.1
percent of population), as did the Turkmen (1.7 percent for 0.7 percent),
the Estonians, the Kirghiz, and several other groups. Clearly, imbalances
existed: on the high end of the scale, 1.0 million Estonians had 41 deputies, 91,000 Abkhaz had 8, and 173,000 Gagauz had 2, while 6.3 million

16. See table 9 for a comparison of the Supreme Soviet of 1984 with the new Congress
and Supreme Soviet of 1989 on the basis of nationality.

17. Valerii A. Tishkov, "*Assambleiia Natsii ili Soiuznyi Parlament?*" work in progress.
According to Tishkov's analysis (see table 9), 65 nationalities out of a total of 127 won
representation in the Congress. Among those nationalities not receiving representation: Assyrian, Aleut, Bulgar, Vepsy, Dolgan, Persian (Iranian), Itelmen, Karaim, Ket,
Chinese, Kurd, Mause, Iganasan, Negidabze, Nivkhe, Orodrian, Romanian, Saams,
Selkup, Serb, Slovak, Tabasaran, Talsh, Tophalar, Turkish, Udin, Uldies, Finnish, Tsagur,
Taigan, Czech, Shorze, Jikagin, Evenk, and Eskimo. The author thanks Valerii Tishkov, director of the Ethnographic Institute of the Academy of Sciences of the USSR, for
allowing him access to this analysis before its publication.

18. Six groups represented in the Congress—the Karachaev, Greek, Taty, Abazius,
Lak, and Hungarian—failed to gain seats in the Supreme Soviet.

19. Although the Mandate Commission certified these elections—as it did all elections—irregularities clearly occurred. In Latvia, electoral districts of 28,000 voters had
been established in areas where Latvians comprised an overwhelming majority, as compared with districts of 150,000 in certain cities where Russians represented a majority.
Several protests about similar gerrymandering in Lithuania and Estonia appeared in
central newspapers both before and after the elections.

20. See table 9. V. Tishkov counts 71 Georgian deputies (the correct number is 74),
equivalent to 3.1 percent of the Congress, whereas Georgians comprised only 1.3 percent of the Soviet population. Other data of Tishkov's differ slightly from ours, but no
difference is large enough to affect materially the overall picture painted here.

Tatars had 24, 1.9 million Germans had 6, and 1.1 million Poles had 7.[21] The ethnic apportionment in general, however, perhaps surprisingly, most penalized the most numerous ethnic groups. Russians, Ukrainians, and Uzbeks all found themselves proportionately underrepresented.[22]

This ethnic analysis reveals another important result. If we consider the four largest ethnic groups in the USSR across each of the fifteen republics, and compare their representation in the parliamentary delegations with the ethnic structures of each republic, three facts are striking. First, Congress elections favored the "titular" nationality (that is, the indigenous ethnic group—for example, Estonians in Estonia or Abkhaz in Abkhaziia) in ten of fifteen republics. Latvians were overrepresented by 24 percent in the Latvian delegation, Estonians by 16 percent in Estonia, and Kirghiz by 12 percent in Kirghizia. In two-thirds of the republics, then, the electoral mechanism failed to secure an ethnically balanced representation of the populace. This general trend was particularly pronounced in the smaller republics, a trend which in turn redounded to the advantage of those smaller ethnic groups possessing some level of state recognition. The titular nationality was underrepresented in the remaining five republics: Russians by 12 percent in the RSFSR, for instance, and Belorussians by 9 percent in Belorussia. Second, the four major ethnic groups succeeded in securing disproportionately large representation in many republics. Ethnic Russians, although underrepresented in the RSFSR, were overrepresented in nine other republics.[23] Ukrainians won disproportionate shares of four delegations, although not of the Ukraine's own delegation.[24] Third, among major ethnic groups, Russians in Latvia and Estonia were most underrepresented, by 18 percent and 17 percent, respectively; close behind were Uzbeks in Tadzhikistan (−16 percent) and Kirghizia (−7 percent), Ukrainians in Moldavia (−9 percent), Armenians in Georgia (−6 percent), Germans in Kazakhstan (−5 percent), and, most strikingly, Azerbaijanis in Armenia. Before the mass emigration spurred by the Nagorno-Karabakh conflict, Azerbaijanis comprised 5 percent of

21. V. Tishkov, 8. Such situations can be explained by several factors. Although Tatars and Bashkirs enjoyed official recognition as an autonomous group, a majority of each group lived outside its designated republican territory. Germans were not recognized at any territorial level. At the same time, popular fronts in several places not only sparked public political awareness, but also encouraged the expression of national and anti-Russian feelings.

22. See table 9.

23. Russians won 14 percent more than their proportionate share of the Tadzhik delegation, 10 percent more in Armenia, 8 percent more in Belorussia, 6 percent more in the Ukraine and Moldavia, 4 percent more in Kirghizia, and 3 percent more in Uzbekistan, Turkmenia, and Azerbaijan.

24. Ukrainians were overrepresented by 6 percent in the Belorussian delegation, by 3 percent in the Uzbek, and by 1 percent in the Kazakh and RSFSR groups.

Armenia's population, yet had no representatives in the Armenian delegation.[25]

The First Congress, then, clearly was in many ways an "assembly of titular nations."[26] This fact unavoidably influenced the nature of the political struggles at the Congress. Much of the Congress' debate concerned the national question. Even when speakers addressed themselves to other issues—economic and political reform, ecology, social issues, protection of cultural and historical heritages—they often implicitly took positions on ethnic and national issues. No political analysis of the Soviet Union, then, particularly in the 1980s, can ignore the national dimension. The emergence of a multi-party system cannot be explained simply in terms of economic, social, and cultural interests. Ethnic solidarities cut across class loyalties and impeded the formation of all-Union trans-ethnic political groups. The growing strength of nationalism could only contribute to particularism and parochialism in the Soviet political arena.

Of course, the contrasts that emerge from this discussion of the ethnic side of Soviet politics are not new. Nevertheless, through an analysis of the composition and behavior of the Congress, many conflicts can be quantified to an unusual degree. This analysis shows that each of the titular nationalities—particularly those enjoying status as a "republic"— wielded great power in the new legislature, and on a deeper level shows the critical importance of ethno-national issues. Two basic issues, indeed, proceeded in tandem during this period. Democratization of politics and society is usually mentioned by all students of the former Soviet Union and its successor states. The search for a new constitutional solution for the ethnic problem, however—whether it be some form of autonomy, a looser federation, or even a confederation—continues, both within and between states, and may be an even thornier issue than the more obvious ones of political and economic reform. The four-tiered structure of the Soviet Union clearly could not sustain itself. Indeed, this structure in many ways created the quagmire in which the USSR found itself during the Gorbachev era. Now, following the demise of the USSR, each of the fifteen republics needs to confront its multi-ethnic nature, even if the central Commonwealth government fails, as seems likely, to solve the national question.

25. V. Tishkov, 15.
26. The characterization is Tishkov's.

# Different Paths to Political Pluralism

The opening of the First Congress of People's Deputies on 25 May 1989 marked the end of our first model of democratization. It embodied, as we have already noted, compromises on a variety of issues. To summarize the main premises on which the first model was based: (1) it insisted on the maintenance of the one-party state in a predictable political environment; (2) at the same time, it envisioned the beginning of a unitary, relatively homogeneous pan-Soviet democratization process; and (3) its structure was in large part based on the assumption that existing social organizations (and new ones created during the process of democratization) would be able to represent and express all important shades of popular opinion, even while political differentiation increased rapidly.

Clearly, in many ways these premises could not reflect fully the political and psychological changes that had occurred over the previous three years. As we shall see, each was made obsolete by events. Nikolai Shmelev's analogy springs to mind: Soviet civil society was starting to reorganize itself after an interruption of seventy years. Social-interest groups began to organize and to express themselves politically, although their "platforms" remained vague and contradictory. Such informal organizations were analogous to the clubs, laboratories, academies, and masonic lodges that proliferated in France just before revolution broke out. These new bodies served to unify social groups, and acted as a matrix for the birth of new political movements. The "Moscow Tribune," established by a group of Muscovite intellectuals including Andrei Sakharov, resembled the French "Society of 30" that gathered at the home of parliamentarian Adrien Duport. In many ways, the "Clubs *Perestroika*" resembled the "Friends of the Blacks," the "Secret Society of Visoflay," and the "Club of Enrageds." The positions of the miners of Vorkuta, the Kuzbass, and the Donbass—the modern *cahiers des doleances*—started to coalesce in such groups. In the Soviet Union, however, two factors impeded this process: first, the existence of a powerful, preexisting political monopoly; and secondly, the difficulties encountered by these social groups in identifying themselves. Egalitarianism and ideology—each serving as a Marxist "false consciousness"—prevented the real natures and strengths of the various interest groups from being fully reflected or realized.

*Glasnost* had yet to be consolidated into law, and those who availed themselves of its privileges consequently did so at their own risk. Do the lessons of France offer a parallel? In a decree of 5 July 1788 Louis XVI convened the States-General for the first time in 175 years. Less than a year later, in May 1789, he accepted a recommendation to grant full freedom to the press—Article 11 of the "Declaration of Human Rights." Social revolution, however, swept away these last attempts at reform by the *ancien régime*. In the Soviet Union of 1989, too, the mounting tide of social pressures for change threatened to overrun the proponents of gradual, controlled democratic reform. New informal organizations and independent newsmagazines set themselves up in competition with existing social organizations, which by this stage had lost virtually all credibility. The Komsomol and the trade unions, in particular, faced such crises. The third premise enumerated above—that is, reliance on such existing bodies— lost all relation to contemporary reality. Central authorities proved unable to enunciate a clear political line. No conscious decision was taken to allow the new informal organizations to pursue their activities, but the impossibility of suppression was equally clear.

Popular fronts, a mass variant of the informal organizations, also coalesced during this period, throwing all three premises of the first model of democratization into question. The third premise was destroyed, and the first retained only formally. Popular fronts, in fact, formed the first real challenge to the one-party state monopoly of power. As to the second premise, it quickly became apparent that the process of reform as envisioned by the various groups mushrooming all over the country could not be unitary. The extreme differences in experience, worldview, and culture among these groups produced a great diversity of interests and goals. The mass media only added to this new pluralism by disseminating reformist ideas. The media could thus be portrayed as contributing to unity of reform—bolstering the model's second premise—but must also be recognized as accelerating mass politicization, further endangering its third premise.

Popular pressure for a multiparty system grew during this period. An opinion poll conducted in December 1988 had found only 6 percent of

*Table 6-1*

| Parties | % in favor | | % indifferent | | % opposed | | % no answer | |
|---|---|---|---|---|---|---|---|---|
| | Total | CPSU | Total | CPSU | Total | CPSU | Total | CPSU |
| Ecological | 74 | 63 | 6 | 6 | 12 | 23 | 8 | 8 |
| Russian nationalist | 33 | 22 | 10 | 5 | 41 | 61 | 16 | 12 |
| Socialist | 31 | 25 | 14 | 9 | 28 | 46 | 27 | 20 |
| Christian | 33 | 22 | 18 | 14 | 32 | 50 | 17 | 14 |
| Bourgeois-democratic | 16 | 13 | 8 | 2 | 59 | 74 | 17 | 10 |

Muscovites willing to agree with the statement, "It would be preferable to have several political parties in existence."[1] Another 17 percent favored the development of "factions and different platforms within the CPSU." Most people (55 percent) stated that they had no clear ideas on the issue. Only two months later, however, another poll administered to a sample of 1,060 Muscovites revealed significant changes, even taking into account differences in question wording, sample size, the organization administering the poll, and so on. In this later poll, fully 46 percent supported a multiparty system in the USSR. Almost three-quarters of this 46 percent, though, declared opposition to the appearance of various specific parties, apparently favoring strict controls on the *type* of multiparty system that would emerge. Support for a multiparty system was stronger among intellectuals (56 percent) than among workers (39 percent), among men (54 percent) than women (39 percent), and among the younger generation (54 percent of 18- to 30-year-olds) than among its elders (29 percent of those older than 60).

The methodology employed by the sociologists administering the poll also allows us to extract more interesting observations. All those interviewed, 25 percent of whom belonged to the CPSU, were asked to express opinions on five hypothetical new parties: ecological, Russian nationalist, socialist, Christian, and bourgeois-democratic. Their responses are summarized in table 6-1. A clear contradiction seems to exist: 54 percent of those asked did not support a multiparty system in the Soviet Union, yet 74 percent would support an ecological party. Many Soviets apparently believed that the eventual appearance of such a movement could be reconciled with the current single-party system, yielding a pattern of double affiliation. This outlook is understandable in terms of the ecological

1. Unpublished occasional paper of L.G. Byzov, Leonid A. Gordon, and I.E. Mintusov, "*Perspectivy pliuralizma v nashem obshchestve: razmyshleniia sotsiologov o politicheskikh reformakh,*" p. 7. Results are cited by permission of Leonid Gordon, department chief, Institute of the International Workers' Movement, Soviet Academy of Sciences.

problems facing the USSR; indeed, even 63 percent of the CPSU members interviewed expressed support for an ecological movement or party. On the other hand, popular support (and support by the CPSU group) was lowest for a "bourgeois-democratic" party. Although more educated groups tended to support this type of party in noticeable numbers, only 11 percent of workers expressed such support. Workers, by contrast, constituted a plurality of those supporting a Russian-nationalist group (40 percent), far outnumbering intellectuals and technicians (25 percent).

The Soviet sociologists also asked the survey participants to identify the one party they would support in a contested election. Question responses are summarized in table 6-2.[2] According to this poll, then, the CPSU seemed to enjoy a substantial lead, although not majority support, over all of its likely competitors in a multi-party system. We cannot, however, forget entirely the problems attached to such polls: respondents may have tailored their answers to perceived "correct" responses, as public discussions of the Party's role were for many years risky in the Soviet Union.

Despite this caveat, it remains apparent that many such taboos were broken in only a few months during 1989. By as early as February the Party and its relations with the populace had shifted: its members were no longer highly ideological, but more often careerist; its function was more to guarantee the normal functioning of society than to carry out a radical social revolution; it was dominated by the *apparat* and various managerial groups, and no longer wished to play a vanguard role in changing society dramatically. Boris Yeltsin's dramatic successes in the capital only added to the exponential growth of popular hostility towards the *apparat*. This political evolution became plain even among the deputies in Congress. According to another opinion poll, this one conducted among nearly 700 deputies, 42 percent opposed the preservation of a single-party system.[3]

In early 1989 Sergei Andreev published an article in the Leningrad magazine *Neva* that enjoyed great success by expressing this popular mood.[4] Not only did Andreev criticize Gorbachev for the "contradictory nature" of his approach to reform, but he roundly affirmed the need for a multiparty political system. "The creation of new parties, in conditions—as we are accustomed to say—of an 'historically-created single-party system,' is a normal question of normal democracy. Forbidding

2. The scholarly nature of the poll's administrators is beyond question. We need to keep in mind, however, that those interviewed represent only the capital, and therefore this poll, however well conducted, cannot be generalized to the entire country.

3. *Literaturnaia Gazeta*, 21 June 1989, 11. It is difficult to estimate how accurately this poll represented the popular mood, but it clearly related to social realities.

4. Sergei Andreev, *Struktura vlasti i zadachi obshchestva*, in *Neva* 1 (January 1989), 144.

*Table 6-2*

| Parties | Total | CPSU | Non-CPSU | Workers | Technicians | Leaders |
|---|---|---|---|---|---|---|
| | | | % of: | | | |
| Ecological | 16 | 10 | 17 | 18 | 12 | 6 |
| Russian nationalist | 4 | 2 | 4 | 3 | 2 | 2 |
| Socialist | 9 | 5 | 10 | 10 | 12 | 8 |
| Christian | 4 | 3 | 4 | 4 | 3 | 10 |
| Bourgeois-democratic | 3 | 1 | 3 | 2 | 1 | — |
| CPSU | 41 | 62 | 36 | 43 | 24 | 58 |
| Did not respond | 23 | 17 | 26 | 20 | 36 | 16 |

such change in principle means forbidding in principle democracy itself."
Events moved so rapidly, however, that the radical suggestions of this
article, which created a furor in January 1989, had become old news
by June.

The reformist front had several options in mid-1989. First, reformers
in the Party leadership rejected, at least temporarily, any transition to
a multiparty system. The reasons for their position had been expressed
at the Nineteenth Party Organizational Conference—the need to maintain a strong political, ideological, and economic center to oppose various
centrifugal forces. While arguing for such positions on highly ideological grounds a year before, however, they now focused on political and
practical necessity to make their case. Second, the radical position of the
intelligentsia had been well expressed by Andreev: namely, that democratization cannot be pursued by half-measures. Hence, this group favored
the immediate introduction of a liberal-bourgeois democratic parliamentary system. Third, a heterogeneous group within the party supported
a position between these extremes. The one-party system could be preserved for the time being, this group argued, as long as pluralism continued to develop within that party. Appeals to the early history of the
Bolshevik Party, and particularly to the legal existence of factions before
the Tenth Party Congress of March 1921, justified this position.

The authors of the sociological investigation cited above belonged to
this third group, although they anticipated more radical developments in
the medium to long term. "In our current situation," they argued, "we can
only help the expansion of pluralism within existing political structures
and, above all, within the CPSU, which in fact represents the political
avant-garde of our society."[5] This perspective focuses on the growing differentiation within the Communist Party, the subdivisions of which were
becoming publicly recognizable. In this focus, however, it misses a crucial

5. *Perspectivy pliuralizma*, 16.

aspect of ongoing political change: it reflected broader trends and was not simply limited to the CPSU. The CPSU had been superimposed onto the social and economic structure of the country and possessed a nationwide base mediated through that structure. The weakening of its ideological cement produced a new situation, wherein relations between center and periphery were regulated by agreements that tacitly assumed power decentralization in exchange for full *nomenklatura* solidarity and agreement on resource distribution. If, therefore, the Party split into factions during the democratization process, it simultaneously expressed increasingly strong sentiments for republican and local autonomy. These sentiments themselves fed into another layer of division, that of the national-ethnic dimension. Not coincidentally, the year 1989 ended with news of just such a split, namely the division of the Lithuanian Communist Party on basically ethnic lines.

Among the group favoring reconstruction, many critics discerned an increasingly *authoritarian* strain. This tendency gained support in the press even from democratically inclined figures,[6] many of whom felt it necessary to cede sweeping powers to a leader entrusted with the task of carrying out a long-term process of democratic reform. The idea of combining the posts of president and Party general secretary emerged from this group, in the hope that it would allow the leader (assumed by all to be Gorbachev) to free himself from the control of *nomenklatura* oligarchs, perhaps making him subject only to a direct popular vote. Many variations on this theme of a presidential republic were discussed in the Soviet press before the Nineteenth Party Organizational Conference.

The tendencies discussed above were not the only ones operative. An enormous conservative bloc consisting of dogmatic, ultraorthodox Marxist-Leninists as well as anti-Communist (and anti-Western) Russian nationalists also wielded substantial political power. For different reasons, each of these groups opposed the Gorbachev-led political reforms. The old-line Communists denounced the abandonment of socialist ideals, while the modern-day "Slavophile" nationalists objected to the adoption of a Western model of liberal democracy for Russia's future. Both arguments converged on Stalin, viewing him favorably—whether as the savior of communism or as the personification of the Great Russian authoritarian tradition of strong central rule. The alliance of these groups had appeared before, most notoriously in the Brezhnevite restoration after the reformism of the Twentieth and Twenty-second Party Congresses.[7] Magazines such as *Molodaia Gvardiia* and *Nash Sovremennik* again appeared hostile

6. E.g., Andranik Migranian. See *Sovetskaia Kultura,* 24 June 1989.
7. See Alexander Yanov, "The Russian New Right" (Berkeley: Institute of Inter-

to "modernization"—and, as in the early 1970s, such themes served to organize the moderate and reactionary counterattack against *perestroika*.[8]

Both broad camps, then, of reformists and of conservatives, purported to be pan-Soviet movements providing a blueprint for the future. In truth, both were mistaken. The end of the first model of democratization tolled the death knell for any hopes of a pan-Soviet, unitary model for future reform. The only way forward—neither destructive nor tragic, simply realistic—was to recognize the irreconcilable nature of the contradictions within the existing institutional structure of the Soviet Union.[9] Neither side of the political debate—apart from Andrei Sakharov and a few others who had no power to influence events—had yet realized this necessity in late 1989, and the contests between centralizing recipes for reform and centrifugal demands for independence would (and will) continue for years. The ultimate destiny of *perestroika*, indeed, depended on the outcome of this struggle.

---

national Studies, 1978) and *Détente after Brezhnev* (Berkeley: Institute of International Studies, 1977).

8. See chap. 13. Under the editorship of the progressive Anatolii Ananev, the magazine *Oktiabr* (which had in the 1970s been a reactionary stronghold in the struggle against Aleksandr Tvardovskii's progressive *Novyi Mir*) broke with this trend. As a result, Ananev came under heavy attack by the *apparat* and the Party right wing in late 1989.

9. See Mikhail Gefter, interview in *Historia y Fuente Oral* 3 (1990).

# CHAPTER SEVEN

# Main Features of the Political Geography

The task of identifying and defining the currents and political tendencies of the First Congress is, for many reasons, difficult. The assembly of 2,249 deputies had no real historical parallels; many deputies were new to public life, and the political positions of most defied easy categorization. Most deputies themselves did not know precisely which "platform" they supported when the Congress began. Many had not even considered the necessity of forming definite political alliances. Most deputies were aware only of the two extremes of radical reformers and reactionaries. Rather than adhere to either extreme, most tried to locate themselves within a large "center" group, the outlines of which remained vague and changeable.

Formally, deputies were categorized in two ways, the first dividing Party members from "nonparty" (*bezpartiinye*) deputies, and the second listing republican or territorial origins. Neither official classification, however, suffices to explain the political dynamics of the Congress. Fully 750 deputies, after all, bypassed selection by popular balloting, and thus cannot be treated in the same manner as the other 1,500 deputies. For this reason, this chapter proposes a usable, if imperfect, analytical framework within which to view the First Congress' political tendencies. Deputies' speeches to the Congress have been characterized as belonging to one of several groups. Unfortunately, available records do not always identify a speaker by name.[1] Unidentified speeches have, however, been included in the analysis in an attempt to measure the relative activism of various tendencies, yielding a total of 682 speeches to be categorized.[2] When

---

1. As reported in *Izvestiia* and as shown on Soviet television, both live and in newscasts.

2. Also included are speeches to the Congress by nondeputies (by ministers, for instance, or by members of Congress commissions who spoke *ex officio*). The president

combined with information from other sources—personal conversations and further press reports, for example—these speeches reveal a variety of Soviet political identities.

In the best case, we would be able to analyze a speech by each deputy, or at least by a majority of deputies. The speech analysis is necessarily limited, however, by the number of speakers—a minority of the Congress, albeit a reasonably numerous one.[3] We must also remember that the sample of speakers is neither random nor, necessarily, representative. Deputies gaining the floor might, in general, be expected to represent the Congress' active elements—those who felt most strongly about their positions and were willing to fight for podium time to share them with the Congress. Despite these caveats, it seems plausible to argue that each of the most powerful political trends would inspire its adherents to make this effort, particularly with the threat of central reprisals for unpopular opinions being greatly diminished. We will contend, therefore, that all of the most significant contemporary political tendencies represented by the deputies are present in this sample of 682 speeches.

We considered each speech, and evaluated it on a variety of criteria. Expressive forms, language choices, and attitudes towards "democratic culture" were considered along with strictly political comments. Among political criteria were opinions on economic reform, political reform, the Party's role in society and its relations to the state, *glasnost* and civil liberties, and the national question.[4]

This approach is obviously subjective, and therefore classifications cannot be portrayed as being in any sense definitive. Moreover, many speeches were vague, confused, or even contradictory. What should be done with a deputy, for example, who expressed a "progressive" position on one issue or set of issues, and simultaneously a "conservative" position on others? Occasionally a deputy spoke one way early in the Congress but gave a later speech falling into a different—even diametrically opposed—group. Difficult decisions were made in such cases, and, whenever possible, information from other sources has been utilized to define a deputy's position more sharply.

Finally, we run a risk in asserting that any given deputy "belongs" to a certain group, as the groups enumerated here are formally nonexistent. They are theoretical constructs, and our categorizations do not imply the existence of group identity, consciousness, or internal solidarity. The argu-

---

and Gorbachev, however, are both only considered as having spoken once, although each took the floor many times. Chap. 10 treats Gorbachev's tactics in greater detail.

3. Many deputies spoke more than once. Hence, the total of 682 speeches (including the nonidentified speeches) represents at least 464 distinct, identifiable deputies.

4. Cf. the discussion of these concerns in chap. 8.

ment made here, however, is that our political classification is justified. First, our experimental subdivision gives an approximate but realistic, suggestive picture of the main trends, which, as we shall see, were confirmed by the political behavior of the Congress at large. Later statistical analyses of data from roll-call votes in the Second and Third Congresses will show that these criteria work sufficiently well to describe many deputies' political positions. Secondly, this approach yields interesting information on the political behavior of various social groups represented at the Congress. Thirdly, it allows us to predict the major political fault lines along which emerging political parties may coalesce.

One obvious methodological compromise is the ease with which our approach may be taken to imply full acceptance of a conventional "left"/ "right" analysis of political positions. Later chapters will demonstrate that such an approach often obscures more than it reveals. Nevertheless, for the purposes of this analysis, "right" will denote conservative positions interested in preserving the existing system and "left" will denote reformist positions interested in changing that system. Clearly the right wing included advocates of positions that at other periods in Soviet historiography were portrayed as belonging to the extreme left wing, and vice versa.[5] Stalinists, in this view, sit on the right wing, while advocates of the free market and the rule of law sit on the left.

The simple scheme of left-center-right, however, quickly proves too coarse and undifferentiated to represent meaningfully the differences of opinion within the Congress, or indeed the developments which followed the Congress. At the same time, the temptations to draw a multitude of too-fine distinctions must be resisted, despite the variety of interests and themes that impel us toward it. Putting deputies into too many different "boxes" both confuses the picture and reduces the precision with which any one classification may be made. In the end the most functional solution—yielding the most logical clarity while losing the least detail—is a division into seven visible, distinct, important groups. Proceeding from left to right, these groups include:

### Radicals (R)

For three reasons, radicals in the First Congress were the most easily identified of the seven groups. Why? They proved in general to be highly conscious politically, they expressed themselves openly, and they tended

5. Stalin's program of forced collectivization, for instance, was portrayed officially in contemporary political discussion as a revolutionary leap forward towards socialism— that is, as a left-wing policy. Opposition to such policies, as expressed by Bukharin and others, was denounced as "right-wing oppositionism."

to support a coherent program of radical reform in both politics and economics. This group's political program focused on the creation of a law-governed, democratic state in the USSR, and its economic program called for a rapid transition to the free-market system. Three prominent radicals were Andrei Sakharov, Iurii Afanasev, and Gavriil Popov.

## Left-wing independents (LI)

This group also favored reform, but framed its demands in more moderate terms than did the radicals. Occasionally, its differences with radical positions extended to attacking both political extremes and refusing to support radicals against the centrist or conservative alliances built up by Gorbachev. Its defining characteristic, however, was its complete uncontrollability by the *apparat*. Many left-wing independents came from suburban areas, often showing highly critical approaches to politics but without a constructive program of their own. Their positions as a result could be contradictory, and were sometimes even more conservative than those of the Right. Nationalist reformers also constituted an important element in this group. Many deputies from the Baltic republics, Armenia, Georgia, and other non-Russian areas defended reformist agendas and at the same time demanded action on national claims. Not all "nationalists," though, were left-wing independents. Exceptions in particular included those right-wing independent deputies whose concerns with national independence or autonomy far outweighed the defense of *perestroika* and reform in the rest of the USSR.[6] Iurii Boldyrev, K. Antanavichius, and Z. Vaishvila were three left-wing independents.

## Mediators (M)

In general, mediators were moderate reformers. They distinguished themselves by their approach to the tactics of reform and by their avoidance of open conflict with conservatives. They focused on consensus-building and consolidation, and often cooperated with Gorbachev even from independent positions, hoping to assist him in developing Soviet reformism without sending conservatives into full-fledged opposition. Although his tactical approach and freedom of action obviously differed from this general pattern, Gorbachev himself belonged to this group. Roi Medvedev and Fedor Burlatskii were two other mediators.

---

6. Cf. the discussion of nationalism in chap. 8.

## Centrists (C)

Centrists functioned as the Congress' opportunists, sometimes refusing to compromise but often refusing to take explicit positions. Most frequently, they simply voted with the majority. Many deputies who had been active in national politics before and who had refused to renounce the CPSU's official policies in 1989 also belonged to this group, which was as a result relatively experienced politically. Centrists behaved cautiously and protected their own interests. Although they usually supported Gorbachev, they did so mainly because they followed the Presidium's recommendations, not out of motivation to fight for political or economic reform.[7] Anatolii Lukianov, Gennadi Kolbin, and G. Tarasevich were prominent centrists.

## Apparatchiki (A)

As the name suggests, this group consisted mainly of members of the Party *apparat* and the social organizations. Others in this group included those who defended the *apparat* and its position, often in its own language. Clearly a conservative group, *apparatchiki* remained hostile to *glasnost* and economic reform and accepted democratization only insofar as it strengthened the Party's political monopoly. Although sometimes couched in ideological terms, this approach clearly served more or less directly to defend the class positions of its adherents. *Apparatchiki* usually refrained from attacking Gorbachev openly—on the contrary, they frequently shielded themselves with his authority—preferring to influence him privately. Three examples were Vitalii Vorotnikov, M. Mamedov, and V. Polianichko.

## Right-wing independents (RI)

Like their left-wing counterparts, these deputies could not be controlled by the Party apparatus, although their independence directed itself against *perestroika*. As a result, their hostility to reform was not muzzled by respect for or fear of Party or government leaders, and they spoke critically about the failure of Gorbachev and others to defend socialism and the leading role of the Party. This group also included extreme nationalists, anti-Semites, Slavophiles, xenophobes and anticosmopolitans, and those who denounced the "degeneration" of mass bourgeois culture. Had

7. In the absence of indications to the contrary, we have also classified all *ex officio* speeches and speeches on technical points of procedure as centrist. These deputies in general were chosen by Gorbachev, were easily controllable, and argued for a centrist compromise. In any case, the number of such speeches (12) is too small to affect materially the analysis offered here.

Nina Andreeva been elected to the Congress, she would have belonged to this group. Three deputies who did belong were Veniamin Iarin, Vilen Martirosian, and V. Sobolev.

### *Pre*-perestroika (P)

This group, characterized by political and cultural underdevelopment, can be described as the "marsh" or the "swamp" of the Congress. In many ways unclassifiable, pre-*perestroika* deputies often came from Central Asia and gained seats in the Congress through appointments by local Party *apparaty*. Many lived in the countryside and were relatively ill-educated; many were women, and most did not campaign for election. For whatever reason, this group lacked certain political notions. Its members were easily manipulated, usually voting with the Presidium or as directed by local or republican Party leaders. As such, in some ways they represent much of the great nonspeaking majority at the Congress. Often unable to understand the Congress' proceedings or significance, they read anti-progressive speeches prepared by others or reacted in a randomly hostile manner against "scandalous" speeches by radical intellectuals, and particularly against radicals of a different ethnic group. Although lacking a political program and relatively few in number, these deputies did represent an important, distinct group and we are justified in treating them separately. Grouping them with *apparatchiki* would overlook their failure to defend their interests in true *apparatchik* fashion. Mostly consisting of workers promoted as a result of their fidelity to the apparatus, pre-*perestroika* deputies occupied an inherently unstable political position. Grouping them separately makes the transitional nature of this group plain, for, as we will see, most pre-*perestroika* deputies developed a defined position in later Congresses. This group thus steadily decreased in size. Three examples were R. Allaiarov, M. Ibragimov, and T. Kaiumova.

As mentioned above, a major limitation of the foregoing classification is its confinement to a reduced sample, resulting from the inadequate data available on the First Congress.[8] Nevertheless, this approach yields a surprisingly accurate picture of the Congress' political currents. Combined with the social-professional criteria described in chapter 5 and the campaign data from chapter 4, these results confirm the main outlines

8. Beginning with the Second Congress we will supplement this type of analysis with study of the roll-call votes published in the official *Biulletin* of the Supreme Soviet. The introduction of an electronic voting system at this Congress allows the behavior of all deputies to be examined. Finally, many deputies who did not speak during the First Congress did so in later Congresses, giving us the chance to expand our limited sample.

described in chapter 6. Later, in chapter 11, we will consider the results of votes on crucial issues to add another dimension to our portrait of the First Congress' political geography. No single dimension explains any of the seven groups completely, but each of these approaches does illuminate an important part of the framework in which they all acted.

First to recap, however, what this chapter has contributed to our political geography. The reformist front may in broad terms be said to consist of three groups: radicals, left-wing independents, and mediators. Conservatives may be divided into four types: centrists, *apparatchiki*, right-wing independents, and pre-*perestroika*. At the chapter's outset, we posited the existence of a large, ill-defined "center" of the Congress between two clearly defined political poles. Upon closer examination, this center proves neither homogeneous nor compact. As our analysis continues, we will see that in this center there existed a floating mass of deputies that formed a majority—but its opinions and composition varied daily, according to the issues under discussion. The nucleus of this mass, and therefore of the Congress' majority, was the combination of mediators and centrists, joined by other groups depending on the issue.

The final point of our classification into political groups is that each varied in internal stability. Hence, constant migrations of deputies among groups characterized the Congress. Four groups in particular proved unstable: on the left, radicals and left-wing independents, and on the right, pre-*perestroika* and right-wing independents. The accumulation of parliamentary experience steadily whittled down the number of pre-*perestroika* deputies. The instability of radicals stemmed from two main causes: first, as with the left-wing independents, they lost members as clashes on a national-ethnic level increased; and second, different gradations of radicalism were present in the group, and some deputies shifted to a more moderate progressive position. Independents of both right and left belonged to eclectic groupings which tended to lose members to more clearly defined political programs. They were doomed to fragment, although their original nuclei held the potential eventually to form new autonomous political groupings of the center-left and center-right. For their part, right-wing independents included a radical right wing, made up primarily of Russians, which could become a political group of the extreme right.[9] As a result, the most likely scenario was one with intermediate left- and right-wing parties (after the breakup of both left- and right-wing independents and some erosion among mediators and centrists) and two radical extremes (after the breakup of radicals and right-wing independents, plus erosion of the centrist and pre-*perestroika* groups). It remained unclear

9. Such tendencies were already clearly visible in the fall of 1989. See chap. 13.

during the First Congress exactly which direction such political evolution would take, depending as it did on the extent of polarization then developing and the forces, if any, that were present to consolidate the system. In other words, the political future depended on the appearance and triumph of either centrifugal or centripetal forces. As time passed, the former emerged as the stronger, for reasons to be treated in the next chapter.

CHAPTER EIGHT

# The National Dimension

The picture of political forces drawn in the previous chapter is useful in general terms, but remains limited in important respects. In geometrical terms, it aligns political forces linearly, with groups distributed from left to right. As already mentioned, the reductionism in such an approach necessarily loses much of the richness and variety that characterized the Soviet political arena in 1989. Three groups in particular—the pre-*perestroika* and the right- and left-wing independents—defy simple placement in such a linear schema. With the possible exception of the radicals, each of the other groups resists such categorization as well. This chapter argues that the missing element in the political analysis so far offered is the national dimension. Addressing this issue adds "thickness" to the discussion. National and ethnic loyalties, existing independently of other foci of debate (ideological, socioeconomic, cultural, or religious), held the key to the developing Soviet civil society and its democratic structures. We therefore need to use a three-dimensional approach to understand contemporary Soviet (and post-Soviet) politics.

In their essay quoted above,[1] Soviet sociologists Gordon and Nazimova offer a two-dimensional picture of these politics as they appeared in mid-1989. Their reasoning may be summarized by positing the existence of a Cartesian plane, with an x-axis and a y-axis.[2] The abscissa defines economic views, moving from a centrally-controlled, planned economy on the left to a completely free, unregulated market on the right. The ordinate represents political views, running from neo-Stalinism at the bottom to radical democratic reform at the top. The plane is split into four regions,

---

1. Leonid Gordon and Alla Nazimova, *"Perestroika: Vozmozhnye Varianty?"* *Kommunist* 13 (1989).
2. See table 11.

and the views of deputies falling into any one of these regions may be summarized as follows:[3]

*Zone 1 (upper right)*: Support for "global *perestroika*," meaning a total change of the politico-economic system towards a multiparty state governed by law and a free-market economy.

*Zone 2 (lower right)*: Support for "technocratic" reform, meaning the modification of economic structures without corresponding shifts in political mechanisms. This group hoped to bring about an economic revival while preserving sufficiently strong central power to maintain discipline and order throughout the USSR.

*Zone 3 (lower left)*: Support for "reactionary" policies; that is, rejecting reform in either the political or the economic sphere and preserving an administrative-command economic system and the one-party state.

*Zone 4 (upper left)*: Support for political democratization but opposition to tampering with the crucial elements of a planned socialist economy.

Subjectively placing our seven groups on this grid, we find that only two are compact and limited to a single zone—the *apparatchiki* and pre-*perestroika* groups, both falling in zone 3—while the other five spill across zones. In their essay, Gordon and Nazimova admit that this method of viewing the Soviet political space is imperfect since, they write, the four groups they describe

. . . do not at all exhaust the possible approaches. It is necessary [also] to consider the enormous importance of the national and national-regional questions. On these issues, each of the specified strategies could be further subdivided. Actually, each (apart from the most reactionary) includes varying opinions, both economic and political, on the question of degrees of permissible autonomy; on the preservation of central powers; and so on.[4]

In this recognition Gordon and Nazimova implicitly realize the need for a third dimension to "stretch" their Cartesian plane. In terms of our seven-group categorization, left- and right-wing independents, along with pre-*perestroika* deputies, particularly require this additional variable in order to be placed accurately. Without this third, national dimension, Soviet politics cannot be understood. As a result, we will modify the simple Cartesian plane by adding a z-axis to represent national feelings. This third axis runs from a high of "nationalist democratic federalism" to a low of "national separatism and neo-Stalinism."[5]

3. These summaries of deputy positions are original, and cannot be blamed on Gordon and Nazimova if faulty.
4. *Kommunist* 13 (1989): 41.
5. See table 12.

The addition of this axis at a stroke doubles to eight the number of categories into which deputies may be placed, and represents much more fully the variety of political strategies in the Soviet Union of 1989. The first sector, then, represents an entirely new Soviet Union—featuring a federal constitution, a multiparty political system, and a socialist market economy. The centrist group protruded into this sector only slightly. Left-wing independents were located mainly in this area, albeit with a sizable minority below the x-y plane (that is, favoring democratic reforms within their republics but too nationalist to favor the extension of these reforms throughout a preserved Union). The entire radical group, most left-wing independents and mediators, and a few centrists, then, located themselves above the x-y plane, favoring a "reformed confederal" structure for the USSR.[6] These deputies represented the Congress, but also reflected general social and political movements in Soviet society during *perestroika*'s fifth year.

This detailed treatment of the national question is not an abstract exercise in political analysis. It is needed to understand why radical reformers both inside and outside the leadership failed to comprehend the importance of the national question. The reformist intelligentsia, while working for a thorough democratic transformation of a colossal *Eurasian* country, reasoned only in *European*, or more accurately *West* European, terms. That is, in conceiving the Soviet Union as a basically unitary state they underestimated the necessity of building, in Gefter's words, "a new house as an unprecedented projection of the entire world community. A sovereign union of completely different people!"[7] As a result they underestimated the strength of particularism and separatism, which grew in tandem with three other developments: the extension of democratization, the creation of new, pluralist institutions, and the end of decades of attempts to use repression to prevent national cultural and linguistic self-expression.

Unfortunately, Gefter's was only one voice, and in pointing out the impossibility of a unitary, pan-Soviet approach to reform and democratization it was in a tiny minority. Few shared his opinion that the problem was one of "carrying out gradual transformations, at different paces, with a full range of different priorities and different forms," at all times remaining conscious of local peculiarities and conditions.[8] Only a minority understood that the processes of *perestroika* and democratization resembled the Copernican revolution in science. Centuries of strong cen-

6. The "reformed confederation" position is represented by the area of zone 1 in table 11, projected above the x-y plane.

7. See Mikhail Gefter, "*Zaslon smute—v kom on?*" *Moskovskie Novosti* 52 (31 December 1989).

8. See Gordon and Nazimova, p. 41.

tralist rule in Russia, where even the great reformers—Peter the Great, Alexander II, even Lenin—had acted from positions of central power, had to be cast off in an attempt to construct a democratic polity and civil society. Hence, Gorbachev's indecision on national issues, probably the only area in which his policy was so seriously deficient, is understandable. His ability to forge compromises, to sense instinctively the proper tactical course, proved dangerously inadequate to cope with the depth of ethnic and national passions. He constantly sought the center of political debates, in order to control the situation, but too often defined this center in terms of political and economic issues, to the exclusion of ethnic and national concerns. Defining a two-dimensional "center" meant that he often found himself "above" or "below" the true political center. This lack of recognition of the national dimension more than once endangered Gorbachev's own political position.

# The First Congress

We will not here attempt to recreate the entire, very rich debate of the First Congress of People's Deputies. Instead, we will focus only on those moments which were particularly important. These moments have been selected on the basis of two criteria. First, they are those which show most clearly the political, cultural, and historical conditions in which the Soviet parliament began functioning. Second, they best reveal the strengths and dynamics of the various political forces that vied for power in, and helped to shape, the Soviet political arena.

## Democratization and the Mass Media

"It is evident to everyone that the deputies are beginning to lay the foundations for a state of law in a situation where the culture of democracy is still in a preliminary stage of formation." So, at least, wrote V. Nadein in an editorial in *Izvestiia* in March of 1989. External observers watching the Congress on television "from countries where parliamentary procedures have repeated themselves for centuries," Nadein continued, may have been astonished—even bewildered—at what they saw happening in Moscow. During the Congress, tens of millions of people, both in the Soviet Union and abroad, felt themselves to be present at an unprecedented spectacle. The sacredness of the old power networks crumbled in the face of an almost total *glasnost*; political, social, and national tensions revealed themselves with full force and unadorned crudity; and the political struggle, once hidden away from public view in the Kremlin, became visible, explicit, and very public. In Nadein's words, "we are who we are, . . . [even if] we are no longer who we were."[1] His remark neatly

1. V. Nadein, editorial in *Izvestiia*, 26 May 1989.

sums up the Congress' historic significance, both recognizing the current limits of, and outlining the future possibilities for, Soviet democracy.

However one judges the Congress, whether in terms of its actual proceedings or of its ultimate results, it must be admitted that the novelty of live, near-total television coverage affected the assembly greatly, and increased dramatically its already marked cultural impact. In discussing the Congress, we are not simply considering the convening of a new parliament, even of one completely unprecedented in Soviet history. The USSR was reaching for democracy only after a delay of many decades; citizens' democratic rights had been restored. This restoration, however, can only be understood as the result of an interplay of traditional political forces with the disruptive strength of the modern mass media. The media dimension is crucial because the modern media wield an extraordinarily powerful influence in shaping public opinion. The integral nature of this connection was realized by many observers, both Soviet and foreign, but many (especially of the foreign observers) simply considered it "normal." They did not trouble themselves about the basic questions of how and why it came into being. Allowing a live telecast of the Congress, though, was by no means a foregone conclusion; indeed, until the last moment there were serious attempts to prevent it. Only Gorbachev's personal intervention resolved the dispute in favor of such an ostensibly "normal" state of affairs.[2]

The media, especially television, played two critically important roles in the drama of the Congress: it allowed millions to observe Gorbachev's tactics and enabled them to guess at his intentions; and equally, its presence influenced the course of the Congress decisively. Reformist leaders had taken to heart the experience of the Nineteenth Party Conference. Just before that conference, voices still were being raised against a too-extensive *glasnost*. Politburo conservatives, using their strength in the Party to pressure the general secretary, fought to keep the conference working in closed session. Their fears of being exposed to public criticism, moreover, were well-founded.

An aggressive anticonservative minority, led by Boris Yeltsin, was prepared on the other side to do battle over this issue of media coverage. A fierce struggle resulted. Yeltsin's group initially failed to force a formal decision to allow sessions of the conference to be televised. On the contrary, it was announced on the eve of the conference that information would be disbursed only at special evening press conferences. With this apparent conservative victory, the conference opened. Already by the second day,

2. According to Boris Yeltsin, "Gorbachev made the important decision that the entire session should be broadcast, live, on national television." (Boris Yeltsin, *Against the Grain* [Summit Books: New York, 1990], 245).

however, the situation seemed to be changing. Television cameras transmitted speeches from the conference. Radio and television journalists received *carte blanche*, buttonholing delegates for interviews and scrutinizing speeches for blunders and indiscretions—and broadcasting whatever was found. *Pravda* commenced publishing integral texts of the debates. The *apparat* had been either tricked or forced to submit. For the first time in CPSU history members of the Politburo found themselves exposed to independent, and very harsh, public criticism. Solomentsev, Gromyko, and Shcherbitskii (who left the Politburo a year later), in particular, faced sharp attacks from the delegates. Egor Ligachev, when forced to take the floor to respond to Boris Yeltsin, turned in a far from brilliant performance.

The experiment was a complete success for Gorbachev, who emerged as the country's only credible leader. Even so, the situation was highly volatile. Live television was risky even for Gorbachev, a fact he probably knew only too well. An assembly of 2,250 deputies with real power was dangerous, and replete with unknowns. The elections of 26 March had altered and significantly broadened the Soviet political space. Decision-making became more difficult, requiring compromises between groups that were intractably opposed. Clearly tactics, too, had to change. The Soviet leader held one strong card: the rules and procedures governing the new parliament had not yet been defined. This fact gave Gorbachev considerable latitude of action, especially as most deputies had little, if any, parliamentary experience. Even Gorbachev lacked parliamentary experience, though, and he often found himself forced to invent on-the-spot solutions to a multitude of procedural, technical, and political problems that the main architect of the Congress, Anatolii Lukianov, neither had foreseen nor could resolve.

In some ways Gorbachev had no real alternative to pressing for the maximum possible publicity at Congress sessions. He faced a conservative majority, and needed to use popular pressure as a counterweight. At the same time, though, favoring media exposure was a strategic choice that fit well with his vision of the Soviet Union's future. In his view, the Congress had rapidly to gain the prestige necessary to become a real alternative power base to the Party. Only by doing so could it eventually become the focus of a new order based on a pan-Soviet compromise of all fifteen Soviet republics. Gorbachev realized that the CPSU by itself could no longer support or sustain the process of rapid reform in the USSR. Hence, he wanted the Congress gradually to assume state power as well as a share of political responsibility, thereby both alleviating pressure on the Party and simultaneously broadening the bases of reform. In short, Gorbachev felt that the USSR needed to pass through a "school of democracy." This sincere pedagogical impulse was an important contributing factor in convincing him to show millions of Soviet citizens the value—and the difficulties—of democratic debate. The Soviet leader was fully aware of the risks inherent in such an exercise, though, and only allowed it to begin after taking a variety of precautions.

## The Agenda Battle

Only three days before the Congress began, virtually no one knew what would happen there. Some commentators have interpreted the feverish, last-minute activity as a skilled maneuver by Gorbachev and his allies, designed to take their adversaries on both the right and the left by surprise. In fact, real uncertainty characterized the period leading up to the Congress. Gorbachev had had to deflect direct attacks by conservatives at the plenum held in April 1989, which had revealed a largely panicked *apparat*. Conservatives at the plenum knew that in constitutional terms the Congress would have the power to determine the new government and to define the nature and powers of a wide range of state offices. They further realized that, although the character of this new state power remained undefined, it depended heavily on choices which could easily imply a fundamental redistribution of power within the Party leadership.

The plenum first considered these issues on 22 May. Its official statement, however, revealed none of the Party infighting. Instead, it simply stated that the plenum had nominated Gorbachev as its candidate for the office of president of the Supreme Soviet.[3] Members of the Party leadership clearly wanted to present a united front and wanted not to seem to challenge the preeminent role of the Congress. In truth, the plenum had also discussed—and, at least in broad outline, approved—Gorbachev's overall program for the Congress, a program which was not debated publicly until two days later, at the republican and regional "Conference of Group Representatives."

This conference, consisting of 446 deputies (many of whom had been participants in the plenum), took place on 24 May—the eve of the Congress—and lasted for nine hours.[4] It showed in a general way the relative strengths of the political forces to be mobilized at the Congress. It had no legal authority, but enabled Gorbachev to gain support for his agenda from a widely based, yet nonparty, body. He was therefore able to present the Congress with a package of procedural and organizational proposals that had been made, at least formally, by deputies from all fifteen Soviet republics. Republican delegations to the conference were nominated in

3. *Izvestiia*, 23 May 1989.
4. *Sovetskaia Rossiia*, 25 May 1989.

such a way as to guarantee this result. The conference's short final statement reported tersely that the delegates had discussed "questions of the work agenda, proposals about the composition of the Supreme Soviet of the USSR, candidacies to high office that the Congress will have to elect or to ratify, and other matters."[5] The only coherent opposition—or even alternative—at the Conference was that presented by representatives of the three Baltic republics and by radicals of the "Moscow Group." This alliance fought bitterly against much of Gorbachev's agenda but in the end was defeated by a crushing majority of 85 percent.[6]

The radicals' main fear was that conservatives, holding a majority at the Congress, might elect a homogeneous Supreme Soviet in their own image, thereby creating a standing sovereign body impervious to pressures for change. They thus stressed the importance of the Congress as a place of legislative production and of political debate. Gorbachev, for his part, did accept two radical proposals, each further elevating and empowering the Congress. The first, requiring a constitutional change, called for not one, but two sessions of the Congress each year. The second required both that half of the members of Supreme Soviet committees and permanent commissions be members of the Congress *not* elected to the Supreme Soviet and that all committee and commission members have an equal vote.[7]

Even after winning the agenda battle—and thus being relatively sure of his ability to control the Congress—Gorbachev clearly did not want irreversibly to oppose the radical reformers. He evidently shared, at least partially, the radicals' fears, and maneuvered to ensure that the radical minority would retain a certain degree of influence in, and control over, the Supreme Soviet. As it turned out, such worries were perhaps overblown; in the end, the Supreme Soviet—elected by a conservative Congress majority—proved surprisingly autonomous from the apparatus.

Nevertheless, the manner in which Gorbachev proposed his agenda for the Congress revealed exaggerated defensiveness. He was determined to dictate, not to negotiate, the exact rules for the Congress to follow, even though his brutal determination threatened his personal popularity. Deputy Nursultan Nazarbaev was given the job of presenting Gorbachev's platform to the Conference, and elucidated it in ten points. The first four dealt with election procedures: the first with the mandate commission to certify deputies' election, and the next three with the elections

5. *Pravda*, 25 May 1989. See also the speeches at the First Congress by Gavriil Popov, Chingiz Aitmatov, E. Stroev, and V. Statuliavichius.

6. According to Gavriil Popov's speech at the opening session of the First Congress, broadcast on Soviet TV, 25 May 1989.

7. *Izvestiia*, 26 May 1989.

of, respectively, the president of the Supreme Soviet, the Supreme Soviet itself, and the vice president of the Supreme Soviet. Only in the agenda's fifth point was provision made for a political report by the president, followed in the sixth by a similar report from the head of government. The seventh concerned the election of the president of the Council of Ministers, and nominations to other state offices followed until the tenth point, which allowed "other business."

Nazarbaev's agenda, however, the best insight we have into the mind of Gorbachev at this critical juncture, was marred by contradictions and inconsistencies. The election of a president, for example, preceded any political discussion whatsoever. Neither did elections to the Supreme Soviet allow time for preliminary debate, discussion, or campaigning. Only after allowing candidates to speak, on the other hand, was the head of government to be elected. Political calculation was clearly aided by widespread confusion in its attempt to craft an agenda to restrict debate. Efforts to curtail or impede discussion, however, only backfired, and an intense political debate sprang up almost immediately after the Congress was called to order on 25 May. Indeed, theatrics characterized the proceedings from the very first, starting with the Latvian deputy Vilen Tolpezhnikov, who marched up to the platform—without being given leave to speak—and abruptly proposed a minute of silence in memory of those killed by government forces in Tbilisi. Tacitly foregoing a vote, the entire hall immediately stood in silence.[8]

Shortly afterwards, Gorbachev's agenda was again challenged by Andrei Sakharov, who called for constitutional changes and whose mere presence in some ways implied an alternative to the official line. Sakharov's was only the first of many demands for constitutional modification at the Congress. Did the deputies, he demanded, wish to transform this assembly into an "electoral Congress"? It was unacceptable, he continued, simply to delegate legislative power to the Supreme Soviet, which would contain only one-fifth of the Congress' members. Furthermore, the proposed rotation of the Supreme Soviet's members was misleading, since "Only 36 percent of the deputies could take part." Sakharov presented the Congress with the text of a proposed decree to affirm its full sovereignty. The rest of his speech was a direct warning to Gorbachev personally. "We will cover ourselves with shame before the people," Sakharov announced, by dodging the universally accepted practice of allowing candidates and their platforms to be discussed before being elected. The Congress must also consider multiple candidates for high state offices. His support for

8. The reconstruction of events which follows is based on the stenographic record published in *Izvestiia* starting on 26 May 1989 and on the live coverage of Channel 2, Soviet TV.

Gorbachev was, he declared, beyond dispute. But the reason—"I do not see another person of rank to lead the country"—ominously bespoke support that was half-hearted and conditional.

Gavriil Popov then challenged the legal inconsistencies of the existing constitutional structure. There should be no mystery, he said, about why the Congress' majority would want to elect the Supreme Soviet without preliminary discussions. The Congress could not meaningfully discuss the Supreme Soviet's composition, as it had already been decided[9] that the principle of territorial representation would be applied to both legislative houses, instead of only to the Soviet of Nationalities as had been planned originally. This decision obviated any discussion at the Congress and ensured that although each republic and region would be represented in central decision-making, deputies would not be able to elect members of the Supreme Soviet according to their political abilities and beliefs. In reality, the Party machine lurked behind this chimera of territorial representation. Members of the Supreme Soviet were chosen by their republican and regional delegations, but these delegations in turn were dominated by Party oligarchs. Reformers thus found themselves isolated within their delegations, and could not join forces effectively with like-minded men and women from other parts of the country to secure election to the Supreme Soviet. Conservatives could eliminate proponents of democracy from the standing legislature, and, ironically, could do so "democratically."

This technique had no parallel in the history of world constitutional law, and left reformers at a loss. It also precluded a real decision by the Congress on such matters as those alluded to by Popov. In the end, it guaranteed that each delegation had virtually absolute control in selecting members to sit in the Supreme Soviet. An unspoken agreement meant that each republic would accept the lists of deputies presented by the others. By doing so, each could be sure that its own list would remain unchallenged. Later we shall see that it was on this issue that the reformist alliance would shatter, with a majority of the Baltic deputies supporting the same technique that Popov and the Moscow radicals denounced.

At the end of his speech, Popov proposed a constitutional change to eliminate republican and regional quotas to the Soviet of the Union. He also announced that no matter what the Congress decided on the question, the Moscow deputies had resolved not to engage in what they considered the undemocratic practice of allocating Supreme Soviet seats in a manner that was strictly territorial and that allowed the Congress at large no choice of candidates. Rather, multiple candidates would be proposed

9. By a constitutional amendment endorsed by the Supreme Soviet in October 1988.

to fill seats allocated to the Moscow delegation. The remaining more than two thousand deputies would choose among the candidates presented. The Moscow group was the only contingent consciously to permit the Congress to influence the selection of its Supreme Soviet delegation. It could thus boast of a victory for democratic principle, but of a victory only morally. This victory was costly: the Congress' conservative majority used the opportunity afforded by the Moscow radicals' democratic ideals—and by the evenhanded way in which the Moscow nominees had been selected, including both conservatives and radicals—to exclude nearly all of Popov's radical Muscovite allies from the Supreme Soviet.

## Procedural Confusion

Gorbachev had won the pre-Congress agenda battle. Once the Congress actually opened, however, his juridical experience was quickly exposed as insufficient. Indeed, from the opening stroke of the gavel, the First Congress was marked by a nearly total lack of legal, technical, and procedural preparation on the part of all participants, Gorbachev included. Having never needed such knowledge before, it was not particularly surprising that most Soviet leaders in 1989 lacked even a rudimentary grasp of parliamentary procedure. Procedural improvisation and jury-rigged solutions to problems were commonplace. When Gorbachev's agenda was placed on the table, for instance, deputies took a variety of positions towards it. Hence, the issue was not so much one of deciding whether to approve the proposed agenda as it was one of choosing amongst a variety of alternatives. Gorbachev, however, cut the discussion short and demanded a straightforward "yea/nay" vote.[10]

Procedural snarls and deviations from the planned agenda kept cropping up. Before long the debate resembled a Russian *matrioshka* doll: inside every problem waited another, and then another, and still another, with the difficulties never entirely disappearing. Unforeseen obstacles arose at every step. In the discussion of the agenda, for example, the Muscovite deputy Iurii Boldyrev asked that all voting be done by roll-calls, so that the public would know how each legislator had voted.[11] After the agenda

10. The agenda was approved with 379 votes against and 9 abstentions.
11. The Boldyrev proposal was considered in an unusual manner. Gorbachev countered Boldyrev's motion by presenting an alternative proposal made by the Presidium and asking the deputies to vote on this second proposal. Deputies Shchedrin and Landsbergis objected—in vain—that this approach was incorrect, and that the two proposals should be considered against each other. Moreover, Landsbergis protested, deputies had never even been allowed to vote on the Sakharov decree. These two examples suffice to show the near-total absence of procedural protection for the rights of minority legislators.

had been approved, it took three hours for debate to begin on Nazarbaev's first point. When the debate on the mandate commission finally did start, a speech by the film director Shengelaia quickly derailed it by raising the explosive issues of Tbilisi and Sumgait. Radicals also contributed to the confusion with repeated outbursts of parliamentary anarchism that only infuriated the "swamp" of *apparatchik* and pre-*perestroika* deputies. During a discussion that ostensibly concerned the rules of the assembly, for instance, the writer Ales Adamovich raised the unrelated issue of the Supreme Soviet's Presidium decree on public demonstrations. The next day, a badly informed deputy Zaslavskaia announced in an emotional voice that government troops the night before had quashed a demonstration near the Kremlin. Many other examples of such behavior could be given.

It fell to deputy Plotnieks to point out that there were, in fact, no rules of procedure. A provisional set of such rules had been drafted and distributed to the deputies, but a discussion of them had been omitted from the agenda. The draft, in any case, had addressed only a few, limited problems and made no attempt to provide a comprehensive procedural blueprint for the Congress. It did not define the division of functions between the Congress and the Supreme Soviet, and in particular said nothing about the relative limits of each body's legislative authority. It specified little about the composition of commissions or about their relation to the Supreme Soviet, nor did it define legislative procedures or address the organization of deputies into groups. In short, the poverty of rules was near-total, and resulted from the past lack of real functions and power on the part of Soviet state institutions. The academic Kudriavtsev explained to the Congress that the preceding Supreme Soviet as a rule had approved only one or two laws per session, of which "it was almost impossible to discuss their contents," and had normally approved about seventy decrees that the Presidium [12] had issued since the last Supreme Soviet session. When his turn came to speak, Lukianov—already under sharp attack for the *ukaz* of 8 April [13]—explained further that decrees from the Presidium had

---

12. Before the approval of a series of constitutional amendments in the autumn of 1988, the Presidium of the Supreme Soviet was a collegial body empowered to issue legislation during the interval between two Supreme Soviet sessions. Taking into account the relative infrequency of such sessions, the Presidium had a formally significant—albeit substantively limited—role in the issuing of decrees and the naming of nominees to fill state posts. Mainly composed of members of the central and republican *nomenklatura*, the general secretary of the CPSU generally presided at its meetings.

13. This decree (*ukaz*), approved by the Presidium of the old Supreme Soviet, introduced severe administrative and criminal penalties for actions and opinions deemed to "discredit" state organs and functionaries. The vagueness and ambiguity of the defi-

been approved "unanimously." His speech, however, did little to clarify exactly who had prepared such decrees and what procedure and legal basis they had used to do so.

We have mentioned only a few of the procedural snafus that plagued the First Congress. They illustrate the primitive technical conditions that, especially at first, impeded its smooth functioning. Matters improved and the Congress' work became more efficient as its president and deputies acquired more experience, but such difficulties never disappeared completely. Their continuing presence cannot be forgotten. We need always to remember the Soviets' starting-point, and the limited internal and external resources available to them, when evaluating the success of, and attempting to predict the likely speed and extent of, Soviet democratization. Furthermore, as the political apex of the country faced these problems during the First Congress, there is no reason to believe that the rest of the country was any more advanced politically. Only the Baltic groups had a developed, mature political culture and program at the Congress. Even though political change was proceeding rapidly in many areas, the rest of the USSR—along with many deputies—had to start from the beginning in democratizing itself. Gorbachev showed that he was well aware of this when, at the close of the First Congress, he stated candidly that "to say the truth, many of us were mentally, and perhaps even intellectually, unprepared [for the Congress]."[14]

## President Gorbachev, Obolenskii, and Yeltsin

Not surprisingly, the election of a president, too, featured errors, procedural bungles, omissions, and political blunders sufficient to provoke protests from many deputies and to alienate the public at large. We will begin our discussion with Gorbachev's nomination. In Soviet practice, candidacies were normally proposed by some designated person. In this case, a formal presentation was hardly necessary, since everyone knew Gorbachev. A few simple words sufficed to fulfill the requirements of ceremony. Beyond that, only a literary genius—one specially picked for such a job—could avoid being swept away by painful hagiographical exaltations of such an illustrious candidate. The writer Chingiz Aitmatov had been specially selected for the task, but even he did not escape

---

nition of such "crimes," however—particularly the notorious paragraph "11 *prim*"—provoked bitter protests from radical democrats. These radicals accurately understood the twin purposes of the decree to be the curtailing of free expression and the harassing of political oppositionists.

14. *Pravda*, 10 June 1989.

such pitfalls. Others followed Aitmatov, adhering to an apparently tightly crafted script. Vitalii Vorotnikov, the session's chair, insisted on opening the discussion of Gorbachev's candidacy immediately, riding roughshod over objections from deputies who wanted first to allow possible other candidacies to be proposed.

An atmosphere of absurdity prevailed. Another candidacy, after all —that of Aleksandr Mitrofanovich Obolenskii—already existed, having been formalized by the Presidium at the beginning of the session. An obscure, "nonparty" (that is, non-Communist) deputy hailing from the small northern city of Apatite (near Murmansk), Obolenskii had realized that Gorbachev's agenda would be approved *in toto*. Hence, basing himself on Articles 48 and 120 of the Soviet constitution, he wrote to the Presidium to nominate himself for the position of president. Obolenskii then asked to address the Congress so as to set forward his own political program, neatly upsetting Gorbachev's carefully constructed agenda and implicitly proposing a procedure that was more just and democratic than Gorbachev's. Vorotnikov gave in, but announced that the Congress would begin the debate by considering first the candidacy of Gorbachev and then, separately, that of the unknown Obolenskii. Many deputies argued that it was impossible to consider one candidate in isolation, since by definition all candidates in a democratic election are considered in relation to one another. Such repeated objections, however, amounted to nothing; Vorotnikov showed no concern about the illogicalities and contradictions. When his turn to speak finally came, Obolenskii took the floor to attack the farce. Although this farce had been created by Anatolii Lukianov, Obolenskii contended that simply for countenancing it Gorbachev shared in the blame.

As Stepan Sulakshin, a deputy from Tomsk, noted, if the Congress had the ability easily to reject unwanted candidates by a simple majority, then the final, secret vote for president would lose much of its meaning. The majority could eliminate, one after another, all but one of the presidential candidates before reaching the final ballot. As a result, the Congress of People's Deputies could transform itself into one of its sycophantic predecessors, meekly pursuing the objective of filtering out a single candidate before holding an officially "secret" final vote. Obolenskii concluded his short speech with a remark that made him famous: "I am not a fool." He knew that he would not be accepted as a candidate for president, he said, but he had at least to try, hoping thereby to affirm the principle that a proper election involved a contest between candidates. Indeed, Gorbachev would have demonstrated great wisdom in accepting Obolenskii's challenge, while not exposing himself to much risk. He nevertheless declined, probably fearing that making such a concession would throw succeeding Congress elections open to a myriad of new, unpredictable candidates. Obolenskii's name never reached the final presidential ballot. The deputy from Apatite, however, did collect the highest number of votes from the opposition, supported by 689 affirmative votes and 33 abstentions.

The barrage directed against Obolenskii actually served another, more important, purpose. By preventing another candidate—any other candidate—from being proposed for the post of president, the danger of Boris Yeltsin also becoming a candidate could be forestalled. Gorbachev saw this danger as real—and his perception of such danger was another example of his exaggerated defensiveness. Nearly fifty deputies spoke on the issue of who should be president; roughly half declared unqualified support for Gorbachev. Twenty other deputies announced that they would vote for Gorbachev, but tempered their support with political and personal criticisms. Twelve of these deputies, for instance, felt that the offices of general secretary of the Party and president of the Supreme Soviet should not be held by the same person. Several of the twelve in turn conceded that an exception should, for political reasons, be allowed in Gorbachev's case, but argued that it should be made clear that this was "for the last time." Only three deputies—B. Kryzhkov, N. Fedorov, and P. Falk—openly opposed Gorbachev. Two others, V. Biriukov and G. Burbulis, proposed that Yeltsin become a candidate for president, and V. Iavorivskii (with Kryzhkov) supported them by inviting Yeltsin to enter the race. Deputy A. Kraiko then took a pragmatic line, asking Yeltsin to renounce his nascent candidacy, so as not to endanger Gorbachev's political position. "Remember, however," Kraiko continued in a warning to the conservative majority, that such a step by Yeltsin would be anomalous in the extreme. Yeltsin had, after all, been elected with five million popular votes, yet "inside here hostile shouts arise every time his name is mentioned." The Congress was out of step with the country, he concluded.

For essentially tactical reasons, Yeltsin did not at this time wish to undercut Gorbachev. Thus, whatever Gorbachev's fears, Yeltsin posed little real danger to the Soviet leader. Indeed, if such a danger existed, Gorbachev could easily have used the Congress' conservative majority to quash it. In the end, Yeltsin took the floor to remove his name from consideration. Significantly, however, he withdrew only at the end of a long debate. He allowed his name to remain in discussion during successive stages of the debate, and ended his candidacy only after gauging the assembly's mood and recognizing the likely dimensions of a near-certain defeat. With his decision, the vote began. With 2,123 votes in favor, 87 against, and no reported abstentions,[15] Mikhail Sergeevich Gorbachev was elected president of the Supreme Soviet.

## Electing the Supreme Soviet

As the Congress shifted its sights to the next item on the agenda, that of electing members to the new Supreme Soviet, another legislative fight erupted. Battle lines were quickly drawn on what would prove to be one of the sharpest disagreements to face the Congress. Two distinct chambers, the Soviets of the Union and of Nationalities, had to be elected, each containing 271 deputies. The existing constitution mandated slight differences in the way members were chosen for each chamber, but in practice the composition of both bodies was determined by strictly proportional representation of all republics and autonomous regions. As discussed above, this approach minimized deputies' freedom of maneuver. It also reduced political outlook—or even basic competence—below territorial origin as a criterion in selecting deputies for either chamber. Each of the fifteen republican delegations (plus the Moscow delegation as a separate group) chose its own nominees to these upper houses, and thus the final (secret) ballot contained sixteen lists for each chamber. The agreement among delegations,[16] however, provided that each would present blocked lists, offering only one nominee for each seat. The Congress as a whole could not propose new candidates, but could only approve or reject those candidates put before it. Any nominee obtaining the support of more than fifty percent of the valid votes cast was elected.

A small number of Party powerbrokers who controlled their respective republican delegations, therefore, could tailor the lists to their liking. Independent-minded or meddlesome deputies were easily excluded. Denouncing this practice, the Ukrainian deputy A. Boiko declared that, "In many republics candidates have been proposed by the 'apparatus method.' We all know very well what this system is. We also know what outcome will result. . . ." The Uzbek deputy V. Zolotukhin illustrated the problem as it existed in his own delegation. The slate of candidates from Uzbekistan presented to the Congress included such figures as the Uzbek Party's first secretary and three of its first regional secretaries, the president and first vice president of the Uzbek Supreme Soviet, the president of the Uzbek *Gosplan* agency, and the president of the Uzbek Committee of Popular Control. Zolotukhin's point was clear: Uzbek *apparatchiki* at-

15. In fact, 2,221 ballots had been distributed. Eleven deputies did not participate.
16. As mentioned, the Moscow group refused to participate in the agreement.

tempted to protect their interests by occupying the maximum number of seats in the new national bodies.[17]

Many radicals and independents on the Left attempted to force a change in this method of deputy selection, but had little success. As already mentioned, therefore, the Moscow delegation, dominated by reformists, decided to set an example by presenting an open list of fifty-five names to fill the twenty-nine spots available to it in the Soviet of the Union. The Congress at large could choose amongst them, and thus had a voice in determining the makeup of the final Moscow contingent in the Soviet of the Union. The conservative majority expressed this voice eagerly, using the trappings of democracy to cancel many radical deputies.

The reformist alliance itself split over this issue of deputy selection. Baltic delegations—from Lithuania in particular—joined conservatives in wanting to eliminate the formal pretense of a Congress vote, preferring to allow each republic openly to select its own delegation to the Supreme Soviet. If enacted into law, this clearly would have altered the meaning of the Supreme Soviet, transforming it into a simple chamber of republican representatives, elected by republics rather than by the Congress. Mutual distrust characterized the relations of the Baltic delegations with other republics; partly as a result, their position was understandable. Under the territorial system Baltic nationalists would be guaranteed a certain presence in the Soviet of the Union. In the radicals' democratic plan, on the other hand, a bloc of the larger, conservative republics could shut them out entirely. Consequently, Latvians, Estonians, and Lithuanians tenaciously resisted perceived interference from other republics in preparing their own lists for both houses of the Supreme Soviet.

The Presidium of the Congress understood perfectly well the nature of this rift in the radical front, and sought to drive the wedge still deeper by satisfying completely the Lithuanian demands. A guarantee was given, agreed upon by all republics: if any Supreme Soviet lists were left incomplete after the Congress had voted—that is, if one or more deputies on a blocked republican list were cancelled by a Congress majority— then not only would the vote be repeated but names on the new list

17. They did not, however, take the new political situation into account. Parliament no longer held only fictitious power as it had in the past. Deputies now had to work for many months of the year. "Duplicity" of Party appointments and parliamentary functions was still permitted, but many Party bosses were unable in practical terms to apply themselves assiduously to the work of the Supreme Soviet and its standing committees. Hence, in subsequent months it became evident that reformers were far more active in these bodies than conservatives (a situation that changed in the Second Congress). Indeed, reformers won many votes through better attendance at meetings of Supreme Soviet commissions. The *apparat*'s avid zeal to hold *all* positions of power, then, boomeranged, rebounding to hurt conservatives and to undercut their real power.

could only be cancelled by deputies from the republics concerned. This guarantee was designed to reassure Baltic deputies that their lists would remain untouched, but Landsbergis, the leader of *Sajudis*, remained stubbornly opposed. "This machinery," he declared, "is absurd." It forced the Lithuanian delegation, he continued, to accede without any real guarantees, since the promise of nonintervention was not binding. Hence, other delegations—especially from the larger republics such as Russia—could change their mind if they wished and still cancel other republics' lists. Landsbergis announced that the Lithuanian delegation would not participate in the vote for the Supreme Soviet. Long discussion finally persuaded the Lithuanians to take part and, in the end, ballots presented to the Congress had only three open lists out of thirty-two.[18] All three exceptions were in the RSFSR: as we know, Moscow presented fifty-five candidates for twenty-nine posts in the Soviet of the Union. The Russian Republic, too, nominated four extra candidates to the Soviet of the Union, and put forward twelve names for the eleven posts allocated to it in the Soviet of Nationalities.[19]

This last, apparently small, difference, only involving one too many nominees, might seem almost insignificant. It, however, actually stirred the largest scandal when the Supreme Soviet vote was finally taken. Boris Yeltsin—the Congress' most popular deputy—finished last of the twelve in the Congress vote, with 964 cancellations. Conservatives of all stripes had joined forces to prevent him from entering the Supreme Soviet, and the apparatus had taken its revenge.[20] Indignation swept the country. Conservatives apparently were determined not to relinquish their iron grip on the country, nor to compromise in any way with progressives. Only the intervention of Aleksei Kazannik, an unknown deputy from Omsk, rescued the Congress from complete disrepute. Kazannik challenged the vote as it stood, offering his seat in the Supreme Soviet to Yeltsin and demanding an eleventh-hour revote to legitimize such a transfer. Despite the procedural irregularity, Gorbachev seized this opportunity to resurrect the Congress' prestige and to restore to it a measure of credibility. Gorbachev brought his personal prestige to bear, pressuring the

18. Sixteen lists each for the Soviet of Nationalities and the Soviet of the Union.
19. During a heated discussion, in fact, it emerged that many deputies from the Russian Republic were dissatisfied with the way in which Vitalii Vorotnikov had determined the composition of the lists. Representatives of autonomous republics and regions protested particularly sharply. In the end, mostly as a result of the confused nature of the debate (as opposed to the Moscow delegation's conscious decision), the Russian Republic's two lists remained open.
20. Rumor had it that the RSFSR list for the Soviet of Nationalities was enlarged simply to prevent Boris Yeltsin from being elected to the Supreme Soviet. It certainly is at least possible that this widespread suspicion had some basis in fact.

conservative Congress majority to accept Kazannik's offer. Perhaps not surprisingly, therefore, the second vote righted the perceived wrong of the first, and Yeltsin entered the Supreme Soviet. The conflict, however, left a bitter aftertaste. It showed the depth of the political divisions wracking the Soviet Union, and progressives could only resent the exclusion of almost the entire Muscovite radical intelligentsia from the Supreme Soviet. A Supreme Soviet so composed, with a majority so obviously disdainful of democratic norms, appeared to many as a body fatally flawed. Apparently dominated by the *apparat*, it seemed to offer little promise as an alternative power base to the party. To reformists' surprise, however, this same Supreme Soviet soon displayed an unexpected vitality and a startling degree of autonomy from the apparatus.[21]

## The "True" Right Wing

We have already seen that radical reformers dominated many debates during the First Congress. Indeed, we shall return at length to this theme in chapter 11. Progressives, however, did not represent the only emerging political force in the Soviet Union. We must also consider the powerful role played—and the enormous potential influence wielded—by those reinvigorated conservatives whom we have dubbed "right-wing independents." This group, in fact, contained the likely embryo of a future conservative party.[22] Extrapolating from its early tendencies, we can guess that this still-unformed party is likely to frame itself as the heir of various classic European extreme-right-wing parties, but with a large dollop of Russian (or Great-Russian) nationalism added. Various (particularly radical) deputies saw the growing threat of such a movement on the right, and denounced its most sinister and dangerous symptoms. In attempting to show briefly as much as possible of the spectrum of political conservatism and Russian nationalism evinced at the Congress, we will concentrate on the speeches of two deputies, Vasilii Belov and Valentin Rasputin.

Belov's speech was masterful.[23] He seemed at first to be defending Gorbachev both against the attacks of the Moscow radicals and against popular criticism. What he really wanted to defend, however, was not Gorbachev or his program but rather the power and authority of the president. Belov accused the intelligentsia, academics, and Soviet scientists of undermining this authority. In doing so, he provided a rallying cry to unify anti-intellectual elements in both the Party apparatus and the

---

21. See chap. 12.
22. See chap. 13.
23. Broadcast on Soviet TV, 1 June 1989.

working class. First addressing ecological concerns, Belov blamed "the scientists" for Chernobyl. Playing on the widespread resentment of high cooperative (private enterprise) prices, he argued that Soviet economists had produced little besides "the farmers' market at Riga Station."[24] He tapped into the rich vein of popular discontent with bureaucracy and meaningless parliamentary niceties. The Congress, he asserted, until then had been nothing but a "waste of time," since it had been hijacked by the Moscow radicals. These radicals allegedly had diverted the deputies with endless "procedural questions" and had thereby prevented any real discussion. In a remarkably short time, Belov struck chords that resonated strongly with millions of Soviet citizens. Gathering protests of both Right and Left to frame his populist message, he deflected blame for the country's predicament from the *apparat* onto the intellectual advocates of change.

Reviving a major theme of the *derevenshchiki* literary school,[25] Belov declared his opposition to "the degeneration [found in] urban culture." He then combined a demand for the privatization of land—a left-wing position—with a polemic against the bureaucratic incompetence of central ministries and a vigorous defense of *sovkhozy* and *kolkhozy*, thereby mixing in a conservative element. He became the first at the Congress to argue for the reconstitution of the Russian Republic's Communist Party and for the Russian Republic's assertion of the same sovereign rights claimed by other republics.[26] He denounced rampant "pornography" and accused many pro-*perestroika* newspapers—particularly *Moskovskie Novosti*—of being instruments of crass, foreign, mass culture, and thus of moral degeneration. Switching gears slightly, but still stressing his pan-Slav credentials, Belov then bemoaned the slight rates of demographic growth shown by the

24. A large cooperative and private market flourishes around the Riga Railway Station (*Rizhkii Vokzal*) in Moscow. Much, if not most, of the commerce at this market was (and is) illegal, and it was widely reputed to be a hub of criminal activity. As such, it was resented by Muscovites and became a symbol of the problems associated with a Soviet free-market economy.

25. Representing the continuation of a persistent strand of Russian literature, the *derevenshchiki* represented a literary-cultural movement in the 1970s which called for a "return to the land." Members of this school opposed rapid industrial development and its consequences, extolling rural culture and denouncing the uncontrolled growth of urban areas and the concomitant erosion of traditional family values.

26. After being abolished by Leonid Brezhnev in the mid-1960s, the Russian Republic did not have a *Biuro* of its own. Instead, the Russian Federation had only a distinct government and Supreme Soviet, as did each of the other 14 republics. Besides the restoration of the *Biuro*, Russian nationalists requested the creation of a Russian Academy of Sciences and other cultural and scientific institutions to exist independent of central Soviet organizations. The plenum of the CPSU Central Committee held in December 1989 endorsed these requests in part, allowing the Russian *Biuro* of the Party to be reestablished.

Soviet Union's Russians, Ukrainians, and Belorussians. The steady reduction of the Slavic proportion within the USSR, he continued, menaced the continuing supremacy of both these Slavic peoples and their cultures. Also on nationalist grounds, Belov expressed his opposition to the integration of the Soviet Union into the world economic system. Joint ventures were tantamount to treason, he argued, since they delivered Soviet territory and resources into foreign hands. International traffic, commerce, and cooperation should be shunned.

Much of Belov's speech denounced the excesses and shortcomings of the Party apparatus, but the main target of his ire remained radical intellectuals, towards whom he exhibited implacable hostility. These radicals themselves, he proclaimed, despite their lofty words, represented the greatest threat to true pluralism. Again appropriating pet issues of both the Left and the ecological movement, he demanded a popular referendum on the continued use of atomic energy in the USSR, and asserted that he favored a Congress that would assume real power. At the same time, he rather cryptically accused radicals of having seized power. This accusation at first seems curious, since radicals were clearly in the minority at the Congress. Belov plainly intended, however, to deliver a barely veiled threat, to warn the radicals that he and his conservative brethren knew what reformers were trying to do. Because now, he proclaimed to loud applause, "we at the Congress have no power; on the contrary, power is in the hands of others, some of whom we do not even know." Belov made it clear that he was not alluding to *apparatchiki* or the KGB when he spoke of "others." Instead, he said that "the power is in the hands of those who control the television cameras and the editing of newspapers. Of those who sit near the tribune and who have learned to use the photocopiers. Even here in the Congress, the power is in their hands."

Belov's targets were obviously radical reformers, particularly those from Moscow (who sat in the front rows at the Congress, near the Presidium, or tribune) and those who had learned to use modern mass communications for political ends. Everyone present realized to whom he was referring, even though he carefully avoided being explicit. As a finale, he then redirected his euphemistic attacks to assail "the Zionists." Although he never spoke of "Jews," thousands of anti-Semitic potential allies who read Belov's speech understood him perfectly. In appealing to the dark underbelly of Soviet and Russian society, Belov hoped to revitalize anti-Semitism as a unifying force, and hoped to use Jews as a convenient scapegoat for his country's ills.

Soviet democracy was so new at the First Congress that most political positions were still coalescing. Where their platforms were not confused, inconsistent, or contradictory, both right- and left-wing groups often took stands that overlapped or were indistinguishable from each other. Valentin Rasputin's address, delivered in a later session of the Congress,[27] revealed much of the same odd ambivalence as Belov's speech. This very ambivalence gave "right-wing independents" great potential for developing popular support. Distinctions between "Right" and "Left" had not yet developed meaning for many Soviet citizens, most of whom were only just beginning to become politically active, and few had developed strong political loyalties. For many, indeed, the labels of "progressive" and "reactionary" had taken on completely different meanings through their past service in the name of authoritarian Soviet socialism.

Valentin Rasputin, a deeply religious man and a famous writer affiliated with no political party, received a stormy ovation at the conclusion of his politically ambiguous, but mostly conservative, speech to the Congress. Many enthusiastic Party members and *apparatchiki* apparently did not realize that part of Rasputin's speech attacked them, but they appreciated his stinging attack on radical reformers. Rasputin's vigorous defense of the electoral mechanism as a safeguard against the "excessive power" of intellectuals pleased members of the Party's right wing, who also applauded his accusation that radicals wished "to take power in order to create a state system of repression of the counterrevolution."[28] Above all, the most dogmatic section of the Right appreciated his subtle distinction between "political pluralism" and "ethical pluralism." The first type of pluralism, Rasputin affirmed, was positive. The second, he called "more dangerous than any bomb." In making this argument, Rasputin asserted that he expressed the philosophical outlook of the silent majorities that existed in Russia as well as in the West, opposing the "glorification of sex, of violence, of the throwing off of every moral standard." Here, however, he broke from his passionate, at times almost delirious, moralizing to make a clear political choice.

Rasputin knew very well that many of the wrongdoings he denounced

27. Broadcast on Soviet TV, 6 June 1989.
28. Rasputin's expression was revealing. Although himself opposed to it, he apparently considered *perestroika* to be a revolution. At the same time, he feared the radical reformers who were, in his estimation, the real promoters of this "revolution." If these radicals achieved victory, he thought, they would dub their political enemies "counterrevolutionaries" and then repress them. Rasputin thus reproduced the old model of the Stalinist repression, simply reversing the political affiliations of the protagonists. He obviously overstated the real danger posed by progressives, as radicals were very far from power in the summer of 1989. On a more fundamental level, however, he neglected the issue of how the different political principles and premises of most advocates of democracy might alter the way in which they approached the process of political struggle. Simply reversing the labels on the old model might not accurately describe the situation that would follow the victory of a new "revolution," particularly if the makers of the new revolution were committed, above all else, to avoiding the replication of that old model.

—real, dramatic transgressions of his moral code—were the result of decades of violence carried out in the name of revolutionary ethics. He was not as aware, however, that they were just as much the product of historical developments in Russia before that revolution. He finished painting for the Congress his bleak picture of Soviet society, concluding with a denunciation of the "race to liberation," a race for which, he maintained, the intelligentsia bore full responsibility. His argument implied that all depravity—a category in which he included modern music ("cacophony"), sex education, widespread violence, and moral pollution—had begun only recently, and was indeed only the product of the bitter winds of *perestroika*. Life, he said, had been better "before."

Belov took popular grievances and offered his own explanations about who was to blame. In the same manner, Rasputin considered the issues of the day by recasting them in terms of his moral vision. He criticized the Afghan war, but drew a parallel between it and the "undeclared war" on morality that beset contemporary society. Red Army veterans who survived the Afghan conflict to return home, he continued, deserved compassion. Due "as much" compassion as veterans, however, were Soviet youths who had been poisoned by the entertainment industry's need to feed on human weakness. Although remaining unaffiliated with any party, Rasputin defended the CPSU from the attacks of reformers, and even defended—albeit not by name—Egor Ligachev. There was a time, Rasputin continued, when Party membership had helped boost one's career. That time, however, had passed, and "to be in the Party is no longer an advantage; on the contrary, [now] it is dangerous." Hence, those who left the Party at this juncture were cowards. "A real sign of courage," he maintained, "would have been leaving the Party ten or even five years ago."

He quickly moved on to other topics, having ensured by his generally pro-Party tone that the *apparatchiki* would listen favorably to the remainder of his speech. Abandoning his defense of socialism and of the Soviet system, he returned to his main theme, that of Russian nationalism. Russia's tragedy, he stated, resulted from "the oppression of the administrative-industrial machine, which revealed itself to all of us as even more terrible than the Mongol joke." This formulation, using for satiric purposes the total political domination of Mongolia, was the more diplomatic version of a theme which Rasputin had proclaimed openly in a number of articles and interviews. He felt that the October Revolution was a Jewish conspiracy directed against the Russian people, and that therefore the command-administrative system which had evolved from the revolution—and which had destroyed Russian culture—resulted from a Jewish conspiracy. Rasputin implied that socialism as a whole should go on trial, and then, glibly abandoning Communists to their fate, returned lyrically to the "instructive" mission of the Russian people toward the non-Russian Soviet peoples. This lyricism was followed by a passionately nationalist attack on Baltic nationalists, whom he called the "ungrateful instigators" of the anti-Russian feeling currently spreading along the country's periphery. You want to leave the Union, he demanded of the Balts? Very well, then, go ahead; it is your decision to make. But what would you and the others say, he continued, if we Russians were to leave? Rasputin and the "true" Right in essence were preparing a program of Russian nationalist revenge against the "unruly" subject peoples who demanded independence.

Whether such ideological appeals as Belov's and Rasputin's can overcome the damage done by the *coup* attempt of August 1991 to create a conservative mass movement remains to be seen. The final outcome depends heavily on how successful the Russian reformist intelligentsia is in using this same nationalist theme while redefining it in progressive, democratic terms. The two converging and colliding forces which threatened to rip the USSR away from a continued *perestroika*—"right-wing" anti-Communism and "right-wing" dogmatic Marxism-Leninism—had this root of anti-Russian hostility (and the resulting pro-Russian nationalist backlash) in common. First transforming this conflict into one that is both constructive and civilly conducted, however, and then unifying the Soviet peoples, required superior political consciousness and skill on the part of Soviet ruling groups. Gorbachev started with a heritage of a rigidly unitary state packaged in a frail federative wrapper, a state in which, in reality, the center deprived the periphery of any meaningful autonomy. Here, on the one hand, lies the root of the systematic Soviet violation of the rights of minority nationalities, and hence the root also of the systematic and cyclical resurgence of centrifugal tendencies. Perhaps the most lucid treatment of this issue at the Congress came in a speech by K. Khallik, a young Estonian deputy.[29] Himself not ethnically Russian, Khallik nevertheless asked the Congress to accept the legitimacy of Russian national aspirations and to use them as a point of departure for finding a democratic solution to the national question. "The fragmented structure of the Russian national state," he argued, "the administration of Russia not as a country but as a conglomerate of regions, leads to the disappearance of national self-consciousness and to its substitution with a (fictitious) pan-Soviet identity. Under these conditions, the main obstacle is to national renewal, and consequently many in Russia wind up perceiving the battle of the other republics against bureaucratic centralism as a struggle against Russia."

29. Broadcast on Soviet TV, 6 June 1989.

# Gorbachev's Tactics

Gorbachev himself explained his tactics on the third day of the First Congress. "I will try to find the middle ground," he said, "so that [various] points of view may be expressed and the atmosphere will remain calm. I believe this is the main objective."[1] Gorbachev was well aware that political battles would occur at the Congress, but he knew that at least outwardly he needed to remain above the fray, ensuring that all sides enjoyed equal opportunity to express their positions. Although not always successful in doing so, he therefore tried to control himself. Visibly tense at the Congress' outset, he nonetheless remained willing to use all the prerogatives of his powerful position. Many even expected a power play at the Congress. When deputy Iurii Boldyrev proposed the introduction of roll-call voting, Gorbachev remarked, "I think this motion . . . attempts to drag us to where the Congress should not be dragged." He then proposed a motion of his own against Boldyrev's, and calling it "the Presidium's motion" put it to a vote. Despite the procedural irregularity, Gorbachev's motion won Congress approval.

Immediately afterwards, though, Gorbachev demonstrated his ability to adapt to new conditions and to correct his mistakes. When Sergei Stankevich raised the question of roll-call voting again, half an hour later, by referring (correctly) to Article 18 of the provisional regulations,[2] Gorbachev did not object. Rather, he made substantial changes in the motion, modifying it to require roll-call voting whenever a Congress majority requested it. Showing that he had learned from his encounter with Boldyrev and Rodion Shchedrin, he then put the two motions to a vote in the proper order—first the Stankevich motion, then his own. Stankevich's

---

1. Unless otherwise indicated, all quotations are taken from the stenographic account published in *Izvestiia*, beginning 26 May 1989.

2. Stankevich's motion called for roll-call voting whenever it was requested by at least 100 deputies.

motion received only 431 votes in favor and was rejected, but Gorbachev attempted to conciliate liberal reformers after their defeat. "Your motion, comrade Stankevich," he said, "has been carried with amendments." This episode illustrates Gorbachev's tactics well. Clearly the Congress rejected the effort to safeguard the rights of minority voters, but—once sure of victory—Gorbachev tried publicly to minimize the differences separating both sides.[3]

Over the course of the Congress the Soviet leader repeatedly demonstrated his capacity to adapt to unforeseen developments and to modify his positions. When radicals protested that certain procedures were too hasty, for example, he sought a compromise. During the debate on his own candidacy for the post of president of the Supreme Soviet, Gorbachev ostentatiously corrected the presiding officer Vorotnikov, calling for all scheduled deputies to be allowed to take the floor, even if only briefly. He also accepted an unsolicited motion of Andrei Sakharov's that called for Gorbachev to present his political program to the Congress before the vote was held. Realizing that it would be a mistake to reject this request, Gorbachev declared—in words echoing Sakharov's—"I have to respond in some way to the questions that have been put to me." The agenda had been changed substantially, then, at the behest of radicals.

Gorbachev did not always support attempts to modify his agenda. He kept one foot in both camps, supporting each side of the political spectrum alternately. Since conservatives were usually less active than reformers, the Soviet leader often balanced the debate by reading notes sent from the floor. Obviously, he did not read every such message, but only those that were useful. Once, to counteract radical pressure, for instance, he read a message from three deputies of the "swamp": "When is the Moscow group going to stop disrupting the Congress?" He sometimes selected written messages to make his own views heard through the voices of others, as when he read aloud the protest of one Tadzhik deputy that "of the three Tadzhik candidates to the Supreme Soviet, two are the first and second secretaries of the Party of the republic."

At certain important points, Gorbachev simply refused to do anything, lest it be precipitate. This was an effective approach, and he often resorted to it when he personally came under attack. Listening in silence, without interruption or emotion, he absorbed every word uttered by his attacker. He behaved this way, for example, during the crisis of the Left

3. We must note that the minority request for roll-call voting would have been impractical at the First Congress, where voting was carried out by a show of hands. A roll-call vote in these conditions would take hours. With the introduction at the Second Congress of an electronic vote-counting system, the radicals' request became practical, and in fact several roll-call votes were published in the official Congress *Biulleten*.

on 27 May. Iurii Afanasev and Gavriil Popov had reacted strongly to the results of the vote on the Supreme Soviet, and radicals had sustained a major defeat with the exclusion of Boris Yeltsin and many of the most intellectually qualified candidates from the Supreme Soviet. The Congress majority was clearly in no mood for compromise, and Afanasev declared the need for a break, to formalize the obvious political division.

Afanasev then launched two main attacks. The first denounced the "aggressive and subordinate" majority that had elected a "Stalinist-Brezhnevite" Supreme Soviet; the second attacked Gorbachev personally, asserting that he "relies judiciously on this majority for support and at the same time is able to use it with great skill." Popov then took the podium and asked, "Why has all this been arranged? Why did anyone want this mechanical voting? There can only be one answer. Because they wanted to create a Supreme Soviet that would take orders from the *apparat* and continue to pressure the progressive wing of the leadership, this time through the Supreme Soviet." Nothing remained for the minority to do but organize an opposition, as it seemed to have been cut completely out of positions of real power. Hence, reformers laid their cards on the table; both speeches, vigorous and decisive, were addressed more to the nationwide television audience than to the Congress itself.

Ironically, much could be said about how mistaken were the radical predictions. In following months the Supreme Soviet showed itself to be far less "Brezhnevite and Stalinist" than it seemed in May.[4] Even at the time, many thought—with some justification—that Afanasev's move would only further isolate the minority before many deputies had even decided their political loyalties. A moment's reflection, however, shows this opinion to be overhasty. Radicals could not silently accept their exclusion from power by an increasingly out-of-touch Congress majority. Had they done so, they themselves would have lost popular credibility. Furthermore, radicals by this point had realized that they had more power, even within the Congress, than originally expected. The first votes, particularly when reformers won 831 votes to oppose the *ukaz* of 28 July (which had substantially limited the right of public demonstration), showed great political fluidity. These votes implied that maintaining a superficial unanimity would only curtail the minority's potential for expanding its support.

The threat of a political break also served as a warning to the apparatus. Its members in effect had been given notice that they could not act with impunity, even if they did control a Congress majority. Backbenchers expressed indignation at the "divisive" actions taken by Afanasev and Popov, but few wanted to denounce these actions on national tele-

4. See chap. 12.

vision. While Gorbachev remained silent, the first reply to the radicals, by deputy V. Stepanov, showed that conservatives were deeply disturbed. "They are trying," Stepanov announced, "to split the Congress off from the people!" Over the next two days the Congress majority showed all the signs of having taken a major blow; the radicals, partially aided by Gorbachev, brought even stronger pressure to bear.

The Soviet leader himself did not respond immediately to the radicals. After gathering his thoughts during Stepanov's speech, he stated frankly that "We have to discuss this, since we are now at a critical moment for our Congress." Despite his attempts to control words and gestures, the intensity of his emotion was apparent. "The comrades [from Moscow] know what they are doing," he said. "They probably have several other moves like this prepared in advance." He paused, and then added drily, "[But] there are some things we cannot accept." Given the vehemence of the attacks directed at him, it was perhaps surprising that he tried to mend the rupture. "I do not think we should reject everything comrades Afanasev and Popov have said." Gorbachev clearly recognized both that the conservative backlash would need to be restrained and that discussion was necessary and inevitable. He understood that the division had to be overcome immediately to head off the danger of the Congress being torn apart.

At this point, Gorbachev abruptly distanced himself from the conservative majority, which wanted only a condemnation of "factionalism." He realized that the radicals' move was for its own sake ineptly timed, but also that it held great potential danger. The ineptness could be measured in the isolation that radicals would bring upon themselves at the Congress; the danger lay in the possibility that Gorbachev, the great mediator himself, would now be exposed to, and swallowed by, the Right. Furthermore, Yeltsin's exclusion from the Supreme Soviet had inflicted a severe blow on the Congress' authority and credibility as a popularly elected, representative organ; to the millions of Muscovite voters who had chosen Yeltsin, the exclusion reeked of shameful hypocrisy.

After a series of speeches and back-room negotiations, when Popov again requested to speak Gorbachev resisted countervailing pressure from the "swamp." "We have to give him the floor," Gorbachev argued. "It is important." Perhaps Gorbachev knew that Popov would accept his proffered hand. In any case, Popov granted that Gorbachev had conducted the discussion on this issue democratically, adding that, "As long as there is the least possibility of working together here, we must do so. I am convinced that it is possible." The opposition's solidarity crumbled, and Gorbachev concluded, with sardonic understatement, "It has been an interesting discussion." The importance of this episode, however, was deeper than its surface threat of a political schism. The entire First Congress proceeded along similar lines, with Gorbachev making concessions to the Left as long as doing so neither threatened the delicate balance within the Party leadership nor restricted his own ability to maneuver.

The Congress elected a president of the Supreme Soviet, a first vice president, and a head of government without opposition. Gorbachev must have known that many deputies' irritation with him over his refusal to permit multi-candidate elections accurately reflected widespread sentiment throughout the USSR. His own position was secure, however, and he intended to hold his ground. When deputy Gennadi Filshin protested the lack of opposition to Lukianov's candidacy, Gorbachev replied, "I'll have to disappoint you. . . ." He explained to Filshin that the only alternative open to the opposition was to reject Lukianov's candidacy when Gorbachev proposed it. In that case, it would then fall to the president (Gorbachev) to propose a new candidate. By relying on this procedure[5] to prevent deputies from nominating their own choices for high office, Gorbachev could, despite the damage to his own popularity, remain intransigent. When he received several written requests to suspend television coverage of the Congress, however, Gorbachev made them public and invited the writers to retract their request. Conservatives clearly had more to fear from public exposure than Gorbachev. They, after all, were winning votes in the Congress but losing face in the country.

Such tactics allowed Gorbachev, the general secretary of the CPSU, to win one of the toughest battles of *perestroika* almost single-handedly, although not without sustaining political damage. Perhaps overconfidence led him to risk a final defeat in what was his only major mistake during the twelve-day Congress. On the Congress' penultimate day, deputies addressed themselves to the issue of the Constitutional Control Committee. We have already seen how reformers considered this committee to be one of the Congress' most important innovations, since it introduced the concept of a separation of powers into Soviet government for the first time. As during the election of the Supreme Soviet, however, a serious crack appeared on this issue in the united front of radicals and progressives on the one hand, and radical Baltic nationalists on the other. The nationalists' position was, from their perspective, reasonable: while the current Constitution remained in effect, a Constitutional Control Committee could only limit the sovereignty of republican parliaments, thereby strengthening central authority. Approving the creation of such a body would only make future conservative seizures of power easier.

On this issue Gorbachev allied with the "Moscovia." He wanted to

5. This procedure was codified in the constitutional changes of autumn 1988.

consider the question of the committee in the context of strengthening the Congress' own authority. To decide nothing, he declared, "would be tantamount to cutting the branch upon which we are sitting." To postpone a decision would only slow the transition to a rule-of-law state. Discussion soon became heated, and many reformers and mediators realized it would be impossible to persuade Baltic nationalists to change their minds. Roi Medvedev suggested that the Congress avoid passing a majority decision, even one with reformist support, that would alienate important ethnic groups and lend itself to centralist pressure. Gorbachev, too, seemed reluctant to force the issue in the face of the Balts' resolute opposition and imaginative tactics. The Soviet president, though, again showed his Achilles heel—namely, his superficial understanding of nationalities issues. When the matter was put to a vote, the 433 negative ballots and sixty-one abstentions showed that opposition to the committee was not only located in the Baltic. Dissent was strongest there, however, and the fifty-member Lithuanian delegation walked out of the hall in protest. Lithuanian Party First Secretary Algirdas Brazauskas left the Presidium to join his delegation.

The substantial majority cobbled together in favor of the Constitutional Control Committee represented a Pyrrhic victory for Gorbachev. His sudden decision to put the question to a vote in effect split deputies on the national question, the most explosive issue facing the Congress. The Soviet president realized only later the extent of the damage, and in his hesitant response seemed to have lost confidence. A motion by Fedor Burlatskii, seeking temporarily to postpone the committee's establishment in order to reexamine its powers and to allow time for negotiations with the Baltic deputies, appeared to Gorbachev as a life preserver. On the last day of the Congress, therefore—the day after the walkout—the newly created committee was quietly annulled. The Congress chose an *ad hoc* committee to write a new bill to regulate the functions of a future Constitutional Control Committee. The question was held over until the Second Congress; as we shall see, it reappeared there, as thorny and insoluble as ever.

This chapter has discussed a few of the most important moments in the proceedings of the First Congress in order to create a political and psychological profile of the Soviet leader. A full portrait, of course, has many superimposed layers and rich, subtle shading: no simple picture renders Gorbachev or his motivations accurately. For this reason, the foregoing illustrations of Gorbachev's tactics are incomplete. The Soviet president's relationship with Andrei Sakharov, for instance, is itself an entirely different chapter, shedding light on another side of Gorbachev's personality—

a side in which humanity transcended the practical exigencies of political struggle.

At the Congress Sakharov was the most vigorous exponent of a political line opposed to Gorbachev's. Thus, two and a half years after Gorbachev released Sakharov from internal exile in Gorkii, the two men found themselves adversaries. Both remembered history, however, and although they recognized their differences of political opinion, neither saw the other as an enemy. Gorbachev remained convinced that the wrong done to Sakharov by the Party and the government could never fully be righted. Sakharov realized that Gorbachev represented the only hope for the Soviet Union to move towards his own political and humanitarian goals. As a result, they continued to struggle, but minimized attacks on each other.

Sakharov was among the first to take the floor at the Congress, although Gorbachev was well aware that his words were likely to be combative. Indeed, Sakharov managed to address the Congress—and with it the nation—eleven times during the First Congress. While his life history testifies to his extraordinary courage, it should be remembered that at the Congress Sakharov was also permitted uniquely generous opportunities to speak. Every time Sakharov took the podium, Gorbachev showed his respect for the elderly academician and former dissident, sometimes even protecting and defending him against the hostility of plebian, intolerant deputies. On the Congress' final day, Sakharov again asked for the floor, and again it was clear that his speech intended to make a break explicit. Gorbachev could easily have denied him the floor, even justifying himself by the majority sentiment—hostile shouts erupted as Sakharov waited by the tribune. Nevertheless, Gorbachev put Sakharov's request to a perfunctory vote, quickly announcing (without a vote-count) that the Congress had approved the academician's request for five minutes of podium time. Even when Sakharov spoke for much longer, Gorbachev interrupted only when the uproar from the audience threatened to become uncontrollable.

Gorbachev achieved all the basic goals he had set out to attain during the Congress, but allowed the Left the privilege of concluding the Congress. Any objective balance sheet of the Congress, in fact, must recognize that Gorbachev actually *guided* the majority of deputies to approve much of the radical political program: creating commissions of inquiry to investigate the Tbilisi massacre, the Molotov-Ribbentrop Pact, and the Uzbek Mafia; modifying the Congress vote that had excluded Boris Yeltsin from the Supreme Soviet; postponing any decision on the Constitutional Control Committee; calling two, rather than one, convocations of the Congress each year; cancelling a section of the decree of 8 April that had mandated criminal penalties for the criticism of public officials and government organs; and creating a special commission at the Congress to study constitutional change.

Seeing the conduct of the First Congress as an example of *enlightened authoritarianism*, or of *astute manipulation* of an assembly that had not yet become a full parliament, is a useful simplification. Such simplifications, however, do not convey the full picture. Through Gorbachev's conscious choice, the First Congress represented the end of an era of *democracy bestowed from above*. It marked the beginning of a new democratic dialectic, of a *democratic chorus* in which all participants had much to learn and in which the *sacredness* of power disappeared forever. The Party's entire leadership faced a merciless, public critical pounding. Millions of Soviet citizens heard deputy L. Sukhov, an unknown chauffeur from Kharkov, compare Gorbachev with Napoleon—who, Sukhov argued, had also used "this adulation, and his wife" to transform a republic into an empire. In May the Politburo had been seated at a special tribunal on the president's right. By the start of the Second Congress in December, however, television cameras showed them seated in strict alphabetical order, mixed together with the other deputies.

# CHAPTER ELEVEN

# The First Congress:
# Political Forces and Behaviors

This chapter develops the assumptions made in chapters 4 and 5, using as evidence both roll-call votes and speeches from the First Congress. The 682 speeches, made by at least 464 different deputies, provide us with important information about those deputies who chose to take the podium; the roll-call votes yield material useful in analyzing the behavior of the Congress as a whole. Although we might desire more data, these large bodies of evidence are more than sufficient to support this chapter's analytic tasks. These tasks include, first, examining the political activity of various republics as represented by their delegations to the Congress. We then consider the behavior of the seven political affiliations identified earlier, and carry out a similar analysis of political behavior by social-professional groups, in both cases attempting better to understand the interrelationship between various social and political groups. Finally, we analyze the votes themselves in order to approximate the main political forces' relative strength. The validity of linking these two types of analysis (based on speeches and votes) will be defended later, in our analyses of the Second and Third Congresses, as the records for these later Congresses also give roll-call vote information for each individual deputy.[1]

## The Republics

Many hypotheses put forward at this book's outset, particularly those regarding various regions of the USSR, are confirmed by considering

1. Obviously, space is insufficient to permit detailed exposition of each deputy's individual behavior. Such details, however, giving information on speeches to all three Congresses, and votes in the Second and Third Congresses, may be found in the "List of Deputies" following the text.

the behavior of our seven political groups. Immediately apparent, for instance, is the total absence of radicals—and the small number of left-wing independents—among speakers from the five Central Asian republics.[2] Mediators were also proportionately underrepresented among the speakers from these republics. While our data, taken alone, do not prove the total absence of radical or reformist deputies from Central Asia, they do suggest that such political positions were rarely held by deputies from this region. This supports the observation made in chapter 4 that the electoral campaign in Central Asia, at least partly because of the region's relative political underdevelopment, remained largely under the control of local apparatuses. Moreover, while deputies from Kazakhstan, Kirghizia, Turkmenia, Tadzhikistan, and Uzbekistan together comprised only 6.3 percent of left-wing independent speakers and 6.6 percent of mediator speakers, they were overrepresented among centrist (15 percent), *apparatchik* (22 percent), and *pre-perestroika* (28 percent) speakers. Central Asian conservatism and apparatus control were readily apparent.

Central Asian delegations also produced only a small number of right-wing independent speeches. Four of the five republics, indeed (all except Kazakhstan), had no right-wing independent speakers. This absence only confirms the comparative lack of independence among Central Asian deputies of *any* political stripe, and the comparatively rigid control exerted over them by Party bosses. The figures are even more impressive when we consider that only a tiny proportion of the 365 Central Asian deputies spoke at all, a much lower participation rate than among deputies from other regions. Although Central Asian delegations filled 16.2 percent of the seats in Congress, they generated only 10.1 percent of speeches.[3] This passivity was itself most likely the product of the area's relative political immaturity, and it reveals shortcomings in both preparation and determination.

The most active region, on the other hand, was the Baltic. The 158 deputies from Estonia, Latvia, and Lithuania took the floor 62 times during the First Congress. As a result, while holding only 7 percent of the seats at the Congress, they represented 9.6 percent of speeches; their "activity coefficient" was more than double that of their Central Asian counterparts (1.37 to 0.53).[4] Similar figures show that deputies from the Slavic republics and Moldavia, while less active than those from the Baltic republics, also far exceeded those from Central Asia and Transcaucasia. The Slavic delegations (with the Moldavians) had the overwhelming ma-

2. The analysis that follows draws on tables 13 and 16.
3. See table 20.
4. For participation figures, see table 20. For details of the "activity coefficient," see table 21.

jority of both deputies (67.1 percent) and speeches (73.8 percent) at the Congress, and had an activity coefficient of 1.10. Transcaucasian deputies also spoke more often than did Central Asians: the delegations from Georgia, Armenia, and Azerbaijan held 216 seats (9.6 percent of the total) and made 7.9 percent of the speeches. With 9.8 percent of speakers, Transcaucasian deputies' activity coefficients of 0.82 and 1.02 were between the Central Asian and Slavic figures.[5]

The Baltic group displayed political behavior almost completely opposite that of the Central Asians. The Lithuanian delegation's "political geography" was particularly stark, with every speaker supporting a reformist position, whether radical (17.6 percent), left-wing independent (52.9 percent), or mediator (29.4 percent). None of the Baltic delegations produced a single centrist, *apparatchik*, or pre-*perestroika* speech. The Lithuanian delegation, though, exhibited greater political and ethnic homogeneity than the other two. While Latvian and Estonian delegations also generally supported reformist policies, they included a sizable number of right-wing independent speakers (22.2 percent and 6.7 percent, respectively). This indicated the presence of a greater number of allochthonous (in this case, mostly Russian) deputies, many of whom supported more conservative positions.[6]

The delegation from Turkmenia distinguished itself as the most primitive and reactionary at the Congress.[7] Although with only four speeches (only the Kirghiz delegation, with three speeches, was less vocal) the sample size is too small to generalize, it is noteworthy that two of these four speeches were pre-*perestroika*, while one each was centrist and *apparatchik*.

In looking at the Slavic republics' participation, we note that the numbers involved—both of deputies and of speeches—are larger, giving us greater confidence in the statistical picture that emerges. At the same time, however, we need to remember that the figures themselves are distorted: reformists more vigorously sought podium time than did conservatives, and as a result counting speeches alone overestimates the strength of liberal reformers. The group from Moscow, for example, seems dominated by the left wing: 74.5 percent of its speeches fell into the radical, left-wing independent, or mediator categories. At the same time, the Moscow delegation was deeply split between liberal reformers and conservative *apparatchiki*. The Russian Federation delegation's speeches, by contrast, were more centrist; speakers from the Ukrainian and Belorussian delegations

5. See tables 20 and 21.
6. See table 16.
7. See tables 13 and 16.

were both more often centrists, *apparatchiki*, or right-wing independents. Moreover, apart from Moscow the three Slavic republics each showed more left-wing independent than radical speeches, indicating how slowly extreme positions gained support outside central urban areas.

One further observation is that the radical group was most numerous among the delegations from Moscow, Georgia, Estonia, and Latvia. The left-wing independent faction was spread primarily among six delegations: those of Armenia, the RSFSR, the Ukraine, Belorussia, Lithuania, and Tadzhikistan. Mediators were particularly prominent among Estonian and Uzbek speakers, as were centrists among Belorussian, Moldavian, Kazakh, and Tadzhik speakers. *Apparatchiki* could most easily be located in Azerbaijan, Kirghizia, and Uzbekistan; right-wing independents were scattered throughout the republics. The pre-*perestroika* position was prominent only among the small group of speakers from Turkmenia.[8]

## Political Groups

It emerges from the foregoing discussion (and from table 19) that political activity, as measured by speeches to the Congress, steadily decreased across the political spectrum from left to right. The progression is perfect when we consider the overall number of speeches made to the First Congress, and is nearly so when the analysis is based on the number of individual deputies who made these speeches. As already noted, radical deputies fought to defend their positions, taking the podium disproportionately often during the Congress. In absolute terms, however, the 80 radical speakers were outnumbered by both the 112 left-wing independents and the 91 mediators. In other words, left-wing independents and mediators—although individually less pugnacious than radicals—as groups exerted greater influence on Congress debates.[9]

Another anomaly concerns the right-wing independents and pre-*perestroika* deputies. Twenty-four right-wing independent deputies took the floor (5.2 percent of speakers) making a total of 32 speeches (4.7 percent); fully 25 pre-*perestroika* deputies (5.4 percent) spoke, but made only 26 speeches (3.8 percent). Only one pre-*perestroika* deputy spoke more than once. Most important to note is the tendency for conservative deputies to address the Congress only once, whether to fulfill a preassigned rhetorical task or simply to react to reformers. As a result, the technical competence as well as motivation of conservatives lagged behind that of reformers.

Taken as a whole, the three reformist groups (radicals, left-wing independents, and mediators) dominated the debates, whether measured by

---

8. See table 16.
9. See chap. 7.

total number of speeches (66.8 percent) or of speakers (60.9 percent).[10] Clearly this dominance reflected reformers' superior pre-Congress preparations, and showed their willingness to take the political offensive. Just as clearly, it revealed Gorbachev's own inclination to grant the left wing, with its greater dynamism, cultural and political supremacy at the Congress. This is particularly apparent when we recall that the political composition of the entire 2,249-member Congress differed markedly from that of the sample of 464 deputies who spoke, the sample upon which table 19 is based. Subsequent chapters probe this divergence more deeply by utilizing the evidence provided by roll-call votes at the Second and Third Congresses.

## Social-Professional Groups

Discrepancies between the number of deputies from each of the seven social positions and their relative participation rates in Congress debates can be seen when we consider the figures in tables 8 and 22. The only exceptions are the *nomenklatura* (comprising 13.5 percent of deputies, and 12.7 percent of speakers) and technicians (362 deputies total, or 16.1 percent of the Congress, producing 17 percent of speeches and 15.5 percent of speakers). Deputies holding cadre, military, or managerial social positions, however, spoke less often than would be expected from their numerical prominence in the Congress. The 6.8 percent of "cadre" deputies produced only 4.3 percent of speeches to the Congress; comparative figures for military deputies were 4 percent and 2.8 percent, and for managers 17.1 percent and 9.7 percent.

The largest "participation gap," though, was displayed by workers. Despite being the largest single group at the Congress, with 503 deputies (22.4 percent of seats), workers comprised only 8.2 percent of speakers. Deputies holding social positions among the intelligentsia represented the opposite extreme, with more than 40 percent (156 of 384) making speeches. (By contrast, the comparable figure for worker deputies was 9 percent.) Although comprising only 17.6 percent of the Congress's deputies, therefore, the intelligentsia made more than a third (33.6 percent) of speeches. Hence, perhaps not surprisingly, debate at the First Congress was dominated by intellectuals—*intelligenty* and technicians. Those deputies in more traditional, productive employment—workers and managers—remained in the shadows, unable to compete in technical skill or political dynamism.[11]

10. See table 19.
11. The term "manager," we should note, in Soviet usage means something quite different from what it does in the West. Although changing greatly in the past two

Our analysis may be deepened by considering the social composition of various political groups.[12] Radical speakers were drawn largely from two social groups—55 percent from the intelligentsia and 26.7 percent from the technicians. Workers, on the other hand, comprised only 3.7 percent of radical speakers, and managers only 5 percent. Radical political positions, then, were taken primarily by the "diffuse intelligentsia," while other social groups were generally more conservative. This general picture of social composition is borne out among left-wing independent speakers. Once again first place belonged to the intelligentsia (41.1 percent) followed by technicians (23.2 percent), although managers (10.7 percent) and workers (9.8 percent) were somewhat more in evidence. "Cadres" represented 6.2 percent of left-wing independent speakers, meaning that some reformist positions enjoyed broad social support—roughly one quarter of those defending such positions came from social groups outside the "diffuse intelligentsia."

Significant shifts occur farther to the right on the political spectrum. A plurality of mediators (40.6 percent) was still drawn from the intelligentsia, but the *nomenklatura* (19.8 percent) took second place. Technicians were third (14.3 percent), followed at a distance by managers (6.6 percent) and workers (3.3 percent). The relative prominence of the *nomenklatura* in this group shows that Gorbachev could rely upon the support of a significant portion—if still a minority—of the apparatuses.

Considered as a whole, the intelligentsia was best represented among reformers—radicals, left-wing independents, and mediators. Not surprisingly, the *nomenklatura* enjoyed a plurality (28.3 percent) among centrist speakers, followed by the intelligentsia (19.4 percent), with managers (14.9 percent) and workers (10.4 percent) also present in significant numbers. The *nomenklatura* dominated the political affiliation of *apparatchiki* even more, with 38.6 percent of speakers. Once again, the intelligentsia took second place (20.4 percent), with managers and workers both at 11.3 percent.

Taking the *nomenklatura* itself as the object of scrutiny, we see that its members were most numerous among centrists and *apparatchiki*; that is, among more conservative groups, particularly among moderate conservatives of the center-right and right. Again, this should not be surprising, since the *nomenklatura* by definition was composed of men and women from the apparatuses, who naturally defended the existing system. It is

---

decades, both in social status and in means of selection, Soviet managers still largely achieved their positions through the *nomenklatura*'s system of selection. Equally, their professional competence was generally limited to activity within the confines of a centrally planned economy.

12. See tables 22 and 25.

equally important, however, to stress the less-expected prominence of the intelligentsia among right-wing speakers. Although less visible on the Right than on the Left, the presence of such intellectuals revealed a deep split within a crucial stratum of Soviet society. The intelligentsia was mostly left-wing in sympathy; many of its members in the apparatuses, however, supported the Right.

Interestingly, the group of right-wing independent speakers was drawn in disproportionate numbers from the ranks of the military. Comprising 25 percent of all right-wing independent speakers, the military outnumbered workers (16.7 percent), the intelligentsia (also 16.7 percent), and cadres (12.5 percent). This situation was important in later debates, when a conspicuous number of (especially lower- and middle-ranking) military personnel in the Congress defended independent positions harshly critical of the Party leadership.

The final group to be considered is that of pre-*perestroika* deputies. The most common social position in this group was "manager," with 24 percent of speakers. Workers (20 percent) were second, while technicians and *nomenklatura* each followed with 16 percent. As we might have expected, deputies from the intelligentsia were least prominent here (8 percent).

We now turn to the figures in tables 26 and 29 to analyze the political tendencies that dominated each of the seven social positions, starting with the *nomenklatura*.[13] Our first observation is that these speakers tended not to support "independent" positions, whether of the Right or of the Left.[14] Secondly, a large minority (32.2 percent) supported reformist (radical or mediator) positions, although most spoke in favor of conservative (centrist, *apparatchik*, or pre-*perestroika*) policies. While the overall picture confirms the generally conservative nature of the *nomenklatura*, then, it also points out flaws in a too-simple equation of the *nomenklatura* with conservatism.

The group of cadre speakers showed a clear reformist bent. With 60 percent supporting radical, left-wing independent, or mediator policies, their speeches showed that the lower and middle ranks of the Party and government—those in more direct contact with the public—were significantly more sensitive to, or reflective of, shifts in the popular mood than their superiors.

Deputies addressing the Congress from military social positions, by

13. Once again, the reader should remember that these analyses utilize the sample of deputies who spoke, not all deputies present, at the Congress.

14. This supports one of our earlier hypotheses, namely that the independent groups of both extremes remained outside the control of Party leaders (the *nomenklatura*). While progressive positions did exist within the *nomenklatura*, it would have been strange to find substantial numbers of deputies from this group attacking their own interests.

comparison, were more conservative, with 84.7 percent classified as right-wing independent, centrist, or pre-*perestroika*. Nearly half (46.7 percent) of military speakers, indeed, were right-wing independents. Before generalizing this observation to the military at large, however, we must remember that the sample is small, and masks an important split within the military. Although the high command was disproportionately represented at the Congress, its conservative beliefs were not necessarily shared by lower-level officers. Simply pointing to the 84.7 percent of speeches that were conservative, therefore, does not accurately render the state of military opinion.

"Managers" were almost evenly split between the Right and the Left. Fully 51 percent of their speeches supported the four conservative political affiliations (centrist, *apparatchik*, right-wing independent, and pre-*perestroika*), but 49 percent lent support to the two most radical groups (radicals and left-wing independents). The diversity implied by these figures reflects the uncertainty felt by this group, situated as it was at the cutting edge of economic reform. Moreover, managers were already permitted, even compelled, to take crucial day-to-day decisions without either supervision or experience. The group's political indecision played a fundamental role in determining the Congress' overall political position.

As already noted, the intelligentsia produced primarily left-wing deputies, with 81.4 percent of its speakers supporting radical, left-wing independent, or mediator positions. An analogous situation existed among technicians, where 79.1 percent of speakers were split among these three reformist groups. Workers were more conservative, with a majority of speakers (55.1 percent) adhering to a conservative group—centrist, *apparatchik*, right-wing independent, or pre-*perestroika*. Curiously, however, the largest single affiliation among workers was that of left-wing independent, at 28.9 percent of speakers. (Right-wing independents, by contrast, numbered only 10.5 percent.) Workers exhibited great political fluidity, and as a result were reliable allies for no political program.

The foregoing analysis allows us to conclude that the fissure between conservatives and reformers had deepened by the Congress, and cut through all major social groups. To varying extents, all social strata were divided by different visions of political, economic, social, and state reform. Traditional class analyses of Soviet society, therefore, fail to capture the essence of Soviet political polarization. In the Soviet Union of *perestroika*, a "system of social alliances" had to be constructed on criteria quite different from those called for by classical Marxism.

## Voting Patterns

As the Congress proceeded, it became clear that out of 2,249 deputies roughly 950 were reliably conservative, and approximately 440 were usually reformist. From 400 to 900 deputies thus were left as the political center of the Congress, and swings in their support were crucial. This central group, comprised primarily of centrists and mediators, reacted differently on each issue, splitting between conservatives and reformers depending on the extent to which it had been radicalized.

The preceding analysis was based on the sample of 682 speeches made by at least 464 deputies at the First Congress. By now broadening our view to include voting results, we gain another, complementary yet still quantitative perspective on the Congress that reflects all 2,249 deputies. Over twelve days of debate, some 80 votes were taken at the Congress. Many of these votes meant little in political terms, and others are of little use since the results were published officially only in approximate terms—the assembly's presiding officer often would simply declare that a resolution had passed "by a large majority." In many cases, too, the number of abstentions is impossible to determine from official records. Finally, particularly in the tense first few days of the Congress, the lack of technical experience showed itself most vividly, and many votes were carried out irregularly or even improperly.

The voting pattern shown in table 31, however, reveals the approximate strength of various political groups over time. One of our earlier hypotheses here finds support: many deputies did not fit easily into the Congress' "political geography." Instead, many at the outset did not fully understand the political struggle, or the differences among political groups. Although political organization proceeded apace during the Congress, confused and unpredictable behavior unavoidably characterized the first few days. Factional discipline proved impossible to secure ("factions" themselves remained ill-defined), and even the Communist Party, despite its theoretical claim on the allegiance of a large majority of deputies, often proved unable to influence its members' behavior.

After bitter debate, for example, the proposed agenda attracted only 379 negative votes and 9 abstentions. The left-wing opposition, still in formation, was weak. Similarly, Stankevich's motion calling for the use of roll-call votes[15] won the support of only 431 deputies, a misleadingly low figure reflecting the opposition's almost total lack of organization. The right wing too, however, appeared confused and disorganized at the

15. See chap. 9. Stankevich's proposal would have required a roll-call vote whenever more than 100 deputies requested it. He aimed to make votes public, thereby forcing deputies to be accountable to the electorate. See table 31, second vote.

Congress' outset: a motion proposed by Viktor Alksnis garnered only 246 positive votes.[16] A more accurate rendering of the strength of conservatives versus reformers had to await the Congress' second session. Here Obolenskii's self-nomination for the post of president of the Supreme Soviet was rejected by 1,415 votes to 689, with 33 abstentions.[17] The outcome is not difficult to understand: Obolenskii's candidacy raised the larger issue of single-candidate elections. Radicals opposed such elections and called for more than one candidate; they were joined by left- (and by many right-) wing independents for the same reason. Many mediators, on the other hand, opposed Obolenskii's candidacy in order to support Gorbachev and Lukianov.[18] In any case, the vote attracted a relatively large amount of dissent, with 722 deputies refusing to join the majority.

The opposition later achieved even greater success. On the question of suspending the *ukaz* of 28 July,[19] for example, democratic reformers (including virtually every radical, left-wing independent, and mediator) succeeded in mustering 831 votes in favor and 30 abstentions; the conservative vote shrank to 1,261. Another revealing vote occurred on the question of requiring full-time service by Supreme Soviet members. Reformers favored the proposal, hoping to force Party leaders either to relinquish their local power bases or to forego seats in the Supreme Soviet. Success, however, might have allowed them to go on to question Gorbachev's dual posts of Party general secretary and Supreme Soviet president. Perhaps for this reason, many mediators followed the Presidium's lead in rejecting the proposal, which went down to defeat with 1,419 deputies opposed.

Later votes showed a shifting balance of strength between liberal and conservative forces, but the general trend was a slow, steady erosion of right-wing support. A progressive motion by the deputy Konovalov at the fifth session[20] won the support of 851 deputies and 47 abstentions. Nearly 900 deputies thus opposed Gorbachev, and in one of its worst showings the conservative front drummed up support from only 1,130 deputies. Conservative strength bottomed out at the thirteenth session, near the end of the Congress, when "the deputy from Murmansk" (Obo-

16. Alksnis called for an inquiry into alleged violations of the electoral law in Latvia. His motion was clearly aimed against the Latvian Popular Front and the local Party leadership, both accused of gerrymandering electoral districts to hinder the election of deputies who were not ethnically Latvian. See the third vote of table 30.

17. See fourth vote, tables 30 and 31.

18. This analysis is not entirely based on supposition. Conversations with many deputies have confirmed the different motivations at work.

19. This *ukaz* (decree) restricted the right of public demonstration and meeting. See vote 6, tables 30 and 31.

20. This motion attempted to modify electoral procedures for the most important state positions. See vote 8, tables 30 and 31.

lenskii) nominated himself to the Constitutional Control Committee. This candidacy seemed less dangerous to many deputies than his previous attempt to lead the Supreme Soviet, and Obolenskii won a plurality of 934 votes. He did not win election to the Committee, however, since he had less than 50 percent support (903 deputies voted against him and 114 abstained).[21]

Table 31 shows in graphic form the most important voting patterns at the Congress. The elections to the Supreme Soviet also yielded interesting results, specifically in terms of comparing candidates' frequencies of cancellation.[22] Candidates from Moscow varied widely in this regard; Iaroshenko attracted 1,025 cancellations, while the radical sociologist Tatiana Zaslavskaia received 1,558. The average between these two extremes may well be a fair measure of real conservative strength at the Congress. The figure of 964 negative votes received by Boris Yeltsin is also significant, since it shows the size of the core of intransigent conservatives who refused any compromise with reformers.

A brief overview, then, of our principal findings: (1) the extreme right wing at the First Congress numbered about 950 deputies; (2) the four most conservative political groups (pre-*perestroika*, *apparatchiki*, right-wing independents, and centrists) attracted, on average, about 1,300 votes; (3) the three groups of reformers (radicals, left-wing independents, and mediators) could rely on the support of approximately 950 deputies; and (4) the extreme left wing (radicals and left-wing independents only) fluctuated between 380 and 500 deputies.[23]

Out of 2,249 deputies, therefore, 950 always voted with conservatives and an average of 440 always voted with reformers. A group of 400 to 900 deputies, comprised mostly of centrists and mediators, formed the Congress' political center. This group divided in different ways between the political Right and Left depending on the issue under discussion and the extent to which it had become radicalized. The way in which it split on each issue, though, determined whether and which policies won Congress approval. Understanding the behavior of this large central group is thus tantamount to solving the puzzle of the First Congress' political dynamics.

21. See fourteenth vote, tables 30 and 31.
22. We here consider those deputies receiving more than 1,000 cancellations. (Deputies did not vote *for* candidates, but merely crossed off—"cancelled"—the names of those they opposed. Hence, to win election a candidate had to receive cancellations from fewer than half of the Congress deputies.)
23. These conclusions are supported by those votes in which the political clash was particularly sharp. In these votes, mediators had to align themselves with one extreme or the other.

# The Supreme Soviet's First
# Two Sessions

The new Supreme Soviet, with its 542 members elected by the Congress of People's Deputies, soon revealed unexpected vitality and independence. Its first session opened formally on 26 June 1989 and concluded on 4 August 1989,[1] having elected Presidiums for both chambers and selected members for a number of working commissions and permanent committees.[2] Since all Congress deputies—even those not elected to the Supreme Soviet—could sit on these panels, many deputies continued to take an active part in policy formulation, with 928 participating in at least one such body.[3] After an initial period of uncertainty and confusion, improvements in parliamentary output and procedure became apparent. Preliminary legislative discussions took place in single-chamber or joint commissions; final approval could only be granted by a full plenary session. Two factors led to increased radical and reformist activity: first, the reformists immediately asserted themselves; and second, many conservative members of the Supreme Soviet were local Party officials and therefore split their attention between local and national matters.

Political clashes occurred as soon as nominations were made to fill certain top-level state posts, including the positions of president of the Council of Ministers, president of the State Committee for People's Control, president of the Supreme Court, prosecutor-general of the USSR, and state arbitrator.[4] These nominations did not achieve the expected *pro forma* passage, becoming instead the subject of sometimes acrimonious debate.

1. The two chambers in fact convened for the first time on 3 June (the Soviet of the Union) and 6 June (the Soviet of Nationalities).
2. Twenty-two commissions and permanent committees of the two chambers were formed. See table 32.
3. The membership of these bodies included the vast majority of Supreme Soviet members, along with almost 400 other deputies from the Congress.
4. Constitutionally, such nominations had to be approved by the Congress.

The appointment of Gennadi Kolbin as president of the State Committee for People's Control,[5] in particular, attracted opposition, with thirty-four deputies opposed and fifty-three abstaining. Aleksandr Sukharev, nominated as Soviet prosecutor-general, faced similar difficulties.

In this early stage it seemed that, as expected, the Congress had been more resolute than the Supreme Soviet would be in opposing the high political leadership.[6] Only a month later, however, the picture had shifted dramatically as the Supreme Soviet increasingly sought to affirm its own authority and independence *vis-à-vis* the executive. Every ministerial nominee proposed by Prime Minister Nikolai Ryzhkov faced a barrage of hostile questions and a vigorous public examination.[7] The gauntlet to be run by each included an examination by a Supreme Soviet commission, followed by an examination by the entire Supreme Soviet, with both chambers sitting in joint session. For the first time, Soviet minister-appointees came under intense political, technical, and personal scrutiny. Even Politburo members nominated to ministerial posts[8] did not escape public examination, contributing greatly to the demythologizing of political power. Indeed, even the director-designate of the KGB, Vladimir Kriuchkov, had to undergo an experience that he later characterized as "one of the most difficult" of his political career.[9] For that matter, the Supreme

5. Lenin created the State Committee for People's Control for the purpose of overseeing the executive powers enjoyed by state bodies. It had been intended in this sense to serve as a kind of analogue to the Western principle of a division of powers, yet to exist within a proletarian dictatorship. The kind of control from below that Lenin envisaged, however, although always legally present, never took on practical meaning. Instead, such institutional checks and balances always found themselves subordinated to the Party will, as expressed by its leaders and the *apparat*, and justified in the name of "democratic centralism." Significantly, the partial constitutional reforms of autumn 1988 did not even consider abolishing the Committee for People's Control, and it only became obsolete when the Supreme Soviet established the Constitutional Control Committee. Although the functions of the State Committee for People's Control differed in many respects from those of the Constitutional Control Committee—the former supervising government ministries and the latter considering legislative production—it is still apparent that the transition to a socialist rule-of-law state would proceed by superimposing new juridical structures on old ones. This method, or rather lack of one, only postponed indefinitely the construction of a definitively new juridical structure.

6. Sukharev's nomination received only 27 negative votes in the Supreme Soviet, whereas in the Congress 330 opposed it (and 273 abstained). Kolbin also won Congress confirmation, but with less opposition—252 negative votes and 138 abstentions.

7. Such examinations were public because at this stage live television coverage of the Congress shifted to complete late-night broadcasts of the Supreme Soviet's discussions.

8. Nikolai Ryzhkov, nominated as president of the Council of Ministers (prime minister); Dmitrii Iazov, defense minister; A. Biriukova, vice president of the Council of Ministers; Iurii Masliukov, president of *Gosplan*, the state economic planning agency (*Gosudarstvennyi komitet po planirovaniiu*); Eduard Shevardnadze, foreign minister; and Vladimir Kriuchkov, director of the KGB.

9. Interview in *l'Unità*, 20 August 1989.

Soviet did not limit itself only to interrogation, but also rejected nine candidates for ministerial posts.[10]

The entire process was an unforeseen outcome of the political changes. Ryzhkov later admitted his surprise: "I hadn't imagined that such debates would flare up around each candidate. And I don't think I was the only one to be surprised; I don't think either Presidium of the Supreme Soviet was prepared for such stormy debate."[11] Gorbachev's reaction is also worth noting. Whereas he had stifled discussion of his own nominees for high state posts—stressing his constitutional right to propose candidates and refusing to allow alternatives—he abandoned those men and women defeated by the Supreme Soviet. Such a step could be seen as showing respect for the Supreme Soviet as a decision-making body, but more likely Gorbachev simply took advantage of the votes to rid himself of conservative ministers.[12]

Another episode of great political importance took place during the first session of the new Supreme Soviet, namely the authorization of economic self-governance for Lithuania and Estonia.[13] Both republics presented their joint proposal, which had been approved by their republican Supreme Soviets, but Gorbachev's support proved decisive in achieving passage by the national Supreme Soviet. The economic plan seemed to require substantive constitutional amendments, but any delay would have prevented Baltic economic home rule from beginning on the target date of 1 January 1990. The central leadership was divided: Vice President

10. The rejected candidates were: V. Kalashnikov as first vice president of the Council of Ministers and as president of the State Food Committee; V. Kamentsev, a close aide of Ryzhkov's, as vice president of the Council of Ministers and as chairman of the State Committee for International Economic Relations; V. Zakharov as minister of culture; G. Bogomiakov as energy minister; P. Polad-Zade as minister of hydraulic works; L. Rozenova as president of the State Price Commission; V. Gribov as president of the State Bank; M. Gramov as president of the State Sport Committee; and M. Busygin as minister of the timber industry. The nominee for minister of railways, N. Konarev, also failed to win election but won on the second try when Ryzhkov resubmitted his name on the final day of the first session.

11. *Nedelia* 29, July 1989.

12. This generalization does not hold equally well for all defeated candidates, although it is certainly valid for Kalashnikov, the most important among them. As the former first secretary of the regional Party committee in Volgograd, he had distinguished himself as one of the most assertive Soviet conservatives both at the Nineteenth Party Organizational Conference in the summer of 1988 and at the Central Committee plenum of April 1988. A strong supporter of Egor Ligachev, his appointment would have placed him at a level equal to Iurii Masliukov, first vice president of the Council of Ministers, and thus would have made him a logical candidate for Politburo membership. Another clearly conservative official rejected by the Supreme Soviet was the former regional Party first secretary of Tiumen, G. Bogomiakov.

13. Latvia later, following the discussion of the Lithuanian and Estonian plans, presented a similar proposal for economic self-government.

Leonid Abalkin favored implementing the plan immediately, whereas the director of *Gosplan*, Iurii Masliukov, spearheaded the opposition to it. Masliukov contended that the Baltic plan violated the measured pace of power devolution favored by government ministers. Many other, more conservative republics protested the plan's granting of special status to the Baltic republics. In the end, however, a Supreme Soviet majority followed Gorbachev's lead, granting the two republics authorization for economic self-government.[14]

On nearly every other point of discussion during the first session, almost unprecedentedly frank discussions arose, creating a new form of political dialectics. Deputies expressed divergent opinions, and government ministers found themselves forced to modify their positions or even to accept outright defeat. The Supreme Soviet, for instance, exempted 176,000 university students from compulsory military service, over the objections of the minister of defense. It increased pensions, amended laws regulating state enterprises and taxing cooperatives, and modified the decree of 8 April 1989 that had set criminal penalties for "crimes against the state," all over strong conservative opposition. The last step in particular marked a victory for reformists allied with Gorbachev. Gorbachev himself, who presided over the session, underlined the real importance of deputies' votes and commissions' decisions.[15]

The second session of the Supreme Soviet opened on 25 September and soon confirmed that the growing independence and authority of the first session had not been a fluke. This independence of action also was aided by the popular pressure on deputies stemming from televised broadcasts of the proceedings.[16] Procedural problems gradually found resolutions, and the second session was less obstructed by technicalities than had been either the first session or the Congress. Electronic voting saved hours that had been spent counting raised hands. Draft laws proceeded according to an agreed path of a first and second reading, and a general code regulating procedural matters at both the Supreme Soviet and the Congress was promulgated. Intense political infighting did result in an agenda, one with nineteen "high priority" and thirty-four "lower priority" items. The large number of urgent questions pointed up the legislative vacuum inherited by the new Supreme Soviet, with at least sixty laws requiring immediate consideration. Procedural confusion caused by inexperience, of course,

14. The Supreme Soviet passed the measure with 35 negative votes and 23 abstentions.

15. See *Pravda*, 5 August 1989.

16. See Jeffrey Hahn's essay, 31: "The high level of involvement of citizens . . . indicates the emergence of a civic culture significantly larger than that expected by many Western Sovietologists."

had not been eliminated, but the exceptional pressures for quick action forced immediate consideration of several matters. The first draft law to be discussed was one authorizing urgent action to normalize the chaotic transport system. Another early topic of discussion was the problem of strikes in crucial industrial sectors. Significantly, the parliament on this issue defeated Gorbachev and the Party leadership by approving an initial moratorium of fifteen months. The first law approved by the second session, after all, had been that guaranteeing the right to strike.[17]

As debate proceeded, the subjects and protagonists of political struggle shifted continuously. Sometimes the government defended its reformist legislation against strong conservative criticism, as for instance when Leonid Abalkin fended off an attack by Veniamin Iarin, L. Sukhov, and V. Khmura that portrayed cooperatives as "a cancerous infection of the people." The Supreme Soviet in this case supported the government, allowing cooperatives to develop while simultaneously protecting against excessive speculation. Later, however, when Abalkin argued the government's case in proposing a new law on republican economic autonomy, positions switched as the Supreme Soviet and its permanent commissions twice rejected the proposed law as too strongly centralist.

Even more complicated were the debates over the budget for the fiscal year 1990. The government's original proposal showed a clear reordering of priorities, as heavy-industry expenditure would rise only 0.5 percent, compared with consumer-goods expansion of 6.7 percent. Once given the chance to review this plan, though, the relevant Supreme Soviet commissions criticized its details, if not its general goals, harshly. Many ministries had compiled their budget proposals using old methods, predicting unrealistically high growth rates and ignoring shortages of resources and finance, as well as labor unrest and disintegrating physical plants. Such criticism by Supreme Soviet commissions and by individual deputies was soon taken up by the media, with *Izvestiia*, for example, alleging that "*Gosplan* evidently has not devised any mechanism to integrate the planning system with the market system."[18]

The continued utilization of obsolete planning techniques presented an easy target. Unprofitable enterprises continued to enjoy state subsidies, with 12,500 such establishments creating an annual drag on state finances of thirteen billion rubles. Instead of falling, spending on management continued to rise, largely independent of production incentives. The pro-

---

17. This law won approval on 9 October with 373 votes in favor, 12 against, and 10 abstentions. The bill as adopted avoided the word "strike," preferring instead to speak of "criteria for resolving conflicts in work relations." Despite its many shortcomings, this law represented a fundamental legal and ideological turning point by guaranteeing a previously unsecured basic democratic right.

18. *Izvestiia*, 29 September 1989.

jected reduction in the state budget deficit, from one hundred billion rubles in 1989 to sixty billion rubles in 1990, to most analysts seemed based on hopelessly optimistic economic forecasts. In many ways, then, the government approached new problems with old solutions. Many deputies, while criticizing certain fundamental choices in *Gosplan's* proposed budget, insisted on the preservation of central, administratively directed, state economic planning. These deputies may not have understood fully that, in their reluctance to abandon central administrative directives to economic enterprises, they were clinging to old illusions of a "command economy," and that as a result enterprise autonomy would be reduced and market development impeded or even doomed. Confusion and hesitation characterized equally the government, the Party, and many people's deputies in the Supreme Soviet.

At the same time, the roles played by each group differed significantly from the past. Both reformist and conservative deputies realized the nature and importance of their new powers and responsibilities. The decades-old tradition of acquiescing passively to the expressed will of the Party leadership had, as we have seen, simply collapsed. Ministries remained powerful, and parliament was still feeble, but deputies now had won real elections and consequently felt real accountability to their constituents. Hence, a new dialectical relationship had begun to form between the legislative and executive branches of government.

While remaining cognizant of this new relationship, however, and of the steady increase in parliamentary experience and influence, other practical aspects of the political situation cannot be forgotten. Agenda problems within the Supreme Soviet, for instance, did not disappear. Debates on draft laws to regulate property, land, and rent, and to create a standardized fiscal system, all exposed deep splits within the Party and within society at large. Vague government proposals reflected Party infighting and collective indecision. Even apart from the problem of Party unity, serious, objective difficulties—widespread unpreparedness among cadres, incompetence among managers, and inexperience among financial leaders—impeded any radical move towards economic reform and a "socialist market system."

For the sake of clarity, though, and with less distortion than might seem likely, the Supreme Soviet can be seen as split into three groups. Deputies of the Abalkin (and Gorbachev) persuasion saw reform as qualitatively *different*—that is, not simply as revamping the old, dilapidated system. At the same time, they felt that "the market should not be a bazaar," and that elements of state control and regulation should therefore be retained.[19] The transition envisioned by this group was gradual, as

19. *Pravda*, 14 November 1989.

the new economic system first required the creation of a flexible system of public administration along with a fiscal and financial infrastructure. The Abalkin model, then, was of a "mixed economy," a *controlled* market system, a welfare state not unlike the contemporary European social-democratic ideal. Deputies cherishing this model, however, remained painfully aware that Soviet conditions were such that the transition to this new system would take at least five years. They proposed a three-phase plan for such a transition: initial legislative action in 1990; wage and price reforms in 1991–92, with the phase-in of more flexible planning; and, after the gradual expansion of these two phases in 1993–94, the introduction of the entire system in 1995.

Radicals, the second group, criticized this approach for two reasons. Political opposition and incompetence, they argued, would obstruct any gradual reform. Over five years, the radicals said, such a gradualist approach would change nothing appreciably. Furthermore, they asserted that no time remained for such gradualism. The economic and social crisis had become so severe that drastic measures were needed. The main proponents of this line within the Supreme Soviet were the economics professor Pavel Bunich, who was elected president of the Committee for Economic Reform, and S. Alekseev, who became president of the Legislative Commission. Joined by many other deputies, both men demanded the immediate adoption of a package of new fundamental laws, to be effective from 1 January 1990.

Conservatives comprised the third general group within the Supreme Soviet. In broad terms, their objectives included preserving existing economic and administrative structures, protecting collective agricultural enterprises (*sovkhozy* and *kolkhozy*), limiting the rental of land to private farmers, and obstructing or ending entirely the development of private cooperative enterprises. Such feelings enjoyed diffuse support among large sectors of the public. Perhaps surprisingly, such support was particularly strong among the managerial strata. On 12 November 1989 Gorbachev had called an assembly of more than 1,400 central and peripheral economic managers to determine their views on economic reform. After three days of frank debate, Leonid Abalkin declared, "I had been psychologically prepared for pressure from the radicals, from those who say we are moving too slowly and are taking only half-measures. But on the contrary, pressure came mainly from conservatives. Perhaps this reflects what is happening in the country at large."[20] Gorbachev's sudden retreat, in which the three main draft laws for economic reform were deferred pending "popular consultation," therefore becomes explicable. This step froze

20. *Washington Post*, 16 November 1989.

the laws until the third session of the Supreme Soviet, and indeed until the Third Congress, the opening date of which had not yet been set. A large majority of Supreme Soviet deputies agreed to this postponement.

The proceedings of the Supreme Soviet's second session nevertheless show significant radicalization in its restricted membership. This increasing radicalism is especially marked if we remember that only 15 percent of deputies belonged, as defined in our earlier model based on the Gordon-Nazimova scheme, to any of the reformist groups (radicals, left-wing independents, or mediators) committed to a radical, democratic *perestroika*.[21] Many others, though, helped approve the law on the status of deputies, declaring themselves to be "professional," "full-time" legislators with a monthly salary[22] and the ability to hire assistants at state expense, to requisition an office, and to enjoy reduced rates on air and rail travel—all perquisites to assist them in representing—and keeping contact with— their constituents. Another draft law, this one regulating elections to republican and local Soviets, represented a victory for reformists when— after heated debate—the rule apportioning one-third of deputy seats to social organizations was abolished. This latter change, it should be noted, was not categorical, as it depended on ratification by republican bodies. While nearly all republics adopted this provision after its passage, not all did so: the Supreme Soviet of Kazakhstan, for instance, retained the old system. The all-Union Supreme Soviet also, by a large majority, authorized the Baltic republics' exercise of economic autonomy,[23] and the Permanent Committee for Agriculture and Food Supply rejected Prime Minister Ryzhkov's second nominee for the post of minister of hydraulic works.[24]

The most significant indicator of the changing political climate in the Supreme Soviet, however, was the struggle started by the academic Andrei Sakharov over the abrogation of Article 6 of the Brezhnev-era Constitution, which guaranteed the "leading role" of the Communist Party. Only the strongest opposition by Gorbachev prevented the victory of this

---

21. See chap. 8, table 11, and the analysis of voting in chap. 11.

22. The "full-time" rule actually allowed exceptions, and was adopted only "as a rule." The radicals lost their fight to eliminate this loophole. The salaries adopted amounted to roughly 200 rubles per month for Congress deputies, with about 300 additional rubles per month added for those deputies who also sat in the Supreme Soviet. Smaller supplements to the 200-ruble base salary were also approved for deputies who did not sit in the Supreme Soviet, but who served on its permanent committees or commissions.

23. The vote included 296 for, 67 against, and 37 abstentions.

24. According to the new rules approved by the Supreme Soviet, a candidate for a ministerial post, once rejected by a Supreme Soviet commission, could not be renominated at the same plenary session of the Supreme Soviet. In this case, the loser was Vladimir Loginov, the former RSFSR minister hydraulic works.

radical proposal; in the final vote, indeed, Sakharov's motion fell just three votes short of approval.[25] The Nobel Peace Prize winner made the same proposal at the Second Congress, which again rejected it.[26]

To conclude, in less than six months two sessions of the Supreme Soviet succeeded unequivocally in putting an end to the old political system and in beginning to transfer real power from the Party to parliament. The new political group that emerged from the elections of 26 March 1989 was rapidly becoming a new "leading class." Whether it would prove any more successful than its predecessor in managing the burgeoning crisis facing the Soviet Union, however, was another, as yet unresolved, question.

25. An initial vote in fact yielded victory for the radicals. Gorbachev, pointing to the lack of a quorum, succeeded in calling a revote.

26. The vote at the Second Congress was 839 in favor, 1138 against, and 56 abstentions. On the basis of percentages, however, the proposal gained support between the First and Second Congresses. See chap. 6.

# CHAPTER THIRTEEN

# Pluralism or Conflagration?

The rapid changes in the Congress' behavior unquestionably reflected ongoing social and political changes. This at least partially confirms one of our working assumptions, namely that the Congress of People's Deputies expressed, if still imperfectly, the full range of political forces coalescing in the Soviet Union. In other words, the Congress in some ways lived up to its billing as the USSR's first genuinely representative parliament. For most republics, indeed, it stood as the most democratic and advanced political structure they had ever encountered.

All three trends discussed in the preceding chapters only intensified in the second half of 1989. This chapter treats each in turn, sketching both direction and intensity.

## The National Dimension

Parliaments in the three Baltic republics had already proclaimed full national sovereignty in the spring and summer of 1989. Among other steps, they awarded republican languages official status, resurrected old national flags, and enacted laws to grant privileges to autochthonous (that is, "native" rather than Russian) citizens. Similar, although less sweeping, measures were enacted in Moldavia, Armenia, Belorussia, Azerbaijan, Uzbekistan, and the Ukraine. In each of these republics a "National Front"[1] appeared and grew quickly. Such organizations also sprang up in autonomous republics to defend the rights of smaller ethnic groups against the perceived mistreatment of dominant (at the Union republic level) groups. Inspired by the examples of the European republics, several

---

1. These organizations had different names. The Ukrainian body called itself *Rukh*; the Uzbek, *Birlyk*; the Lithuanian, *Sajudis*; and the Armenian, first the Karabakh Committee and then the National Armenian Movement.

other Central Asian republics proclaimed their respective national languages to be "official" in republican affairs. The legal degree of tolerance shown towards the Russian language varied greatly from one republic to another.

This general picture, though, obscures much unevenness among republics in political maturity, organization, and platform. Wide differences existed, too, in the response of local and central authorities. In the Baltic republics, strong nationalism took exclusively peaceful forms; its leaders kept tight control of the movement and were aided by local authorities' reluctance to use force. In other areas, however, clashes occurred. Police blocked nationalist demonstrations in Minsk, the Belorussian capital; police and Interior Ministry troops forcibly dispersed a similar demonstration in Kishinev, the capital of Moldavia. Most frightening was the clash in Tbilisi, where—possibly connected with political infighting in the upper echelons of the Party leadership—special military units attacked a crowd of Georgian demonstrators, killing twenty-one and wounding hundreds more.

The special forces also took action in the Ukraine, in Kiev in August and in Lvov in September. Crowds of Moldavians and Estonians in their respective republics threatened allochthonous minorities (mainly Russians) who were striking in protest of alleged mistreatment. In broadest terms, the protests and violence expressed general trends towards support for greater autonomy at the republican level, opposition to any extension of central power, and bitterness about perceived Russian domination and colonialism. In some areas, these impulses became entangled with complex local interethnic feuds. In Abkhazia, for instance, Abkhaz fought Georgians in July 1989; in the autonomous region of South Ossetia, Ossetians demanded unification with co-nationals in the Russian Republic and separation from the Georgian republic;[2] and in Uzbekistan, conflict between Uzbeks and Turks exploded into a massive pogrom in June 1989.

Between August and December tensions also mounted in the disputed region of Nagorno-Karabakh, creating a new round of conflict between Armenia and Azerbaijan. Azerbaijani attacks on transport and rail convoys effectively isolated Armenia for several months; neither local nor central authorities could find a peaceful solution to the impasse. In a bid to contain Azerbaijani nationalism, the Supreme Soviet voted to end a temporary system of central administration for the disputed territory. In its place, Azerbaijani control over Nagorno-Karabakh was to be restored under the supervision of a Supreme Soviet commission.[3] This solu-

2. By late November 1989 troops intervened in Tskhinvali to clamp down on violence between Georgians and Ossetians.
3. This vote of 28 November provoked the Armenian delegation to walk out of the

tion, however, only inflamed both Azerbaijani and Armenian nationalists. Police intervention was needed to disperse a large Azerbaijani National Front demonstration in Baku against local Party bosses. Several days later violence again broke out in Nagorno-Karabakh, despite the heavy concentration of peacekeeping military units. The unrest spread into the autonomous republic of Nakhichevan (populated by Azerbaijanis but separated from Azerbaijan proper), where thousands of Azerbaijanis destroyed border fortifications separating them from Azerbaijani populations in Turkey and Iran. By this stage the Azerbaijani National Front had clearly surpassed the Azerbaijani Communist Party in power and prestige, and the ethnic and religious clash with Armenia had transformed the Front into a genuinely separatist movement. The chain of events ultimately led to the intervention of the Red Army in Azerbaijan on 19 January 1990, both to quell an anti-Armenian pogrom in Baku and to impede Azerbaijani attempts to secede from the Union.

Centrifugal tendencies had grown in the preceding months throughout Transcaucasia. In September the Azerbaijani Supreme Soviet had declared its sovereignty and proclaimed its right to secede. The Georgian Supreme Soviet followed suit in November, as did the Armenian Supreme Soviet in January. By the beginning of 1990 Armenia and Azerbaijan had entered an all-but-declared state of war, and only central intervention prevented more massacres than occurred. Central and Party authority, however, quickly eroded in both Baku and Erevan; the National Fronts of each republic boasted thousands-strong armed militias. Civil war had already begun in Transcaucasia.

Russian nationalism was the last to join the turmoil of increasing national self-expression, but many signs at the Congress as well as outside it indicated that Russian national loyalties were gaining in strength.[4] Only in late October, however, did such sentiments appear in organized form with the establishment of the "Russia Club" (*"Rossiia"*). This group, in many ways a classical political party of the Right, is discussed at length later in this chapter.[5]

## The "Communist Multiparty System"

The secession of the Lithuanian Communist Party from the all-Soviet Party organization on 12 December 1989 only added to the turmoil. Party

Congress. Reformists could not agree on a course of action: Andrei Sakharov criticized the Congress' decision, while Anatolii Sobchak favored it.

4. See chap. 9.

5. Such categorizations of Soviet groups are perhaps too conventional. The groups themselves often mixed national and social programs, combining in curious ways features of political and social pluralism with aspects of old, authoritarian political programs.

leaders in Vilnius saw such a secession as the only possibility for avoiding a total Communist defeat in the upcoming elections. As a result the Lithuanian Party split into two groups. The first, smaller group supported the CPSU; its popularity in Lithuania was virtually nil. The second group supported the Party's organizational secession. Algirdas Brazauskas, a member of this second group, won election as general secretary of this new Party and immediately became one of the most popular leaders in Lithuania.[6] All attempts by Party leaders in Moscow to block the secession failed. After a bitter session in which conservatives demanded the use of force, the CPSU plenum managed only to buy time. Gorbachev rebuffed the conservative hard line, but the Lithuanian parliament voted in any case to end the Communist Party's political monopoly. The failure of Gorbachev's own subsequent trip to Lithuania demonstrated the futility of using central pressure to induce the Lithuanian Party to reverse its decision.

The Lithuanian parliament amended the republic's constitution. Openly challenging the Soviet Constitution, this amendment affirmed that "parties and organizations are elements of the political system of the Lithuanian republic." A similar resolution soon won the approval of the Estonian Communist Party, and was widely expected to be passed by the Estonian Supreme Soviet. From late 1989, then, two Union republics had unilaterally decided, against explicit central wishes, to establish a "multiparty" (but still Communist) political system.

Moscow's answer to this explicit challenge was hesitant, defensive, and slow to take shape. Attempting to block the growing centrifugal tendencies within the Party and the growing pressure of Russian nationalists, Gorbachev first created a *Biuro* for the Russian Party.[7] He spoke rousingly of the necessity of defending the unitary structure of the Party: "Our duty," he said, "is to avoid crossing that line beyond which the CPSU will be menaced with destruction as a unifying force and as the vital consolidating force of Soviet society."[8] Alluding only indirectly to events in the Baltic republics, he went on to declare: "Within this framework [of constitutional revision] every article may be modified or eliminated. This is true

6. According to a poll by the Lithuanian Academy of Sciences, 82 percent of Lithuanian citizens approved the creation of a Communist Party independent from Moscow. The same poll indicated that Algirdas Brazauskas ranked as the most popular Lithuanian Party leader. See the *Washington Post*, 10 January 1990.

7. This decision was formalized on 12 December 1989. The Russian *Biuro* included 15 members under Gorbachev's leadership, duplicating the structure of the other 14 *Biuro*s. In the past, the Russian Party was represented only in the all-Union CPSU organization, which, most agreed, it had dominated. On the one hand, Gorbachev therefore bowed to pressure for "Communist decentralization" in creating the Russian *Biuro*. At the same time, he hoped to divert growing Russophile sentiment within the RSFSR.

8. TASS, 9 December 1989.

even of Article 6."[9] Gorbachev essentially offered negotiations towards a future, mutually agreed-upon constitution under the auspices of the Congress of People's Deputies. His offer, however, did not persuade Baltic legislatures to reconsider their actions.

As a result, the Second Congress of People's Deputies, held in December, revealed the growing hostility of most deputies, particularly Russians and conservatives, towards their separatist Baltic colleagues. During stormy discussions of the Lithuanian issue, Gorbachev advanced a new compromise proposal: the new Constitution to be formulated by mutual agreement would include legal mechanisms to safeguard republics' right to secede from the Union. And on the issue of a multiparty system Gorbachev went farther than ever before, announcing that "I do not consider it [a multiparty system] to be a tragedy if it benefits the people. The most important thing is not whether there are one or two parties, but the level of democratization and *glasnost*."[10]

The Communist bastion with which Gorbachev wished to arrest the disintegration, however, had itself already been undermined by profound internal divisions, and not only along national lines. Both the Party plenum in April and the Central Committee meeting of July revealed the increasingly split composition of the upper levels of the apparatus. The Congress of People's Deputies, consisting mostly of Party members, unavoidably reflected these divisions, consisting as it did of men and women with radically different conceptions of the Soviet future. By the end of November, Boris Gidaspov, the first secretary of the Leningrad Party organization, had organized a massive demonstration. This demonstration took as its slogan the phrase "Party revenge," hoping to mobilize the Russian members of the "United Workers' Fronts" in defense of "socialist values." On the opposite side of the political battlefield, the "Democratic Faction" of the CPSU held its first meeting in Moscow during the last half of January 1990. Both sides were little more than fringe groups at this stage, but foreshadowed the direction in which conflict within the Party would develop. This conflict, indeed, ultimately transformed the Twenty-eighth Party Congress into an open confrontation between alternative platforms.

## "Classical" Parties

The broadly based, almost general strike of miners in July 1989 closed one and opened another, qualitatively different, phase of political development. For two years before the strike, tens of thousands of informal

9. *Washington Post*, 10 December 1989.
10. *Washington Post*, 14 January 1990.

organizations had proliferated throughout the country. This intermediate phase of "capillary politicization" proceeded spontaneously, without any significant central organization. The massive participation of tens of millions in the elections of 26 March, however, produced a qualitative leap in the collective political consciousness. This leap was evident in the miners' demands, which far surpassed simple trade unionism. Instead, the miners' "fighting platforms" represented the birth of a new *class consciousness* throughout much of the working class. The reformist "revolution from below" had begun to consolidate organizationally and to find institutional targets. Indeed, sixty-one deputies elected from districts in which the miners struck later joined the progressive Interregional Parliamentary Group (*Mezhregionalnaia Deputatskaia Gruppa*, or MDG) proposed by Gavriil Popov on the third day of the First Congress.[11] Equally, the miners' powerful political movement clearly helped catalyze the radicals' decision to constitute themselves formally as an opposition group in the Congress.

We have already seen that the decision by radicals to create a formal parliamentary opposition group was postponed by pressure from mediators, from reformers inside the Party, and probably from Gorbachev himself.[12] By the end of July, however, a new wave of protests seemed about to wash over the country, and radicals again intensified their organizational work and political activism. Roughly 300 Congress deputies met at the *Dom Kino* on 29 and 30 July to discuss a united opposition platform and to elect leaders for its parliamentary faction. Journalists attending this meeting received an initial list of 273 members of the MDG. Iurii Afanasev, however, an MDG leader, simultaneously announced that another 116 deputies had joined the group since the list had been printed, and that the MDG could count on the support of more than 450 deputies at the Congress.[13] These numbers held constitutional significance, as they were, if accurate, sufficient to permit MDG members to call an extraordinary session of the Congress.[14] Afanasev's preliminary estimate, however, overestimated radical strength. It soon became clear that the radical opposition contained deputies of dramatically different temperaments, goals, and strategies. Boris Yeltsin was universally acknowledged to be the most

11. *Sotsialisticheskaia Industriia*, August 1989.
12. See chap. 9.
13. Data collected by Giulietto Chiesa.
14. Article 110 of the amended Constitution specified that "extraordinary sessions [of the Congress] will be held on the initiative of the Supreme Soviet of the USSR upon the proposal of one of the chambers of the Supreme Soviet of the USSR, of the Presidium of the Supreme Soviet of the USSR, of the President of the Supreme Soviet of the USSR, or of not less than 20 percent of the People's Deputies of the USSR, or on the initiative of one of the Union Republics through its supreme organ of state authority."

popular member of this group, but after Yeltsin the picture muddied considerably. Only after long discussion could a collegial body of five MDG members be selected to lead the group: Andrei Sakharov, Boris Yeltsin, Iurii Afanasev, Gavriil Popov, and Viktor Palm.

Subsequent events confirmed the relative fragility and fluidity of the MDG. Five months after this initial meeting MDG membership had fallen to only 159.[15] Part of this drop may be ascribed to the tendency of Baltic deputies to abandon support for a pan-Soviet, radical *perestroika* and to transfer their loyalties to radical-nationalist groups. The absence of any real strategy, however, combined with internal divisions and extremist rhetoric by some MDG leaders to alienate moderate reformers. The decision to call a general strike on 12 December in support of an immediate Congress discussion of Article 6, for example, only weakened the unity of the radical front. Andrei Sakharov's unexpected death during the crisis further undermined group solidarity. The disunity on the Left also partly resulted from the broad conservative rebound in strength that became apparent soon after the Second Congress opened on 12 December 1989.

By this time the economic crisis had deepened, along with public disillusionment over the high price of economic improvements that seemed as distant as ever. Criminal activity expanded rapidly as the extent of the economic, social, and national disintegration became clear. The prevailing public mood still seemed to favor more decisive reformist policy,[16] but by many indicators direct public activism in support of such reform dwindled. Subscription figures to many newspapers and magazines— both progressive and conservative—dropped. Candidates campaigning for election to local and republican Soviets encountered renewed disillusionment and passivity.

Despite all the negatives, the reformist-democratic bloc still commanded considerable support in the Congress and in the country. As noted above, in mid-December 836 deputies at the Second Congress voted to discuss the future of Article 6, and 56 abstained—both groups supporting part of the radical program. Radical strength remained considerable throughout the Congress, and grass-roots progressive activism had not disappeared. Following Gidaspov's demonstration for "socialist values," pro-*perestroika* forces succeeded in holding an even larger demonstration in early December. Further enlivening this demonstration was the active support of the Interregional Association of Democratic Unions (*Mezh-*

15. According to the "*Spisok Narodnykh Deputatov SSSR, podpisavshikh Zaiavlenie MGD,*" distributed at the Second Congress.
16. For example, in a sociological poll published in *Moskovskie Novosti* 1 (January 1990), a near-majority expressed support for more energetic, radical reform.

*regionalnaia Assotsiatsiia Demokraticheskikh Obedinenii*, or MADO), which drew supporters and affiliated organizations from more than forty urban centers of the RSFSR. The panorama of such "informals" remained rich, although they still lacked unity amongst themselves. The miners of Vorkuta resumed their strike in October, and strike committees in the Kuzbass continued to exert political influence and pressure in West Siberia. Social-democratic groups in Estonia merged in January, while numerous electoral initiative committees reconstituted themselves to influence the new round of republican elections.

The picture of left-wing radicalization plus increasing popular disillusionment, however, is incomplete. The missing element is right-wing radicalization, well illustrated by the small group of twenty-eight conservative deputies from various parts of the RSFSR that met in Tiumen on 20–21 October. This group's concluding resolution represented the first attempt to formulate an organic platform for the right wing in parliament, and to provide the conceptual and ideological bases for a new, conservative Russian party.[17] Many themes in the resolution echoed the positions of Vasilii Belov and Valentin Rasputin, discussed in chapter 9. Belov, in fact, helped found this new group, along with Viktor Astafev, Iurii Bondarev, and the editor of *Nash Sovremennik*, Stanislav Kunaev. This group, calling itself the Russia Club, was formed officially in Moscow three days after the Tiumen meeting closed. From the beginning *Rossiia* enjoyed explicit, public support from major periodicals such as *Nash Sovremennik*, *Molodaia Gvardiia*, *Literaturnaia Rossiia*, and *Sovetskaia Rossiia*.[18] Especially revealing of *Rossiia's* political orientation was the list of political and cultural organizations, both formal and informal, that lent it their support. These organizations included the United Workers' Fronts of Russia, the Writers' Union of the RSFSR, the Committee for the Salvation of the Volga, and the *Edinstvo* ("Unity") movement. The well-known workers' leader and deputy from Sverdlovsk, Veniamin Iarin, was elected president of the club.

The political significance of the club, therefore, far exceeded the number of the twenty-eight founding deputies, but extended to their powerful outside support and extensive organizational preparation. In our system of political classification, *Rossiia* corresponds almost exactly to the group of right-wing independents. Even more precisely, it represented a subgroup corresponding to a stage in the evolution of right-wing indepen-

17. The document was published in *Nash Sovremennik* 12 (1989): 3–6.
18. Curiously, the MDG did not control any mass media organs. Despite the sympathies shown for the radical cause by many papers and magazines, none acted as an official mouthpiece. The listed media organizations, however, directly and explicitly promoted the Russia Club and its program.

dents. We argued above that the nature of this group dictated its relative instability. This instability in fact led to the formation of *Rossiia* as some "independents" acquired organizational ties.

This evolution corresponded with events on the Left, where the group of radicals lost members in two different directions, towards the left-wing independents and towards national (republican and ethnic) groups.[19] The latter tendency manifested itself particularly strongly among Baltic deputies. With the growth of movements for national independence in Lithuania, Latvia, and Estonia, deputies from these republics gradually abandoned the Congress of People's Deputies, either refusing to attend or refusing to participate in important discussions. This tendency became clear and irreversible by the Third Congress in mid-1990.

To return to *Rossiia*, we have seen that it possessed a range of powerful political allies. Even further, we can say that *Rossiia* represented all three tendencies towards a multiparty system isolated in chapter 6: it was a right-wing group in the classical, European sense; it was a national, Russian group; and it remained essentially a faction within the CPSU, enjoying a measure of official support. Valentin Chikin, for instance, the editor of *Sovetskaia Rossiia*, belonged both to the CPSU Central Committee and to the *Biuro* of the Russian Party in addition to the club. Boris Gidaspov, Leningrad Party first secretary, also belonged both to the Russian *Biuro* and to the United Workers' Fronts. *Rossiia* announced that it would fight to defend "the political interests of the Russian Federation" as well as the rights of those "Russians who live in other republics."[20] It self-consciously assumed the leadership of strikes "in Kuzbass, Estonia, and Moldavia" (although such an assumption might well have been disputed by many strikers), contrasting these movements with "separatist hotheads and those seeking the support of Party functionaries who have thrown off their internationalism and their statesmanlike wisdom." *Rossiia*, then, attacked both radicals and the reformist wing of the CPSU while trying to gain mass support by co-opting the strike movement.

Its platform contained an explicit threat: we are ready, the conservatives declared, to defend our interests "by parliamentary means"; nevertheless, if these means fail, "the people itself will begin to fight using all means at its disposal." Conservatives thus utilized a *national* tactic. *Rossiia* declared that it had "no intention to reject the importance [of the radical platform]," and even professed "to share some MDG theses." What it

19. The same shift to national groups occurred among left-wing independents themselves between the First and Second Congresses.

20. This and all subsequent quotations from *Rossiia* are taken from the platform published in *Nash Sovremennik*.

considered erroneous, however, was the "concentrating [of] attention on general political problems . . . forgetting Russia and Russians." Naturally, it continued, "all nations possess equal rights and equal dignity," but it then implicitly threatened any nationalities wishing to secede from the Union. "The outflow of wealth from Russia to other republics continues," it asserted, while "Russians have become unwanted immigrants not only in Estonia, Latvia, and Lithuania, but even in Georgia, which Russians once saved from destruction."[21]

The platform affirmed the continuity of the tsarist and revolutionary heritages by paying tribute to Stalin. "Instead of serious analysis of the work of the People's Commissariat [for Nationality Affairs] under Stalin,[22] there are attempts to further the disintegration of the country." The background to these attempts, the *Rossiia* document continued, is that of "wild attacks on Russian language and Russian history." "In this context," it added, "the contribution of the Russian people to the development of many nations and peoples of our country is completely ignored." These statements amounted to a declaration of war against radical reformists, the intelligentsia, and nationalists, and broadly targeted Gorbachev's political program as well. It reiterated much of Nina Andreeva's "anti-*perestroika* platform." Its umbrella spread widely enough to include Boris Gidaspov, Viktor Astafev, Valentin Chikin, and Veniamin Iarin. It included both the writer Aleksandr Prokhanov, who glorified the Afghan War, and Afghan War veteran Sergei Chervonopitskii, who reproached Gorbachev during the Congress for never using the Stalinist catchphrase "Power, Motherland, Communism."

Most fundamentally, *Rossiia*'s founders rejected in principle the "new thinking" that underlay *perestroika*. The Soviet youth of the future, these men and women argued, should be raised to believe in "the greatness of the Soviet Motherland, the inviolability of its frontiers and the monolithic integrity of the country." They resurrected the notion of "Power" (*Vlast*) as basic to the USSR. This "Power" took many forms, among them "Power as conception, Power as consciousness, [and] Power as military structure."

Democratization, then, allowed these and other tensions to emerge, and led to the unveiling of secrets hidden by decades of violent, repres-

21. This platform plainly mixed elements of diverse political programs, attempting to reconcile positions normally perceived as diametrically opposed. In point of fact the Estonian and Moldavian strikes were revolts of those republics' Russian minorities against autochthonous nationalities' independence movements.

22. Stalin directed the People's Commissariat for Nationality Affairs from shortly after the October Revolution of 1917 until the Commissariat disappeared during an administrative reorganization of the mid-1920s.

sive rule. Stirring the stagnant waters of Soviet society to effect change also lifted ugly debris from the bottom: ancestral imperial loyalties; nostalgia for autocracy; the slave mentality; popular anti-Semitism; old notions of the Russian people's unique, divine mission; and belief in Stalinism as a revolutionary formula of modern Russian messianism. Among this "debris" lurked the remnants of Marxist-Leninist dogmatism. Both the Russian right wing and the remaining dogmatic, orthodox Communists pressed for immediate, authoritarian termination of the ongoing democratization. And both, possessing deep social roots, served notice of their intention to play a major role in political struggles in the years to come. At the same time, the emergence of such secrets and tensions showed that Soviet society, despite the obstacles, had already begun to change. These contradictory pressures, indeed, were known to Party leaders, thus explaining how, given a few more years of *glasnost*, with the gradual weakening and elimination of the one-party system, and with the gradual expansion of free expression and rights of political, cultural, and religious organization, Gorbachev and his allies could foresee the emergence of a relatively mature, democratic, modern public opinion and civil society. Full transition to the rule-of-law state envisioned by reformers, however, could only be possible after defeating these forces from the past.

# CHAPTER FOURTEEN

# The Second Congress: Debates

The Second Congress opened on 12 December 1989, one of the most con-fused and difficult moments of the entire five-year period of *perestroika*. Contradictory signals came from a torn, restive country enmeshed in a serious economic crisis and increasingly beset by powerful centrifugal forces. At the September Politburo plenum Gorbachev had succeeded in driving out a group of conservatives, including Viktor Chebrikov, the former KGB director, but he was far from free of bureaucracy and re-mained uncertain of what line to take at the Congress. Right-wing criti-cism of his leadership only grew with the intensification of the Lithuanian crisis, the resurgence of ethnic conflicts in other parts of the country, and the collapse of allied governments in Eastern Europe. The Left criti-cized him for allowing economic reform to stagnate. To use an historical analogy, Gorbachev was being forced to play the roles of both Luther and the Pope—while moving ever closer to a Counter-Reformation.[1]

The Soviet leader in October had committed himself personally to op-pose any attempt by the Supreme Soviet to alter Article 6 of the Consti-tution, which guaranteed the CPSU's "leading role" in Soviet society. At the same time he bitterly attacked the Left, accusing it of holding "irre-sponsible" and "incendiary" attitudes.[2] Gorbachev's personal popularity, already sinking over the past several months, continued to decline.

The Party leadership had become paralyzed by internal disagreement and remained unable to take decisions. Some high leaders began to prepare an antireformist counteroffensive, and many technocrats of the

---

1. This original yet appropriate historical comparison was first made by Evgenii Ambarzumov in an interview with an Italian newspaper.

2. He made these statements to the press on 12 October. Cf. *Washington Post*, 17 Octo-ber 1989.

governmental, managerial, and ministerial apparatuses moved to the right. The general gain in conservative strength became apparent in mid-October, when Gorbachev summoned a pan-Soviet conference of 1,400 economists, government enterprise managers, and Party cadres to devise a solution to the problems facing the country.[3] He had hoped, in fact, at this conference to introduce a new, compromise political reform program that had been hammered out with great difficulty by the Politburo. This program set a goal of a "regulated market economy," to be achieved after a five- to six-year "transition period." During the transition period, though, it remained unclear how (or even if) the old control mechanisms for the command-economy system were to be dismantled. The entire program was carefully worded, and its prudence reflected the influence of Prime Minister Nikolai Ryzhkov as well as, at this stage, of Gorbachev himself. Conservatives nonetheless attacked it as too radical. As already noted, Leonid Abalkin, a defender of reformist policies within the government, publicly expressed his surprise at the conservative reaction.[4]

Popular discontent had grown rapidly in the face of a worsening food- and consumer goods-supply situation combined with inflation, general social disorder, and a veritable explosion in criminal activity. Conservatives tried explicitly to harness waves of popular unrest, and to direct them against political and economic reform. The Leningrad Party, for example, organized a demonstration against "speculators," "millionaires," "the market," and "anarchy" on 22 November. The possibility emerged that popular protest over declining standards of living—protests that, although certainly anti-Communist, were not necessarily antireformist— and political pressure from consciously antireformist conservative "lobbies" might fuse. At this critical moment, the Left managed only a weak, toothless response. Barely overcoming its own internal divisions, the Interregional Parliamentary Group (MDG) called for a general strike the day before the Second Congress convened, in order to demand the abolition of Article 6. The general strike largely failed, showing that the radical opposition's organizational network was too weak and dispersed to carry out effective nationwide action.

At the opening of the Second Congress, therefore, the political atmosphere was more strained than it had been six months before. The Right was on the offensive, and Gorbachev had been seriously compromised and embarrassed. The unexpected death of Andrei Sakharov early in the

3. The meeting was to last three days, from 13 to 15 October, and was to consider the general theme of "The Problems of Radical Economic Reform." Leonid Abalkin, the vice president of the Council of Ministers and responsible for directing economic reform, was the presiding officer.
4. See quotation at n. 20, chap. 12.

Congress further weakened the Left by depriving it (and the country) of one of its most compelling leaders, a man whose rare moral and political prestige had held great potential for introducing stability amid chaos. As we shall see, these internal developments played a major role in influencing the course of the Second Congress.

## The Agenda and the Question of Article 6

Everyone present knew that the first battle of the Congress would concern its agenda. Gorbachev opened the proceedings with an announcement that the task of drafting an agenda had been entrusted to a committee of eighty people, including the entire Presidium of the Supreme Soviet as well as representatives of various parliamentary groups, including the MDG.[5] A Congress majority approved the draft agenda, even though it did not include a debate on Article 6's guarantee of the CPSU's "leading role" and political monopoly. The eighty-member commission also decided that the Congress should not discuss many basic economic reform laws. Some of these laws—on ownership, land, local autonomy, vacations, pensions, and the press—already had been approved by the Supreme Soviet. Others, such as a law on land rent, had been sent directly for "consultation with the people."

The ratification of most legislative work completed by the Supreme Soviet, in fact, was to be carried over to a later Congress. Anticipating strong radical opposition, Gorbachev tried to preempt criticism by saying that such a postponement was necessary to avoid mistakes being made in haste. He then tried to reassure the radicals, adding, "We believe it entirely realistic to plan on these laws being approved by next spring." Objective difficulties, however, made it virtually impossible to implement rational, well-planned legislation. This left Gorbachev in a quandary since, despite the delays, the Congress' constitutionally-mandated legislative role meant that sooner or later it would attack the resulting flaws. Although laws were needed to redefine in practice the entire legal structure of the state, Soviet officials almost universally lacked experience or knowledge of the mechanics of rule-of-law states and market economies. The legislative vacuum was so severe that the Supreme Soviet had drawn up a priority list, with nineteen draft laws deemed "high-priority and

5. The Interregional Group was, in effect, the only nonterritorially defined *political* group at the Congress. Some representatives of *professional* groups also participated in drafting the agenda, as did Vasilii Starodubtsev on behalf of agrarian deputies. No information ever was made public on the method of selection used to determine the membership of this agenda-setting committee, but the Party apparatus clearly achieved representation for itself as well.

essential" and a further forty called "necessary" and placed on a waiting list. All concerned, however, knew that the fundamental reason for postponement was the deep political disagreement within the Party.

The urgency of the political situation imposed its own rhythms. The danger of being surpassed by republican parliaments forced the Supreme Soviet to debate proposals for constitutional change hurriedly, and to approve laws pell-mell, without waiting for the Congress' imprimatur. The sheer speed that seemed to be necessary was the first symptom of a major political development, a landslide that was to shake the foundations of central power in the months to come. Despite its own feverish activity, the all-Union Supreme Soviet had indeed already been surpassed in legal reform by many republican legislatures, which had approved electoral laws in conflict with the Soviet Constitution.[6] Similar problems arose in the field of republican economic autonomy: in its first two sessions the Supreme Soviet had made concessions to two Baltic republics, but the questions of dividing property between, and determining the priority of economic plans made by, central and republican governments remained unresolved.

Gorbachev, despite pointing out the practical difficulties of his situation, still failed to win radical support. One Mariu Lauristin, a deputy from Estonia, immediately raised the issue of Article 6, demanding that it be added to the discussion already planned on electoral reform. The debate that followed quickly degenerated, with conservatives and reformers attacking each other aggressively. "Rightists" like Lithuania's Arnold Klautsen and the Ukraine's Leonid Sharaev faced off against such radicals as Lauristin, Vilen Tolpezhnikov (also from Lithuania), Evgenii Evtushenko (from Moscow, but elected in the Ukraine), and Igor Shamshev (from Iaroslavl). Sharaev denied the Congress' right to legislate on the issue before hearing the "people's opinion"; in reply, radical Leningrader Aleksandr Shchelkanov presented recent sociological data showing that 70 percent of Muscovites and 71.9 percent of Leningraders favored abolishing Article 6.[7] Shchelkanov also noted that a Supreme Soviet majority of 198 had favored such abolition, with 173 opposed; Article 6 would already have been scrapped, he said, if the Supreme Soviet had not been three votes shy of a quorum at the time.

In a heated exchange with Sakharov and Lauristin, Gorbachev cast his lot with the conservatives, rejecting accusations that democratic norms

6. These new laws specifically conflicted with the provisions approved by the old Supreme Soviet on 1 October 1988. See chap. 3.

7. Shchelkanov did not cite the source of his figures, only saying that the data had been gathered in the past few days. Muscovites had been questioned on 1 December 1989, and Leningraders on 10 December 1989.

had been violated. While recognizing the "legitimacy" of the question, he stated that the debate on Article 6 had to be carried out so that it did not compromise "the normal process of constitutional change." It was obvious, he added, that "life and practice clash with the Constitution. Is this a drama, a tragedy? No, it is a normal process. We are passing from one system of social and governmental institutions to another."[8] Plainly Gorbachev, unlike many conservative deputies, had abandoned blindly ideological prejudice; instead, he opposed immediate debate on Article 6 because he knew that the Communist Party was not prepared for its abolition. A majority of Congress deputies ultimately sided with Gorbachev, voting not to discuss the future of Article 6.[9] Gorbachev contributed greatly to this first, short-lived conservative victory. But only three months later, popular pressure from below forced Article 6's abolition, and Gorbachev's popularity sank even further.

After much procedural skirmishing, the agenda favored by Gorbachev won Congress approval. Economic reform, in the ultra-prudent variant favored by Prime Minister Nikolai Ryzhkov, was the first topic of discussion. The plan's very title, though—"Measures to Heal the Economy, Stages of Economic Reform, and a Draft Outline for the Thirteenth Five-Year Plan"—showed that continuity had prevailed over drastic change. Second was a debate on constitutional modifications to effect electoral reform. Following in order were discussions of procedural rules for the Congress, rules defining deputies' own status, and the establishment of the Constitutional Control Committee. Elections to this committee were to follow, and then a debate on anticrime measures; the Congress would finally hear reports on the work of commissions established at the First Congress. A complete analysis of such wide-ranging discussion is clearly outside the scope of this work; once again, we will only highlight the most important moments of the Congress, those that shed the most light on the Congress' own political development and on the tactics used by the various groups active there.

## The Government's Economic Program

Economic discussions dominated the Congress' first four days and showed that the situation had changed substantially since the First Congress. Ryzhkov's draft project had emerged from the strength of mod-

8. *Izvestiia*, 13 December 1989.

9. The vote had 862 in favor of debating Article 6, 1,188 opposed, and 57 abstaining. These figures at the Second Congress' outset—with 919 deputies opposed to Gorbachev—nearly equalled reformers' best showing of the entire First Congress. (On the

erate conservatives in the months leading up to the Congress and had been sanctified by the pan-Soviet conference of mid-October. The prime minister said that he foresaw a six-year transition period leading to the establishment of a "socialist market"; his plan did call for some dramatic changes, but it postponed consideration of the most basic issues, in particular leaving the centralized administrative command system largely intact. Although the Soviet economy was beset with a multitude of problems threatening organizational, technological, and financial collapse, Ryzhkov and his advisors seemed to think that reform, both in industry and in the countryside, could be started with existing administrative and productive methods.

Many deputies, even a majority of those who ultimately supported the Ryzhkov plan, pointed out the inconsistencies and flaws in a plan for change that used only old methods. The plan itself used old-fashioned criteria; only the predictions of macroeconomic performance had changed, based on the needs of the leadership's new political orientation. The respected deputy Genrikh Novozhilov, who opened the debate at a preliminary session, described the near-catastrophic situation that existed even in such key industrial sectors as his own.[10] Management orders continued to be both capricious and contradictory, blocking orderly progress towards a market economy. Such development, left uncontrolled, not surprisingly became unbalanced and even pathological. Enterprises now refused to sign supply agreements based on the Five-Year Plan, Novozhilov continued. They instead awaited a nonexistent financial market, took advantage of rare opportunities to deal directly with other enterprises, and demanded "barter" arrangements that were independent of, if parallel to, the "official" operation of the government's planned economy. In conditions that increasingly resembled general anarchy, with *Gossnab* ever more unable to meet the quotas set by *Gosplan*[11] and with officially regulated prices losing all meaning, economic enterprises exchanged machinery and equipment, construction equipment, spare parts, foodstuffs, and consumer goods both directly and illegally.[12] A market in "deficit"

question of Obolenskii's self-nomination, reformers at the First Congress had mustered 934 votes.)

10. *Izvestiia*, 15 December 1989. Novozhilov worked as the chief design engineer at the Moscow Ilyushin aircraft factory and occupied a seat as a CPSU deputy. After this preliminary session, the Congress was to split into three working groups that would address, respectively: "Measures for the Recovery of the Soviet Economy," "Stages of Economic Reform," and "Fundamental Guidelines for Drafting the 13th Five-Year Plan."

11. *Gossnab* is *Gosudarstvennyi komitet po snabzheniiu*, or State Supply Committee. *Gosplan* is *Gosudarstvennyi komitet po planirovaniiu*, State Planning Committee.

12. The situation described by Novozhilov had existed to some degree since the first Five-Year Plans of the Stalin period, and had been aggravated by the stagnation of the

goods had already sprung up, entirely outside government control. In many cases, Novozhilov concluded, even precious foreign exchange credits were being traded between enterprises.

Nearly all deputies taking the floor agreed with Ryzhkov that it was impossible to pass immediately to a full-fledged market economy. This was only realistic, and many radicals fully agreed. The formulas proposed to alleviate the chaos, however, were diametrically opposed. Ryzhkov's approach, supported with minor differences by such moderate conservatives as Novozhilov, the Ukrainian Vladimir Ivashko, and the Belorussian Mikhail Kovalev, aimed to restore "order" to the relationships between central government and economic enterprises, and among the enterprises themselves. It left untouched, at least for the present, the system of central economic planning. The supporters of this approach were unable to explain why this system could not revert to the old administrative "iron discipline," with all its social, political, and economic consequences.

In an effort to sweeten the pill for reformers, Kovalev proposed allowing market forces to regulate the exchange of goods "not in short supply." Administrative control and "rationing laws" would only regulate other goods. With its premise that the market could only function when merchandise was available in sufficient quantities, however, Kovalev's idea was doomed from the start. By entrusting the economic rescue—that is, the generation of such "sufficient quantities"—to old, non-market-based approaches, Kovalev's supporters failed to recognize that the structural contradictions of these same approaches had caused the supply crisis in the first place.

It was a case of the dog chasing its tail, as is plain in considering the food-supply program. Ryzhkov's program called for a production increase of 10 percent in meat and 8 percent in milk, and even more ambitiously decreed the need to expand overall agricultural productivity by 60 percent through increased use of modern technology during the course of the Five-Year Plan. The Plan included no corresponding increase of investment in agricultural technology, however, despite the widespread recognition that food supply lagged behind even the other sectors of Soviet industry. The Estonian economist Mikhail Bronshtein openly ridiculed the Ryzhkov agricultural program. In the Twelfth Five-Year Plan, he stated, Soviet agriculture had proceeded on a "5 to 1" basis—that is, assuming that an increase of 5 percent in agricultural resources would lead to an increase of 1 percent in agricultural productivity. Now, however, Ryzhkov's plan essentially proposed anchoring Soviet agriculture on a

---

Brezhnev years. In the late 1980s, however, anarchy expanded from marginal status in the Soviet economy to absolute centrality.

"0.8 to 1" basis, without explaining the source of the suddenly expanded productive efficiency. The government forecasts, Bronshtein concluded, had been pulled from thin air, and could only be realistic if a return was planned to either coercive discipline or spontaneous Stakhanovism.[13]

Ideological blinders made it impossible for the supporters of the Ryzhkov approach, even when in good faith, to see the contradictions of their proposals. The government plan caricatured responsible planning. From the perspective of the Right, however, the plan served a purpose: the many speeches by conservatives in its defense showed a conscious attempt to save the mechanisms of administrative command, with their social and political corollaries. From the moderate perspective, too, the plan had its strengths: many deputies agreed with Ryzhkov that a "progressive transition" to a "controlled market" was both possible and desirable, and would avoid undue pain and social rupture. In the view of many radical critics, though, a "passage" between systems necessarily implied a "qualitative rupture":[14] any attempt to avoid it would only further aggravate problems with old productive processes while simultaneously worsening already dangerous social tensions. These critics specifically pointed to the lack of any specific plan for a "transition to a market economy," an economy which in the government's vague program would simply appear at the beginning of the next Five-Year Plan. As Valentin Vologzhin[15] said later, four types of questions could be seen as essential in setting up a market economy, but the government had answers for none.

It remained unclear, for example, what the government document meant by the limited formula of a "plurality of forms of social ownership." Did it mean that only variations on the traditional forms of "social ownership" would be permitted, and that therefore other, "nonsocial" (such as private or collective) forms of ownership would not? On this question Leonid Abalkin defended the government, arguing that the formula used corresponded to that of the "draft law on ownership drawn up by the Supreme Soviet and sent for debate to the people." As his support for "nonsocial" ownership was well-known, Abalkin implicitly blamed the

---

13. The Stakhanovite movement took its name from Aleksis Stakhanov (1905–77), a miner in Donbass and "hero of socialist labor," who in 1935 set a tonnage record for coal mining.

14. Slightly more than a year later, Gavriil Popov, the new mayor of Moscow, pronounced a brutal epigraph to summarize this phase: "Since this society was formed unnaturally, we will need to take unnatural measures to turn back to the way of civilization." (from the record of the first meeting of Boris Yeltsin's Presidential Council, 23 November 1990). Cf. *La Stampa*, 27 November 1990.

15. Vologzhin was president of the Supreme Soviet's permanent commission for economic reform. He was also the director of the Ukrainian productivity consortium *Konveien*, in Lvov.

Supreme Soviet majority for the word choice. But, Abalkin added, if the Congress felt a change was needed, it could propose such a modification. If it did not do so, he continued, it would in effect abdicate to the executive its own power of decision. His appeal seemed almost desperate, as it was clear that the Congress majority had no intention of going farther than the Supreme Soviet. For the rest, Ryzhkov echoed Egor Ligachev's hostility to nonsocial forms of ownership.

Furthermore, Vologzhin insisted, other essential questions had simply been ignored or postponed indefinitely by the government program. Governmental regulation of the economy needed to be recast completely, but Ryzhkov gave no hint of how this rethinking was to be carried out. How, for example, would bids between competing enterprises for government contracts be evaluated? What economic levers did the government hope to utilize once direct administrative command had ended? What criteria would be used to create pricing, fiscal, and financial policies? If the government honestly wanted to begin the transition toward a "socialist market," then these questions and others needed answers in the next few months, Vologzhin argued. Yet answers were nowhere to be found in the government proposal. Most glaring was the complete absence of proposals for a banking system, without which no market worthy of the name could function. The Central Bank's role received no mention, and no ideas on the operation and financing of local government were stated publicly. Similarly, Ryzhkov's team remained silent on antimonopoly regulations, foreign investment, and other crucial questions, while making only vague pronouncements on social policy. The lack of meaningful attention being paid to social issues showed, if not reckless irresponsibility, then either that the government had no intention of dismantling economic structures already in place or that it was unaware of the social consequences and conflicts that would result from economic reform.

The economist Pavel Bunich noted the reduction in the proportion of national income allocated to industrial accumulation: although in previous Five-Year Plans it had been 25 percent, Ryzhkov proposed a reduction to 12–13 percent.[16] The government recognized that heavy industry needed to be cut, but the massive transfer of economic resources and labor could only be carried out as an integral part of an irrevocable, radical reform, not simply to reduce government spending. Deputy Gennadi Filshin pointed out, however, that investment in the consumer-goods consumption sector was only to be increased from 4.7 percent in 1989 to 5.2 percent in 1990 and that neither figure matched the level of spending in 1940, at the outset of World War II.[17] If this proportion did not rise to at least 10–

16. *Izvestiia*, 16 December 1989.
17. *Izvestiia*, 18 December 1989. Gennadi Filshin was a departmental director in the

12 percent, Filshin maintained, the government's reorienting of economic priorities would have no visible effect on consumer goods supplies. The government's proclaimed intentions did not, he argued, compensate for a lack of investment.

The gap between the government and radicals was even wider on the issue of social spending. Ryzhkov stated his intent to devote 35 percent of government expenditures to nonproductive social services by 1995, a substantial increase over the 26.7 percent spent in 1990. Even the higher figure, though, Filshin insisted, was nothing more than a return to the levels of spending during the 1960s. During this earlier period, Soviet spending on social services such as health care had been roughly on a par with other European governments. By the 1990s, subsequent cuts in funding had created a near-disaster situation, with obsolete equipment and long delays in obtaining medical attention and emergency services. Lost ground could not be regained simply by returning to the old levels of investment, Filshin argued, and particularly not when government debt had risen to the immense sum of 411 billion rubles. Most of this debt, in turn, was tied to unfinished industrial projects that were on average only 19 percent complete. Some factories would not commence operations for another five to six years.[18]

Midway between the moderate conservatives and the radical reformers stood a group of moderate reformers. Leonid Abalkin, the vice president of the Council of Ministers whose embarrassed defense of the government's position showed his own disagreement with it, was the most prominent member of this group. Even when defending the government Abalkin made clear the extent to which conservative pressure had influenced the Ryzhkov plan. At the conclusion of the Congress proceedings on "Stages of Economic Reform,"[19] he stated his willingness to meet several deputies' request immediately to sign into effect the fundamental

---

Institute for the Economy and Industrial Organization, part of the Siberian branch of the Soviet Academy of Sciences. He noted that investment in consumer goods during the 12th Five-Year Plan averaged 4.3 percent, "the lowest such proportion in the entire history of the USSR."

18. Filshin pointed to a survey of industrial enterprises with fixed capital greater than 200 million rubles. Nine out of every ten such factories used technology more than 20 years out of date. Only 5 percent of the industrial equipment in Siberia met international standards, and most of the equipment that did had been imported from abroad. In the mining industry the figure was even lower, at 3–4 percent. (*Izvestiia*, 18 December 1989.) Deputy Evgeniia Malkova also stressed Soviet industrial backwardness. The average age of industrial plants was 27, and 90 percent of even new equipment fell short of basic standards of hygiene, sanitation, or safety. Such figures, she continued, explained the high number of industrial accidents in Soviet factories. Approximately 14,000 people in the Soviet Union, more than 40 percent aged between 25 and 40, died in such accidents each year. (*Izvestiia*, 17 December 1989.)

19. See *Izvestiia*, 18 December 1989.

laws of economic reform. He did so despite Gorbachev's own stated intent of postponing such a move until the spring of 1990,[20] feeling it necessary since the government's plan had been drawn up "in the absence" of such laws. The "principal destabilizing factor," Abalkin argued, was the "unbounded growth" of family monetary income. Since "There is no growth in commodity production, no rate of expansion in services can cover the 13 percent increase [in the money supply], either in one year or in any other time frame."[21] Even government agencies, he continued, had accumulated monetary reserves in excess of 100 billion rubles—and this at a time when the budget deficit approached 120 billion rubles. It was now clear, Abalkin concluded, that change could not be delayed. The only question was whether Soviet society was willing to pay the costs of an immediate transition to a market-based economy. Abalkin expressed his conviction that much of Soviet society was in no position to pay such costs, and that (for different reasons) the Congress majority was unwilling to approve such a transition. On the contrary, he said, many deputies were asking themselves, "If *this* is the road that leads to the temple," why not abandon reform and forget *perestroika* altogether?

Abalkin went on, however, to distance himself from the proponents of radical economic reform with the assertion that ". . . the market will not be introduced by decree. It needs a certain amount of preparation. It is impossible to introduce immediately. Our present situation is entirely out of equilibrium due to the enormous amount of deferred demand; productive conditions are monopolistic, without a competitive basis for the economy; and there is no ruble convertibility." Nevertheless, this moderate reformist perspective also differed from Ryzhkov's view, as it called for an immediate start towards a market system, even if "it will take at least three years" to achieve. Abalkin called for the creation of technical and legal structures, and the development of proper politico-psychological conditions. The Soviet economy, he said, had to create commercial and financial exchanges, trade information centers, fiscal and financial controls, and price controls. Furthermore, it needed trained personnel to work in these areas, an effective system of protection for the poor, and means by which to control and direct the flow of labor.

This list essentially duplicated Vologzhin's, showing that Abalkin, a moderate, shared many radical views on the short-term transition to a market system. He tended not to attack the radicals; rather, he saved his harshest words for the theses proposed by Egor Ligachev and Vasilii Starodubtsev's group of more than four hundred agrarian deputies. The

20. The actual approval of these laws did not take place until after the summer of 1990.

21. Family income had increased 13 percent between January and November 1989.

theses' assertion that agricultural problems resulted from insufficient investment, Abalkin argued, was not true. On the contrary, investment rubles had simply disappeared into the morass of unproductive *kolkhozy* and *sovkhozy*. Instead, the real questions, which had not been solved at the plenum of March 1989, were those of changing the relationships between production and ownership and between city and country. These relationships were precisely what the Congress majority had no intention of modifying: most speeches to the Congress had been made by deputies from the "swamp" and by local leaders intent on securing finance, investment, and other advantages for their "parishes." As the academician Iurii Ryzhov remarked, too many people "are asking to reset prices instead of demanding that a new price-setting mechanism be set in place." In Ryzhov's view, this situation culminated the USSR's long development into a "society of beggars and distributors of government handouts." [22]

Reformers made a last-ditch attempt to prevent adoption of the government plan, seeking to have the Congress "take note" of Ryzhkov's document while not voting formally on the plan itself. Gorbachev, less than fully satisfied with the Ryzhkov blueprint for reform, supported this effort. Ryzhkov realized that a vote simply "taking note" of his plan would be a serious political defeat, but he was saved by the radical deputy Iurii Andreev, who proposed a stark "no confidence" motion. Ryzhkov easily replied to such a blunt attack, and argued that a vote "taking note" of the economic plan would now also be tantamount to a vote of no confidence. A Congress majority, on three successive votes, supported Ryzhkov and the government. [23]

Once again, however, the victory was Pyrrhic at best. Within four months it became plain both that the government's program was too impractical to be carried out, and that the Congress majority which had approved it showed political blindness, detachment from reality, and no grasp of strategy. Iurii Afanasev's prophecy proved correct in every detail:

We are against total nationalization of the economy, and we think it is impossible to hold off disaster in the economic system with prohibitions and administrative orders alone. We think it is exceptionally dangerous to postpone for years the changeover to an organic market economy, with independent businesses. For these reasons, we have opposed [approving the government program] because, in spite of some of its original provisions, we foresee an intensification of the crisis

22. *Izvestiia*, 18 December 1989.
23. The first vote, on the question of "supporting" the government's program for economic reform, received 1,532 votes in favor, 419 opposed, and 64 abstentions. The second, which proposed only "taking note" of the program, failed with only 389 votes in favor, 1,532 opposed, and 64 abstentions. The third, which "rejected" the Ryzhkov plan, won only 199 votes in favor, with 1,685 opposed and 98 abstentions.

and a worsening of the conditions [necessary] to carry out further economic and political reform.[24]

## Constitutional Changes in the Electoral Procedures

Increasing conservative strength and pressure became apparent during the discussion of Article 95 of the Soviet Constitution, the article which stipulated that one third (750) of Congress deputies were to be elected by the Plenum of Social Organizations (OOSS). To recapitulate briefly, at its fall meeting the Supreme Soviet had authorized the republics to abolish the OOSS quota and had, over the objections of Gorbachev and Lukianov, approved significant constitutional changes.[25] These changes included allowing republican parliaments to modify the system of indirect election of republican Supreme Soviets and Supreme Soviet presidents. Such permission did not *require* the republics to implement these changes; indeed, Kazakhstan's legislature had moved in the opposite direction by approving new electoral laws consistent with those of October 1988. On the other hand, some republics such as the RSFSR already had eliminated the seats reserved for the OOSS while leaving in place the indirect election of a Supreme Soviet.[26] The three Baltic republics already had approved new electoral laws that went even farther, abolishing seats for the OOSS and indirect election of the Supreme Soviet and also terminating the authority of POSs to "approve" the registration of candidates.[27]

Strictly speaking, each of these new laws was illegal, since each had been passed in violation of the all-Soviet Constitution. The Congress thus faced a series of *faits accompli* and was forced to approve constitutional changes to ratify the laws that had already been passed by supposedly subordinate bodies at the periphery.[28] Conservative deputies tried to make

24. Afanasev showed a document supporting this position signed by 140 radical deputies, and to which, he said, the support of the "Baltic group" had also been given. His document thus purported to represent the sentiments of "at least 250 deputies" (*Biulleten Vtoroi Sezd Narodnykh Deputatov* 16:87–90). As shown by the figures in the preceding note, radical positions actually received somewhat greater support.

25. According to the Constitution, such changes required the approval of the Congress of People's Deputies.

26. *Sovetskaia Rossiia* published the complete text of the RSFSR's new electoral law on 2–3 November 1989.

27. See chap. 3. Kazakhstan maintained the POSs, while the Ukraine, Belorussia, and the RSFSR also abolished them.

28. Challenging these laws would have been dangerous for the Congress and for central authority as a whole. The experience of the previous months showed that the center's ability to assert its power had dwindled dramatically, both in areas with strong Popular Fronts and in areas where Party rule faced little opposition. On 10 November 1989, for example, the Presidium of the Supreme Soviet declared several laws passed by four republican parliaments (including the Estonian parliament) unconstitutional. The assertion that these laws were null and void, however, had little discernible effect.

a virtue out of this necessity, attempting at a minimum to prevent the political situation in the Union and in the Congress from worsening. One commission at the Congress, under the direction of deputy Iurii Manaenkov,[29] proposed reintroducing a seat quota for the OOSS under the ambiguous formula: ". . . a portion of the people's deputies of the USSR and also, if so specified by the Constitution of the [given] republic, a portion of the people's deputies of the republics and autonomous regions of the USSR, is to be elected by the OOSS." Manaenkov's commission clearly hoped to legitimize Kazakhstan's decision, and also to influence the draft laws being considered in Moldavia, Belorussia, and the Ukraine. Preserving seats for the OOSS seemed likely to save many (malleable, conservative) local officials from near-certain defeat in upcoming territorial and national-territorial elections.

Lukianov helped the commission by attempting to prevent the Congress from modifying Article 109 of the Constitution, which specifically authorized the selection of 750 deputies at the all-Soviet Congress of People's Deputies by the OOSS. While the Supreme Soviet had modified Article 95, it apparently forgot to abolish Article 109; with Lukianov's assistance, therefore, conservatives nullified one of the Supreme Soviet's most important reformist decisions.[30] Despite his reputation as a mediator *par excellence*, Fedor Burlatskii lost his patience and denounced such maneuvers: "Come on! Let us be clear and say it like Bolsheviks, as we used to say, what we really want. Do we want to keep the OOSS representatives, but at a minimum, hidden in some way? [Do we want to hide] the old version that the Supreme Soviet has already rejected?" In that case, he continued, deputies should ask themselves, "How could the Supreme Soviet, which has our confidence, ever have taken that decision?"[31]

The Manaenkov Commission found it difficult to implement its plan. Constitutional changes required the approval of two-thirds of all depu-

29. Manaenkov was the former Party first secretary in Lipetsk, and recently had been appointed a member of the CPSU Central Committee Secretariat.

30. As the deputy Liudmila Arutiunian later pointed out, the Congress in fact annulled much of the Supreme Soviet's work of the preceding months (*Biulleten Vtoroi Sezd Narodnykh Deputatov* (20 December 1989). On the one hand, therefore, the Supreme Soviet was to the *left* of the Congress. On the other hand, the lack of a clear division of powers between the Congress and the Supreme Soviet helped conservatives maneuver, playing the two bodies against each other. By this stage, conservatives and radicals had reversed their initial strategies, radicals now concentrating on the Supreme Soviet and conservatives using the Congress to stop them.

31. *Izvestiia*, 19 December 1989. The Right found an unexpected ally in this discussion in the person of Aleksandr Neumyvakin, president of the Russian Association of the Blind and a deputy appointed from a social organization. Neumyvakin proved to be the staunchest defender of electoral corporatism, thereby dramatically shifting his own position. At the First Congress he had delivered a left-wing independent speech, but here at the Second Congress he began to sound like an *apparatchik*. Thanks to him,

ties, and neither the proposal of the commission nor that of the Supreme Soviet garnered sufficient support.[32] As a result, problems arose. A solution had to be devised, since the electoral laws of 1988 were still in force, and therefore many republics remained in open violation of the Constitution. After another vote again failed to achieve the necessary majority, the Congress finally approved a modification to Article 95 close to that sought by the Manaenkov Commission. This victory too, however, was only apparent, since as already noted nearly all republics had already rejected the OOSS quota. The 750 deputies at the Congress who represented social organizations, then, had much reason to feel insecure in their seats. The events of 1990 and the inexorable approach of a new Union treaty led many to believe that the Congress—the Soviet Union's first democratic parliament—would last far less than its originally stipulated five years. The Second Congress recognized that reality continued to change rapidly, and thus granted the republics extensive rights in making their own electoral legislation—rights which the republics had in any case already assumed and begun to use.

## The Constitutional Control Committee

Six months after the Lithuanian delegation walked out of the First Congress on 8 June 1989 to protest the establishment of a Constitutional Control Committee (*Komitet Konstitutsionnogo Nadzora*, or KKN), history seemed about to repeat itself.[33] Gorbachev had been forced to retreat in the First Congress after trying to force a decision; the KKN had been disbanded and a commission had been appointed to draft a bill to regulate its future tasks and powers. Deputies from the Baltic republics had made explicit their reasons for opposing the formation of such a body as the KKN. Although it would introduce the principle of a division of powers into Soviet government, they said, and thus assist the transition to a rule-of-law state, its establishment within the existing constitutional framework and political context would inevitably help those wishing to

---

too, in protecting their own positions conservatives managed to portray themselves as defenders of the handicapped. Ilia Zaslavskii, another handicapped deputy but one elected from a territorial district in Moscow, said sarcastically, "I wonder by what right the 750 deputies of the OOSS hide behind the suffering backs of the invalids" (*Izvestiia*, 19 December 1989). The Party first secretary in Belorussia, Efrem Sokolov, attempted similarly to try to maintain a quota of twenty-nine seats for war veterans and workers, and seven seats each for three organizations for the handicapped.

32. Despite the confusion and Lukianov's procedural manipulations, the Supreme Soviet proposal won a majority of 1,350 (70.9 percent), with 510 opposed and 42 abstaining. Although still roughly 150 votes shy of the necessary 1,497, the reformist front here achieved its greatest success to date, as even many moderate conservatives refused to support the Presidium's position.

33. See chap. 10.

preserve central power and hinder the development of republican sovereignty. The dispute arose over Article 125 of the Constitution, which granted the KKN power to block any laws, whether passed by central or republican legislatures, which conflicted with the Soviet Constitution.

The commission appointed by the First Congress had worked hard, eventually finding a compromise supported by some, but not all, Baltic deputies. Under its terms, the KKN would be empowered to "formulate its conclusions" and to suspend ordinary laws passed by republican legislatures; if the republican parliament still dissented, the "sovereign" arbitrator would be the all-Soviet Congress of People's Deputies. The KKN would not, however, have any power over the *constitutions* of the individual republics. Such a compromise, although perhaps still possible a year earlier, was now not acceptable to the majority of Baltic deputies. On the one hand, nationalist and separatist movements had snowballed in strength, and increasingly had become both aware of their own strengths and peremptory in their demands. On the other hand, the all-Soviet Congress, with its conservative majority, did not seem to these deputies a reliably impartial judge in matters concerning the periphery.

Conservative attacks on every manifestation of republican sovereignty only fed Baltic diffidence.[34] The compromise seemed from the Balts' perspective to deprive them of room for maneuver, and to make their republics' future entirely dependent on the goodwill of the central bureaucracy. Even Gorbachev's personal guarantee failed to calm these worries. The Baltic deputies' position was perfectly understandable—Gorbachev himself was not immune to centralizing temptations, and in any case there was no guarantee that he would remain in office.

Moderate reformers, for their part, for other reasons also opposed the compromise. As a result, Aleksandr Iakovlev, who enjoyed the trust of both the Left and Baltic nationalists, took the floor to persuade both groups instead to support it. Without the KKN, he argued, the Congress' and Supreme Soviet's legislative powers would be weakened enormously. In this initial phase of transition the executive clearly was better-equipped than the legislature to rule through decrees, regulations, and unchecked directives. The KKN's authority, however, included acts promulgated by the Council of Ministers; those contrary to the will of parliament would be declared null and void. The KKN therefore not only promised to safeguard the interests and rights of the republics, but also represented a

34. The Baltic mistrust proved fully justified. When the Second Congress discussed the Molotov-Ribbentrop Pact, a Commission chaired by Iakovlev presented its report on the matter to the Congress. This report recognized the existence of various "secret protocols" and declared that the Soviet government of the time had acted "illegitimately" and "immorally." Only strong pressure from Gorbachev and Lukianov, however, forced the conservative Congress majority to accept the Iakovlev Commission's report.

necessary structural mechanism in a rule-of-law state. Such divisions of power, Iakovlev insisted, were essential.

Baltic deputies responded equally forcefully, arguing that the KKN was being established while the Constitution was in flux. What kind of constitutional "controls," they asked, were possible in these circumstances? What guarantee existed that the KKN would not become the guardian of the old Constitution? Deep political disagreements underlay such questions, and the Baltic reaction sprang from the Baltic republics' own long experience of centralist, authoritarian abuses. To men and women with memories of such abuses, the fact that Moscow now *said* it wished to expand republican autonomy meant little. The compromise offered by Gorbachev's central government could not be accepted, because trust was impossible where the center was concerned. As deputy Viktor Skudra stated, the only federalism possible was that based "exclusively on the interests of the republics in the Union's existence."[35] The fact remained, however, that perceptions of such interest had declined. It could only be revived, Skudra argued, by an overall reform in the relations among republics and a thoroughgoing economic reform package to end administrative centralism. These changes, though, even if begun immediately, would take years to complete, while the institutional crisis was measured in months and while old centralizers petitioned the Congress immediately to discipline the disobedient periphery.

One example of such petitions will suffice. The deputy Ivan Tikhonovich made a particularly bitter speech to the Congress: "Our great and free country threatens to split into a series of microscopic principalities in which the nation, the citizens, and the languages will be distributed on the basis of a scale of hierarchical and caste values."[36] From such a conservative, Great-Russian nationalist viewpoint the call to oppose separatism was clear. Simultaneously, however, from the national progressive camp emerged a more realistic view, expressed most eloquently by Lithuanian President A. Gorbunov: "Let us not rush to cover the case for republics' independence with invective," he said. Such impulses result not only from the central government's inefficiency over the preceding decades, he continued, but also from "disappointment in the results of the First Congress in [achieving] the legal regulation of the republics."[37]

While Gorbunov's language was moderate, he implied that more foresight six months earlier might have mitigated the current, bitter tensions.

---

35. *Biulleten Vtoroi Sezd Narodnykh Deputatov* 17:21. Skudra was the Latvian minister of justice.

36. Ibid., 18. Tikhonovich worked as an instructor at the Pedagogic Institute in Vilnius.

Now, he left little room for doubt: "We can escape this crisis only by decentralizing, and with a strict division of powers between the Soviet Union and the republics, to the advantage of the latter." Acting otherwise, he warned, would only "strengthen the centrifugal forces." He therefore proposed a "transitional phase" in which the all-Union Supreme Soviet could approve laws even in conflict with the Constitution. Similar powers should be entrusted to republican Supreme Soviets pending the approval of a new, entirely revised Constitution. In the meantime, they would be empowered to veto laws of the all-Soviet body on the principle that "on federal questions laws of the Union take precedence; on republican issues, republican laws [take precedence]." The Congress, however, did not even consider his proposal.

In the intervening six months, the Left had developed a position on the issue of the KKN much stronger than its stance at the First Congress. Both Aleksei Kazannik (speaking for the MDG) and Roi Medvedev saw the danger of direct confrontation, and suggested that the Congress again postpone any decision.[38] Gorbachev angrily disagreed, rejecting Kazannik's suggestion and telling him not to "push things." Even on formal grounds, however, those who called for an immediate vote on the KKN opened themselves to criticism, since such a vote violated at least the spirit of Article 113, which stipulated that matters of concern to the republics could "normally" be considered by the Congress only "after their consideration, in a first and second reading, by the Supreme Soviet." Gorbachev contended that the Baltic republics had already embarked upon a separatist path; he preferred to face that separation immediately, in the Congress, as long as the Congress created a political structure to assist the central government in impeding future secessionism.

Realizing what Gorbachev wished to do, separatist Baltic deputies on 19 December approved a declaration of principles read by deputy K. Moteka:

The people's deputies from Lithuania and the overwhelming majority of the deputies from Estonia and Latvia will not participate in the discussion of the draft law on constitutional control in the USSR. Neither the representative from Lithuania, nor any other Lithuanian citizen, will take part in the work of the KKN of the USSR.[39]

On the ballots that followed, a majority of MDG deputies abstained, while others opposed the law authorizing the KKN. Some deputies of the ex-

37. *Izvestiia*, 17 December 1989.
38. *Izvestiia*, 22 December 1989. Kazannik spoke as a radical, Medvedev as a mediator.

treme Right also abstained on proposals further limiting the powers of the KKN. As Moteka had warned, the Baltic deputies walked out of the hall.

## Conclusion

Gorbachev's tactics had not changed materially since the First Congress. He still hoped to maintain his position at the center, carefully avoiding the enmity of the conservative majority. This majority, however, had moved even farther to the right by the Second Congress, and hence the Congress' political center of gravity—the spot at which Gorbachev situated himself—stood to the right of where it had been six months earlier. Even the official Soviet press confirmed this trend, which was also well expressed by a statement of a group of academicians during the Congress: ". . . we are convinced it is obvious that rightist extremism has grown, as have attempts to bring us back to the period that preceded *perestroika*, and to restore the Stalinist order of stagnation."[40] This general tendency is confirmed by the statistical analysis related in subsequent chapters.

Boris Yeltsin used this opportunity to launch an energetic attack on Gorbachev. We are proceeding "blindfolded," he exclaimed; the "initiators of *perestroika*" bear heavy responsibilities for choosing such a slogan "without drawing up an adequate plan [for its realization]." "Concrete tactical proposals were presented to the leadership three years ago," Yeltsin continued, obviously referring to his own personal history, "but they were deemed politically mistaken," and thus remained undeveloped. What the Soviet Union now faced, therefore, was a picture of "halfway measures, indecisiveness, [and] compromises halfway between the interests of government and those of society. All this has made us lose three years, and has brought us to a general crisis."[41] Despite his words, the Congress continued to veer rightward, even as the country, albeit confusedly, moved leftward. Gorbachev's popularity sank even lower.

39. *Biulleten Vtoroi Sezd Narodnykh Deputatov* 17:35. Moteka worked as a lawyer in the first legal office in Vilnius.
40. *Izvestiia*, 18 December 1989. Deputies signing this statement belonged to all three of the leftist groups we have identified: mediators such as Georgii Arbatov and Sviatoslav Fedorov; left-wing independents like Vitalii Goldanskii; and radicals such as Gavriil Popov, Aleksei Iablokov, and Tamaz Gamkrelidze.
41. *Izvestiia*, 18 December 1989.

# CHAPTER FIFTEEN

# The Second Congress:
# Changes in the Political Geography

The social turmoil of middle and late 1989 strongly reverberated in the national political arena, but the Congress' response was contradictory. The Communist Party still formally enjoyed a political monopoly, although even without a formal opposition politics had become *de facto* pluralist. This chapter follows the development of various political tendencies at the Congress, attempting to take the pulse of the new political elite which appeared as a result of the constitutional changes of October 1988.

Several processes shaped this elite, processes which varied in intensity and speed of diffusion across social strata and geographical regions. Political participation increased more rapidly, for instance, in large urban centers and the European sections of the USSR than it did in rural areas and Central Asia. The nationalities question posed itself more sharply in the Baltic areas and Transcaucasia than it did in the Slavic and Muslim republics. Equally, the crisis in the Communist Party varied in intensity from one region of the country to another. We must, then, analyze the influence of these complex interactions on the behavior of people's deputies during the interval between the First and Second Congresses. We will do so first by utilizing the same analytic criteria applied to the First Congress in chapter 11, and then by considering the new information provided by records of Second Congress roll-call votes. This statistical analysis complements our earlier approach and allows new insight into the behavior of all Congress deputies, rather than into the behavior of only those deputies who spoke to the Congress.

## The Republics

Even a cursory glance at tables 13, 14, 16, and 17 shows the durability and consistency of certain basic political trends isolated at the First Congress. The absence of radical speeches—and the infrequency of left-wing independent or mediator speeches—by deputies from Central Asia, for example, is again prominent. Equally, four of the five Central Asian delegations failed to produce even a single right-wing independent speech, supporting our earlier contention that these delegations showed little political independence of any type. Instead, deputies from Central Asia remained under the control of their respective Party apparatuses. Little seems to have changed since the First Congress.

Elsewhere, however, change did occur. In Transcaucasia, for instance, the Azerbaijani delegation failed to make any radical or left-wing independent speeches, showing increased conservatism. (At the same time we must note the need for caution when using Transcaucasian summary data, as the sample size decreased greatly, from forty-two speakers at the First Congress to twenty-nine at the Second.) The Lithuanian delegation changed its behavior, with no radical speeches and fewer left-wing independents and mediators. Similar reductions in reformist activity characterized the Latvian and Estonian delegations. The Baltic shifts, however, should not be seen as evidence of the conservative trend discussed in the previous chapter. Rather, they—and, to some extent, the Azerbaijani shift as well—reflected the increasing absenteeism among reformist deputies, symptomatic of the political rift that later intensified to a nearly total rupture at the Third Congress. In these regions the drive for independence became paramount, and radical nationalists no longer saw any need to struggle alongside other reformists to influence the Soviet future. They saw their priority as being the struggle for secession, and opted to abandon pan-Soviet *perestroika* to its fate.[1]

The group of deputies who spoke to the Second Congress differed greatly from that which had addressed the First Congress. Roughly two-thirds of those speaking at the First Congress did not do so at the Second Congress. The high turnover of speakers, though, only underscores the continuity of the major political trends and the defensibility of our political categories. A total of 539 deputies made 772 speeches to the Second Congress; we therefore can classify roughly 400 new deputies who had not spoken at the First Congress.

The data in tables 20 and 21 allow us to make other, important observations. The Transcaucasian and Baltic delegations' "activity coefficients" fell significantly between the First and Second Congresses. By contrast, the Slavic republics became slightly more active, while the Central Asian delegations increased their activity by a great margin. These figures, given

1. This observation also applies, to varying degrees, to the cases of Georgia, Armenia, and Moldavia.

in table 19, reveal a changed political situation. If the reduction in public activity on the part of "progressive" republics heralded a "flight from the Congress," then the increase in participation by "conservative" republics showed the beginnings of a conservative recovery—a recovery led by the Party apparatus.

## Political Tendencies and Groups

First of all, the activity of the most radical reformers declined at the Second Congress. Whereas 192 radical and left-wing independent deputies took the floor at the First Congress, representing 41.3 percent of all speakers, at the Second Congress the same figures fell to 174 and 32.3 percent, respectively. The percentage decline is particularly significant, since the absolute number of speakers increased from 464 to 539. On the Left, only mediators increased their activity at the Second Congress. Taken as whole, the three reformist groups' dominance decreased, from 60.9 percent to 52.5 percent. With the exception of centrists, who sent more deputies to the podium than at the First Congress yet registered a lower overall percentage, all conservative groups enjoyed correspondingly enhanced roles at the Second Congress.

The pause in *perestroika* and the rebound in conservative strength and confidence emerge clearly from these figures. We observe the situation from other angles later in this chapter, but it is already apparent that conservative groups had begun to reorganize following the initial shock of electoral defeat. They now aimed to utilize their unquestioned numerical superiority at the Congress to prevent the implementation of radical policies. Gorbachev's own line undoubtedly aided conservative assertiveness. Noticing the increased pressure from the apparatuses, he did not oppose it; instead, on occasion he even lent it his support. He thus showed his own growing hostility towards the radical groups which now attacked him openly. In the face of these attacks, Gorbachev became more intransigent, often refusing even to consider radical requests.

## Social-Professional Groups

This turn to the right at the end of 1989 was a first symptom of a major psychological change among conservative and reactionary groups. The trauma of the spring elections and the First Congress clearly had been felt, and had had a galvanizing effect. Disorientation within the apparatuses gradually disappeared, replaced by a renewed desire to struggle to preserve existing social and political structures. The Left, preoccupied by internal divisions and an imminent loss of popularity expected from public disappointment with reform, remained uncertain how to respond. The economic crisis continued to worsen as the administrative command system collapsed; social classes with interests served by this system became increasingly concerned about the threat posed by reform. These groups had no coherent response to the challenges facing the country, however, and so could play no role in any radical social and economic transformation.

The conservative backlash of such elites, clearly evident at the Congress, at the same time corresponded only in part to political trends in the country at large. Outside the Congress, painful processes of political radicalization continued; hence, the dichotomy between the Congress and the public mood grew ever sharper. Even with all its limits, however, the Congress still reflected—albeit imperfectly—the major political trends in Soviet society. Analysis of the data in tables 26 and 27, for instance, shows striking reversals in the political behavior of certain social-professional groups. The group of *nomenklatura* became more mistrustful of *perestroika*'s political innovations—its proportion of radical, left-wing independent, and mediator speeches declined from 32.2 percent to 28.1 percent. A similar shift occurred among managers, and particularly among cadres. These three social groups, therefore, exhibited proclivities to rein in what they saw as too-radical reform. The "diffuse intelligentsia" of technicians remained roughly constant in political behavior, making speeches more progressive than any other group except the intelligentsia. Interestingly, this latter group became even more progressive, largely due to its expansion in proportion of mediators (from 23.7 percent to 31.2 percent).

Although our model does not replicate the Soviet Union's social composition exactly, it does capture important social phenomena. Representatives of the apparatus—taken in the widest sense of that term—expressed greater intolerance for *perestroika*, while representatives of more "cultured" groups pushed for further reform. The twin processes of radicalization and polarization deepened the political gulf.

The political behavior of the military group is particularly noteworthy, as it shows some of the most conspicuous changes. At the First Congress only 7.7 percent of military speakers supported reformist positions, but at the Second Congress many more favored radical or left-wing independent policies. On the right wing, *apparatchik* positions gained at the expense of right-wing independents. The picture therefore shows tension between two separate, mutually opposed, trends. First, the military hierarchy had become more active politically, and sought to exert greater control over lower-ranking soldiers. At the same time, ongoing radicalization within the army led many soldiers, particularly in the junior ranks, to exhibit independent judgment and courage sufficient to express independent reformist positions. Both developments complement each other to reveal the military's new intention to involve itself more aggressively in public political life. The "colonels" of both right and left, indeed, were prominent on both sides of many political battles in the succeeding months.

Employed workers, the largest single social position represented at the Congress, proved to be both the most amorphous and the most stable in political behavior. Worker deputies maintained generally conservative to centrist positions, as they had in the First Congress. While this may have shown uncertainty about the future, we cannot forget that many worker deputies won election in relatively tame contests in a variety of republics and regions. Most thus remained under apparatus control, with little freedom of judgment or behavior. Not coincidentally, this group produced a disproportionate number of pre-*perestroika* speeches at the First Congress—and this proportion actually increased at the Second Congress.

## The Evolution of Political Groups

Keeping such considerations in mind, we need now to examine each political group's consistency. In so doing we also hope to evaluate the validity of the criteria we have used to classify deputies. We will evaluate consistency by considering the deputies who spoke at both Congresses, paying particularly close attention to migrations of deputies from one political group to another. In table 41 the rows correspond to deputies who spoke at the First Congress; the columns correspond to those who spoke at the Second. While the low number of deputies necessitates caution when generalizing, using the data to complement the qualitative analysis of speeches permits us to make some interesting observations.

The diagonal demonstrates that the criteria we used to classify deputies are defensible, as the largest number of each group in the First Congress speaking again in the second remained with that same group.[2] The pre-*perestroika* group was the only real exception, as could be expected, since it has been defined as provisional, comprised of deputies with little political experience and therefore the most subject to influence by conflicts and other groups at the Congress. Of the twenty-two pre-*perestroika* deputies at the First Congress, only four spoke again at the Second Congress; none expressed a pre-*perestroika* position.[3]

2. As a partial exception, equal numbers of First Congress *apparatchiki* spoke as *apparatchiki* and centrists at the Second. This stability does not contradict our earlier hypothesis, which posited constant shifts from one group to another due to the volatility of the political situation and many deputies' inexperience. This instability did not exceed the stability; if it had, we would find it impossible to define any group meaningfully.

3. Two made *apparatchik speeches*, and one each spoke as a centrist and as a mediator.

Other groups displayed a certain fluidity, but most transfers of political loyalty occurred between groups adjoining one another on the political spectrum. Radicals, for instance, lost twelve deputies to the left-wing independents but only five to all other groups, including three to conservatives. Radicals in exchange gained thirteen deputies from the left-wing independents and three from the mediators, but only one from any of the right-wing groups. Radicals, moreover, at 61.4 percent (by column) and 60 percent (by row), showed one of the highest levels of stability: only mediators, at 65 percent and 63.4 percent, were higher. More than the other groups, therefore, radicals and mediators can be seen as members of coherent political entities, with clearly-defined programs and goals. Left-wing independents showed substantially less stability, losing thirteen deputies to the radicals, ten to the mediators, and four to right-wing groups. At the same time left-wing independents gained less from other sources than did radicals and mediators—in total, only six deputies from the right. Much consistency characterized the behavior of *apparatchik* and centrist deputies. From another vantage point, the social positions of intelligentsia, technicians, and *nomenklatura* exhibited the greatest shifts in political loyalties.

Shifts between political extremes did occur, but for the most part deputies transferred allegiances between politically contiguous groups. Individual cases may be examined by consulting the "List of Deputies." Prime Minister Ryzhkov (deputy #1650), for example, began as a mediator but became a centrist. Anatolii Sobchak (#1788), the future mayor of Leningrad, first spoke as a radical but then moved to a left-wing independent position. Vytautas Landsbergis (#1095), the future president of Lithuania, supported radical causes at the First Congress but moved to strict separatism at the Second. Boris Gidaspov (#436), the first secretary of the Leningrad Party organization, after speaking as a centrist at the First Congress became a rare *nomenklatura* right-wing independent at the Second. Developments in later months confirmed many such changes; deputies frequently altered their political views after the First Congress.

Equally, of course, some shifts reveal initially dubious classifications. Sergei Stankevich (#1813), for example, the future deputy mayor of Moscow, radical leader and personal advisor to Boris Yeltsin, was counted as a mediator at the Second Congress. Another future radical leader, Vladimir Samarin (#1692), was identified as a mediator at both Congresses. Finally, the military man Vilen Martirosian (#1202) supported the right-wing independents at the First Congress, then shifted to a radical position at the Second, only to revert to the right-wing independents at the Third. Such individual cases are useful in pointing out the unavoidably subjective nature of our classifications; it is dangerous to rely on only a few (or even one) short speeches to categorize a deputy, and the limits imposed by such subjectivity restrict our ability to generalize. Nevertheless, even these cases—and these cautionary notes—do not invalidate our methodology.

A final note concerns the differential "shift rates" noted in each of our main political groups. As shown in table 41, fewer than half (30 of 74) of the radical speakers at the First Congress did not also speak as radicals at the Second Congress. These 30 deputies in turn were replaced by 20 new radical speakers. Left-wing independents had a higher replacement ratio: of 100 such speakers at the First Congress, 56 did not speak at the Second, and they were replaced by 41 new deputies. The turnover among conservative speakers was even more dramatic. Of 53 First Congress centrist speakers, 39 did not address the Second Congress; their places were more than filled, however, by 47 new centrists. Similarly, only 27 of 44 First Congress *apparatchik* speakers took the floor at the Second Congress, but 46 new speakers more than compensated for the lost 17. From yet another perspective, therefore, these data confirm the increasing vitality, assertiveness, and organizational skills of conservatives. On the whole, nevertheless, reformists continued to dominate Congress debates. Left-wing independents were the most numerous groups over the first two Congresses, with 141 deputies total; mediators produced 134 speakers; centrists, 100; radicals, 94; *apparatchiki*, 90; pre-*perestroika*, 39; and right-wing independents were the least numerous group, with only 31 deputies over both Congresses.

## The Roll-Call Votes: Methodology

Apart from a brief glance at First Congress votes, we have restricted our analysis thus far to the sample of deputy speeches at the first two Congresses. Starting with the Second Congress, however, the introduction of an electronic voting system allows us to broaden our view to consider the political behavior of all deputies, even those who never made a speech. Happily, nearly complete results of the roll-call votes have been published by the Supreme Soviet.[4] Our statistical analysis of these results has been carried out along the lines of the criteria set out below.

The most straightforward manner in which to denote each deputy's average relative political position is to assign him or her a *score*. While summarizing anyone's political views with a single number is clearly a simplification, and thus dangerous, it is, when used in combination with

4. The roll-call data has been taken from the *Biulleten Vtoroi Sezd Narodnykh Deputatov* series, which contains the official stenographic record and results of 23 roll-call votes. The *Biulleten* was published daily throughout the Congress. See table 44.

other data, not without value. To assign such scores, we first determined the *political content* of each of the recorded roll-call votes at the Second Congress. Each deputy could vote on any question in one of three ways: "for," "against," or "abstain." For the first two options, values of $+10$ were assigned to "progressive" votes, and values of $-10$ were assigned to "conservative" votes—obviously, "for" and "against" changed political meanings depending on the question under discussion. Abstentions did not necessarily show a simple failure to choose a position, but rather often carried political meaning, particularly on votes with an uncertain quorum.[5] Hence, abstentions received an intermediate value of either $+5$ or $-5$, depending on the issue. Deputies absent from the session (and the handful recorded as "not voting," *ne golosovalo*) received scores of 0 for that vote.

Plainly this methodology is at root subjective, since it unavoidably depends upon the author's own evaluations of the issues under discussion. We therefore make no claims to have determined in absolute terms the political behavior of deputies, either individually or collectively. The problems of validity faced by such subjective criteria must be kept in mind throughout the statistical analysis that follows. Nonetheless, these criteria are not simply arbitrary. First of all, the meaning of most issues under discussion at the Congress was clear to all present. In order to define the "progressive" and "conservative" sides of each issue, we considered both the speeches leading up to the vote and the meaning of the vote in the Congress' broader political struggles. Such data most often led to only one possible interpretation of each vote.[6]

While defensible, the procedure outlined above fails to distinguish between the *political value* of different votes. A $+10$ progressive vote on one issue, for instance, may represent far less commitment to progressivism than a $+10$ or even $+5$ vote on another issue. We applied a series of coefficients to the conventional values to rectify this shortcoming, thereby distinguishing those deputies with extreme radical or reactionary sympathies from those with more moderate views. In general terms, low coefficients were applied to deputies voting with large majorities, since these deputies' votes did not necessarily express extreme views. (Such votes could be seen as following the crowd, or perhaps as taking the "correct" side of an issue so self-evident that nearly all deputies—including those normally on the other side of the political fence—voted the same

---

5. For most votes to pass, Congress regulations required a majority of 50 percent plus one, measured over *all* deputies eligible to vote, rather than only over those present. (Constitutional proposals faced higher hurdles, requiring a two-thirds majority.)

6. Readers may consult table 44 to see how these values were assigned.

way.) Only on closer votes can we be more confident that deputies show their true political loyalties.

Going a step farther, we contend that we are *most* certain of the political opinions of those deputies who voted in a conservative or progressive manner when those positions were in a tiny minority. Willingness to stick one's neck out in a clearly losing cause, that is, shows one's political loyalties in the most visible way. As a result we employed a sliding eight-point scale, in which majority and minority votes were weighted differently, to determine a series of coefficients:

1. Majority > 87%.
   Deputies voting with majority: coefficient = 1.
   Deputies voting with minority: coefficient = 8.
2. 80% < Majority < 87%.
   Deputies voting with majority: coefficient = 2.
   Deputies voting with minority: coefficient = 7.
3. 66.6% < Majority < 80%.
   Deputies voting with majority: coefficient = 3.
   Deputies voting with minority: coefficient = 6.
4. 50% < Majority < 66.6%.
   Deputies voting with majority: coefficient = 4.
   Deputies voting with minority: coefficient = 5.

The values of +10 or −10 are then multiplied by the appropriate coefficient for each vote. Abstentions valued at +5 are multiplied by the same coefficient applied to that issue's +10 vote, whether majority or minority; abstentions of −5 similarly share the coefficient of a −10 vote. In the end, therefore, each deputy has 23 numbers, one for each vote, ranging from −80 to +80. Zeros in this list denote absences or failures to vote. Adding together these 23 numbers and dividing by the number of votes for which that deputy was present yields a mean deputy score, with a theoretical range of −80 to +80. The entire process was carried out separately with the results of the Third Congress, and both sets of results—averages for all deputies in both the Second and Third Congresses—are presented in the "List of Deputies," following the text.

This approach reduces the subjectivity of determining "extreme" positions, as it is based on the voting results themselves.[7] The four categories

---

7. Even this approach, however, while the best available, does not eliminate the possibility of the data being skewed systematically, as for example in the type of questions that are presented to the Congress for a vote. For this reason, caution must be used in comparing averages from one Congress with those from another. Equally, it should be noted that extremely high or low averages often resulted from sparse attendance. A deputy attending one vote, receiving a +10 but with an 8 coefficient for voting in a small

emerge from the results as well; as table 44 shows, most votes achieved majorities typical of plebiscites. Such large majorities reflected the Congress' composition, and resulted in part from voters' experience of mindless unanimity over preceding decades. The system we have adopted, of course, is limited insofar as it yields only a *linear* representation of deputies' political views, placed along a simple right-center-left continuum. "Two-dimensional" and "three-dimensional" information, though, is not so easily quantifiable, and any attempt to use more than one number to summarize each deputy would introduce an unacceptable degree of complexity and confusion in the analysis. Even this linear system, however, allows great latitude in exploring the political dynamics of the Congress. As we shall see, it permits useful analyses of deputies by themselves and by groups, whether delineated by republics, social positions, speeches, or manner of election.

## Roll-Call Statistics: The Congress' Political Spectrum

Basic statistical analysis of the roll-call data from the Second Congress yields the general figures given in table 15-1. Actual deputy behavior, therefore, extended almost throughout the range of possibilities. Some deputies attended no roll-call votes, some attended all 23; the average deputy attended nearly 20 votes (mean attendance 19.76), allowing us to gauge his or her behavior over many different issues. The most conservative average voting score was −50 (out of a possible −80), and the most radical deputy boasted an average of +70 (compared with the theoretical maximum of +80). The mythical, typical deputy fell between these extremes, with a marginally left-of-center average of +0.50. The sizable standard deviation of 16.87, though, shows that deputies did not cluster tightly about this mean.[8]

With no comparable data available for the First Congress, we cannot make direct comparisons to confirm the rightward shift detected in the earlier analysis of speeches. If we distinguish deputies by means of election, however, and treat the 746 deputies from social organizations separately from the 1,497 elected in national and national-territorial districts, we find striking confirmation of the hypothesis put forward in chapters 4 and 5.[9] In this earlier discussion, we posited that the supporters of constitutional change in autumn 1988 wished to establish a relatively more democratic Soviet parliament, but at the same time wanted carefully to

---

minority, for example, appears in our list as far more progressive than one casting +10 votes at every opportunity, since many votes had coefficients lower than 8.
   8. See the histogram, figure 1.
   9. See table 35 and figure 2.

*Table 15-1*

|  | Votes | Average |
|---|---|---|
| Number of cases | 2,245 | 2,245 |
| Minimum vote/average score | 0 | −50.0 |
| Maximum vote/average score | 23 | +70.0 |
| Mean | 19.76 | +0.50 |
| Standard deviation | 5.26 | 16.87 |

guard against the possibility of the apparatus losing control. A primary means to ensure such control was the reservation of one-third of the Congress' seats to the social organizations, "the Party's transmission belts." This plan could not be carried out fully in practice, since the Party's control of the social organizations had already weakened, but the roll-call data show that the idea was not entirely ill-founded. The nearly 750 deputies from the social organizations did help the Party leadership keep a measure of control over the Congress. With an average score of −4.02, these deputies behaved more conservatively than did those who were popularly elected, who had an average score of +2.75. This difference continued at the Third Congress.

## Roll-Call Statistics: Republican Behavior

The analysis carried out in the first section of this chapter with a limited sample may now be broadened to consider the Congress as a whole.[10] In so doing, we confirm many of our earlier conclusions, while simultaneously providing them with a stronger quantitative base. Reformist political behavior, for instance, clearly characterized the three Baltic republics: the average scores for deputies from Lithuania, Estonia, and Latvia were +35.27, +25.75, and +19.04, respectively. Following at a distance were the other three republics in which independence movements had matured rapidly: Georgia at +8.37, Moldavia at +3.17, and Armenia at +2.42.[11]

The close connection between nationalists and reformists is made plain by these figures. Perhaps also worth noting, the average among the more than 900 deputies from the Russian republic, at +0.93, also sat slightly to the left of the overall Congress average of +0.50. On the other hand, deputies from the Ukraine (−1.24), Moscow (−1.84), and Belorussia (−3.18)

10. See table 37 and figures 3–8.
11. These figures foreshadowed the events of early 1991, when these six republics refused to participate in drafting a new Union treaty, thereby setting themselves on a *de facto* road to secession.

voted in a more conservative manner than did the Congress at large. Most conservative of all were the five Central Asian republics and Azerbaijan. Uzbeks, with an average of $-12.59$, held the most extreme right-wing group score. As stated in chapter 4, the Central Asian electoral campaigns remained under the tight control of Party leaders, who generally succeeded in producing easily controlled Congress delegations. These Party organizations sent most regional first secretaries to the Congress, usually in single-candidate elections. We can, therefore, now delineate more precisely the outlines of the conservative/reactionary "swamp" that strongly influenced the Congress' political behavior. This "swamp" represented a silent, maneuverable majority of deputies, elected according to the *nomenklatura*'s own rules and not at all influenced by the first winds of democratization.

## Roll-Call Statistics: Social Group Behavior

A similar analysis of roll-call voting data, carried out along the lines of the various social-professional groups, provides equally valuable insight.[12] Starting once more with the extreme left wing, it should come as no surprise that the intelligentsia ($+11.26$) demonstrated the greatest reformist tendency, nor that it was followed by the group of technicians ($+5.23$). These two groups, representing about 750 deputies in total, were the only two with averages to the left of the Congress average of $+0.50$. Moreover, these two groups' scores also had the highest standard deviations, at 19.64 and 17.20, respectively, showing that *intelligenty* and technicians were more widely dispersed along the political spectrum than other groups. (For comparison, *nomenklatura* scores had an s.d. of 12.89, and workers' scores an s.d. of 12.82.) The intelligentsia included deputies with scores ranging from $-40$ to $+70$. This 110-point span shows the immense variety of political opinions held by intellectual men and women.

Managers ($-0.16$), cadres ($-1.71$), and workers ($-2.13$) all supported moderately conservative positions. Farther to the right, military deputies ($-5.05$) and the *nomenklatura* ($-9.38$) were unabashedly right-wing in sympathy. As already noted, these results correspond with our earlier hypotheses, and with the analysis of the restricted sample of deputy speeches.

## Roll-Call Statistics: Speaker Behavior

We need now to utilize our new statistical data to consider the political behavior of those deputies who spoke at the Congress. Since their

12. See table 39 and figures 9, 10, and 11.

speeches have already been characterized for political content, this perspective should allow us to evaluate our earlier, qualitative analysis of speakers.[13] As we shall see, the classification by speeches complements the roll-call data very well. The 64 radical speakers, for example, as a group possessed far and away the most left-wing average score (+26.37). The 82 left-wing independents scored an average of +14.56; their large standard deviation showed the group's great heterogeneity. Mediators averaged +1.92, near to the Congress average of +0.50, as we would expect for a progressively inclined group pushing for a political compromise. The conservative groups of centrists (−8.30) and *apparatchiki* (−10.44) also fell roughly where expected to the right of center.

Two anomalies, however, also appeared. The group of right-wing independent speakers, expected to fall near the conservative extreme, actually had an average score of −2.22, only slightly right of center. Its low standard deviation, moreover, shows this group's unexpectedly low dispersal. In their political behavior, right-wing independents seemed less conservative than either centrists or *apparatchiki*. The 19 pre-*perestroika* deputies (−6.46), furthermore, also fell to the left of centrists and *apparatchiki*.

Perhaps our original criteria for classifying speeches of these two types —right-wing independent and pre-*perestroika*—were deficient. Certain problems are apparent in individual cases. As mentioned, for instance, the military deputy Vilen Martirosian (#1202), spoke as a right-wing independent at the First Congress, then became classified as a radical at the Second Congress. This political shift seems at first glance confirmed by his roll-call score of +13.04, significantly left of center. Other deputies also changed positions (as gauged by their speeches) just as abruptly. Nevertheless, Martirosian in the Third Congress again spoke as a right-wing independent, yet his roll-call average moved even farther left (+14.23), implying a classification error of some kind.

Similar discrepancies mark the records of Anatolii Shchelkogonov (#2190), Vakhit Diusembaev (#628), and Valerii Kucher (#1078), among others. Even if such cases do show classification mistakes, the subjective basis of our categories has been clear from the outset. In other deputies' cases, moreover, discrepancies between speeches and roll-call scores do not necessarily imply that either is invalid. Two examples will suffice, both of deputies who later achieved notoriety but who at this stage remained comparatively unknown. Colonel Viktor Alksnis (#75) later showed his extreme right-wing sympathies by helping found and lead the *Soiuz* parliamentary group. Alksnis even expressed views critical of the Party's own conservatives; his classification as a right-wing independent is beyond doubt. As expected, his average at the Second

13. See table 33 and figures 12, 13, and 14.

Congress of $-3.50$ stood close to that of the right-wing independent group as a whole ($-2.22$). While remaining a right-wing independent at the Third Congress, however, his score moved unexpectedly leftward, averaging $+8.89$—noticeably more progressive than the group of right-wing independents ($+4.94$). The case of Alksnis reflects the contradictory nature of the political struggle, wherein a particular deputy could take progressive positions on economic reform (as Alksnis did) while simultaneously adopting conservative or even reactionary views on political reform and questions of republican sovereignty.

Sverdlovsk worker Veniamin Iarin (#2238) serves as our second example. Iarin also consistently spoke as a right-wing independent, but his voting averages in the Second and Third Congresses fell far to the left of the right-wing independent group averages. In addition to the considerations brought up in Alksnis' case, we can explain the skewed averages at least in part by pointing to the small sample size of the group of right-wing independents. The same proviso applies to generalizing the pre-*perestroika* group average, as the two were the least numerous political groups at the Congress.

Furthermore, the pre-*perestroika* group in any case was defined in large part by its indeterminate and provisional nature. As discussed in chapter 7, these deputies had little political experience and no defined political loyalties. Hence, it should not be surprising that their votes showed contradictions, nor that many proved unable to understand the issues under discussion. As for the group of right-wing independents, similarly unexpected voting patterns could easily result from the very independent characteristics of its members. Right-wing independents certainly did express conservative views, but with varying intensity and in a less dogmatic or clearly defined fashion than centrists or *apparatchiki*. Thus, many deputies expressing right-wing independent positions in speeches on certain issues could vote for progressive or reformist positions on others.

In the end, the results of this analysis are clear. Despite the caveats and exceptions, the difference in voting patterns among the three reformist groups (radicals, left-wing independents, and mediators) and the four conservative groups (centrists, *apparatchiki*, right-wing independents, and pre-*perestroika*) is plainly visible. Reformists showed positive voting averages, and conservatives showed negative averages. This result conforms to our expectations, and insofar as both approaches bolster each other, provides a measure of confirmation for both the qualitative speech and statistical roll-call analyses.

# CHAPTER SIXTEEN

# Power Struggle, Party Crisis: The Third Congress Debates

The year 1990 would prove to be crucial for the reform efforts of *perestroika*. The democratization "from above" that had begun at the CPSU Central Committee plenum of January 1987 had now become unstoppable. Soviet society seethed with activity, and all previous political and social relationships seemed in danger of being overturned. The Communist Party leadership, which had supported the accession of Gorbachev in March 1985 following the death of Konstantin Chernenko, was divided and incapable of dealing with the challenges facing it. The Party itself, which its leaders had hoped would act as the vanguard of transformation, proved similarly incapable of change and democratization, and unable to adapt to new conditions. It remained the only organized force that reached all corners of the USSR; it held a huge membership, boasted enormous economic and financial resources, and maintained tenacious control of virtually all mass media and governmental institutions. Nevertheless, by 1990 the Party's structural ossification, hostility to change, and rabid conservatism were readily apparent. The Party (or, more precisely, its bureaucracy) had itself become the main obstacle blocking a revolutionary transformation of Soviet society.

The perception throughout society of this obstacle's presence helped shape the dramatic events that followed, and made them take on their aura of inevitability. When Communist reformers were backed into a corner by events—events only dimly foreseen—even these Communists realized that risks had to be taken in order to prevent greater chaos and bloodshed. "For decades," wrote Aleksandr Iakovlev in February 1990, "we have postponed an examination of the principles and methods on which we based our conduct. Added to this are all the past abuses, on whose pervasiveness and importance we now substantially agree. This is why it has become necessary to start a transformation simultaneously in all directions. If we had done this at the proper time, we would not now face such a critical situation, nor would we need so radical or painful a *perestroika.*"[1]

## The Party Crisis

Matters came to a head in early 1990, with the Party crisis leading the way. As we have seen, the Second Congress abruptly halted economic reforms and at the same time attempted to reestablish central control against the centrifugal pressures that became apparent during the second half of 1989. In both actions, Party bureaucrats sought to protect and re-emphasize their own "command" positions. Their refusal to consider the abolition of Article 6's codification of the CPSU's "guiding role" serves as only the most glaring example. The conservative majority at the Congress, with Gorbachev's support,[2] felt sufficiently powerful to postpone debate on this issue indefinitely. The consequences of this error in judgment quickly became apparent: the Party's refusal to respond to broadly-based pressure for change created a wave of disgust that irreparably damaged its last vestiges of popular support.[3]

The signs of incipient collapse were inescapable, widespread, and multifarious. As already seen in chapter 6, for example, "national" Communist parties began to appear. The Lithuanian Communist Party split on 20 December 1989, soon followed by the Estonian and, a few weeks later, the Latvian Parties.[4] Developments in the Moldavian,[5] Armenian,

1. *Izvestiia,* 23 February 1990, "*Na rubezhe.*"

2. On the Congress' first day, Gorbachev had an angry exchange with Andrei Sakharov over the radicals' request for a debate on Article 6.

3. According to a survey of 3,823 people in 14 regions during December 1989, 35 percent of the population favored the immediate abolition of Article 6. A further 33 percent favored abolition after a specified period of time. Only 19 percent of respondents thought it best to retain Article 6. This survey, carried out while the Second Congress was in session, was administered by the Department of Applied Sociology and Social Psychology of the Academy of Social Sciences of the CPSU, a body far from the vanguard of radicalism (*Izvestiia,* 1 January 1990).

4. At its second session of early January, the Estonian Party Central Committee reached a compromise position requesting "genuine autonomy for the republican [Communist] parties within the CPSU." Further discussion was postponed pending the Party's Twentieth Congress, scheduled to open on 23 March, where a split was planned paralleling that of the Lithuanian Party (*Izvestiia,* 5 January 1990). In Latvia, a conference of militant Party members in late February declared itself in favor of creating a Latvian Communist Party entirely independent of the CPSU. Fully 60 percent of this conference supported the immediate establishment of such a Party, and called for an inaugural Congress on 14 April. The plenum of the existing Latvian Party called its Twentieth Congress for 6 April, and the final outcome was a schism leading to the foundation of a Party outside Moscow's control. Unlike the Lithuanian case, in Latvia this breakaway Party remained in the minority, while the preponderance of Communists remained with the CPSU (*Pravda,* 7 March 1990).

5. Thousands of people took to the streets in Kishinev in early February to par-

Georgian, Ukrainian, and Russian Parties took a similar course. The first months of 1990 witnessed genuine revolts of vast numbers of the Party rank and file against local leaders.

A street crowd in Volgograd proclaimed its lack of confidence in the entire Party regional committee (*obkom*), forcing four members of the regional secretariat to resign in addition to first secretary V. Kalashnikov.[6] Similar protests had occurred in previous months at Tiumen, Chernigov, and Sverdlovsk. In Donetsk, demonstrators demanded the revocation of the parliamentary status of *obkom* first secretary A. Vinnik.[7] A crowd in Ulianovsk similarly demanded the resignation of *obkom* first secretary Iu. Samsonov,[8] while the entire citizens' Party committee of Kremenchug was forced to resign. As a final example, after a protracted struggle the regional plenum in Sverdlovsk accepted the resignation of first secretary L. Bobykin.[9]

The list could go on, but the episodes reported in the central press likely only faintly reflect the dimensions of change in peripheral Party organizations. In Bashkiria, the entire regional Party committee was forced to step down, ceding authority to a provisional secretariat.[10] The Voroshilovgrad plenum removed First Secretary I. Liakhov, as the Altai plenum did First Secretary F. Popov.[11] The Twenty-eighth CPSU Congress had been scheduled for the summer; as it approached, pressure from below intensified. Frightened Party *apparatchiki* at the February plenum tried to postpone local Party committee reports until after the Congress, although their attempt failed when Gorbachev opposed it. The problems cannot be located simply between leaders and the rank-and-file, however; nor was it only among leaders themselves.

## The Power Struggle

Indeed, the entire society was being rent apart. Central government repression diminished and the beginnings of democratization and *glasnost* appeared, but unsolved social problems also emerged into public

---

ticipate in a demonstration called by the Popular Front and by the Presidium of the Moldavian Supreme Soviet. The public discussion of an independence program included the issue of establishing a Communist Party independent of the CPSU (*Izvestiia*, 12 February 1990).

6. *Izvestiia*, 28 January 1990.

7. *Izvestiia*, 10 February 1990. Vinnik's voting average (#362) in the Second Congress was −3.70, and he was absent from all votes at the Third Congress.

8. *Izvestiia*, February 1990. Samsonov is deputy #1701 in our list; his voting averages were −10.43 and −10.00 at the Second and Third Congresses, respectively. The special *obkom* plenum forbade him to run for reelection.

9. *Pravda*, 13 February 1990.

10. *Izvestiia*, 14 February 1990.

11. *Pravda*, 16 February 1990; *Izvestiia*, 17 February 1990.

view, complicated by the pressing needs of a developing modern society. Violence, an intrinsic part of the preexisting social fabric, appeared concomitantly with the loss of central authority. Between 31 December and 2 January thousands of Azerbaijani demonstrators tore down barriers along the border between Iran and the autonomous republic of Nakhichevan. New violence erupted in Nagorno-Karabakh in early January, and on 13 January a popular revolt broke out in Baku. Erevan witnessed a series of massive demonstrations, and large pro-independence rallies in Tbilisi between 5–20 January paralyzed the Georgian capital. On a non-violent level, representatives of Soviet Germans—deported by Stalin to Kazakhstan—met in Alma-Ata to demand the establishment of an autonomous German republic on the lower Volga.[12] The Crimean Tatars, also victimized by Stalin, started returning to their homeland, creating serious problems for the Ukrainian government.[13]

The central government again responded slowly and confusedly. The Presidium of the all-Union Supreme Soviet on 10 January annulled various decisions of the Azerbaijani and Armenian parliaments,[14] but the real struggle was now located in the streets and mountains of the Caucasus, not in arguments over empty decrees. On 15 January the Presidium resolved to send troops to Azerbaijan, and declared a state of emergency in Nagorno-Karabakh. Four days later a state of emergency was decreed in Baku, and popular demonstrations came to an end when quelled with gunfire: official casualty lists had 20 dead and 260 wounded in Nagorno-Karabakh, with 93 dead and nearly 600 wounded in Baku. Thousands of Armenian and Azerbaijani refugees fled their homes in an exodus of almost Biblical proportions.

All these developments, whether violent or peaceful, clearly showed the rapid disintegration of old state structures and the Party's inability to mediate among opposing interests. Although local leaders managed to contain popular unrest in Belorussia,[15] ethnic strife increased in Moldavia[16] and served as a harbinger of future violent clashes. It was in the

12. *Izvestiia*, 8 January 1990.

13. *Izvestiia*, 6 January 1990. A plenum of the Crimean *obkom* called the wave of returning Tatars "disturbing" and called for government funding to help defray resettlement costs, lest the returnees cause a "destabilization of the region's economy."

14. Included were resolutions of the Armenian Supreme Soviet, passed on 1 December and 9 January, which purported to annex Nagorno-Karabakh and incorporate its economy into that of Armenia proper. Decisions of the Azerbaijani parliament on 4 December that opposed the central government's plan to "normalize" the situation were also annulled.

15. The Belorussian Supreme Soviet approved a "law on languages," which declared Belorussian to be the republic's "official language" and Russian to be its "language for relations between nationalities" (*Pravda*, 31 January 1990).

16. The Russian minority in Moldavia organized a popular referendum to reject the

Baltic republics, however, that events completely escaped central control. The Estonian Supreme Soviet made the first move with its consideration of a declaration of sovereignty on 16 November 1988. This declaration won approval two weeks later, after the all-Union Supreme Soviet passed the requisite constitutional amendments to create the new Congress of People's Deputies. Harsh reaction in Moscow and bitter reprimands from Estonian Communists sympathetic to the declaration, however, temporarily halted the movement and derailed similar measures in the other two Baltic republics. The Lithuanian Supreme Soviet waited six months, until 18 May 1989, before following the Estonian example; the Latvian parliament followed suit on 28 July 1989.

The great democratic awakening produced by the electoral campaigns of that spring had taken a deeply nationalist turn in the Baltic republics, a turn that proved critical in subsequent months. Popular independence movements grew exceptionally strong in all three republics; popular fronts became *de facto* political parties, with highly trained leaders capable of crafting and implementing detailed, sophisticated political strategies. "One by one," wrote the journalist L. Kapelniushnyi, "laws were approved that like a scalpel separated vessel after vessel, nerve after nerve from the pan-Soviet organism. They skillfully used sutures, bandages, and modern equipment. The operation was performed energetically and without loss of blood."[17] As for real blood, though, Kapelniushnyi was unfortunately mistaken—its appearance was only a matter of time.

The last months of 1989 and the first of 1990 witnessed a continuous stream of Baltic attempts to create *faits accompli* that in sum would amount to *de facto* independence. Lithuania now led the pack, as the republic's Communist Party appeared to have disintegrated on 20 December 1989. On 4 January 1990 Gorbachev received a delegation of Lithuanian Communists led by Algirdas Brazauskas in a last-ditch, unsuccessful attempt to repair the rupture. The general secretary himself then flew to Vilnius on 11 January in an attempt to persuade the populace not to force the issue of Lithuanian separatism within the CPSU, but even this extraordinary effort failed to halt the nationalist momentum.

While Gorbachev met the leaders and people of Lithuania, the Supreme Soviet in neighboring Latvia was, with the consent of the Latvian Communist Party, modifying Articles 6, 7, and 49 of its republican constitution

---

Moldavian parliament's language law and to establish an "Autonomous Republic of Transdnestr." Of the republic's "non-Moldavian" citizens, 92 percent participated in this referendum, 96 percent of whom supported both propositions (*Izvestiia*, 31 January 1990).

17. *Izvestiia*, 6 March 1990.

to establish a multiparty system. A few days later, on 15 January, the Lithuanian parliament elected the pro-independence Communist Brazauskas as its president and declared the Second Congress' just-approved law on constitutional control invalid. The Estonian Supreme Soviet followed on 26 January, when an overwhelming majority of 187 deputies (with 20 opposed and 27 abstaining) voted to abolish Article 6 of the constitution, which codified the Party's "leading role."[18] An assembly of Estonian deputies at Tallin on 2 February adopted a declaration of separation from the Soviet Union and requested an immediate start to negotiations with the central government. The Lithuanian Supreme Soviet, in its turn, on 7 February proclaimed Lithuanian sovereignty.

In the tense atmosphere that ensued, Party leaders in Moscow decided to convene a plenum of the CPSU's Central Committee, not even two months after Gorbachev had rejected brusquely Andrei Sakharov's request for a debate on Article 6. The CPSU was forced to focus on damage control, and had to adopt under pressure what it had tried to drag out with a majority vote at the Congress of People's Deputies. The plenum met for three days, from 5–7 February 1990, and witnessed bitter political struggles. Gorbachev, now hated by the Left as the betrayer of democratic reform, faced at the same time an even more hostile conservative opposition, one totally opposed to any compromise. As rumors of an imminent *coup* circulated on 4 February, the eve of the plenum, radicals organized an enormous demonstration in Moscow to demand the abolition of Article 6. Many on the left feared that Gorbachev would once again feel forced to yield to conservative pressure, but the Soviet leader managed again to use the remnants of his popularity to force conservative internal opposition to retreat. He announced at the plenum the end of the Communist Party's political monopoly. "The Party," he said, "can survive in a society in the process of renewal and take a leading role, only if it is a democratically accepted group. This means that its position must not be imposed by constitutional legitimation."[19]

With only Boris Yeltsin dissenting (on the grounds that the Party's self-criticism was insufficient), senior Party leaders voted to support this motion. A special session of the Congress of People's Deputies was now indispensible, both to define the constitutional changes flowing from the Party's decision and to face up to the depths of the crisis facing the coun-

18. The amendment did not pass, however, as it failed to attract the required support of two-thirds of the 283 deputies. Bitter controversy ensued, with the pro-independence faction accusing Party conservatives of vote manipulation and of resorting to parliamentary technicalities.

19. *Pravda*, 6 February 1990.

try.[20] Support for an emergency expansion of presidential powers to allow one-man rule rapidly grew among deputies of the political right and center and even among moderate reformers; the question, as we will see, was central to the proceedings of the Third Congress.[21]

The Third Congress of People's Deputies opened on 12 March 1990 at the Palace of Congresses in the Kremlin. Even before the Congress officially began, however, it had become clear that its influence over events would be minor at best—change had already far surpassed, for better or worse, the comparatively minor political and psychological targets for democratization proposed by Gorbachev the previous year. The entire USSR was caught up in the ongoing election campaign that promised to shake up republican elites: nearly all republican parliaments were to be re-elected in the first months of 1990, together with regional, town, district, and village Soviets.[22] These elections showed continued erosion in the CPSU's strength; exploding support for popular fronts; a mushrooming of new political groups; and an overall trend towards localist, separatist, pro-independence politics.

Only in the five Central Asian republics did the Communist leadership succeed in controlling popular sentiment and in producing electoral results that substantially—albeit less than totally and with greater difficulty—replicated those of April 1989. Popular fronts won overwhelming majorities in the Baltic republics. Even with fewer voters, opposition forces in the RSFSR, the Ukraine, Belorussia, and Moldavia all improved their showings dramatically from the earlier general elections. By mid-1990, then, the Soviet political picture had been completely transformed, and the country was fractured by a myriad of divisions. The center in Moscow clearly had lost its ability to decide the country's fate without reference to the wishes of new, popularly invested political organizations and institutions.

20. The Presidium of the all-Union Supreme Soviet, meeting on 12 February, decided to refer to the entire Supreme Soviet the constitutional changes required to establish the office of President, and to call an extraordinary session of the Congress.

21. Fedor Burlatskii published a detailed article in *Izvestiia* on 10 February ("*President i razdelenie vlastei*," or "The President and the Separation of Powers") that addressed the issue. He proposed a variety of solutions to the crisis, among them the direct election of the president by the people, although not immediately. Burlatskii's views on the creation of a Presidential Council and on the relations between president and parliament found substantial expression in the proposals for constitutional changes set before the Third Congress.

22. Only Armenia, Georgia, and Azerbaijan had to postpone these elections, essentially for reasons of public order.

## The Third Congress Debates

It should come as no surprise, therefore, that the Third Congress debates were characterized by extraordinary developments. The empty chair of the Lithuanian representative on the stage of the Palace of Congresses symbolized the entirely new situation, one to which most of the 2,092 deputies present did not know how to respond. Fully 153 deputies from the Baltics and other rebellious republics either did not come to Moscow at all or attended the Congress while refusing to recognize its authority. Gorbachev did not attempt to hide his concern as he opened the proceedings. Reports from Vilnius, where the Lithuanian Supreme Soviet had just declared the republic's independence, were "rather disturbing," he said.

The preceding weeks witnessed an ongoing struggle between centripetal and centrifugal forces. The special session of the all-Union Congress of People's Deputies had now been convened, but before its second round of voting ended the Lithuanian Supreme Soviet had also been called into special session, in an attempt to beat Moscow to the punch by presenting it with an openly defiant *fait accompli* of separation. The Congress in Moscow clearly faced issues of cardinal importance: what remained of the country's unity was at stake. Nevertheless, the Congress' activity remained confused, even deliberately obfuscatory.

Deputies heard calls to delegate new executive powers to the president in order to prevent a general collapse and to impose a modicum of order in the country. In truth, Gorbachev as general secretary of the CPSU and president of the Supreme Soviet already enjoyed immense powers, mostly inherited from the autocratic structure of the Party. He did not lack power—but his ability to exercise this authority presupposed an ultimate reliance on the use of arbitrary rule and coercion. Gorbachev's powers, in short, clashed with the imperatives of the rule-of-law state that he wished to create. He therefore required a formal parliamentary legitimation of these powers, but failed (as did others) to realize that the problem was at root one of politics as much as of institutional engineering. Mere formal legitimation no longer sufficed to guarantee authority. Without a new system of consensual relationships among new political and institutional interests—republics, parties, movements, and social groups—coercion would once again become necessary.

Contradictions flowing from a variety of countervailing purposes marked the Congress' multifaceted reform impulse. The proposed institutional architecture reflected a variety of conflicts: that within the Party and that between the Party and the opposition, as well as that between the center and the republics. Gorbachev's proposed agenda for the Congress amounted to an attack on the republics' independence and a retreat in the face of pressure from pro-democracy forces. It was ambiguous on questions of land- and property-ownership reform. In the third item on the agenda, however, a proposal that the CPSU renounce its "leading role," reformers won a clear victory.

Conservatives, having seen that the strength of the presidency could be a double-edged sword, were forced to renounce their political monopoly. They responded in different ways to this change of fortune, but generally—and perhaps oddly—sought to substitute an even stronger, authoritative presidency for the positions of strength they had lost. While they did not trust Gorbachev, these conservatives still believed they could strongly influence his actions. This belief in turn created great suspicion in the democratic Left, which trusted Gorbachev's intentions no more than did the Right. With its own pragmatic interpretation, only the center around Gorbachev embraced wholeheartedly the idea of creating a Soviet presidency as a new, dramatically stronger institution. Centrists shared conservatives' concern about the potential disintegration of the country and wished to replace the declining authority of the Party with a new, strong, popularly legitimated central authority.[23] In the final analysis, however, Gorbachev strengthened his personal position and increased his independence from the Party by this solemn investiture of power in the Congress, which had been directly elected by the people.

Lukianov tried to alleviate radical-democratic suspicions about a possible "dictatorial" interpretation of the presidency. In the first place, he stated, constitutional changes allowed in principle for the election of the president through universal, direct, and secret ballots. The fact that the first president of the USSR was to be elected by the Congress rather than by the people—one of the points most bitterly contested by the democratic opposition—should be seen, he argued, as nothing more than a transitional measure. Other constitutional provisions limited any president to no more than two terms in office, Lukianov pointed out; presidents could be forced to resign by the Congress of People's Deputies "in the case of violation of the Constitution and laws of the USSR"; the president's actions were to be restricted by the existing laws of the USSR; and finally, the Congress retained the right to annul presidential decrees,

---

23. Lukianov made this argument explicit when he requested the Congress to establish "a more exact system of power relationships which . . . should operate as the Party relinquishes its role as the direct instrument of governmental and economic leadership, and this function is removed from the Party structure and placed in the government" (*Vneocherednoi Tretii Sezd Narodnykh Deputatov SSSR, Biulleten* 1:15). Shortly afterwards, he stated that the presidency, "when *perestroika* has entered its most acute phase, must be a means for sharply increasing the efficiency of the entire power mechanism, and fostering stability and respect for law and order" (Ibid.).

while the Constitutional Control Commission could judge the legitimacy of all proclamations.

Despite Lukianov's attempts to minimize them, the new powers conferred on the president at the Third Congress were extensive and substantial. The president gained direct control of the government and acquired the power to appoint ministers. He (or theoretically she, although all present presumed Gorbachev would retain the position) was empowered to appoint a Presidential Council—without consulting the Congress—for securing assistance in matters of foreign and domestic policy as well as national security. In a measure clearly aimed at the coming secession of Lithuania, the president also received the power "to take the necessary measures for the defense of the Soviet Union's sovereignty and that of the republics in the Union, for the security and territorial integrity of the nation."[24] Furthermore, the president gained veto power over decisions of the all-Union Supreme Soviet, could propose to the Congress that the Supreme Soviet be dissolved and reelected, could suspend government decisions and even, in exceptional circumstances, declare a state of "temporary presidential control."[25] He or she also won authorization to put votes of confidence in the Council of Ministers to the Supreme Soviet, and to appoint and dismiss senior armed services commanders. Finally, in a nod to the increased powers of the republics, the president was to be assisted by a Federation Council composed of the most senior representatives of each republic.

These changes plainly aimed to deal with crisis situations, but many were destined never to be used, while others failed when tried. The "paralysis of power," as deputy Sergei Alekseev dubbed it,[26] resulted not so much from an unclear definition of various governmental bodies' powers as from deep disagreements among top Party leaders on the choices which needed to be made. True, all political currents at the Congress still agreed that parliament was the body best situated to introduce reforms. Nevertheless, the Party apparatus neither desired nor knew how to yield power. Hence, even moderate reformers supported the institution of the presidency as an interim measure until a permanent division of powers could be devised and until parliament became sufficiently strong to safeguard its prerogatives. Alekseev's succinct analysis echoed the words of Lukianov: "Without power that is sufficiently civilized and strong, the presence of many parties would fragment our social system even farther; it would be an explosive tendency. Furthermore, under

24. Ibid., 20.
25. Ibid., 21.
26. Alekseev was president of the Constitutional Control Commission. Ibid., 29.

present conditions the institution of the presidency could perhaps be the only possible means of transmitting *de facto* powers from the Party apparatus to the government."[27]

More surprises emerged during the course of Congress debate, as political groupings at the Congress and in the Party rapidly became more complex. Nursultan Nazarbaev, president of the Kazakh Supreme Soviet's Presidium, gave an astonishingly critical speech. He did not oppose the institution of the presidency, but attacked shortcomings in the constitutional framework that had been established in the fall of 1988. He called this framework "a power on two levels, a vicious circle within which every concrete decision is blocked."[28] Nazarbaev, a republican Communist leader, revealed a vertical split in the conservative front by denouncing the rift between central and republican Party leaderships. Part of the conservative camp, that is, saw attempts to centralize power as dangerously threatening to its own authority. "The bastions of administrative and ministerial *diktat*," exclaimed Nazarbaev, "are still entrenched and confident of their power even five years after *perestroika* began."

It was therefore no accident that the Kazakh leader launched one of the strongest attacks on Nikolai Ryzhkov's government. "The government must finally make a clear choice," he declared, "which god it bows to and which it serves: ministerial ambitions or the Soviet people." Claims to power by republican Party leaders had grown increasingly strident and, by the time Nazarbaev spoke, sounded eerily similar to those of anti-Communist republican leaders. What is the meaning, Nazarbaev asked, of the "absolutely confused" notion of "social ownership"? "If we want to avoid returning to the old bureaucratic ways," he continued, "we must recognize that the ownership of rights to land and to natural resources do not belong legally to the people, but to the republics, since they are sovereign state bodies." These bodies in turn, "according to the Declaration of the Establishment of the Union of Soviet Socialist Republics, approved in 1922, have not delegated to anyone the property rights to their territory. [They] have only delegated voluntarily certain of their rights to the center."[29] Plainly, Nazarbaev's remarks avoided entirely the topic of reforming production relationships, instead focusing on transferring ownership from the center to republican Party leaderships, thus hoping to establish a new division of powers between the center and the periphery. The blossoming of a Communist multiparty system in turn derived from this request.

27. Ibid., 30.
28. Ibid., 35.
29. Nazarbaev's speech may be found in ibid., 36.

The coalescing democratic opposition, on the other hand, appeared at the Third Congress with an entirely different position. The Interregional Group (MDG) again gave Iurii Afanasev the task of launching the attack against Gorbachev's proposed agenda. The MDG did not oppose a strong presidency in principle, Afanasev stated, as the group had proposed this idea itself several months earlier. However, he continued, instituting such a post at the Congress without taking certain precautions would be a "dangerous step, with unforeseeable consequences, which will make our problems much worse."

In setting forth five "preliminary" points, the radical leader sketched a political strategy diametrically opposed to that of the Soviet president. First, the Left proposed to draw up a new "Pact of Union among Sovereign States," which would be followed by the establishment of a multiparty Supreme Soviet with genuine powers—unlike the largely formal Congress—to be a counterweight to the executive. The election of the president should be by direct, secret, and universal suffrage, Afanasev argued, and only after and on the basis of the Pact of Union. Finally, he repeated the request now common to the radical opposition: Gorbachev as president should cease diluting his power as head of state by continuing his presence at the head of the CPSU.

The democrats thus put forward a line that Gorbachev did not support and could not accept. First, it paid no heed to the difficult compromise he had reached in the Party's Central Committee. To break this compromise would lead to renewed conflict, from which Gorbachev might emerge beaten and excluded from power—perhaps a foretaste of a Party vs. people battle awaiting the country. Second, the radical line ignored the power relationships present at the Congress. Third, especially in asking Gorbachev to renounce his position of Party general secretary, it seemed to assume falsely that the Party, once led by others, would be willing to cede its power to the democratic state institutions then in formation. Radicals thus remained in Gorbachev's view unable to perceive existing power relationships, let alone to distinguish between those positions forced upon him by necessity and those he had deliberately chosen. His insistence on retaining his post as general secretary, for instance, was clearly his own, but also resulted in part from political considerations. Only by preserving his status as Party leader could Gorbachev neutralize or prevent possible (indeed, probable) illegal antidemocratic moves by the unreconstructed Party bureaucracy.

In the abstract, Afanasev's proposal of successive stages to reform the political system appeared to have merit. As events showed, however, a new "Pact of Union," a new Constitution, and multiparty democratic elections all remained impossible without endangering the USSR itself, at least in its then-existing form. Criticism of Gorbachev for holding onto the illusion that mounting chaos could be controlled with enhanced presidential powers was justified. Equally, though, his critics tended to overlook the persistent conservative stranglehold on the nerve centers of government power, and thus to ignore the need to block the most acute centrifugal forces in order to prevent a unified conservative counter-reaction. To put it in slightly different terms, each alternative carried great risks. Delaying needed social reform increased the danger of social explosions; accelerating such reform could potentially spark a political crisis and endanger the peaceful, gradual nature of democratic change. Finding himself between a rock and a hard place, Gorbachev opted for the first alternative.

The limits of the Soviet leader's perception and his occasional blindness to the depth and irreversibility of the social transformation he started are plain. Afanasev's alternative, however, seemed far from capable of solving the difficult problems facing the Congress. Indeed, on the contrary it seemed much more likely to lead to bloody confrontations than would Gorbachev's plan. In their responses to this dilemma a clear political break occurred between radical democrats and the originator of *perestroika*. "This hasty attempt to introduce the institution of the presidency," Afanasev announced, "is a very serious and important political error. . . . The line taken by the country's leadership, under the guidance of Mikhail Sergeevich Gorbachev, has gone wrong and become dangerous in the last few months."

Iurii Afanasev, however, more a philosopher and historian than a politician, saw the deeper causes of the crisis more clearly than did Gorbachev. His prognosis turned out to be correct—as had the views he expressed at the Second Congress. The reason for the governmental paralysis, he stated, lay not "in the lack of force, but in the lack of agreement," in the incapacity to "renounce the Communist ideal, which is now defunct. We must recognize that the path we have taken over these seventy years has been shown to have no way out."[30] The Congress greeted these remarks noisily, and the hubbub continued when Afanasev announced that Gorbachev, the first democratic parliamentarian in modern Soviet history, was largely unable to "stare truth in the face." His limitations were plainly visibly in his design for Party-led democratization, Afanasev concluded, a design that already had been superseded by events.

Practically as Afanasev spoke, the Lithuanian Supreme Soviet in Vil-

---

30. *Vneocherednoi Tretii Sezd Narodnykh Deputatov SSSR, Biulleten* 1:42.

nius provided confirmation of his words. On 13 March, as he opened the Congress' third session, Gorbachev informed the deputies of events in Lithuania:

The session of the republic's Supreme Soviet—which has now been renamed 'Sejm'—has made an appeal to our Congress, to the Supreme Soviet of the USSR, to the president of the Supreme Soviet of the USSR, to the government of the nation. It emphasizes . . . that a legal examination of the events of 1940 and the entire process of Lithuania's association with the Soviet Union leads to the conclusion that they amounted to a Soviet occupation of Lithuania, and that they prevented the expression of the people's will. Thus, the declarations of that time are declared invalid. It follows that the Constitution of 1938, the bourgeois constitution, is reestablished and all the acts based upon it are declared valid. This is how the comrades in Lithuania put the matter.

Gorbachev's account was succinct, avoiding qualifying adjectives that would prevent him from appearing objective. The hall of the Congress, though, boiled with indignation. One deputy shouted from the floor: "But what comrades?" Gorbachev, visibly tense and on edge, was hard put to hold back invective that would only have made matters worse, considering the fact that much of Lithuania was then watching the Congress proceedings on television. He therefore replied calmly, but in words laden with allusions: "What comrades? I think they are comrades. Perhaps there are some differences [between us]. But I'm talking about Lithuania, about the Lithuanian people, about Communists, and about those representatives of other nationalities who live there. I think the decisions they took have no juridical value. But now I don't want to anticipate anything. . . ." Still hoping for a Lithuanian retreat, Gorbachev spoke as the leader of a central government unwilling to cede its prerogatives: "You have noted that the Lithuanians have proposed negotiations, and that the Estonian and Latvian representatives have joined them. I believe that there is no question of negotiations of any kind. We conduct negotiations with foreign countries."

This was the real stumbling block facing the Congress. The first real reply to Gorbachev's words came from the elected Latvian deputy Andris Plotnieks, who spoke in a moderate tone but remained sharply critical of the central government's political line. "They state," Plotnieks said, "that they want to renew the federation, but they approve laws that reinforce the principle of unity." On 6 March, for instance, he pointed out, the Supreme Soviet had approved a new law on property ownership. The attached list of properties belonging to the central Soviet government was so extensive, however, that the republics were left with only crumbs. On 27 November 1989, in another example, the USSR Supreme Soviet had recognized the Baltic republics' economic autonomy. The USSR Council of Ministers, though, had since then transferred control to republican authorities of only fifty-one of more than three hundred enterprises in the Latvian republic. As far as proposals for constitutional change went, Plotnieks added, the new post of president plainly took its powers from the parliament and republics, not from the executive, thereby alienating moderate progressive nationalists. The Latvian deputy concluded with a veiled warning: "At this moment, Latvia's status is not defined. It is subject to negotiation." This was his answer to Gorbachev, then, in terms of what must follow: "Let us call them negotiations or whatever we like. But they must be discussions between equals, based on equality and not command." [31]

Plotnieks' words met a frigid silence. Uproar, however, greeted Lithuanian deputy Vaidotas Antanaitis when he announced abruptly that the Lithuanian Supreme Soviet refused even to consider any "mechanisms" of secession from the Union for the simple reason that "Lithuania was taken into the USSR by force and [by] an arbitrary act of Stalin. Therefore it is not a question of secession, but one of violated independence." The Lithuanian deputies, Antanaitis shouted against protests from the floor, "are attending the Congress as observers." [32]

A speech by Iurii Blokhin, a Russian from Moldavia, made plain the differences that divided the Congress. He announced to fairly widespread surprise that he spoke in the name of *Soiuz* ("Union"), a still relatively unknown parliamentary group of three hundred deputies. After the MDG, *Soiuz* had been the second political group to make its formal appearance at the Congress. At first, *Soiuz* had held a variety of positions: its members, in our scheme, came mostly from the group of right-wing independents, but also numbered centrists, *apparatchiki*, and pre-*perestroika* deputies among their ranks. The conservative-reactionary nature of *Soiuz* became increasingly clear during successive confrontations in the Congress and the USSR Supreme Soviet.

Now Blokhin asked the Third Congress to place the Lithuanian question on the agenda for discussion, hoping obviously to secure a vote condemning the Lithuanian Supreme Soviet's action. He appealed "to all citizens who hold Soviet positions" to support the request for "an approval without delay at the Third Extraordinary Congress of a law that establishes procedures for secessions from the Union." On the proposal for introducing the institution of the presidency, Blokhin continued, *Soiuz* concurred but did not believe that Gorbachev should be the only can-

---

31. *Vneocherednoi Tretii Sezd Narodnykh Deputatov SSSR, Biulletin* 3:11.
32. Ibid., 18.

didate. He proposed a slate of three candidates "in alphabetical order," chosen carefully to appeal to various sectors of the Congress: Interior Minister Vadim Bakatin, Mikhail Gorbachev, and Prime Minister Nikolai Ryzhkov.

Surveying the proceedings of the Third Congress as a whole, one notes the rapid emergence of increasingly clearly defined political groups, even when these groups still remained formally enclosed within the shell of the Communist Party. *Soiuz* in substance amounted to a parliamentary group of "conservative Communists" who enjoyed great freedom of action. After Blokhin another extreme-right-wing speaker took the floor: Ivan Polozkov, first secretary of the Krasnodar Party organization, an *apparatchik* and Russian Communist leader who was Boris Yeltsin's primary competitor for the post of president of the Supreme Soviet of the Russian Republic. Polozkov took as his *leitmotif* an attack on the "parliamentary-journalistic-cooperative lobby," whose best-known representatives he identified as Vladimir Tikhonov, Anatolii Sobchak, and Egor Iakovlev, editor of the *Moscow News* newspaper.[33]

Conservative anger and discomfort at facing a situation that was "out of control" found expression in the thunderous applause that greeted Polozkov's speech. The Congress majority had not yet determined what line to follow, but on the Right many felt that Gorbachev had not defended their interests strongly enough and suspected that the general secretary could not be relied upon to take the drastic, forceful actions they deemed necessary. Emblematic of this sentiment was the speech of Marshal Ivan Kozhedub, who announced that he spoke in the name of the "Heroes of the USSR and the Knights of the orders of glory of three levels."

Kozhedub also began by supporting the institution of presidential powers and declared himself—albeit without much enthusiasm—in favor of Gorbachev's candidacy. He then, however, shifted into a violent attack on Gorbachev's foreign policy cast in broadest terms, calling it a policy of "indifference to the security of the state." Kozhedub deemed this approach nonsensical at a time when NATO countries allegedly "are not reducing but [are rather] increasing their military potential," and stated that it bore responsibility for "dismantling the armed forces of our allies and for the accelerated withdrawal of Soviet troops from Europe," which in its turn "changes the strategic equilibrium of the world." The cry of anguish that followed provoked more enthusiastic applause from sympathetic deputies: "We have forgotten the words of the great Lenin: the socialist fatherland is in danger! The 'pacifist syndrome' is upon us."[34]

33. Ibid., 35.
34. Ibid., 42.

Only at the Congress' fourth session, on the afternoon of 13 March, did Gorbachev finally make his views explicit, just before a vote was to be taken. The central question before the Congress, he argued, was whether the Soviet Union was to move forward towards democracy, or backward away from it. Gorbachev said that his preference was clear: "This [constitutional change] is a giant step towards democracy and its defense," which "will help us to radicalize the reforms taken in the framework of *perestroika*." Answering republican fears about excessive centralization of power, the Soviet leader promised that "presidential power has a basic task to fulfill, [namely] the establishment of a federation in the interest of all the peoples." Such words remained too vague, however, to convince the Lithuanian "observers"; Estonian deputies threatened also not to participate in the vote, and Latvian representatives had not yet decided on their parliamentary tactics.

The danger arose that the vote would fail due to the lack of a quorum, as constitutional questions required a two-thirds majority of all deputies elected. Gorbachev proposed bending the rules, namely measuring a majority based on the number of deputies voting rather than, as the Constitution required, on the total number of people's deputies. The Congress refused to go along with this scheme, but the first two votes laid fears to rest by reaching the required quorum by a large margin.[35] The vote on abolishing Article 6's "leading role" for the Communist Party, however, revealed much about the Third Congress' atmosphere, and about the new, complex power relationships at work in it.

The Uzbek deputy Pulatzhan Akunov requested a vote to change the proposed rewriting of Article 6, aiming to eliminate all references to the Communist Party from the Constitution.[36] While this proposal fell shy of the needed quorum, a majority of voting deputies favored such a change.[37] Even some moderates and conservatives, then, realized that granting the Party a special constitutional role of any kind was not only juridically indefensible, but also completely anachronistic. Principles of a "rule-of-law" state gained support rapidly, even though procedural violations, parliamentary maneuvering, and inexperience all marred the voting.[38]

---

35. See table 45. The first vote concerned the establishment of an office of president of the USSR, and the second regarded other modifications to the Soviet Constitution.

36. The Commission's proposed version of Article 6, which the Congress later passed, still seemed to grant the Communist Party a special place: "The Communist Party of the USSR, other political parties, as well as union, youth, and other social organizations . . . will take part in formulating Soviet state policies. . . ."

37. Fully 1,067 deputies voted in favor of Akunov's proposal, with 906 opposed and 37 abstaining.

38. We have often returned to the topic of the deputies' general lack of technical and legal training. In this case, though, these problems appear to have been exaggerated

A procedural trick, for example, worked to end the controversy over Article 127. The majority of deputies voted for a constitutional provision to prohibit the Soviet president from holding a leading role in any political party, that is from mixing governmental and party authority. Once again, however, no quorum could be attained and thus the amendment did not pass.[39] This vote nonetheless remains important for its political meaning. In the majority that voted for this change, radical and reactionary positions fused. As no one doubted that Gorbachev would be elected president, most radicals firmly opposed Gorbachev's remaining at the head of the CPSU. They feared exactly what conservatives hoped, namely that the president would be subject to strong, permanent political influence. On the other hand, this vote also shows that some Party bureaucrats were not at all averse to the idea of freeing themselves from Gorbachev's no doubt "malign" influence.

A similar fusion, this one between conservatives and moderate progressives, could be seen in the minority vote on the question of Article 127. Both groups preferred to maintain Gorbachev at the head of the Party, at least for a transitional period. The concept was best expressed by Aleksandr Kraiko: "I think that when the [Party] reform is complete, when its functions are completely different, [then] the question will fall of its own weight and no one will pay it any more attention."[40] At the same time, some conservatives plainly hoped to keep the two loci of power together for their own sake. In any case, the outcome of this vote on Article 127 effectively weakened the movement to abolish the Party's "leading role."

A further definitive moment of the Third Congress came during the vote on the third section of the constitutional changes—the "transitional" section stipulating that "the first president of the Soviet Union will be

---

for deliberate effect, and Gorbachev seems to have participated in the effort. *Izvestiia* on 16 March 1990 reported that deputy Grigorii Novikov moved during the fifth session of the Congress that all 14 votes taken up to that point be declared invalid, on the (indisputably correct) grounds that procedural rules had been violated. Novikov particularly denounced the procedure of voting first on the sections of the Constitution to be changed and then on each separate amendment to rewrite these sections (in each case, a two-thirds majority was required), without then passing on to a vote on the overall text. Hence, deputies who voted for the overall changes could not later propose modifications to the result. The anomaly resulted that no changes could be introduced in a previously approved text, even when (see table 45) at least a simple majority of the Congress approved such changes. This procedure violated common rules of logic and democracy, and indeed clashed with the regulations already passed by the Congress (articles 140–42). Gorbachev, however, reacted badly, insinuating that Novikov had some (unspecified) "job to do," rather than being motivated by a desire to follow the rules. When the matter was put to a vote, though, Gorbachev obtained his victory: 409 deputies sided with Novikov, 1,398 opposed his motion, and 163 abstained.

39. The vote saw 1,303 in favor, 607 opposed, and 64 abstentions.

40. *Izvestiia*, 15 March 1990.

elected by the Congress for a period of five years."[41] This time, discussion took place almost entirely within the reformist camp. The spectrum of disagreement extended from Aleksandr Shchelkanov's blunt refusal to support such a motion, through Boris Nikolskii's evident indecision, to Aleksei Eliseev's proposal to adopt Gorbachev's device of calculating a quorum on the basis of those deputies voting.[42] Others, such as Ilia Zaslavskii and Vladimir Desiatov, stressed the necessity of holding popular presidential elections immediately. Two MDG leaders, however—Anatolii Sobchak and Nikolai Travkin—came out strongly in favor of the transitional regulations.[43]

Aleksandr Iakovlev's speech proved decisive, as his influence with radicals was strong enough to persuade many to support the transitional regulations. "Let us not pretend anything," announced Gorbachev's principal advisor. "We gathered here to elect the first president of the country, especially in view of the current situation and the possibility of advancing our democracy. . . . [I]n substance, in these hours, in these minutes, we are deciding our country's future. . . ." Iakovlev, who was still secretary of the CPSU Central Committee, then addressed the objections of the reformist forces with his own arguments, arguments very different from those of the conservatives. "The idea of popular election is very attractive," he agreed. "And it is just." But postponing urgent decisions now simply to await an election, he continued, "can [only] push us backwards."

Indeed, what purpose would such an election serve, Iakovlev mused? "To seek a new leader? Or what else?" Once again, the issue of timing had to be addressed: should a popular election be held now or later? "A popular election," Iakovlev argued, "will be much more democratic in a system where there are many parties; I am convinced that the logic of *perestroika* will not wait—it is driving us forward." The issue of one man being both Soviet president and CPSU general secretary, he admitted, "really is a problem." At the same time, though, he warned the critics that it could be dangerous for reformers to divide over comparatively unimportant issues. Iakovlev maintained that Gorbachev should not be weakened as Party general secretary while "he is on the eve of making his account to the Party Congress."

In concrete terms, Iakovlev concluded, only one specific person existed to elect: Mikhail Gorbachev. Bursting into passionate oratory, Iakovlev

41. *Vneocherednoi Tretii Sezd Narodnykh Deputatov SSSR, Biulleten* 5:36.

42. As discussed above, this proposal would have made passage of any measure significantly easier, since at the time Eliseev spoke roughly 300 deputies were either absent or had announced that they would not vote.

43. Travkin, it should be noted, proposed that the first presidential term be reduced to three years.

then declaimed, "It is apparent that nearly all of us agree on that. But then, on the basis of what morality and justice can we today fit him for that heavy crown of Monomakh[44] and then shut him up in some dusty storeroom? It is impossible to die twice, just as it is impossible to be born twice."[45] The final vote removed all uncertainties, and Iakovlev achieved his aim. With 1,542 deputies in favor (77.6 percent), 368 opposed, and 76 abstaining, a quorum was achieved. The Left had been split in half; the Right remained silent, but obediently lined up in favor of the transitional regulations. Public opinion, though, was unmistakably and unadulteratedly critical.

Historians will possess ample material to judge the controversies concerning this delicate moment in the struggle to transform the USSR democratically. Nevertheless, for now, writing less than two years after the actual events and, with the benefit of hindsight, knowing the effects of Boris Yeltsin's triumphant election as president of the RSFSR and the ultimate collapse of the USSR, it is still fair to ask whether Gorbachev should not have risked a direct presidential election. At the time, his domestic popularity had clearly declined, but with the single possible exception of Boris Yeltsin—fresh from his stunning victory in the Moscow national-territorial district—Gorbachev remained incontrovertibly stronger than any candidate who could oppose him.

Furthermore, at that moment the likelihood of Yeltsin opposing Gorbachev in a presidential election was small, for both tactical and strategic reasons. In March 1990 Yeltsin remained a member of the CPSU Central Committee—he left the Party only four months later, during the Twenty-eighth Party Congress. In the spring, however, Yeltsin could not be at all sure that he would win a victory on a pan-Soviet scale, especially not in a contest in which he would face the combined organizational machinery of the Party and the state, and particularly not while many reformers still openly supported Gorbachev. Perhaps in March he might have won a clear victory in Russia, but his electoral strength in the rest of the USSR could only be a matter of guesswork. The risks Yeltsin would have faced can be seen in the referendum on the Union in March 1991, where despite the precipitous fall in his popularity Gorbachev still managed a political victory.

Yeltsin, then, in March 1990 likely remained unwilling to risk his newly promising political career on a dubious run for Soviet president. His plans for the future no doubt already included such hopes, but at the time

44. Vladimir Vsevolodovich Monomakh, Grand Prince of Kiev, was scion of a dynasty which ruled over Volyn, Galicia, Smolensk, Vladimir, and Suzdal in the twelfth and thirteenth centuries.
45. *Vneocherednoi Tretii Sezd Narodnykh Deputatov SSSR, Biulleten* 5:45–46.

patience best suited his personal interests. Furthermore, Yeltsin must have realized—if he considered running for president in 1990—that a defeat would end Gorbachev's political career, and would likely terminate his tenure as Party general secretary as well. While his main political rival would thus be eliminated, as president, Yeltsin would face all of the unsolved problems still confronting Gorbachev in 1990, in the face of unremitting hostility from conservatives. The right wing was far from tamed in March 1990, as became clear in the autumn when it forced Gorbachev to retreat by abandoning the radical "500 Days" economic reform program.

Such discussions obviously benefit from twenty-twenty hindsight, and much that now seems self-evident was completely unpredictable in March 1990. At the same time, though, Gorbachev might reasonably have been expected to foresee more than he did. Yeltsin showed in July that he realized the state of power relationships when he came to Gorbachev's aid against conservatives before stalking out of the Twenty-eighth Party Congress.[46] We do not know whether Gorbachev and Yeltsin held talks during these weeks, or whether they had indirect contacts, although this possibility seems remote. If both men had managed to overcome their mutual hostility, the course of events might well have differed significantly.

The "Yeltsin factor," however, cannot be portrayed as the only variable in Gorbachev's decision to push for approval of the transitional regulations. Gorbachev certainly realized that appearing to flee from a popular vote would cost still more of his popularity. On the other hand, the most likely outcome, given the already diminished state of that popularity, may have seemed to be a narrow victory. Such a victory would itself have altered the president's stature and diminished his authority. Nor should it be forgotten that a pan-Soviet election would only make clear the refusal of many republics (the Baltic republics, Armenia, Georgia, Azerbaijan, and the Ukraine) to participate at all, thereby reducing Gorbachev's appearance of legitimacy even further. Finally, Iakovlev's argument cannot be seen as merely self-serving: the Soviet crisis *was* becoming ever more severe. A presidential campaign, in addition to losing precious time, would likely have embittered other electoral campaigns, possibly increasing illegal maneuvering, electoral provocations, and even violence. Choosing to hold the election in the Congress, therefore, while not without its problems, turned out to be the best option available. No time existed to consider the longer-term consequences, and short-term tactics won out in the end.

The Congress of People's Deputies, however, did not see its role as

46. See Giulietto Chiesa, "The 28th Congress of the CPSU," *Problems of Communism* (July–August 1990).

simply recording events. We have already seen from the voting how often majorities favored changes in the procedures to amend the constitution. When it came to the procedures used to choose candidates and to elect a president, Gorbachev soon found himself fighting on two fronts. First, as if reading from a script, Vladimir Ivashko[47] rose to announce that a plenum of the Central Committee had designated Gorbachev as a candidate. Colonel Viktor Alksnis then advanced three candidates in the name of *Soiuz*, once again "in alphabetical order": Vadim Bakatin, Mikhail Gorbachev, and Nikolai Ryzhkov.[48]

Tension filled the subsequent discussion. Most speakers favored Gorbachev, but many criticized him or posed questions; some even tried to impose conditions on the president. Dissonant voices refused to be silenced: *Soiuz*'s Nikolai Engver supported Alksnis' proposal; Aleksandr Chernykh and Aleksandra Zemskova announced their support for Bakatin; Valentin Dikul came out for Ryzhkov; and General Albert Makashov refused to support anyone, limiting himself to firing a barrage of questions at the candidates, in the name of all "who consider themselves men and defenders of the nation."

Bakatin immediately disavowed his candidacy, upon which eleven deputies followed one another to the podium in a vain attempt to persuade the interior minister to change his mind. Most of these speakers belonged to the *Soiuz* group and were clearly more interested in undermining Gorbachev than in helping Bakatin to win. Other deputies, too, persisted in the effort to change Bakatin's mind. Many feared the repetition of an election with no alternative candidates, a circumstance which would discredit the Congress even further in the public opinion. Colonel Nikolai Petrushenko made this argument most forcefully: "Even if it was correct not to include Comrade Obolenskii in the list of candidates at the First Congress, this time we must not serve the future president ill by electing him with no alternatives."[49]

Part of the Congress did not in the least share this opinion. "I think Gorbachev should be the only candidate," one deputy exclaimed, "because if it weren't for Gorbachev there wouldn't have been any *perestroika* and 70 percent of us sitting in this hall wouldn't be here. That's all. Other people would be here."[50] Of the twenty deputies who spoke regarding the candidacies of Gorbachev and Ryzhkov, only five—including Ryzhkov, who also withdrew his candidacy—gave unqualified support to Gorbachev.

---

47. Ivashko was first secretary of the Ukrainian Party. He later became deputy general secretary of the CPSU at the Twenty-eighth Party Congress.
48. *Vneocherednoi Tretii Sezd Narodnykh Deputatov SSSR, Biulleten* 6:4.
49. Ibid., 28.
50. Ibid., 21. The identity of the deputy speaking is not given in the official record.

One declared himself for Ryzhkov; nine expressed support for no candidate, but voiced doubts and criticisms regarding the leadership in general and Gorbachev in particular; in harsh language, four attacked Gorbachev specifically.[51] The secret ballot that followed awarded Gorbachev, the only candidate considered, 59.2 percent of the vote and thus the post of president.[52]

The final task facing the Congress, one apparently of secondary importance, was the election of a new president of the Supreme Soviet. As president of the USSR, Gorbachev had, according to the Constitution, to relinquish his positions as people's deputy and as president of the Supreme Soviet. Political struggle, however, broke out once more. The Congress, as if realizing belatedly its mistake after voting yet again for a single candidate, now poured an avalanche of candidacies on the table. Aleksandr Dzasokhov, in the name of the outgoing Presidium, had led the way by proposing the (expected) candidacy of Anatolii Lukianov, the Supreme Soviet's outgoing vice president. But this time no such obvious candidacy could be so easily imposed on the Congress, and none could sail to victory. Deputies in the hall proposed no fewer than eighteen other candidates: academicians Evgenii Velikhov, Aleksandr M. Iakovlev, and Iurii Ryzhov; CPSU Central Committee secretary Aleksandr N. Iakovlev; Kazakh Party first secretary (and, from 22 February, president of the Kazakh Supreme Soviet) Nursultan Nazarbaev; University of Omsk instructor Aleksei Kazannik, the man who had left the Supreme Soviet at the First Congress to make room for Yeltsin; president of the Union Soviet Evgenii Primakov; Konstantin Lubchenko, a jurist and instructor at Moscow State University; Chuvasha University instructor Nikolai V. Fedorov, nominated by the delegations of the five autonomous republics; Leningrad jurist Anatolii Sobchak; Muscovite historian and researcher Sergei Stankevich; Arkadii Volskii, department chief of the Party Central Committee and later president of the special administrative body for Nagorno-Karabakh; Ukrainian physicist Sergei Riabchenko; Siberian economist Gennadi Filshin; Kalmuk poet David Kugultinov; Gennadi Kolbin, former Kazakh Party first secretary and recently nominated president of the People's Control Committee; Ilia Zaslavskii, researcher at the Moscow Textile Institute; and Nikolai Ryzhkov, president of the Council of Ministers.

---

51. The speeches of Teimuraz Avaliani and Aleksandr Shchelkanov were particularly bitter, arguably sinking from the realm of criticism into that of gratuitous insult.

52. *Vneocherednoi Tretii Sezd Narodnykh Deputatov SSSR, Biulleten* 7:3–4. According to the electoral commission's report, of 2,245 deputies only 2,000 picked up ballots and only 1,878 voted. Fifty-four ballots were declared invalid. In the end, 1,329 deputies voted for Gorbachev, as against 495 opposed.

The contest remained bitter even after eleven of these candidates withdrew immediately, one after another.[53] Of those remaining, Lukianov became the target of choice for the radicals; *Soiuz* deputies, as well as much of the vast hall of Party bureaucrats and centrists, came to his defense. The Right counterpunched by attacking two reformist candidates, Kazannik and Sobchak. The conservatives' greatest fear, though, was that the possible dispersal of votes among the eight remaining candidates would prevent Lukianov from attaining the required 50-percent-plus-one margin needed to secure victory. Deputy Iurii Komarov even tried the questionably ethical tactic of excluding Kazannik from consideration; if his attempt had worked, it might have proved equally easy to eliminate other candidates.

Komarov's attempt is worth mentioning because it recalls the First Congress' exclusion of Obolenskii's self-proclaimed candidacy by a simple majority vote. On this earlier occasion, the elimination of a candidacy was justified on the grounds that the Congress' rules gave it the right to "approve" candidacies. Plainly, however, if this rule were so interpreted, the Congress majority would be able to turn any election into a single-candidate farce—as in fact happened at the First Congress.

Gorbachev supported Komarov's maneuver, trying in a variety of ways to exclude Kazannik from the list of candidates. Under the unremitting eye of television cameras and in front of millions of viewers, Gorbachev led one of the worst, most shameful episodes of antidemocratic abuses. His actions, indeed, did far more harm to his personal position than a loss by Lukianov would have done. The absurdity of his attempt seemed so obvious that even the moderate deputy Vladimir Kudriavtsev, a jurist with the complete confidence of both Gorbachev and Lukianov, felt obliged to intervene to prevent the Congress from degenerating into tragicomedy. Gorbachev seemed oblivious to the danger, and resisted Kudriavtsev's arguments. Conceding the inadmissibility of Komarov's request seemed tantamount to conceding the illegitimacy of the earlier exclusion of Obolenskii, but finally even Gorbachev relented. The names of all eight candidates remained on the ballot, and Lukianov still managed to pull off a modest victory with 53.7 percent of the votes cast.[54]

The Third Congress, however, could not conclude without giving a political answer to the question that had motivated its convocation, namely the independence of Lithuania. Gorbachev, now elected presi-

53. For various reasons, the following men left the race: Primakov, both Iakovlevs, Nazarbaev, Ryzhov, Stankevich, Volskii, Kugultinov, Kolbin, Ryzhkov, and Zaslavskii.
54. Of 2,244 deputies on the general list (Gorbachev no longer counted as a deputy) only 1,896 voted, casting 1,890 valid votes. Lukianov received 1,202 votes, with 682 cancelled ballots. The other candidates followed at a great distance.

dent, needed a solemn, formal statement as a mandate to block Baltic (and other) secession drives. A committee led by Rafik Nishanov, president of the Soviet of Nationalities, had drafted a final resolution for the Congress on this subject. The harsh text presented to the Congress, though, provoked so many objections that Gorbachev accepted a compromise proposed by Valentin Falin that was "less weighed down by excessive detail and argument." Gorbachev essentially sought a text short of one that would provoke a total break, and hence the untenable assertion that Lithuania's presence in the Union was "voluntary" disappeared from the resolution.

The reply to the Lithuanian attempt to create a *fait accompli*, however, remained otherwise uncompromising, leaving no room for misunderstanding. The decisions of "the Supreme Soviet of the Soviet Socialist Republic of Lithuania," the resolution declared—ignoring the Vilnius parliament's new name of *"Sejm"*—"have no legitimate juridical validity." The resolution went on to assert that, even though "it has the constitutional right of self-determination, a constituent republic of the Soviet Union cannot ignore the political, economic, social, territorial, and juridical problems deriving from such a move, whether it stays in the Union or not." In conclusion, the Congress repeated that "the sovereignty of the USSR continues to include the territory of the Soviet Socialist Republic of Lithuania" and, "repeating the right of every republic to leave the USSR freely on the basis of Article 72 of the Constitution of the USSR," declared invalid the decisions taken between 10 and 12 March 1990 by the Lithuanian parliament "until a law is approved that defines the means and consequences of secession from the Soviet Union."

President Gorbachev thus received the mandate he wanted. He had the power to "defend the legitimate rights of every citizen living in the territory of the Soviet Socialist Republic of Lithuania, and to respect the rights and interests of the USSR and the other republics of the Union on Lithuanian territory." The Congress approved this mandate by a large majority, with 1,463 votes in favor and only 94 against (128 abstained). Many democratic reformers and radicals voted in favor of this resolution. Nevertheless, it soon became plain that neither the president nor the Congress possessed the power to reverse or even slow the course of events.

# The Third Congress: Changes in the Political Geography

The exceptional nature of the Third Congress was also apparent in the sheer speed with which it introduced reforms, starkly contrasting with the antireformist slowdown of the Second Congress. Soviet society remained riddled with contradictions and racked with convulsions, all reflected in the Congress and many influencing deputies' votes in easily predictable ways. In this chapter we will return to our methodological schema of chapter 15 to define the resultant changes in the Congress' political geography. The first step is to develop a statistical analysis of the twenty-six roll-call votes held at the Third Congress, using the same system as for the Second Congress.[1] Next, we need to consider and classify the deputies' speeches in order to indicate the main political trends. This enables us to trace changes in the views of the deputies who addressed the Congress, and also suggests changes occurring over the entire group of deputies as well. Finally, we compare the results of this speech classification with the statistical analysis to gauge the extent to which such a broad reading of the speeches' importance is justified.

## Roll-Call Statistics: The Congress As a Whole

The overall picture of the Third Congress' voting behavior is summarized in table 17-1.[2] Some deputies, then, took part in all twenty-six of the

1. See table 45.
2. Note that the number of deputies remains constant. This actually masks small variations; some deputies were replaced in supplementary elections, while others changed social positions during the intervals between Congresses. Both types of change affected only a handful of deputies, however, and imply only minor theoretical problems for using the structure of the Second Congress as a basis for comparison. The only serious criticism of doing so hinges on changes in the types of roll-call votes facing each

*Table 17-1*

|  | Votes | Average |
|---|---|---|
| Number of cases | 2,245 | 2,245 |
| Minimum vote/average score | 0 | −50.00 |
| Maximum vote/average score | 26 | 55.00 |
| Mean | 22.79 | 2.14 |
| Standard deviation | 7.74 | 10.86 |

roll-call votes, while others participated in none. The average of nearly twenty-three, though, remains high enough (roughly equivalent to the Second Congress data) for us to be confident that the data are not flawed systematically by the disproportionate influence of a few active deputies. Voting averages extended from a right extreme of −50 to a left extreme of +55. This represents a noticeably smaller range than that present at the Second Congress (the standard deviation, furthermore, dropped from 16.87 at the Second Congress to 10.86 at the Third), but as will be seen this narrowing is more an artifact of our coefficient system than indicative of any reduction in political conflict.

As the Third Congress witnessed more hotly contested votes than the Second, the average majority remained closer to 50 percent. Hence, the average coefficient applied to any given vote was lower, and thus deputy averages tended to fall closer to the central mark of zero. The overall compression of deputies reduced the range of deputy scores by about 40 percent. Since these variations are only relative, however, and because the compression flows largely from the method used to calculate averages, we may still usefully consider the variations present among deputies' roll-call data. Furthermore, despite the narrowing, deputies' average score moved noticeably leftward, from +0.50 to +2.14. The Third Congress had responded to the influence of the republican elections during early 1990, and shifted its tone from that of the Second Congress' conservatism.

Important distinctions may once again be noted between deputies with

---

Congress—for instance, did the Third Congress simply vote on more self-evidently correct reformist measures than the Second, and therefore only *appear* to be more reformist? While this is a real problem on a statistical level, the other analyses carried out here (judging the matters put to a vote, and speech classification) suggest that such changes were not meaningfully present. Indeed, struggles over issues became, if anything, even more bitter. If such a difference *was* present, indeed, it would itself only reveal a reformist shift in the selection of matters upon which to vote. Hence, this chapter proceeds—with these caveats—to use the Second Congress figures as a basis for comparison.
3. See table 36 and figure 2.

mandates from social organizations and those representing territorial or national-territorial districts.[3] As at the Second Congress, the former behaved more conservatively than the latter, but differences between the two narrowed. The mean voting average for deputies appointed by social organizations shifted from −4.02 at the Second Congress to +0.07 at the Third, while elected deputies moved from +2.75 to +3.18. While this compression no doubt follows in part from the coefficient effects outlined above, the fact remains that social-organization deputies moved leftward more rapidly at the Third Congress than did those popularly elected.[4]

The reality of continuing differences of political outlook between these two groups only months after the Second Congress should come as no surprise. Psychological and political change usually occurs only slowly in large groups; here the interests represented by each group remained at odds, and hence total fusion of political views cannot be expected. Shared membership in the CPSU by many deputies, both appointed and elected, only obscured the underlying differences between them. At the same time, though, ten months of parliamentary experience in a completely new atmosphere had begun to change deputies' political consciousness. The realities of parliamentary struggle forced all sides to agree on common rules of behavior. Differences remained and even sharpened, but shifted in unpredictable ways as well—indeed, the overall picture of the Congress resembled nothing so much as an enormous kaleidoscope, spinning under the influence of both internal and external factors. These influences themselves were not free from contradictions and confusion, and hence deputies in some ways only reflected the main currents of unrest in the society at large.

## Roll-Call Statistics: The Republican Delegations

The range of voting averages narrows still farther when calculated on the basis of republics. The Second Congress had seen great variation, from Lithuania's +35.27 to Uzbekistan's −12.59.[5] The range at the Third Congress shrank from 47.86 to 18.02, with the extremes represented by Estonia's +13.18 and Azerbaijan's −4.84.[6] While some of the causes of this

4. The difference between the two groups' mean voting averages had been 6.77 at the Second Congress, but fell to 3.11 at the Third. Consider also the changes in standard deviations, which show an increased clustering around the new averages. Social-organization deputies' s.d. fell from 15.21 at the Second to 9.13 at the Third Congress, and that of elected deputies fell from 17.22 to 11.49. The range of deputy averages shrank from 100 to 74.29 for the appointed deputies, and from 120 to 105 for those elected.
5. See table 37.
6. See table 38.

shift may be located in the coefficient system, some real political changes can be seen in the figures. The most progressive republics at the Third Congress, for instance, were Estonia and Latvia: Lithuania, the previous leader, fell to tenth place with a negative average of $-0.60$. While at first glance curious, this shift is easily explained by the decision of most Lithuanian deputies to boycott the Congress. As a result, Lithuania was represented at the Third Congress almost exclusively by non-Lithuanian minorities, a group that supported conservative positions almost without exception.[7]

Similar dynamics marked the Georgian case, where the republican mean score fell from $+8.37$ (fourth most progressive) at the Second Congress to $-0.89$ (eleventh) at the Third. The Estonian and Latvian delegations experienced some of these developments, although in a less extreme form. The shift in these two republics was less dramatic because their delegations were more heterogeneous to begin with than either their Georgian or Lithuanian counterparts, as shown by the large standard deviations of their voting averages. Although Latvia and Estonia remained generally at the cutting edge of reformism in the Third Congress, their averages thus fell far below those of the Second Congress radicals.

Among other republics with strong pro-independence movements, the Armenian delegation became more reformist at the Third Congress, with an average of $+5.34$ as compared with $+2.42$ at the Second. This shift may reflect the political decision of Armenian separatists, unlike that of their Lithuanian colleagues, to continue their struggle within the Congress and other pan-Soviet institutions. Similar conclusions apply to the Moldavian case as well.

Massive shifts occurred in the parliamentary behavior of delegations from the Slavic republics and from Moscow. These changes are illuminating in comparison with the overall Congress shift of 1.65 points leftward (from $+0.50$ to $+2.14$). Belorussian deputies, for instance, outpaced the Congress by moving a full 6.62 points leftward, from $-3.18$ to $+3.44$. The Ukraine and the RSFSR also moved to the left more quickly than did the overall Congress, by 3.30 and 2.46 points respectively. On the other hand, the Moscow average moved only 0.55, from $-1.84$ to $-1.29$, and remained on the conservative side of zero. How should we best interpret these figures? Their general import is to show a relatively more rapid shift to reformism on the periphery than at the center. The presence of senior bureaucrats of the central *nomenklatura* in the Moscow delegation accounted for its conservative bent, while the recent electoral campaign

7. Note that the Lithuanian delegation also showed the lowest standard deviation at the Congress (6.67).

likely bore much responsibility for the expansion of political participation and reformism throughout the European portion of the USSR.

The Muslim republics continued their general conservatism, but apart from Azerbaijan all nonetheless moved leftward more rapidly than the Congress average. Uzbekistan's average moved leftward by 10.42 points, and Kirghizia's by 10.11. Kazakhstan's shift of 10.67 even pushed it onto the progressive side of neutral, with an average of +2.03. Delegations from Turkmenia and Tadzhikistan changed more modestly, but still did so more dramatically than the Congress as a whole. In sum, then, the basic characteristics of republican political behavior that emerged during the First and Second Congresses continued during the Third. At the same time, significant changes appeared, particularly in the growing independence of deputies previously beholden to their republican *nomenklatura*.

The Azerbaijani delegation found itself located at the rightmost extreme of the Third Congress, according to these figures, a circumstance following from two separate causes. Conservative-reactionary forces, fearful of a repetition of the pro-independence outburst of January 1990, flatly refused to countenance any further reform. In addition, pro-independence forces moved towards extreme nationalism, and away from an alliance with reformists and radicals at the center, under the influence of the territorial conflict with Armenia over Nagorno-Karabakh. From this perspective, Azerbaijani nationalists followed a route similar to that already taken by some of their Baltic colleagues.

## Roll-Call Statistics: Social-Professional Groups

The general compression of voting averages is also visible when the data are broken down by social and professional categories. Whereas the averages of the extreme groups at the Second Congress—the intelligentsia (+11.26) and the *nomenklatura* (−9.38)—had been separated by 20.64 points, at the Third Congress the range shrank to only 11.37.[8] Technicians, moving from +5.23 to +5.62, now supplanted the intelligentsia (+5.55) as the most progressive group, while the *nomenklatura* (−5.75) remained on the right extreme. After technicians and the intelligentsia, managers remained the third most progressive group, but shifted leftward 3.38 points (−0.16 to +3.22), outpacing the overall Congress average. All other groups' means fell to the right of the Congress as a whole, but nonetheless moved leftward more rapidly than did the overall Congress—workers' average score, for example, shifted 4.48 points left.

The Congress' leftward shift, then, was caused primarily by a change

8. See tables 39 and 40.

in the behavior of its most conservative groups, which converged on the center more rapidly than did reformist groups. Notwithstanding the influence of our coefficient system, the relatively greater move on the part of conservatives toward the political center reflects the strength of popular pressure on deputies. Congress proceedings, after all, continued to be televised throughout the USSR; conservative deputies from territorial and national-territorial districts faced thousands of disgruntled constituents and hundreds of angry telegrams after the Second Congress. To explain the apparent rightward shift of the intelligentsia, on the other hand, we must remember that many of this group's most radical members, from the Baltic and other republics, had decided to boycott the Third Congress.

## Roll-Call Statistics: Speakers

The sample of deputies who spoke at the Third Congress numbers only 222, and thus is statistically less reliable than the larger group of speakers at the First or Second Congresses.[9] Nonetheless, the general criteria laid out in chapter 7 for categorizing speeches again finds a measure of vindication here, as the statistical data complement the speech analysis quite well. The forty deputies classified as radicals again showed the highest mean voting average (+15.72), followed at a distance by the forty-six left-wing independents (+9.70). At the opposite, conservative extreme fell the expected pre-*perestroika* (−5.77),[10] *apparatchik* (−5.05), and centrist (−0.87) deputies. The only apparent anomaly is the unexpectedly progressive score of the twenty-one right-wing independents, which at +4.94 fell to the left of the group of mediators (+0.17) and almost equalled the group of left-wing independents.

Keeping in mind once again the effects of the coefficient system, we need to observe relative shifts more than absolute changes when evaluating such apparent anomalies. In this case, right-wing independents as a group moved leftward by 7.16 points between the Second and Third Congresses, from −2.22 to +4.94—that is, almost five times as much as the Congress itself shifted leftward. Certain deputies may have been mistakenly categorized, but the peculiar characteristics of the group of right-wing independents discussed in chapter 15 apply here as well. In many cases, to put it simply, deputies' behavior *was* contradictory, as men and women changed their positions at the Congress from day to day and from issue to issue.

9. See table 34.
10. We should note that the "group" of pre-*perestroika* deputies at the Third Conference consisted of only one deputy.

The case of deputy V. Iakushkin (#2232 in our list) stands as an example of a possible classification error. Placed in the right-wing independent group at the Third Congress, his voting average of +13.00 puts him closer to the radicals' mean score. Furthermore, his voting average of +7.04 at the Second Congress might be taken as evidence suggesting that Iakushkin already stood somewhere between mediators and left-wing independents on the political spectrum. Deputy V. Matiukha (#1221) represents a similar case. Classified as a right-wing independent at the Second Congress, his average voting scores were high: +9.13 at the Second Congress, and a startling +21.15 at the Third. As a final example, deputy A. Chernykh (#2078) appears anomalous among right-wing independents with his averages of +11.74 and +17.69, respectively, at the Second and Third Congresses.

Many other right-wing independent deputies, however, did undergo a process of political evolution. Consider, for example, the case of N. Kondratenko (#960), a right-wing independent at the Second Congress whose voting average of −11.50 shifted to +2.50 at the Third Congress. In most cases, furthermore, our classification system does no more than faithfully record the natural variations within political groups. Deputy P. Shetko (#2147), for instance, classified as a right-wing independent at the First Congress, plainly shifted to the left, joining the group of left-wing independents at the Second Congress. The evolution in his thought can be confirmed by his voting averages of +10.24 and +10.19 at the Second and Third Congresses, respectively.

## Speeches to the Congress: Republican Delegations

Comparing table 18 with tables 16 and 17, we see clearly the stability of certain political trends isolated at the First and Second Congresses. No Central Asian made a "radical" speech, for example, and only two Central Asian republics (Kazakhstan and Uzbekistan) produced any left-wing independents. Equally plain, four of the five Central Asian republican delegations had no deputies categorized as right-wing independents. Once again, in other words, the Central Asian delegations remained largely under the control of republican Party bureaucracies.

The Azerbaijani delegation also behaved in a manner consistent with its activity at the Second Congress, producing no radical or left-wing independent speeches. The Transcaucasian group as a whole showed a slight overall increase in speech activity,[11] although it remained below the level of participation seen at the First Congress. The slight increase can

11. See tables 20 and 21.

be seen only in relative terms—the twenty-two speeches made by seventeen Transcaucasian deputies lagged behind the figures of the First and Second Congresses.[12]

The Baltic groups, on the other hand, altered their speech activity dramatically during the Third Congress.[13] The overall presence of Baltic speakers at the Congress declined, thanks in large part to Lithuanian absenteeism. As shown in table 18, neither Lithuania nor Latvia produced any radical speeches at the Third Congress, while neither Estonia nor Lithuania produced any mediator speeches. At the same time, the percentage of right-wing independent speeches among the Baltic delegations increased due to the greater weight of conservative, mostly ethnically Russian deputies.

The activity rate of the Central Asian republics, when compared with the Second Congress, declined at the Third, while that of the Slavic republics and Moldavia continued to increase. This latter group, indeed, made more than three-quarters of the Congress' speeches. In total, the Third Congress saw 231 individual speeches, and only 68 deputies who had addressed neither preceding Congress received the chance to take the podium. Over three Congresses, therefore, a total of 697 deputies had the chance to speak.

## Speeches to the Congress: Political Trends

The leftward shift of the Congress not surprisingly found expression in an increased percentage of reformist speeches relative to the Second, although not necessarily the First, Congress.[14] Radical, left-wing independent, and mediator speeches taken together comprised fully 66 percent of the speeches and 60 percent of the speakers at the Third Congress. Such a broad view, however, conceals important variations among the various reformist groups themselves. Radicals became more active at the Third Congress, but failed to reestablish the dominance of debate they had enjoyed at the First Congress. Left-wing independents gained in the percentage of speeches made, but lost ground in the number of deputies speaking. Only the group of mediators rose to new heights in both categories, revealing a new moderation among reformers.

12. This observation applies to all republics, and indeed across all types of categories, since as shown in table 20 the Third Congress was so much shorter than either of its predecessors that many fewer deputies received the opportunity to take the floor. As a result, the regional groups of speakers from the Transcaucasus, the Baltic republics, and Central Asia all remained too small for us to be confident of their representativeness.

13. See tables 20 and 21.

14. See table 19.

Centrists and particularly right-wing independents experienced similar gains, achieving their highest levels of activity at the Third Congress. *Apparatchiki*, on the other hand, were less evident in debates, falling to their level of the First Congress. Finally, the pre-*perestroika* group became almost invisible, with only one such speech being made to the Congress. This disappearance confirms the hypothesis of chapter 7 and demonstrates the growth in political maturity of the assembly. Pre-*perestroika* sentiments shrank as their adherents gradually determined that their allegiances lay with one or another of the more formal groups of either Right or Left.

### Speeches to the Congress: Social-Professional Groups

Despite the smaller size of the sample of speeches in the Third Congress compared with the first two Congresses, useful information regarding the behavior of our social-professional groups can still be extracted from it. Consider, for example, the proportion of reformist (radical, left-wing independent, or mediator) speeches among each of the groups.[15] Among the *nomenklatura* this proportion rose higher than it had in either of the first two Congresses, to 40.5 percent, although the preponderance of these speakers was classified as mediators, and indeed none were radicals. The group of cadres also reached a new high of reformist sentiment, with 63.7 percent of speeches falling into one of these three categories—a dramatic increase from the 37.5 percent at the Second Congress. Among military deputies, this proportion remained at its lowest ebb, yielding only 15.4 percent reformist speeches.

The case of the managerial group is interesting, since the proportion of reformist speeches given by managers fell continuously, from 48.9 percent at the First Congress to 44.7 percent at the Second to 30.7 percent at the Third. A possible explanation may be the intensification of economic difficulties, which could well have produced an almost reflexive conservatism among this group. The trend among managers stands in stark opposition to that among workers, who progressed from 44.7 percent progressive speeches at the First Congress to 45.7 percent at the Second to 57.8 percent at the Third. The intelligentsia and technicians, however, remained far and away the strongest in terms of reformist sentiment, and variations between Congresses in this proportion were minimal.

Different political positions dominated each of the social-professional groups we have isolated. Centrist views predominated among *nomenklatura* speakers (40.5 percent), as during the previous two Congresses. Left-

15. See tables 26–28.

wing independents (dominant at the First Congress), centrists (dominant at the Second), and centrists all shared equal proportions (27.3 percent) of cadre speakers. As in the First Congress—*apparatchiki* had prevailed in the Second Congress—right-wing independents enjoyed a plurality (38.5 percent) among military deputies. Managers remained divided: after left-wing independents gained the largest fraction of support at the First Congress, centrists held a narrow edge at both the Second and Third (29.6 percent) Congresses. As at the first two Congresses, left-wing independents predominated among the intelligentsia (34.2 percent) and technicians (28.2 percent). Workers' loyalties were more unstable: from a left-wing independent advantage at the First Congress to a mediator-*apparatchik* split at the Second, radicals seized the edge at the Third.

## Speeches to the Congress: Changes in Political Groups

We must now consider the relative stability of the political groups here discussed, taking into account the shifts between the First, Second, and Third Congresses.[16] Upon examination, it becomes plain that political stability and cohesion were increasing by the Third Congress, as changes between the Second and Third Congresses were less dramatic than those between the First and Second. This increasing stability may in part be misleading, insofar as it results from the shorter interval between the Second and Third Congresses. At the same time, however, it likely reflects the rapid growth of political sophistication and experience on the part of the deputies.

Considering the percentages on the main diagonal of table 42, we can see that all have increased from those of the diagonal of table 41. Hence, the number of repeating speakers maintaining their political positions in the Third Congress increased across the political spectrum, and dispersion of speakers from the Second Congress into other groups decreased. (It should be recalled that small sample sizes here require caution when inferring anything more than an apparent stabilization.) Nearly 90 percent of radical speakers who spoke again, for example, maintained their affiliation. Only three previous radicals spoke for another group (two for the group of right-wing independents), and the six new radicals with previous affiliations had all been drawn from the comparatively sympathetic groups of left-wing independents and mediators. Left-wing independents as a group—insofar as they may be discussed as such—also enjoyed growing stability. *Apparatchiki* maintained more than half of their number in the Third Congress; the earlier pre-*perestroika* group dispersed entirely.

16. See tables 42 and 43.

Comparing positional changes over the longer period between the First and Third Congresses (June 1989 to March 1990), on the other hand, yields a picture midway between the maximum fluidity of the First-Second Congress shifts and the maximum stability of the Second-Third Congress period. That is, after the violent shock of December 1989 induced widespread political conversions among deputies, political groups coalesced at a more gradual, deliberate pace. Two other details, however, may be worth noting. First, all of the First Congress' right-wing independents who spoke again remained with that group at the Third Congress, although five new members from the reformist groups were added.[17] Second, left-wing independents must be judged the most unstable of all political groups.

## The Behavior of Well-Known Deputies

The last task of this chapter is an examination of the absolute and relative positions at the Third Congress of some of the best-known deputies. Table 46 shows the behaviors of fifty such men and women, drawing figures from all of the major political groups. Almost all those listed held important positions in national politics, and therefore more information is available on their political views than what is implied by their actions in Congress alone.[18]

A variety of observations may be made. Take, for example, the views of Mikhail Gorbachev. In the analysis given in preceding chapters, Gorbachev has been placed among the reformers, and specifically within the group of mediators. Our analysis is not flawed, and this is indeed the proper place for the CPSU general secretary. But why, then, did Gorbachev vote at the Second (and Third, albeit less totally) Congress as the most rabid of conservatives? His voting behavior, indeed, paralleled that of deputy S. Umalatova, who later requested a formal vote of no confidence in his leadership at the Fourth Congress of December 1990. The

17. As noted above, however, this result is weakened by an examination of specific voting averages. Deputy V. Voskoboinikov (#395), for example, counted as a right-wing independent at the First Congress and continued to hold a highly progressive voting average of over +40 at the Second Congress. At the Third Congress, although moderating his views, Voskoboinikov remained far to the left of the right-wing independent mean, with a score of +17.38. The case of deputy B. Dadamian (#549) is similar. Deputy L. Sukhov (#1851), on the other hand, showed an entirely different voting pattern. Categorized as a left-wing independent at the First Congress, he voted conservatively at the Second, with an average of −3.08. At the Third Congress, however, Sukhov shifted again back to a radical stance, with an average of +14.58.

18. The list for the Second Congress contains exactly 50 names. The Third Congress list contains the same names, although Boris Yeltsin did not vote in any of its roll-call votes.

need to explain this apparent anomaly becomes even more pressing when we realize that Gorbachev voted in a manner more conservative than General B. Gromov, Colonels N. Petrushenko and Viktor Alksnis, and even slightly to the right of his rival Egor Ligachev.

A logical political explanation does in fact exist for this apparent inconsistency, an explanation that follows from the discussion of Gorbachev's tactics presented in chapter 10. In Congress debates the Soviet president often acted shrewdly to create a balance, using both right-wing uncertainty and left-wing naiveté for his own purposes. The radical Left served conveniently to restrain conservatives, just as reactionary outbursts could be utilized to counteract overly strong reformist pressure. At the same time, though, Gorbachev knew that deputies took note of his votes as recorded in the official *Bulletin*. He also knew that the large majority of the Congress held conservative, even reactionary views. One imprudent vote might ruin his chances of success in the delicate balancing act of neutralizing the conservatives while at the same time not ceding outright power to radicals.

Gorbachev's actions, then, appeared conditioned by the need he perceived not to lose contact with conservative groups, lest he endanger his ability to "guide" the Congress. The Soviet leader's own personal sympathies, of course, may be debated, and perhaps they were more right-wing than has been argued here. The possibility that his voting record accurately reflected his views, however, should not be accepted too easily, and his behavior seems more likely to have followed from his own unique position as general secretary and president. Indeed, Gorbachev's voting record placed him among the most reactionary of Soviet deputies— to the right of General Albert Makashov at both the Second and Third Congresses, and to the right of the mean score of both centrists ($-8.31$) and *apparatchiki* ($-10.44$). This record cannot but have resulted from the tactical requirements he perceived of his political battle.

At the conservative end of the political spectrum, too, other deputies categorized as mediators also voted in an ultrareactionary manner. Iurii Golik and the first secretary of the Odessa *obkom*, G. Kriuchkov, are two examples. These apparent discrepancies, however, do not necessarily imply a flaw in our classification system. More likely, they indicate the political "team play" of many mediators, who felt obliged to support Gorbachev. Such a motive was particularly plain, for instance, in the behavior of "mediator" Aleksandr Iakovlev at the Second Congress. Without doubt his political views can be called progressive, yet he voted well to the right of the Congress average, and well to the right of the mediators' group average as well.

The case of Roi Medvedev is equally interesting. A mediator at the

First Congress, Medvedev continued to hold a clearly progressive position at the Second Congress, where indeed his voting average fell to the left of the mediators' group mean. At the Third Congress, however, he supported ultraconservative positions and showed an average of $-16.92$, far to the right of Gorbachev himself. Medvedev's Third Congress average placed him in the company of conservatives Gennadi Ianaev—the future Soviet vice president and "coup plotter" of August 1991—and Anatolii Lukianov. In Medvedev's case the shift rightward cannot be seen as purely tactical, but rather as reflective of his own political evolution. In subsequent months, indeed, he held increasingly conservative positions, to the point of supporting Nikolai Ryzhkov against Boris Yeltsin for the presidency of the RSFSR.

Many other interesting points could be made by considering this table carefully, but overall the picture shows the clear evolution of views on the part of deputies whose political classifications cannot be doubted. Radical P. Bunich, for instance, took left-radical positions at the Second Congress but then changed to support the extreme right at the Third. Furthermore, at the Third Congress Bunich's voting average of $-10.00$ placed him squarely in the middle of a fascinatingly heterogeneous group: Leningrad Party first secretary Boris Gidaspov, a right-wing independent at the Second Congress and *apparatchik* at the Third; *apparatchik* Egor Ligachev; Gorbachev advisor Anatolii Cherniaev, who although not a speaker at the Congress should be considered a mediator; mediator *par excellence* Fedor Burlatskii; and Gorbachev's moderate conservative military advisor Marshal S. Akhromeev, who spoke as a centrist at all Congresses. The future CPSU deputy general secretary, V. Ivashko (an *apparatchik* at the Second Congress and a centrist at the Third), on the other hand, supported moderate positions throughout the Congress and showed a more progressive voting average than the three well-known mediators Gorbachev, Cherniaev, and Volskii (the prefect of Nagorno-Karabakh).

Such peculiarities of voting averages on the Right should not surprise the reader, considering the heterogeneous nature of issues facing the Third Congress. The Congress had to deal with a variety of new challenges: political reform, interethnic feuds, and republican relations, in addition to the creation of new civil rights laws and state structures to guarantee a division of powers. The traditional reliance upon Marxist-Leninist doctrine no longer served as a guide to action, and deputies reacted to these challenges in unpredictable ways.

Deputy behavior on the Left was in general less contradictory and more predictable. Boris Yeltsin's average ranked among the Congress' most radical, even exceeding that of Sergei Stankevich, deputy mayor of Moscow, and Nikolai Travkin, future leader of the Democratic Party. Progressive leaders S. Belozertsev, Galina Starovoitova, and Iurii Afanasev all showed voting averages higher than the radical mean score. Leningrad mayor Anatolii Sobchak, also a reformer, took positions noticeably more moderate than the radical or left-wing independent averages.

On the Left, too, we find some of the well-known right-wing independents mentioned above. E. Kogan, for example, at the Second Congress had shown an average slightly more progressive than the *left*-wing independents' mean score. Colonel Viktor Alksnis appeared at the Third Congress as a reformer, together with V. Iarin and Colonel N. Petrushenko. Such groupings may appear anomalous with respect to the voting averages' linear representation of "left" and "right," but they in fact show some of the diversity that would be visible if the three-dimensional approach suggested in chapter 8 had been applied to the voting statistics.

# Reflections and
# Provisional Conclusions

This book concludes with the (not unexpected) demise of its subject, the Congress of People's Deputies. During the first days of September 1991, the Soviet Union's first democratic parliament essentially decreed its own suicide. The astute actions of the now-defeated Mikhail Gorbachev, however, forestalled the violence that might have accompanied this event. The Congress resisted as long as possible, but by September only about 1,800 deputies remained—more than 400 had been swept away by political events in the republics and refused to participate—that is, to assert the Congress' sovereignty.

Despite all the limitations set out in preceding chapters, the elections of spring 1989 represented an extraordinary leap forward in the Soviet Union's ongoing democratization. The parliament that emerged, although by 1991 already a dinosaur, had attempted to do the impossible: namely, to reform Soviet communism. At the same time, this parliament witnessed a complex, largely hidden struggle among at least three opposing forces: Gorbachev, his conservative adversaries, and emerging democratic public opinion. Each of these forces pursued its own objectives at the Congress, allying with others only when it seemed necessary to do so.

In the end, however, conservative bureaucracies suffered the greatest defeat. In much of the USSR they emerged decimated by the electoral campaign, despite—or perhaps because of—their misguided confidence that the dangers of popular political involvement could be limited. At least initially, this confidence did seem justified, as a variety of precautionary laws (for example, those regarding the POSs) secured a solid conservative majority at the Congress. This short-term victory, however, proved ultimately fatal by persuading conservatives that they could withstand mounting popular pressures for reform indefinitely. Hence they failed to grasp the reality that the Communist Party at this time missed its last chance to participate in an inevitable, thoroughgoing social transformation.

Such was Gorbachev's gamble. As president and general secretary, he continually delayed implementing democratic and market reforms in the hope that the Party would catch up with his ideas, thereby rescuing itself. As a result, Gorbachev himself, caught in the middle, paid the unavoidable political price of postponing change in the face of popular pressure. Yet at the same time government and Party bureaucracies remained resistant and slow to change—a ruling class that failed to realize the futility of resisting change. Having learned nothing from recent events, these bureaucracies continued to oppose all types of reform, failing even to devise workable tactics to delay or minimize them. Orthodox Communists had become the high priests of a religion they no longer understood, and failed even on their own terms—not recalling the most elementary of Marx's lessons, namely that at a certain point developing productive forces irresistibly overwhelm established productive relationships.

In Marxist terms, this is what transpired in the Soviet Union seventy-four years after the October Revolution. The evolution that Gorbachev had hoped to lead became transformed into a revolution. In one of the many ironies of the Soviet situation, though, Gorbachev—the Louis XVI of the second Soviet revolution—was not yet shunted aside. His role was to sign the death certificate of the first stage of change—the stage which he himself had begun—and to determine the birth date of next phase, the phase which now has only begun in the former Soviet Union. Only then, in December 1991, did he resign. To many in the West, Gorbachev had appeared a leader of virtually limitless power; yet as the Marquis de Custine wrote one and a half centuries ago, "One must go to Russia to understand what cannot be done by the person who can do anything." Gorbachev realized the need to "restore politics to the people," but those around him failed to share this realization.

Historian Iurii Afanasev contemptuously dismissed the Congress deputies who surrendered at Gorbachev's behest on 5 September 1991 as formerly, at the First Congress, "aggressive and subordinate," but as having now lost their "bellicose aggressiveness." The only property these deputies still possessed was their "supine subordination" to the leader, a characteristic that followed from their position as *apparatchiki*. They could have defeated Gorbachev in the Congress, using his own democratic institution. What the so-called "Emergency Committee" tried to accomplish during its three-day *coup d'état* of August 1991 could have been achieved strictly legally. Outside the Congress hall, however, in the streets of Moscow and throughout the country, popular sentiment remained implacably hostile to such a move, as became clear during the failed *coup* of August.

Hence, Gorbachev's opponents never dared to force such extreme measures in the Congress.

The *coup* of 19 August changed, but did not obliterate, the course of development we have dubbed "transition to democracy." The *coup*, in fact, abruptly pushed events forward towards the "conflagration" discussed in chapter 13. To return to our interpretative model, we might say that all the major actors in the drama of August 1991—Gorbachev, the conspirators, Boris Yeltsin and other radicals—behaved as though imprisoned in a two-dimensional geometry, trying to find a solution to the Soviet crisis by working within the old, accepted system. The perceived possibilities—Gorbachev's first model of democratization, the Right's explicit restoration of authoritarianism, or even the Left's radical transformation to a rule-of-law, market-based democracy—all sprang from the Western political culture of the last three centuries.

No such easily visible solution based on Western antecedents, however, ever existed as a real possibility for Soviet development. All three models ignored the likelihood of a total breakup of the Soviet state-empire. The Soviet Union spanned the Eurasian landmass and contained peoples at vastly different levels of development, peoples who had been held together by force alone. The failure of August 1991's attempted restoration made this breakup inevitable. Total disintegration—of the USSR and the RSFSR within it—and civil war might still have been avoided after August, but only if an entirely different solution could have been found. As suggested in chapter 8, specifically, the "third dimension" of nationality had to be factored in to any possible solution; the tragedy of the Soviet crisis lay in the failure of all sides to appreciate its multidimensional nature.

Even without the *coup d'état*, however, the entire Soviet state-institutional edifice that had been erected since 1989 was destined to collapse, most likely quickly, and certainly within a year. The agreement signed by nine of the fifteen republics at Novo Ogarevo on 23 April 1991 marked the end of a transitional phase. This pact mandated a new Constitution; it thereby signified the loss of the Congress' legitimacy once state and territorial boundaries shifted with the creation of a new "Federation of Sovereign States." Deputies elected in republics not signatories to the pact could no longer be considered "Soviet" representatives, and the Congress—with its underpinnings removed at Novo Ogarevo—no longer reflected the new division of power, role, and function between the center and the republics.

The electoral system that had reserved one-third (750) of all seats to the social organizations had been abandoned by nearly all republics, to be superseded by a more directly representative approach. The two-tiered structure of the Congress and Supreme Soviet, with its cumbersome 2,250-member parliament and no real division of powers, was swept away along with most of the political figures who had emerged in the elections of 1989. By the middle of 1991, with or without a *coup d'état*, the Congress of People's Deputies had become an historical relic.

Looking back on the Congress after the demise of the Soviet Union itself, however, we can see its importance in an essential transitional stage, the stage in which the formal vestiges of a one-party system faced the realities of a *de facto* multiparty democracy. True democracy cannot be created by fiat, but rests on the weight of accumulated experience and requires the presence of certain psychological and objective conditions characteristic of a relatively developed, civilized society. Virtually none of these elements existed in the Soviet Union of 1989; all could develop only gradually, and at greatly differing rates in the different national communities that comprised the Soviet state.

This development of the social preconditions for democracy, however, proceeded much more rapidly than it had in other Western, particularly European, democracies. Despite apparent backwardness in many areas, Soviet society showed great democratic vitality and promise. The ideological burden of Marxism-Leninism that had paralyzed intellectual life for a time concealed, but did not altogether prevent, various characteristics typical of developed, urbanized, industrial society from emerging. Once freed to influence public life, these characteristics created a Pandora's box of energies, some creative and some destructive. The shape of the new society that will emerge from today's tumult depends on the outcome of the struggle among these energies.

The development of real pluralism will no doubt encounter difficulties stemming from the former USSR's specific historical, political, and social conditions. The abolition of the Communist Party, paradoxically, may only deepen these troubles and hinder the emergence of pluralism. The birth and development of political parties, that is, requires not only competing social interests, but also a public awareness of their existence, an identification of the social forces that they express, and proper institutional and political conditions for them to organize.

Some of these conditions already exist, while others are still developing. The illusion of social homogeneity is disappearing, but disruption is possible when market mechanisms take effect on a large scale. For the forseeable future, ideology and egalitarian economic structures will continue to distort reality. Nevertheless, the society formerly known as "Soviet" has irrevocably set out towards political diversification and multiparty pluralism. In doing so it replicates only partially the experience of other countries. Some of the concepts sketched here in the first few chapters may prove useful in understanding the perhaps unique Soviet road to democracy.

One such concept is that of the Communist multiparty system. By mid-1991—just before the August *coup*—this system had become established to differing degrees in several republics. A second Communist Party, independent of Moscow, had appeared in all three Baltic republics in late 1989 and early 1990, following the split of the CPSU along republican lines. The birth of the Russian Communist Party in July 1990, explicitly directed against Gorbachev's continued leadership of the CPSU, was followed a year later by the formation in Russia of the Party of Democratic Communists, a group which supported Russian vice president Aleksandr Rutskoi. Furthermore, Communist leaders of several other republics began to express their desire to separate from the CPSU. The formation of the Communist multiparty system, then, proceeded simultaneously along two lines. The first saw the CPSU itself fragment along republican lines, and saw Moscow increasingly lose control of lower-level Party organizations. The second witnessed the division of these republican and lower-level organizations into groups of independent reformers and centralist conservatives.

The *coup d'état* of August 1991 only catalyzed these processes, causing them to accelerate dramatically. Yeltsin suspended the activities of the CPSU throughout the RSFSR and nationalized its property; Gorbachev cast off his post of general secretary and suggested that the Central Committee dissolve itself. Both actions helped bring about the total collapse of the Party's central structures. One after another, republican Communist Parties quickly declared complete independence from the now defunct CPSU. In some cases, these republican parties retained the name "Communist," while in others (such as in Kazakhstan and Azerbaijan) they adopted the new title of "Socialist."

Despite such outward signs, though, it remained clear that many of these changes represented nothing more than a cynical attempt on the part of local Communist bureaucracies to retain Party property and maintain old power structures. Although the process continues as of this writing, many Communist Parties—under whatever name—plainly continue to exist and to wield great influence over political life in certain republics. In areas such as Lithuania, moreover, where the Communist Party has been banned by legal decree, it will likely revive under another name, if only as a defender of national minorities.

The second main vector of political development, at least for the present, will continue to be expressed by the popular fronts. The formation of these groups preceded the breakup of the CPSU, and began in the Baltic republics in 1988. The popular fronts represented essentially the first legal, organized opposition to the Communist Party since the 1920s, and they spread (with varying degrees of success) to all of the Soviet republics and the largest autonomous republics. The fronts won important victories in the republican elections of 1990, gaining majorities in the Baltic republics, Georgia, and Armenia, and securing positions of influence in Russia, the Ukraine, Belorussia, and Moldavia. We have already seen how local *nomenklaturas* retained control in Central Asia and Azerbaijan, due in part to the relative cultural and political backwardness of those areas.

The eclectic groupings known as popular fronts were needed to direct the common struggle against perceived central oppression. The failure of the center and the CPSU, in turn—the efforts of which paradoxically only further unified republican separatists—inevitably led to the breakdown of the popular fronts themselves into their constituent parts of opposed social and political groups. The fronts' conquest of power allowed them to begin to carry out economic reform. In addition to marking their new-found independence, though, this power also marked the beginning of the end for these broad alliances.

Once again the Baltic region foreshadowed later developments, which occurred on a gradient running from west to east. Already by mid-1990 Estonia had twenty-five (mostly small, even miniscule) political parties of record. In Georgia and Armenia, the proliferation of political parties was accompanied by the establishment of nationalist movements that, broader and larger in scope, paralleled the popular fronts. In Russia developments took a somewhat different course, although still following the same basic pattern. The birth of "Democratic Russia" on 21 October 1990 marked the establishment of a Russian analogue to the popular fronts. This "front" as elsewhere amounted to a collection of nascent political parties: the Constitutional Democrats, the Republicans, the Social Democrats, the Christian Democrats, and fifty other, lesser-known groups drawn from throughout the RSFSR. Democratic Russia spearheaded the electoral group that supported Yeltsin during the struggles of autumn 1990 and spring 1991, leading up to the signing of the Novo Ogarevo Pact and Yeltsin's victory in the race for the Russian presidency on 12 June 1991.

The strength of Democratic Russia, however, remained much greater as a loose bloc than as the sum of its parts. At the end of summer 1991, that is, the Republican Party possessed roughly 4,000 members, while the Social Democrats numbered barely 2,000. The only party with a noticeable organizational foundation was Nikolai Travkin's 36,000-member Democratic Party, and even here successes were modest. Democratic Russia as a whole, though, made progress by committing itself wholeheartedly against the CPSU and for Yeltsin, and by playing the card of Russian sovereignty against the USSR. Like other popular fronts, it expressed disdain if not open hostility toward any unitary state. Russian reformers, then, threw in their lot with the forces of fragmentation, while conservatives increasingly became associated with centralist policies.

Gorbachev had been forced to seek support from conservatives in order to protect his own goal of democratizing the old, unitary USSR, and therefore found an ever-increasing gulf between himself and radical reformers. His strategy, though, did seem to achieve a measure of success in March 1991, when a referendum on the future of the USSR showed majority support, particularly in Russia, for retaining a unitary, albeit altered, Soviet structure. Plainly, many "yes" votes in this referendum had been cast by democratic reformers.

Yeltsin himself, while linking his own proposal for a directly elected Russian presidency to Gorbachev's conservative referendum, still openly recognized the need to preserve a "center"—even one, as he said, that would be "this small." The Novo Ogarevo process and subsequent agreement, however, signified the substantive end to the cooperation between Russia and Gorbachev's own center. Yeltsin attained an important victory, but nonetheless embarked on a program of "minimal reconstruction," meaning the creation of a "9 + 1" federation that would recognize Baltic independence and allow a partial withdrawal of Armenia, Moldavia, and Georgia.

At this point, the latent divisions within Democratic Russia began to emerge. One current of opinion that favored reconstructing a new "Union of Sovereign Republics" had long been visible. Now the equally important group on the other side of the issue, led by historian Iurii Afanasev, emerged as well. On the eve of the *coup* of 19 August 1991, he and a group of radicals published an appeal that criticized Yeltsin for allegedly giving in to Gorbachev's overly centralist approach.

During the summer, at the height of the CPSU crisis, another attempt to create an organizational base to underlie a "pan-Soviet reconstruction" appeared within the reformist camp. The Democratic Reform Movement, supported by Eduard Shevardnadze and Aleksandr Iakovlev, named itself the mouthpiece of all democratic and progressive forces, including those still trapped within the CPSU. Shevardnadze's movement clearly saw itself in many ways as constituting an alternative both to the CPSU and to Democratic Russia. Its purpose, however, was different, and in some ways more ambitious. The Democratic Reform Movement set itself the goal not only of unifying Russian pro-democracy forces, but also of operating throughout the territories of the nine republics that had signed the Novo Ogarevo Pact. When the name of Aleksandr Rutskoi, the Russian vice president, also appeared on the list of this movement's supporters, it seemed obvious to many that Boris Yeltsin implicitly supported this approach.

Shevardnadze and Iakovlev shared an assumption not held by Democratic Russia. They both expressed the third tendency discussed in this book's opening chapters, namely the establishment of pan-Soviet parties, this time with much greater consistency of ambition and outlook than found in Travkin's Democratic Party. Their movement foresaw a transitional period in which it would need to compete with the declining CPSU, gradually whittling away the Communist electoral base by allying with democratic forces in each republic and in the renewed Soviet parliament. By doing so, Shevardnadze and Iakovlev hoped to force the CPSU into opposition.

Gorbachev now held an ambiguous, although not necessarily hostile, position. By preserving his Party position, he hoped to force the extreme reactionaries out and thereby to save a "purified" CPSU. At the same time, though, he kept the option open of himself breaking with the Left, should these reactionaries prove to be a majority.

This was the situation on the eve of 20 August 1991, the day on which the new Union Treaty was to have been signed. The *coup* that intervened instead and its ignominious defeat, however, jarred this equilibrium and forced developments to proceed at a radically accelerated pace. Centrifugal forces found themselves abruptly strengthened, not least because a new Russia—democratic instead of Communist—emerged as a possible center. Those republics led by ex-Communist *nomenklaturas* feared a re-aggregation of the old USSR for this very reason, not to mention the simple fact that Russia remained too strong not to arouse fears that its "imperialist" tendencies would reappear in any reconstituted Union. Yeltsin's revolution added to such fears with a stream of decrees that demolished the old center's power only to reestablish it in Russian hands.

Hence a wave of independence declarations followed the defeat of the Emergency Committee. The Pact of Novo Ogarevo faced unforeseen obsolesence, as it no longer represented a compromise acceptable to eight smaller republics and gigantic Russia. When the Fifth Congress ratified the termination of the Soviet Union's existence, then, no one knew what would take its place. A transitional period had begun, one with a duration impossible to predict. At the last minute, a temporary lowest common denominator was reached by the ten republican presidents and Gorbachev to avoid the total collapse of the USSR. The Council of State, ratified by the Congress, comprised a directorate of equals—all of whom, except Soviet president Gorbachev, enjoyed a veto—and it is with this Council that this book closes.

If these eleven men preserved order and established a series of ground rules, they could conceivably have created a viable new structure. The situation, though, would be unprecedented in the modern era: a state allowing different forms of association to its members, in a manner reminiscent of the old Holy Roman Empire or Habsburg Monarchy. Full members need to cede power to the central organization, however, which makes it difficult to imagine anything more than a transitory, *sui generis* confederation—the Commonwealth of Independent States—marking this period of development. The existence of any supranational parliament with lawmaking authority is very doubtful, as is the formulation of any universally binding constitution. Clearly the bicameral Supreme Soviet ratified by the Fifth Congress could not function as a true pan-Soviet parliament, if only because every republican delegation possessed what amounted to a veto.

Even looser forms of association are required in this fragile confederation for those republics which shun all political integration and concede only the need to remain in a common economic space. Possibly—or rather probably—the confederation and its constituent republics will both adopt their own currencies, distinct from the old ruble. Finally, certain republics such as the Baltics which have already achieved full, internationally recognized independence, will continue to refuse political participation in the Commonwealth and will accept only a small and continually shrinking economic role. Such republics will agree only to negotiations that codify their formal withdrawal from all formerly Soviet organizations and structures.

The possibility of a differentiated confederation, such as it is, remains the best hope for the former Soviet Union's future in the medium term. Other outcomes, however, are at least as likely. Enormous numbers of people now act as autonomous, uncontrollable forces in a variety of newly freed nations. A collective stand is needed: parliaments must be renewed, since the August *coup* cancelled previous legitimate authority. First the Council of State, and then the Commonwealth, have been threatened by powerful separatist sentiments. Even though the center is no longer Communist—even though the center, for all practical purposes, no longer exists—inertial and inherited hatred for the Communist center continues to inundate the successors to the old Soviet central government. The legacy of oppression is too great and runs too deep to be forgotten or overcome. Much more time would be needed fully to neutralize this legacy with the experience of a balanced, democratic, pluralist political culture.

An appalling economic crisis, a maze of ethnic conflicts, innumerable territorial disputes, and immense social disequilibrium stand in the way of any peaceful, consensual, unified solution to the current crisis in the new Commonwealth of Independent States. If efforts to create unity among the disparate peoples of the former Soviet Union fail, though, the specter of another, much deadlier Yugoslav crisis looms on the horizon.

# Figures and Tables

*Figure 1.* Voting Positions

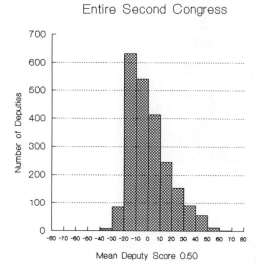

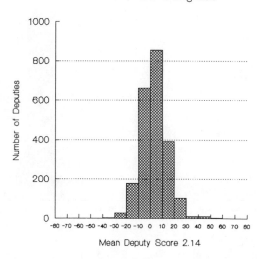

*Figure 2.* Voting Positions by Means of Election

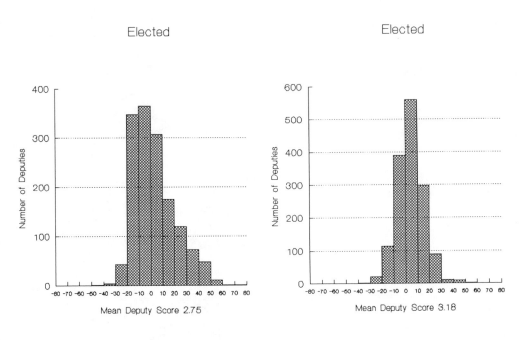

SECOND CONGRESS

Elected

Number of Deputies

Mean Deputy Score 2.75

THIRD CONGRESS

Elected

Number of Deputies

Mean Deputy Score 3.18

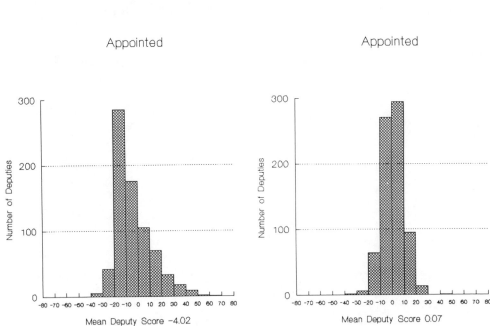

Appointed

Number of Deputies

Mean Deputy Score −4.02

Appointed

Number of Deputies

Mean Deputy Score 0.07

*Figure 3.* Voting Positions by Republic

SECOND CONGRESS

THIRD CONGRESS

Armenia

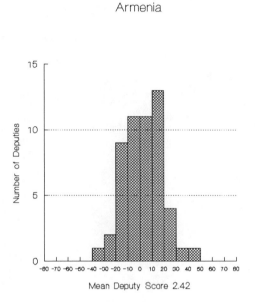

Mean Deputy Score 2.42

Armenia

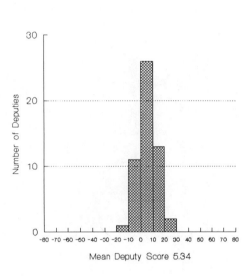

Mean Deputy Score 5.34

Azerbaijan

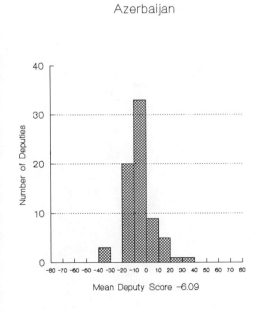

Mean Deputy Score −6.09

Azerbaijan

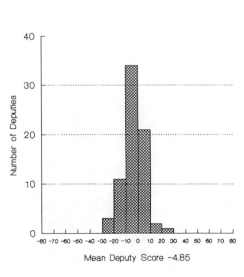

Mean Deputy Score −4.85

213

*Figure 3.* Voting Positions by Republic *(continued)*

SECOND CONGRESS

THIRD CONGRESS

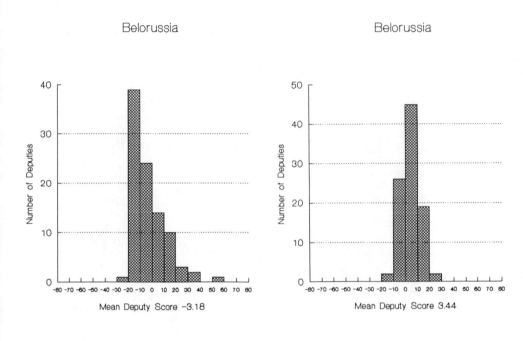

Belorussia

Belorussia

Mean Deputy Score −3.18

Mean Deputy Score 3.44

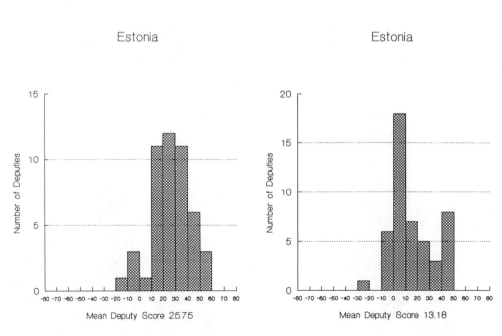

Estonia

Estonia

Mean Deputy Score 25.75

Mean Deputy Score 13.18

*Figure 3.* Voting Positions by Republic *(continued)*

SECOND CONGRESS

THIRD CONGRESS

Georgia

Georgia

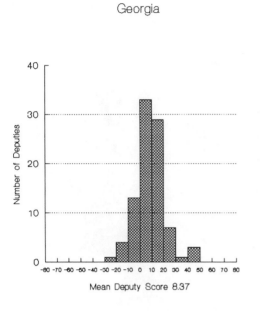

Mean Deputy Score 8.37

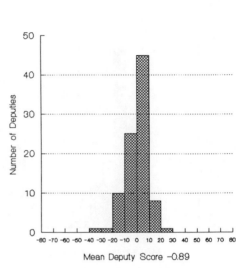

Mean Deputy Score −0.89

Kazakhstan

Kazakhstan

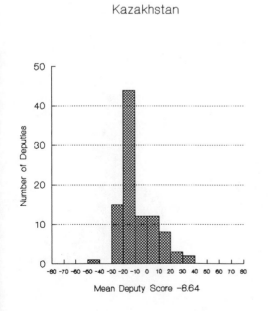

Mean Deputy Score −8.64

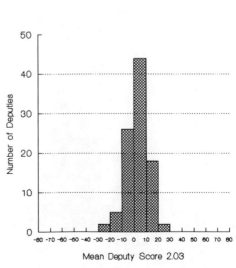

Mean Deputy Score 2.03

*Figure 3.* Voting Positions by Republic *(continued)*

SECOND  CONGRESS

THIRD  CONGRESS

Kirghizia

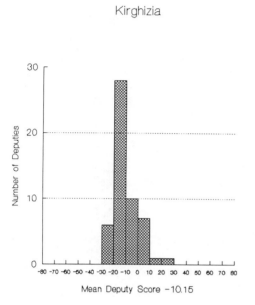

Mean Deputy Score −10.15

Kirghizia

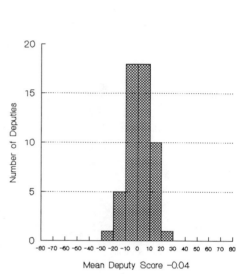

Mean Deputy Score −0.04

Latvia

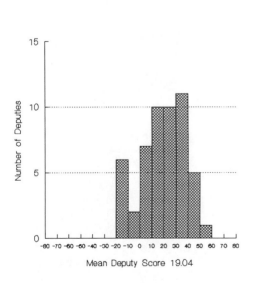

Mean Deputy Score 19.04

Latvia

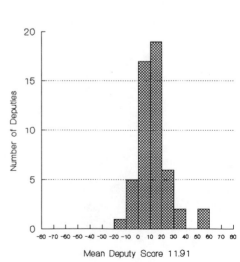

Mean Deputy Score 11.91

*Figure 3.* Voting Positions by Republic *(continued)*

SECOND   CONGRESS

THIRD   CONGRESS

Lithuania

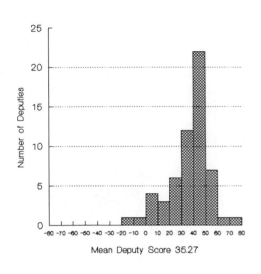

Mean Deputy Score 35.27

Lithuania

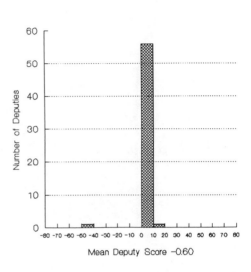

Mean Deputy Score −0.60

Moldavia

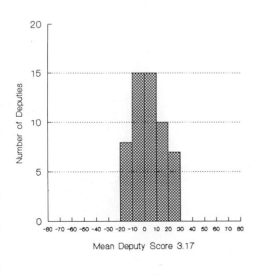

Mean Deputy Score 3.17

Moldavia

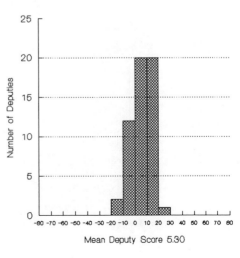

Mean Deputy Score 5.30

*Figure 3.* Voting Positions by Republic *(continued)*

SECOND CONGRESS

THIRD CONGRESS

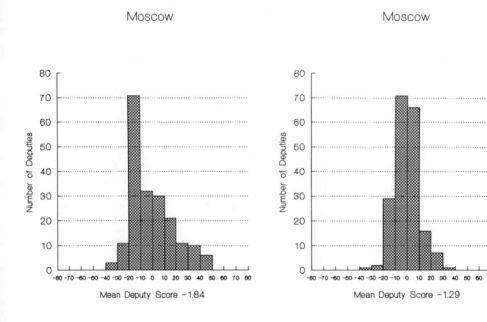

Moscow

Mean Deputy Score −1.84

Moscow

Mean Deputy Score −1.29

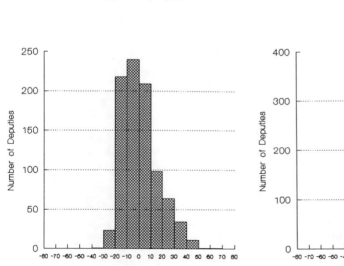

Russian SFSR

Mean Deputy Score 0.93

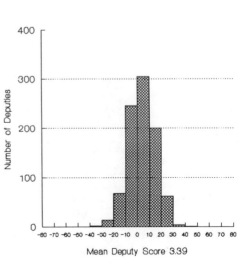

Russian SFSR

Mean Deputy Score 3.39

*Figure 3.* Voting Positions by Republic *(continued)*

SECOND CONGRESS

THIRD CONGRESS

Tadzhikistan

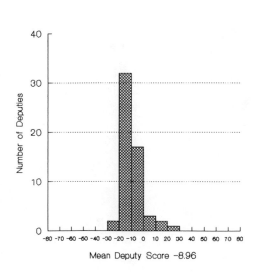

Mean Deputy Score −8.96

Tadzhikistan

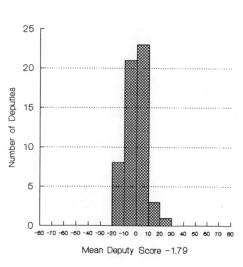

Mean Deputy Score −1.79

Turkmenia

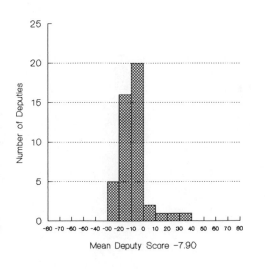

Mean Deputy Score −7.90

Turkmenia

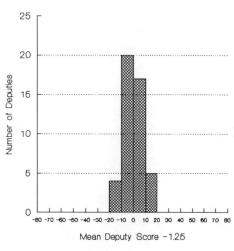

Mean Deputy Score −1.25

## *Figure 3.* Voting Positions by Republic *(continued)*

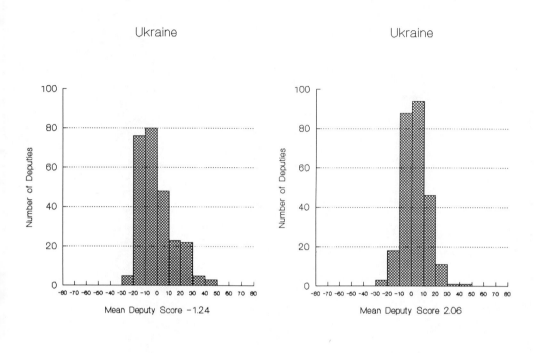

SECOND CONGRESS

THIRD CONGRESS

Ukraine

Ukraine

Mean Deputy Score −1.24

Mean Deputy Score 2.06

Uzbekistan

Uzbekistan

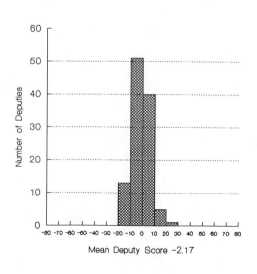

Mean Deputy Score −12.59

Mean Deputy Score −2.17

*Figure 4.* Voting Positions by Social Position

SECOND CONGRESS

THIRD CONGRESS

Nomenklatura

Nomenklatura

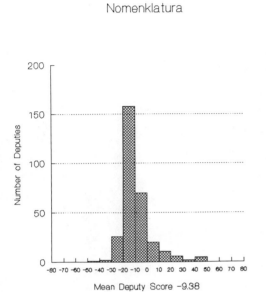

Mean Deputy Score −9.38

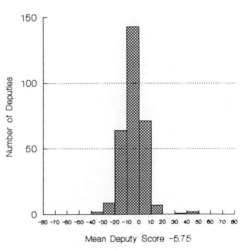

Mean Deputy Score −5.75

Cadres

Cadres

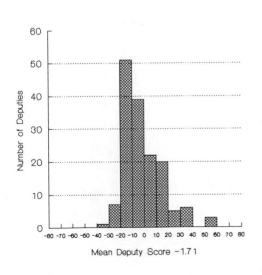

Mean Deputy Score −1.71

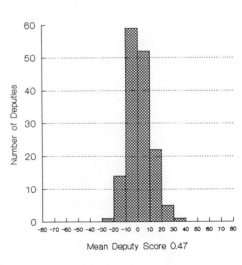

Mean Deputy Score 0.47

221

*Figure 4.* Voting Positions by Social Position *(continued)*

SECOND CONGRESS                    THIRD CONGRESS

Military                                   Military

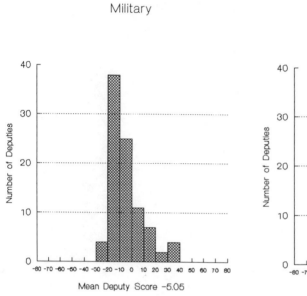
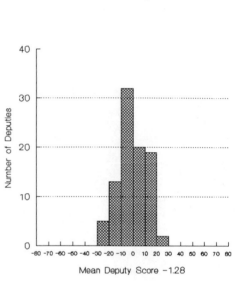

Managers                                   Managers

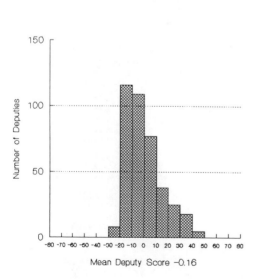
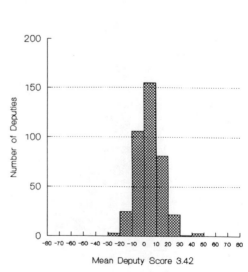

*Figure 4.* Voting Positions by Social Position *(continued)*

Intelligentsia

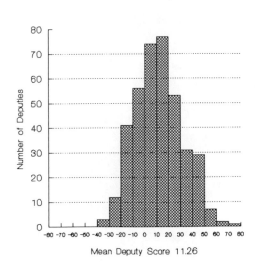

Mean Deputy Score 11.26

Intelligentsia

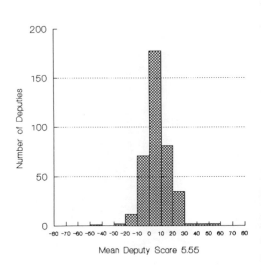

Mean Deputy Score 5.55

Technicians

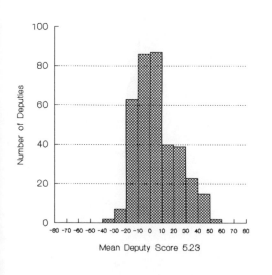

Mean Deputy Score 5.23

Technicians

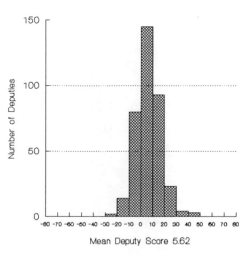

Mean Deputy Score 5.62

*Figure 4.* Voting Positions by Social Position *(continued)*

SECOND CONGRESS

THIRD CONGRESS

Workers

Workers

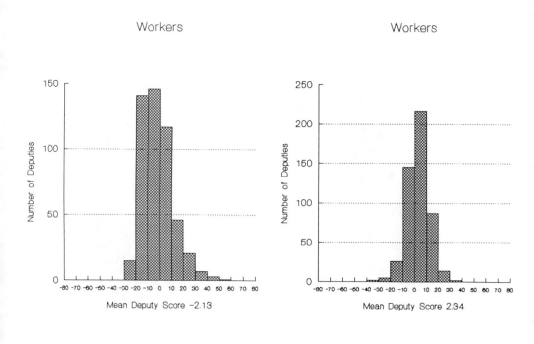

Mean Deputy Score −2.13

Mean Deputy Score 2.34

Other Social Groups

Other Social Groups

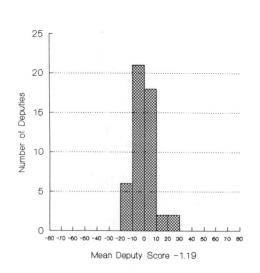
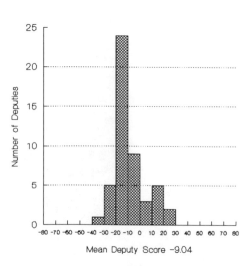

Mean Deputy Score −1.19

Mean Deputy Score −9.04

*Figure 5.* Voting Positions by Political Affiliation

SECOND CONGRESS

THIRD CONGRESS

Radicals

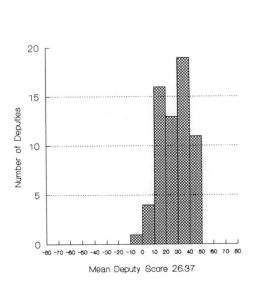

Mean Deputy Score 26.37

Radicals

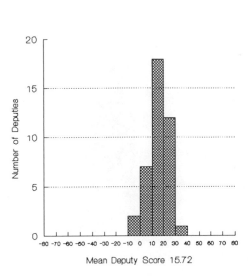

Mean Deputy Score 15.72

Left-wing Independents

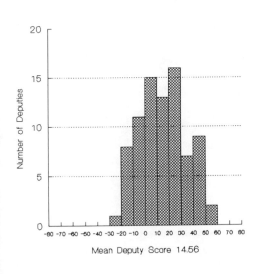

Mean Deputy Score 14.56

Left-wing Independents

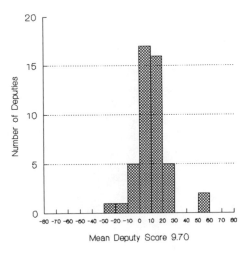

Mean Deputy Score 9.70

225

*Figure 5.* Voting Positions by Political Affiliation *(continued)*

SECOND CONGRESS                    THIRD CONGRESS

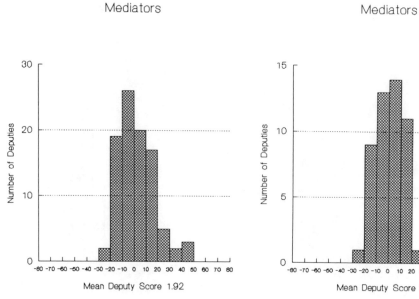

Mediators

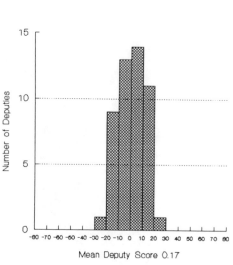

Mediators

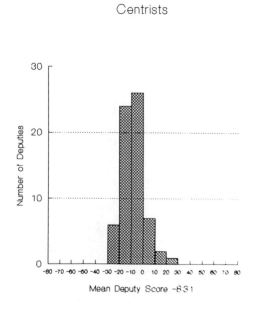

Centrists

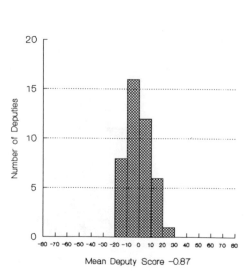

Centrists

*Figure 5.* Voting Positions by Political Affiliation *(continued)*

SECOND CONGRESS                    THIRD CONGRESS

Apparatchiki                      Apparatchiki

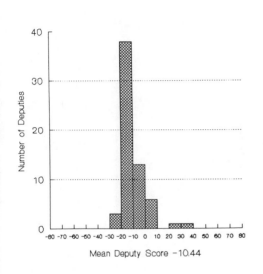

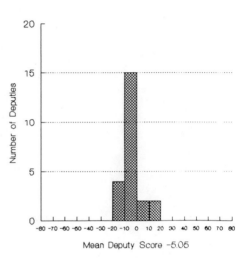

Right-wing Independents            Right-wing Independents

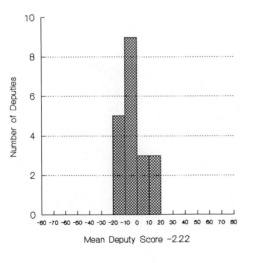

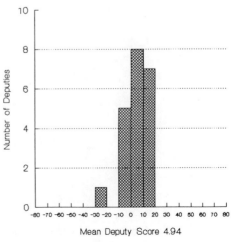

*Figure 5.* Voting Positions by Political Affiliation *(continued)*

SECOND  CONGRESS

THIRD  CONGRESS

Pre-perestroika

Pre-perestroika

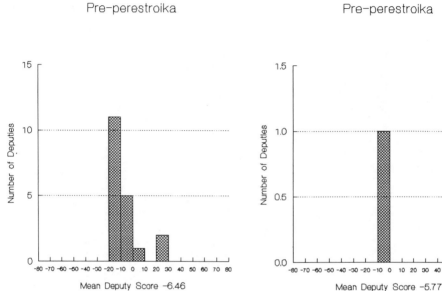

Mean Deputy Score −6.46

Mean Deputy Score −5.77

Non-Speakers and Not Categorized

Non-Speakers and Not Categorized

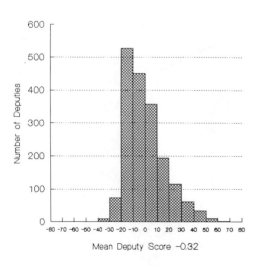

Mean Deputy Score −0.32

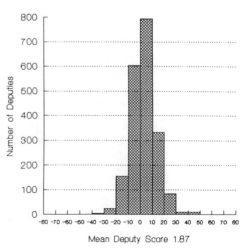

Mean Deputy Score 1.87

*Table 1.* Restriction of Candidacies by POSs in Electoral Campaign (1989) [1]

| Candidacies | | Total Seats | Rate |
|---|---|---|---|
| Candidates from<br>  Preliminary Assemblies | 9,950 | 2,250 | 4.2:1 |
| Registered Candidates<br>  of which: | 5,074 | 2,250 | 2.1:1 |
|   Territorial Districts | 2,195 | 750 | 2.9:1 |
|   Nat.-Territ. Districts | 1,967 | 750 | 2.6:1 |
|   Social Organizations | 912 | 750 | 1.2:1 |

[1]Source: *Pravda*, 6 October 1989.

*Table 2.* "Multi-Candidate" Election among Social Organizations (1989) [1]

| Name | Seats Assigned | Candidacies |
|---|---|---|
| CPSU | 100 | 100 |
| Central Council of Trade Unions | 100 | 114 |
| *Komsomol* | 75 | 102 |
| Veterans' Union | 75 | 102 |
| Women's Committee | 75 | 76 |
| Council of *Kolkhozy* | 58 | 58 |
| Consumer's Societies | 40 | 40 |
| Academy of Sciences | 20 | 23 + 25 |
| *DOSAAF* | 15 | 17 |
| Scientific Associations | 10 | 15 |
| Engineering Associations | 10 | 15 |
| Academy of Agricultural Sciences | 10 | 11 |
| Academy of Medical Sciences | 10 | 18 |
| Architects' Union | 10 | 18 |
| Journalists' Union | 10 | 15 |
| Cinema Union | 10 | 18 |
| Composers' Union | 10 | 12 |
| Writers' Union | 10 | 11 |
| Theater Union | 10 | 12 |
| Artists' Union | 10 | 16 |
| Red Cross and Crescent | 10 | 12 |
| *Znanie* Association | 10 | 12 |
| Others[2] | 62 | 91 |

[1]Source: FBIS (Foreign Broadcast Information Service), "Parliamentary Elections in the USSR: Voters Stun Soviet Officialdom," 16 June 1989, as modified by the author.

[2]Soviet Foundation for Peace; All-Soviet Committee for the Defense of Peace; Union of Friendship Associations; Designers' Union; Soviet Foundation for Culture; Foundation for Childhood; Charity Foundation; Academy of Arts; Academy of Pedagogical Sciences; Association of Inventors and Rationalizers; Sports Associations; Union of Fishing Kolkhozes; Anti-Alcohol Society; Book Friends; Cinema Friends; Musical Society; and Philatelic Society.

*Table 3.* Voting Results of the Enlarged CPSU Plenum [1]

| Candidate | Cancellations |
|---|---|
| 1. E. Ligachev (Politburo) | 78 |
| 2. A. Iakovlev (Politburo) | 59 |
| 3. M. Ulianov (Actor) | 47 |
| 4. V. Afanasev (Editor-in-Chief, *Pravda*) | 38 |
| 5. L. Abalkin (Academician) | 32 |
| 6. V. Nikonov (Politburo) | 26 |
| 7. D. Granin (Writer) | 26 |
| 8. L. Zaikov (Politburo) | 25 |
| 9. V. Medvedev (Politburo) | 22 |
| 10. N. Sliunkov (Politburo) | 19 |
| 11. G. Razumovskii (Candidate Member, Politburo) | 18 |
| 12. E. Primakov (Academician, Director IMEMO) | 15 |
| 13. Ch. Aitmatov (Writer) | 15 |
| 14. V. Chebrikov (Politburo) | 13 |
| 15. M. Gorbachev (Politburo) | 12 |
| 16. S. Fedorov (Professor) | 11 |
| 17. I. Laptev (Editor-in-Chief, *Izvestiia*) | 10 |
| 18. N. Ryzhkov (Politburo) | 10 |
| 19. G. Marchuk (President, Academy of Sciences) | 9 |
| 20. V. Oleinik (Writer) | 9 |

This table reveals the hostility of both extreme wings of the Party against the other's best-known candidates, Ligachev and Iakovlev. Two other reformers, Ulianov and Abalkin, also ranked among the most-cancelled candidates (Abalkin, indeed, eventually became Vice-President of the Council of Ministers despite his high cancellations here), along with the well-known conservative editor of *Pravda*, Afanasev, who lost his job a few months later. Some anomalies, however, remained: electors could cancel names presented to them, but could not write in substitutes. In this circumstance, it was only logical that the cancellations focused on those candidates who were well-known, with clear political positions. In the plenum, for instance, fully 52 of the 100 candidates received no cancellations and won unanimous election. This unanimity, however, did not connote universal, unconditional approval, but merely that most electors were ignorant of, or indifferent to, their positions. The CPSU deputies included 21 industrial workers, 6 kolkhoz farmers, and 5 directors of agricultural enterprises. Clearly if more active support had been required to gain election the results would have been significantly different.

---

[1] Sources: *Pravda*, 19 March 1989, and FBIS, "Parliamentary Elections," *op. cit.*, p. 25.

*Table 4.* Electoral Results by Republic (1989) [1]

| Republic | A | B | C | D | E | F | G | Deputies Total | |
|---|---|---|---|---|---|---|---|---|---|
| Armenia | 71.9 | 40 | 19 | 36 | 0 | 4[2] | 13 | 53 | |
| Azerbaijan | 98.5 | 63 | ? | 62 | 1 | 0 | 9 | 72 | |
| Georgia | 97.0 | 75 | ? | ? | ? | ? | 16 | 91 | |
| RSFSR | 87.0 | 618 | ? | ? | ? | ? | 454 w/Moscow | 1099 | w/Moscow |
| Moscow | -- | 27 | 0 | 16 | 8 | 3 | -- w/RSFSR | -- | w/RSFSR |
| Ukraine | 93.4 | 175 | ? | ? | ? | ? | 87 | 262 | |
| Belorussia | 92.4 | 60 | ? | 47 | 3 | 10 | 34 | 94 | |
| Moldavia | 90.5 | 43 | 15 | 37 | 0 | 6 | 12 | 55 | |
| Estonia | 87.1 | 36 | 3 | 30 | 5 | 1 | 12 | 48 | |
| Latvia | 86.0 | 40 | 7 | 29 | 5 | 6 | 12 | 52 | |
| Lithuania | 82.5 | 42 | 0 | 33 | 8 | 1 | 16 | 58 | |
| Kazakhstan | 93.7 | 73 | 35 | 60 | 2 | 11 | 26 | 99 | |
| Kirghizia | 97.0 | 41 | ? | ? | ? | ? | 12 | 53 | |
| Tadzhikistan | 93.9 | 46 | 1 | 44 | 1 | 1 | 11 | 57 | |
| Turkmenia | 96.1 | 39 | 3 | 33 | 2 | 4 | 9 | 48 | |
| Uzbekistan | 95.8 | 81 | ? | 69 | 2 | 10 | 27 | 108 | |
| USSR | 89.8 | 1499[3] | 399 | 1226 | 76 | 198 | 750 | 2249 | |

Key to Column Headings:
- A  Voters %
- B  Seats (Territorial and National Territorial)
- C  One-Candidate Districts
- D  Candidates Elected 26 March
- E  Candidates Elected in the Second Round
- F  Districts Requiring a Repeated Election
- G  Seats for Social Organizations

---

[1] Sources: FBIS, "Parliamentary Elections," op. cit., pp. 34 and 37; *Politicheskoe Obrazovanie*, no. 10, 1989, with some modifications by the author from other sources.

[2] Includes three districts where elections had to be repeated under the terms of the new electoral law when less than 50% of eligible voters participated in the first round of elections.

[3] In the Menzelinskii district of Tataria elections were repeated only after the First Congress.

## Table 5. Electoral Results for Top-Level Officials (1989) [1]

| Republics | First Sec'y. | Second Sec'y. | Premier | Pres. of Sup. Sov. | Regional First Sec'y. Winners | Defeated |
|---|---|---|---|---|---|---|
| Tadzhikistan | W | W | W | W | -- | -- |
| Azerbaijan | W | W | W | D | 1 | 0 |
| Georgia | W | W | W | W | 3 | 0 |
| RSFSR | -- | -- | W | W | 52 | 24 |
| Moscow | CPSU[2] | D | -- | -- | -- | -- |
| Ukraine | W | W | W | W | 21 | 4 |
| Belorussia | W | W | W | W | 4 | 2 |
| Moldavia | W[3] | W | W | W | -- | -- |
| Estonia | W[3] | D[3] | W[4] | W[3] | -- | -- |
| Latvia | W[3] | W[3] | W[4] | W[3] | -- | -- |
| Lithuania | W[3] | W[3] | D | D | -- | -- |
| Kazakhstan | W | W | W | W | 17 | 0 |
| Kirghizia | W | W | W | W | 2 | 0 |
| Tadzhikistan | W | W | W | W | 3 | 0 |
| Turkmenia | W | W | W | W | 3 | 0 |
| Uzbekistan | W | W | W | W | 11 | 0 |

[1]Sources: FBIS, "Parliamentary Elections," *op. cit.*, p. 7.

[2]Elected by the CPSU as a social organization.

[3]Winner with the support of the local Popular Front.

[4]Winner in the second round.


## Table 6. Social Compositions of the Supreme Soviets (1984 and 1989) and of the Congress (1989) [1]

| Group | Supreme Soviet 1984 (%) | Congress 1989 (%) | Supreme Soviet 1989 (%) |
|---|---|---|---|
| Nomenklatura | 41.5 | 40.5 | 33.0 |
| Technocrats | 6.6 | 25.3 | 35.3 |
| Production/Services | 45.9 | 22.1 | 18.3 |
| Intelligentsia | 6.0 | 10.2 | 12.5 |
| Clergy | -- | 0.3 | -- |
| Pensioners | -- | 1.6 | 0.9 |

[1]Source: *Moskovskie Novosti*, no. 24, 1989, data as modified by the author.


## Table 7. Social Composition of the Congress (Partial) [1]

| | |
|---|---|
| Industrial Managers | 152 ⎫ 344 |
| Agricultural Managers | 192 ⎭ |
| Scientists, Academicians, Teachers, etc. | 316 ⎫ |
| Health Services | 96 ⎪ |
| Arts and Culture | 146 ⎬ 616[2] |
| Mass Media | 58 ⎭ |
| Party Functionaries | 237 |
| Military | 80 |
| Clergy | 7 |
| Total | 1284 |

[1]Source: *Pravda*, 6 October 1989, data as modified by the author.

[2]*Pravda* defines this group collectively as "intellectuals."

*Table 8.* Functional Composition of the First Congress [1]

| Group | Deputies | Percentage |
|---|---|---|
| 1. *Nomenklatura* | 303 | 13.5 |
| 2. Cadres | 154 | 6.8 |
| 3. Military | 90 | 4.0 |
| 4. Managers | 403 | 17.9 |
| 5. Intelligentsia | 384 | 17.1 |
| 6. Technicians | 362 | 16.1 |
| 7. Workers | 503 | 22.4 |
| 8. Others | 50 | 2.2 |
| *Total* | *2249* | *100.0* |

[1]Source: *Spisok Narodnykh Deputatov SSSR*, Moscow 1989.
A few discrepancies exist between this table and those used in the statistical analysis of the Second and Third Congresses. First, as is discussed in the text, a few deputies died after the First Congress and were replaced in supplementary elections. Second, some deputies acquired new state and government posts, obligating them to give up their seat in the Congress. They, too, were replaced in supplementary elections. And finally, some deputies shifted their social position between Congresses. None of these discrepancies, however, are statistically significant enough to affect the political conclusions of our analysis.

*Table 9.* Composition of the Congress and the Supreme Soviet by Nationality [1]

| Nationality | Congress Dep. | % | Supreme Soviet Dep. | % | Population Number (x 1000) | % |
|---|---|---|---|---|---|---|
| 1. Russian | 1,026 | 45.6 | 206 | 38.0 | 137,397 | 52.42 |
| 2. Ukrainian | 258 | 11.5 | 60 | 11.1 | 42,347 | 16.16 |
| 3. Uzbek | 87 | 3.9 | 18 | 3.3 | 12,456 | 4.75 |
| 4. Belorussian | 94 | 4.2 | 20 | 3.7 | 9,463 | 3.61 |
| 5. Kazakh | 53 | 2.4 | 13 | 2.4 | 6,556 | 2.50 |
| 6. Tatar | 23 | 1.0 | 5 | 0.9 | 6,317 | 2.41 |
| 7. Azerbaidzhani | 60 | 2.7 | 20 | 3.7 | 5,477 | 2.09 |
| 8. Armenian | 61 | 2.7 | 16 | 3.0 | 4,151 | 1.58 |
| 9. Georgian | 71 | 3.2 | 20 | 3.7 | 3,571 | 1.36 |
| 10. Moldavian | 43 | 1.9 | 10 | 1.8 | 2,968 | 1.13 |
| 11. Tadzhik | 44 | 2.0 | 15 | 2.8 | 2,898 | 1.11 |
| 12. Lithuanian | 52 | 2.3 | 14 | 2.6 | 2,851 | 1.09 |
| 13. Turkmenian | 40 | 1.8 | 12 | 2.2 | 2,028 | 0.77 |
| 14. German | 10 | 0.4 | 3 | 0.6 | 1,936 | 0.74 |
| 15. Kirgiz | 35 | 1.6 | 10 | 1.8 | 1,906 | 0.73 |
| 16. Jewish | 15 | 0.7 | 3 | 0.6 | 1,811 | 0.69 |
| 17. Chuvash | 15 | 0.7 | 5 | 0.9 | 1,751 | 0.67 |
| 18. Latvian | 44 | 2.0 | 11 | 2.0 | 1,439 | 0.55 |
| 19. Bashkir | 11 | 0.5 | 3 | 0.6 | 1,371 | 0.52 |
| 20. Mordvinian | 11 | 0.5 | 4 | 0.7 | 1,192 | 0.45 |
| 21. Polish | 7 | 0.3 | 2 | 0.4 | 1,151 | 0.43 |
| 22. Estonian | 41 | 1.8 | 11 | 2.0 | 1,020 | 0.39 |
| 23. Chechen | 7 | 0.3 | 2 | 0.4 | 756 | 0.29 |
| 24. Udmurt | 4 | 0.2 | 2 | 0.4 | 714 | 0.27 |
| 25. Mari | 9 | 0.4 | 2 | 0.4 | 622 | 0.24 |
| 26. Ossetian | 13 | 0.6 | 6 | 1.1 | 542 | 0.21 |
| 27. Avar | 5 | 0.2 | 1 | 0.2 | 483 | 0.18 |
| 28. Korean | 4 | 0.2 | 2 | 0.4 | 389 | 0.15 |
| 29. Lezgin | 3 | 0.1 | 1 | 0.2 | 383 | 0.15 |
| 30. Buryat | 9 | 0.4 | 5 | 0.9 | 353 | 0.13 |
| 31. Greek | 1 | -- | 0 | -- | 344 | 0.13 |
| 32. Yakut | 11 | 0.5 | 3 | 0.6 | 328 | 0.13 |
| 33. Komi | 2 | 0.1 | 2 | 0.4 | 327 | 0.12 |
| 34. Kabard | 6 | 0.3 | 2 | 0.4 | 322 | 0.12 |
| 35. Karakalpak | 5 | 0.2 | 2 | 0.4 | 303 | 0.12 |
| 36. Dargin | 2 | 0.1 | 1 | 0.2 | 287 | 0.11 |
| 37. Kumyk | 2 | 0.1 | 1 | 0.2 | 228 | 0.09 |
| 38. Uigur | 1 | -- | 1 | 0.2 | 211 | 0.08 |
| 39. Ingush | 3 | 0.1 | 1 | 0.2 | 186 | 0.07 |
| 40. Gagauz | 2 | 0.1 | 1 | 0.2 | 173 | 0.07 |

[1]Source: V. Tishkov, *op. cit.*, 1986 data.
All spellings in tables 9 and 10 have been standardized with the primary spellings given by Ronald Wixman, *The Peoples of the USSR: An Ethnographic Handbook* (London: Macmillan, 1984). With a few exceptions (for example, "Kirghiz" and "Azerbaijani") these spellings have been used throughout the text.

| | | | | | | |
|---|---|---|---|---|---|---|
| 41. Hungarian | 1 | -- | 0 | -- | 171 | 0.07 |
| 42. Tuvinian | 6 | 0.3 | 2 | 0.4 | 166 | 0.06 |
| 43. Komi Permyak | 1 | -- | 1 | 0.2 | 151 | 0.06 |
| 44. Kalmyk | 6 | 0.3 | 3 | 0.6 | 147 | 0.06 |
| 45. Karelian | 4 | 0.2 | 2 | 0.4 | 138 | 0.05 |
| 46. Karachaev | 3 | 0.2 | 0 | -- | 131 | 0.05 |
| 47. Adygei | 4 | 0.2 | 1 | 0.2 | 109 | 0.04 |
| 48. Lak | 1 | -- | 0 | -- | 100 | 0.04 |
| 49. Abkhaz | 8 | 0.4 | 2 | 0.4 | 91 | 0.03 |
| 50. Tabasaran | 1 | -- | 0 | -- | 75 | 0.03 |
| 51. Khakass | 2 | 0.1 | 1 | 0.2 | 71 | 0.03 |
| 52. Balkar | 4 | 0.2 | 1 | 0.2 | 66 | 0.03 |
| 53. Nogai | 2 | 0.1 | 1 | 0.2 | 60 | 0.02 |
| 54. Altai | 2 | 0.1 | 1 | 0.2 | 60 | 0.02 |
| 55. Dungan | 1 | -- | 1 | 0.2 | 52 | 0.02 |
| 56. Cherkess | 2 | 0.1 | 1 | 0.2 | 46 | 0.02 |
| 57. Nenets | 2 | 0.1 | 2 | 0.4 | 30 | 0.01 |
| 58. Abaza | 1 | -- | 0 | -- | 29 | 0.01 |
| 59. Evenk | 1 | -- | 1 | 0.2 | 27 | 0.01 |
| 60. Tat | 1 | -- | 0 | -- | 22 | 0.01 |
| 61. Khant | 2 | 0.1 | 2 | 0.4 | 21 | 0.01 |
| 62. Chukchi | 1 | -- | 1 | 0.2 | 14 | 0.01 |
| 63. Nanai | 1 | -- | 1 | 0.2 | 10 | < 0.01 |
| 64. Koryak | 1 | -- | 1 | 0.2 | 8 | < 0.01 |
| 65. Crimean Tatar | 1 | -- | 1 | 0.2 | ? | ? |
| Other | 0 | -- | 0 | -- | 1,357 | 0.52 |

## *Table 10.* Diasporas Inside the USSR [1]

| Nationality[2]<br>Diaspora | Level of State<br>Representation[3] | Population | Residents[4] | |
|---|---|---|---|---|
| | | (x 1000) | (x 1000) | (%) |
| 1. Jewish | Jewish A.Rg. | 1,811 | 10 | 99.45 |
| 2. Evenk | Evenk A.D. | 28 | 3.2 | 88.80 |
| 3. Tatar | Tatar A.Rp. | 6,317 | 1,642 | 74.01 |
| 4. Mordvinian | Mordvinian A.Rp. | 1,192 | 339 | 71.57 |
| 5. Zakhurian[5] | Daghestan A.Rp. | 14 | 4.6 | 67.14 |
| 6. Nogai | Daghestan A.Rp. | 60 | 25 | 58.34 |
| 7. Lezgin | Daghestan A.Rp. | 383 | 189 | 50.66 |
| 8. Mari | Mari A.Rp. | 622 | 307 | 50.65 |
| 9. Chuvash | Chuvash A.Rp. | 1,751 | 888 | 49.29 |
| 10. Khant | Khanti-Man. A.D. | 21 | 11 | 47.62 |
| 11. Karelian | Karelian A.Rp. | 138 | 81 | 41.31 |
| 12. *Armenian* | Armenian U.Rp. | 4,151 | 2,725 | 34.36 |
| 13. Ossetian | Ossetian A.Rp.-A.D.[6] | 542 | 364 | 32.85 |
| 14. Udmurt | Udmurt A.Rp. | 714 | 480 | 32.78 |
| 15. Bashkir | Bashkir A.Rp. | 1,371 | 936 | 31.73 |
| 16. Komi Permyak | Komi Permyak A.D. | 151 | 106 | 30.19 |
| 17. Koryak | Koryak A.D. | 7.9 | 5.7 | 27.85 |
| 18. Ingush | Checheno-Ingush A.Rp. | 186 | 135 | 27.42 |
| 19. Cherkess | Karach.-Cherk. A.Rg. | 46 | 34 | 26.09 |
| 20. *Tadzhik* | Tadzhik U.Rp. | 2,898 | 2,237 | 22.81 |
| 21. Chukchi | Chukotka A.D. | 14 | 11 | 21.43 |
| 22. Adygei | Adygei A.Rg. | 109 | 86 | 21.11 |
| 23. *Belorussian* | Belorussian U.Rp. | 9,463 | 7,568 | 20.03 |
| 24. Khakass | Khakass A.Rg. | 71 | 57 | 19.72 |
| 25. *Kazakh* | Kazakh U.Rp. | 6,556 | 5,289 | 19.33 |

---

[1]Source: *Rabochii klass i sovremennii mir*, no. 3, 1989. A. Zubov, A. Salmin, "*Optimizatsiia natsionalno-gosudarstvennykh otnoshenii v usloviiakh 'natsionalnogo vozrozhdeniia' v SSSR*," pp. 62-81. Zubov and Salmin utilize the work of S.I. Bruk, "*Naselenie mira*," 1981, which in turn is based on data from the census of 1979.

[2]Only nationalities officially recognized at one of the four levels of state autonomy (union republic, autonomous republic, autonomous region, or autonomous district) are included.

[3]U.Rp. = Union Republic; A.Rp. = Autonomous Republic; A.Rg. = Autonomous Region; and A.D. = Autonomous District.

[4]Population residing in designated national territory.

[5]Not listed in Wixman, *op. cit.*

[6]Autonomous Republic of North Ossetia (part of the RSFSR) and Autonomous District of South Ossetia (part of Georgia).

| | | | | |
|---|---|---|---|---|
| 26. Chechen [7] | Checheno-Ingush. A.Rp. | 756 | 611 | 19.18 |
| 27. *Moldavian*[7] | Moldavian U.Rp. | 3,097 | 2,526 | 18.44 |
| 28. Mansi | Khanti-Mans. A.D.[8] | 7.6 | 6.2 | 18.43 |
| 29. Buryat | Buryat A.Rp.-A.D.[8] | 353 | 288 | 18.42 |
| 30. *Russian* | RSFSR U.Rp. | 137,397 | 113,522 | 17.38 |
| 31. Kalmyk | Kalmyk A.Rp. | 147 | 122 | 17.01 |
| 32. Lak | Daghestan A.Rp. | 100 | 83 | 17.00 |
| 33. Karachaev | Karach.-Cherk. A.Rg. | 131 | 109 | 16.80 |
| 34. Altai | Gorno-Altai A.Rg. | 60 | 50 | 16.66 |
| 35. Dolgan | Taimir A.D.[9] | 5.1 | 4.3 | 15.69 |
| 36. Nenets | Nenets A.D.[9] | 30 | 25 | 15.67 |
| 37. *Uzbek* | Uzbek U.Rp. | 12,456 | 10,569 | 15.15 |
| 38. Komi | Komi A.Rp. | 327 | 281 | 14.07 |
| 39. *Azerbaidzhani* | Azerbaidzhani U.Rp. | 5,477 | 4,709 | 14.03 |
| 40. Dargin | Daghestan A.Rp. | 483 | 419 | 13.43 |
| 41. *Ukrainian*[10] | Ukrainian U.Rp. | 42,347 | 36,489 | 13.84 |
| 42. Avar[10] | Daghestan A.Rp. | 483 | 419 | 13.43 |
| 43. *Kirgiz* | Kirgiz U.Rp. | 1,906 | 1,687 | 11.50 |
| 44. Kumyk | Daghestan A.Rp. | 228 | 202 | 11.41 |
| 45. Abkhaz | Abkhaz A.Rp. | 91 | 83 | 8.80 |
| 46. Agul | Daghestan A.Rp. | 12 | 11 | 8.33 |
| 47. Balkar | Kabard.-Balk. A.Rp. | 66 | 60 | 8.10 |
| 48. *Estonian* | Estonian U.Rp. | 1,020 | 948 | 7.06 |
| 49. Karakalpak | Karakalpak A.Rp. | 303 | 282 | 6.94 |
| 50. *Turkmen* | Turkmen U.Rp. | 2,028 | 1,892 | 6.71 |
| 51. Rutul | Daghestan A.Rp. | 15 | 14 | 6.66 |
| 52. *Latvian* | Latvian U.Rp. | 1,439 | 1,344 | 6.61 |
| 53. Kabard | Kabard.-Balk. A.Rp. | 322 | 304 | 5.60 |
| 54. *Lithuanian* | Lithuanian U.Rp. | 2,851 | 2,712 | 4.88 |
| 55. Yakut | Yakut A.Rp. | 328 | 314 | 4.27 |
| 56. Tabasaran | Daghestan A.Rp. | 75 | 72 | 4.00 |
| 57. *Georgian* | Georgian U.Rp. | 3,571 | 3,433 | 3.87 |
| 58. Tuvinian | Tuvinian A.Rp. | 166 | 162 | 2.41 |

*Note:* These figures show that more than 50 million Soviet citizens live in an internal diaspora. In absolute terms, Russians head the list, with nearly 24 million Russians residing outside the RSFSR. Following at a distance are: Ukrainians (6 million), Tatars (5 million), Armenians (3 million), Belorussians (2 million), and Kazakhs (1.5 million). The three Slavic republics' diaspora together total nearly 33 million people.

[7]Including both Moldavians and Romanians.

[8]Autonomous Republic of Buryats and Autonomous Districts of Agin and Ust-Ordinsk.

[9]Autonomous Districts of Nenets, Taimir, and Yamal.

[10]Including the 13 Ando-Tsezkie nationalities.

*Table 11.* Two-Dimensional (Gordon-Nazimova) View of Soviet Politics in 1989

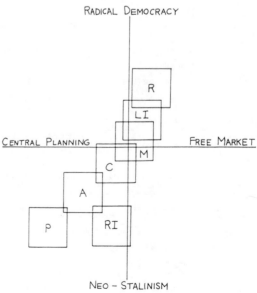

*Table 12.* Three-Dimensional View of Soviet Politics in 1989

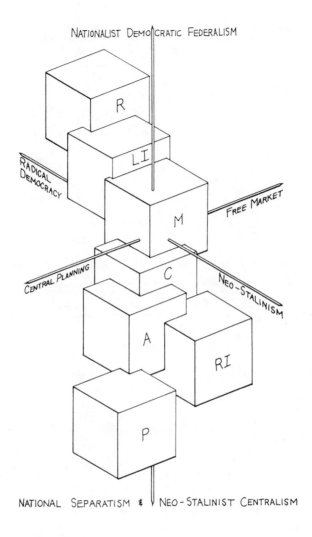

*Table 13.* First Congress — Political Affiliation by Republic [1]

| Republic | Radicals | | Mediators | | | Centrists | | Apparatchiki | | Pre-perestr. | | | | Unknown | | Total |
|---|---|---|---|---|---|---|---|---|---|---|---|---|---|---|---|---|---|
| | | | Left | | Indep. | | | | | Right | | Indep. | | | | |
| | No. | % | No. | % | No. | % | No. | % | No. | % | No. | % | No. | % | No. | % | No. |
| Armenia | 4 | (5.0) | 5 | (4.5) | 2 | (2.2) | 0 | -- | 1 | (2.3) | 0 | -- | 0 | -- | 0 | -- | 12 |
| Azerbaijan | 3 | (3.8) | 1 | (0.9) | 1 | (1.1) | 2 | (3.0) | 8 | (18.2) | 1 | (4.2) | 3 | (12.0) | 1 | (4.8) | 20 |
| Georgia | 4 | (5.0) | 1 | (0.9) | 2 | (2.2) | 2 | (3.0) | 0 | -- | 1 | (4.2) | 0 | -- | 0 | -- | 10 |
| RSFSR | 27 | (33.8) | 41 | (36.7) | 28 | (30.8) | 25 | (37.3) | 13 | (29.5) | 7 | (29.2) | 9 | (36.0) | 6 | (28.8) | 156 |
| Moscow | 22 | (27.5) | 15 | (13.4) | 21 | (23.1) | 12 | (23.9) | 5 | (11.4) | 1 | (4.2) | 1 | (4.0) | 1 | (4.8) | 78 |
| Ukraine | 3 | (3.8) | 16 | (14.3) | 8 | (8.8) | 3 | (4.5) | 4 | (9.1) | 3 | (12.5) | 3 | (12.0) | 0 | -- | 40 |
| Belorussia | 1 | (1.3) | 6 | (5.6) | 3 | (3.3) | 6 | (9.0) | 3 | (6.8) | 2 | (8.3) | 0 | -- | 0 | -- | 21 |
| Moldavia | 1 | (1.3) | 1 | (0.9) | 1 | (1.1) | 2 | (3.0) | 0 | -- | 0 | -- | 1 | (4.0) | 0 | -- | 6 |
| Estonia | 3 | (3.8) | 1 | (0.9) | 3 | (3.3) | 0 | -- | 0 | -- | 2 | (8.3) | 0 | -- | 0 | -- | 9 |
| Latvia | 5 | (6.2) | 4 | (3.6) | 4 | (4.4) | 0 | -- | 0 | -- | 1 | (4.2) | 0 | -- | 1 | (4.8) | 15 |
| Lithuania | 3 | (3.8) | 9 | (8.0) | 5 | (5.6) | 0 | -- | 0 | -- | 0 | -- | 0 | -- | 0 | -- | 17 |
| Kazakhstan | 0 | -- | 3 | (2.7) | 1 | (1.1) | 4 | (6.0) | 2 | (4.5) | 3 | (12.5) | 1 | (4.0) | 0 | -- | 14 |
| Kirghizia | 0 | -- | 0 | -- | 1 | (1.1) | 0 | -- | 2 | (4.5) | 0 | -- | 0 | -- | 0 | -- | 3 |
| Turkmenia | 0 | -- | 0 | -- | 0 | -- | 1 | (1.5) | 1 | (2.3) | 0 | -- | 2 | (8.0) | 0 | -- | 4 |
| Tadzhikistan | 0 | -- | 2 | (1.8) | 0 | -- | 2 | (3.0) | 1 | (2.3) | 0 | -- | 1 | (4.0) | 0 | -- | 6 |
| Uzbekistan | 0 | -- | 2 | (1.8) | 4 | (4.4) | 3 | (4.5) | 4 | (9.1) | 0 | -- | 3 | (12.0) | 0 | -- | 16 |
| Unknown | 4 | (5.0) | 5 | (4.5) | 7 | (7.7) | 5 | (7.5) | 0 | -- | 3 | (12.5) | 1 | (4.0) | 12 | (57.1) | 37[2] |
| Total | 80 | (100) | 112 | (100) | 91 | (100) | 67 | (100) | 44 | (100) | 24 | (100) | 25 | (100) | 21 | (100) | 464 |

[1] Political affiliation measured by speeches to the First Congress. Only those deputies speaking at least once are included. Percentages are vertical--that is, showing proportions of those speaking from each political group rather than from each republic.
[2] Each speech by an unidentified deputy is here assumed to have been delivered by a distinct deputy not already counted. This assumption may not be valid, and therefore this section may include some double counting.

*Table 14.* Second Congress — Political Affiliation by Republic [1]

| Republic | Radicals | | Mediators | | | Centrists | | Apparatchiki | | Pre-perestr. | | | | Unknown | | Total |
|---|---|---|---|---|---|---|---|---|---|---|---|---|---|---|---|---|---|
| | | | Left | | Indep. | | | | | Right | | Indep. | | | | |
| | No. | % | No. | % | No. | % | No. | % | No. | % | No. | % | No. | % | No. | % | No. |
| Armenia | 1 | (1.5) | 5 | (4.7) | 3 | (2.7) | 0 | -- | 0 | -- | 1 | (3.3) | 0 | -- | 0 | -- | 10 |
| Azerbaijan | 0 | -- | 0 | -- | 3 | (2.7) | 0 | -- | 4 | (5.8) | 2 | (6.7) | 1 | (3.3) | 0 | -- | 10 |
| Georgia | 1 | (1.5) | 4 | (3.8) | 2 | (1.8) | 0 | -- | 0 | -- | 0 | -- | 0 | -- | 2 | (3.6) | 9 |
| RSFSR | 25 | (36.7) | 29 | (27.3) | 37 | (33.9) | 23 | (32.4) | 25 | (36.2) | 12 | (40.0) | 9 | (30.0) | 28 | (50.0) | 188 |
| Moscow | 19 | (27.9) | 6 | (5.7) | 21 | (19.3) | 8 | (11.3) | 7 | (10.1) | 2 | (6.7) | 0 | -- | 6 | (10.7) | 69 |
| Ukraine | 11 | (16.2) | 7 | (6.6) | 7 | (6.4) | 6 | (8.4) | 6 | (8.7) | 1 | (3.3) | 3 | (10.0) | 9 | (16.1) | 50 |
| Belorussia | 5 | (7.3) | 2 | (1.9) | 3 | (2.7) | 6 | (8.4) | 3 | (4.3) | 0 | -- | 0 | -- | 3 | (5.3) | 22 |
| Moldavia | 0 | -- | 2 | (1.9) | 3 | (2.7) | 4 | (5.6) | 1 | (1.4) | 0 | -- | 1 | (3.3) | 0 | -- | 11 |
| Estonia | 2 | (2.9) | 5 | (4.7) | 1 | (0.9) | 0 | -- | 0 | -- | 2 | (6.7) | 1 | (3.3) | 2 | (3.6) | 13 |
| Latvia | 1 | (1.5) | 13 | (12.3) | 1 | (0.9) | 0 | -- | 2 | (2.9) | 1 | (3.3) | 0 | -- | 0 | -- | 18 |
| Lithuania | 0 | -- | 7 | (6.6) | 4 | (3.7) | 0 | -- | 0 | -- | 0 | -- | 0 | -- | 1 | (1.8) | 12 |
| Kazakhstan | 0 | -- | 1 | (0.9) | 4 | (3.7) | 3 | (4.2) | 2 | (2.9) | 1 | (3.3) | 1 | (3.3) | 1 | (1.8) | 13 |
| Kirghizia | 0 | -- | 0 | -- | 2 | (1.8) | 3 | (4.2) | 1 | (1.4) | 0 | -- | 2 | (6.7) | 0 | -- | 8 |
| Turkmenia | 0 | -- | 0 | -- | 0 | -- | 1 | (1.4) | 2 | (2.9) | 0 | -- | 1 | (3.3) | 0 | -- | 4 |
| Tadzhikistan | 0 | -- | 0 | -- | 3 | (2.7) | 4 | (5.6) | 2 | (2.9) | 0 | -- | 0 | -- | 0 | -- | 9 |
| Uzbekistan | 0 | -- | 3 | (2.8) | 1 | (0.9) | 8 | (11.3) | 8 | (11.6) | 0 | -- | 3 | (10.0) | 4 | (7.1) | 27 |
| Unknown | 3 | (4.4) | 22 | (20.7) | 14 | (12.8) | 5 | (7.0) | 6 | (8.7) | 8 | (26.7) | 8 | (26.7) | 0 | -- | 66[2] |
| Total | 68 | (100) | 106 | (100) | 109 | (100) | 71 | (100) | 69 | (100) | 30 | (100) | 30 | (100) | 56 | (100) | 539 |

[1] Political affiliation measured by speeches to the Second Congress. Only those deputies speaking at least once are included. Percentages are vertical--that is, showing proportions of those speaking from each political group rather than from each republic.
[2] Each speech by an unidentified deputy is here assumed to have been delivered by a distinct deputy not already counted. This assumption may not be valid, and therefore this section may include some double counting.

## Table 15. Third Congress — Political Affiliation by Republic [1]

| Republic | Radicals | | Mediators Left | | Indep. | | Centrists | | Apparatchiki | | Right | | Pre-perestr. Indep. | | Unknown | | Total |
|---|---|---|---|---|---|---|---|---|---|---|---|---|---|---|---|---|---|
| | No. | % | No. | % | No. | % | No. | % | No. | % | No. | % | No. | % | No. | % | No. |
| Armenia | 1 | (2.4) | 2 | (3.2) | 2 | (3.7) | 2 | (4.2) | 0 | -- | 1 | (4.3) | 0 | -- | 0 | -- | 8 |
| Azerbaijan | 0 | -- | 0 | -- | 2 | (3.7) | 2 | (4.2) | 0 | -- | 1 | (4.3) | 0 | -- | 0 | -- | 5 |
| Georgia | 0 | -- | 3 | (4.8) | 0 | -- | 1 | (2.1) | 0 | -- | 0 | -- | 0 | -- | 0 | -- | 4 |
| RSFSR | 22 | (52.4) | 18 | (28.6) | 16 | (29.6) | 14 | (29.8) | 13 | (50.0) | 12 | (52.2) | 1 | (25.0) | 2 | (33.3) | 98 |
| Moscow | 10 | (23.8) | 6 | (9.5) | 14 | (25.9) | 7 | (14.9) | 2 | (7.7) | 0 | -- | 0 | -- | 2 | (33.3) | 41 |
| Ukraine | 5 | (11.9) | 1 | (1.6) | 6 | (11.1) | 2 | (4.2) | 2 | (7.7) | 2 | (8.6) | 0 | -- | 1 | (16.7) | 19 |
| Belorussia | 1 | (2.4) | 1 | (1.6) | 3 | (5.6) | 3 | (6.4) | 1 | (3.8) | 0 | -- | 0 | -- | 0 | -- | 9 |
| Moldavia | 0 | -- | 2 | (3.2) | 0 | -- | 2 | (4.2) | 0 | -- | 1 | (4.3) | 0 | -- | 1 | (16.7) | 6 |
| Estonia | 1 | (2.4) | 2 | (3.2) | 0 | -- | 0 | -- | 0 | -- | 2 | (8.6) | 0 | -- | 0 | -- | 5 |
| Latvia | 0 | -- | 5 | (7.9) | 1 | (1.8) | 0 | -- | 0 | -- | 1 | (4.3) | 0 | -- | 0 | -- | 7 |
| Lithuania | 0 | -- | 2 | (3.2) | 0 | -- | 1 | (2.1) | 0 | -- | 0 | -- | 0 | -- | 0 | -- | 3 |
| Kazakhstan | 0 | -- | 1 | (1.6) | 2 | (3.7) | 2 | (4.2) | 1 | (3.8) | 1 | (4.3) | 0 | -- | 0 | -- | 7 |
| Kirghizia | 0 | -- | 0 | -- | 1 | (1.8) | 0 | -- | 1 | (3.8) | 0 | -- | 0 | -- | 0 | -- | 2 |
| Turkmenia | 0 | -- | 0 | -- | 1 | (1.8) | 3 | (6.4) | 0 | -- | 0 | -- | 0 | -- | 0 | -- | 4 |
| Tadzhikistan | 0 | -- | 0 | -- | 0 | -- | 1 | (2.1) | 2 | (7.7) | 0 | -- | 0 | -- | 0 | -- | 3 |
| Uzbekistan | 0 | -- | 5 | (7.9) | 0 | -- | 3 | (6.4) | 2 | (7.7) | 0 | -- | 0 | -- | 0 | -- | 10 |
| Unknown | 2 | (4.8) | 15 | (23.8) | 6 | (11.1) | 4 | (8.5) | 2 | (7.7) | 2 | (8.6) | 3 | (75.0) | 0 | -- | 34[2] |
| Total | 42 | (100) | 63 | (100) | 54 | (100) | 47 | (100) | 26 | (100) | 23 | (100) | 4 | (100) | 6 | (100) | 265 |

[1] Political affiliation measured by speeches to the Third Congress. Only those deputies speaking at least once are included. Percentages are vertical--that is, showing proportions of those speaking from each political group rather than from each republic.
[2] Each speech by an unidentified deputy is here assumed to have been delivered by a distinct deputy not already counted. This assumption may not be valid, and therefore this section may include some double counting.

## Table 16. First Congress — Political Profiles by Republic [1]

| Republic | Radicals | Left | Mediators Indep. | Centrists | Apparatchiki | Right | Pre-perestr. Indep. | Unknown | Total |
|---|---|---|---|---|---|---|---|---|---|
| | % | % | % | % | % | % | % | % | % |
| Armenia | 33.3 | 41.7 | 16.7 | -- | 8.3 | -- | -- | -- | 100 |
| Azerbaijan | 15.0 | 5.0 | 5.0 | 10.0 | 40.0 | 15.0 | 15.0 | 5.0 | 100 |
| Georgia | 40.0 | 10.0 | 20.0 | 20.0 | -- | 10.0 | -- | -- | 100 |
| RSFSR | 17.3 | 26.3 | 17.9 | 16.0 | 8.3 | 4.5 | 5.8 | 3.8 | 100 |
| Moscow | 28.2 | 19.9 | 26.4 | 15.4 | 6.4 | 1.3 | 1.3 | 1.3 | 100 |
| Ukraine | 7.5 | 40.0 | 20.0 | 7.5 | 10.0 | 7.5 | 7.5 | -- | 100 |
| Belorussia | 4.8 | 28.6 | 14.3 | 28.6 | 14.3 | 9.5 | -- | -- | 100 |
| Moldavia | 16.7 | 16.7 | 16.7 | 33.3 | -- | -- | 16.7 | -- | 100 |
| Estonia | 33.3 | 11.1 | 33.3 | -- | -- | 22.2 | -- | -- | 100 |
| Latvia | 33.3 | 26.7 | 26.7 | -- | -- | 6.7 | -- | 6.7 | 100 |
| Lithuania | 17.6 | 52.3 | 29.4 | -- | -- | -- | -- | -- | 100 |
| Kazakhstan | -- | 21.4 | 7.1 | 28.6 | 14.3 | 21.4 | 7.1 | -- | 100 |
| Kirghizia | -- | -- | 33.3 | -- | 66.7 | -- | -- | -- | 100 |
| Turkmenia | -- | -- | -- | 25.0 | 25.0 | -- | 50.0 | -- | 100 |
| Tadzhikistan | -- | 33.3 | -- | 33.3 | 16.7 | -- | 16.7 | -- | 100 |
| Uzbekistan | -- | 12.5 | 25.0 | 18.8 | 25.0 | -- | 18.8 | -- | 100 |
| Unknown | 10.8 | 13.5 | 18.9 | 13.5 | -- | 8.1 | 2.7 | 32.4 | 100 |

[1] Political affiliation measured by speeches to the First Congress. Unlike Tables 13-15, which list each deputy once, this table shows the relative proportion of speeches in each political group. Thus, a vocal deputy may be counted more than once. Percentages are horizontal--that is, showing proportions by republic rather than by political affiliation.

## *Table 17.* Second Congress — Political Profiles by Republic [1]

| Republic | Radicals | Mediators Left Indep. | Mediators | Centrists | Apparatchiki | Right Indep. | Pre-perestr. | Unknown | Total |
|---|---|---|---|---|---|---|---|---|---|
| | % | % | % | % | % | % | % | % | % |
| Armenia | 10.0 | 50.0 | 30.0 | -- | -- | 10.0 | -- | -- | 100 |
| Azerbaijan | -- | -- | 30.0 | -- | 40.0 | 20.0 | 10.0 | -- | 100 |
| Georgia | 11.1 | 44.4 | 22.2 | -- | -- | -- | -- | 22.2 | 100 |
| RSFSR | 13.3 | 15.4 | 14.9 | 12.2 | 13.3 | 6.4 | 4.8 | 14.9 | 100 |
| Moscow | 27.5 | 8.7 | 30.4 | 11.6 | 10.1 | 2.9 | -- | 8.7 | 100 |
| Ukraine | 22.0 | 14.0 | 14.0 | 12.0 | 12.0 | 2.0 | 6.0 | 18.0 | 100 |
| Belorussia | 22.7 | 9.1 | 13.6 | 27.3 | 13.6 | -- | -- | 13.6 | 100 |
| Moldavia | -- | 18.2 | 27.3 | 36.4 | 9.1 | -- | 9.1 | -- | 100 |
| Estonia | 15.4 | 38.5 | 7.7 | -- | -- | 15.4 | 7.7 | 15.4 | 100 |
| Latvia | 5.6 | 72.2 | 5.6 | -- | 11.1 | 5.6 | -- | -- | 100 |
| Lithuania | -- | 58.3 | 33.3 | -- | -- | -- | -- | 8.3 | 100 |
| Kazakhstan | -- | 7.7 | 30.8 | 23.1 | 15.4 | 7.7 | 7.7 | 7.7 | 100 |
| Kirghizia | -- | -- | 25.0 | 37.5 | 12.5 | -- | 25.0 | -- | 100 |
| Turkmenia | -- | -- | -- | 25.0 | 50.0 | -- | 25.0 | -- | 100 |
| Tadzhikistan | -- | -- | 33.3 | 44.4 | 22.2 | -- | -- | -- | 100 |
| Uzbekistan | -- | 11.1 | 3.7 | 29.6 | 29.6 | -- | 11.1 | 14.8 | 100 |
| Unknown | 4.5 | 33.3 | 21.2 | 7.6 | 9.1 | 12.1 | 12.1 | -- | 100 |

[1] Political affiliation measured by speeches to the Second Congress. Unlike Tables 13-15, which list each deputy once, this table shows the relative proportion of speeches in each political group. Thus, a vocal deputy may be counted more than once. Percentages are horizontal--that is, showing proportions by republic rather than by political affiliation.

## *Table 18.* Third Congress — Political Profiles by Republic [1]

| Republic | Radicals | Mediators Left Indep. | Mediators | Centrists | Apparatchiki | Right Indep. | Pre-perestr. | Unknown | Total |
|---|---|---|---|---|---|---|---|---|---|
| | % | % | % | % | % | % | % | % | % |
| Armenia | 12.5 | 25.0 | 25.0 | 25.0 | -- | 12.5 | -- | -- | 100 |
| Azerbaijan | -- | -- | 40.0 | 40.0 | -- | 20.0 | -- | -- | 100 |
| Georgia | -- | 75.0 | -- | 25.0 | -- | -- | -- | -- | 100 |
| RSFSR | 22.4 | 18.4 | 16.3 | 14.3 | 13.3 | 12.2 | 1.0 | 2.0 | 100 |
| Moscow | 24.4 | 14.6 | 34.1 | 17.1 | 4.9 | -- | -- | 4.9 | 100 |
| Ukraine | 26.3 | 5.3 | 31.6 | 10.5 | 10.5 | 10.5 | -- | 5.3 | 100 |
| Belorussia | 11.1 | 11.1 | 33.3 | 33.3 | 11.1 | -- | -- | -- | 100 |
| Moldavia | -- | 33.3 | -- | 33.3 | -- | 16.7 | -- | 16.7 | 100 |
| Estonia | 20.0 | 40.0 | -- | -- | -- | 40.0 | -- | -- | 100 |
| Latvia | -- | 71.4 | 14.3 | -- | -- | 14.3 | -- | -- | 100 |
| Lithuania | -- | 66.7 | 33.3 | -- | -- | -- | -- | -- | 100 |
| Kazakhstan | -- | 14.3 | 28.6 | 28.6 | 14.3 | 14.3 | -- | -- | 100 |
| Kirghizia | -- | -- | 50.0 | -- | 50.0 | -- | -- | -- | 100 |
| Turkmenia | -- | -- | 25.0 | 75.0 | -- | -- | -- | -- | 100 |
| Tadzhikistan | -- | -- | -- | 33.3 | 66.7 | -- | -- | -- | 100 |
| Uzbekistan | -- | 50.0 | -- | 30.0 | 20.0 | -- | -- | -- | 100 |
| Unknown | 5.9 | 44.1 | 17.6 | 11.8 | 5.9 | 5.9 | 8.8 | -- | 100 |

[1] Political affiliation measured by speeches to the Third Congress. Unlike Tables 13-15, which list each deputy once, this table shows the relative proportion of speeches in each political group. Thus, a vocal deputy may be counted more than once. Percentages are horizontal--that is, showing proportions by republic rather than by political affiliation.

*Table 19.*  First, Second, and Third Congresses — Political Group Activity [1]

| Group | First Congress | | | | Second Congress | | | | Third Congress | | | |
|---|---|---|---|---|---|---|---|---|---|---|---|---|
| | Speeches | % | Deputies | % | Speeches | % | Deputies | % | Speeches | % | Deputies | % |
| Radicals | 161 | 23.6 | 80 | 17.2 | 120 | 15.5 | 68 | 12.6 | 76 | 20.5 | 42 | 15.8 |
| Left-wing Independents | 155 | 22.7 | 112 | 24.1 | 166 | 21.5 | 106 | 19.7 | 88 | 23.7 | 63 | 23.8 |
| Mediators | 140 | 20.5 | 91 | 19.6 | 159 | 20.6 | 109 | 20.2 | 81 | 21.8 | 54 | 20.4 |
| Centrists | 91 | 13.3 | 67 | 14.4 | 103 | 13.6 | 71 | 13.2 | 55 | 14.8 | 47 | 17.7 |
| Apparatchiki | 56 | 8.2 | 44 | 9.5 | 91 | 11.8 | 69 | 12.8 | 28 | 7.5 | 26 | 9.8 |
| Right-wing Independents | 32 | 4.7 | 24 | 5.2 | 44 | 5.7 | 30 | 5.6 | 33 | 8.9 | 23 | 8.7 |
| Pre-perestroika | 26 | 3.8 | 25 | 5.4 | 33 | 4.3 | 30 | 5.6 | 4 | 1.1 | 4 | 1.5 |
| Unclassified | 21 | 3.1 | 21 | 4.5 | 56 | 7.3 | 56 | 10.3 | 6 | 1.6 | 6 | 2.3 |
| *Total* | *682* | *100* | *464* | *100* | *772* | *100* | *539* | *100* | *371* | *100* | *265* | *100* |

[1] All speeches to the Congresses are considered, including those by deputies not indentified in the official Congress records.

*Table 20.*  First, Second, and Third Congresses — Debate Activity by Region [1]

| Region | Seats in Congress | First Congress | | | | Second Congress | | | | Third Congress | | | |
|---|---|---|---|---|---|---|---|---|---|---|---|---|---|
| | | Speeches | | Deputies | | Speeches | | Deputies | | Speeches | | Deputies | |
| | % $(x)$ | % $(y_1)$ | | % $(z_1)$ | | % $(y_2)$ | | % $(z_2)$ | | % $(y_3)$ | | % $(z_3)$ | |
| Transcaucasia[2] | 216 | 9.6 | 51 | 7.9 | 42 | 9.8 | 34 | 4.8 | 29 | 6.1 | 22 | 6.5 | 17 | 7.4 |
| Slavic Republics and Moldavia[3] | 1511 | 67.1 | 476 | 73.8 | 301 | 70.5 | 527 | 74.6 | 340 | 71.9 | 264 | 78.3 | 173 | 74.9 |
| Baltic Republics[4] | 158 | 7.0 | 62 | 9.6 | 41 | 9.6 | 70 | 9.9 | 43 | 9.1 | 19 | 5.6 | 15 | 6.5 |
| Central Asia[5] | 365 | 16.2 | 56 | 8.7 | 43 | 10.1 | 75 | 10.6 | 61 | 12.9 | 32 | 9.5 | 26 | 11.2 |
| *Total* | *2250* | *100* | *645* | *100* | *427* | *100* | *706* | *100* | *473* | *100* | *337* | *100* | *231* | *100* |

[1] Percentages calculated on the basis of deputies with known republics of origin.
[2] Transcaucasia: Armenia, Azerbaijan, and Georgia.
[3] Slavic Republics and Moldavia: Russian SFSR, Moscow, Ukraine, Belorussia, and Moldavia.
[4] Baltic Republics: Estonia, Latvia, and Lithuania.
[5] Central Asia: Kazakhstan, Kirghizia, Turkmenia, Tadzhikistan, and Uzbekistan.

*Table 21.* First, Second, and Third Congresses — Activity
Coefficients by Region [1]

| Region | First Congress | | Second Congress | | Third Congress | |
|---|---|---|---|---|---|---|
| | $y_1/x$ | $z_1/x$ | $y_2/x$ | $z_2/x$ | $y_3/x$ | $z_3/x$ |
| Transcaucasia[2] | 0.82 | 1.02 | 0.50 | 0.63 | 0.68 | 0.77 |
| Slavic Republics and Moldavia[3] | 1.10 | 1.05 | 1.11 | 1.07 | 1.17 | 1.12 |
| Baltic Republics[4] | 1.37 | 1.37 | 1.41 | 1.30 | 0.80 | 0.92 |
| Central Asia[5] | 0.53 | 0.62 | 0.65 | 0.80 | 0.59 | 0.69 |

[1] For key to coefficients, see column headings of Table 20.
[2] Transcaucasia: Armenia, Azerbaijan, and Georgia.
[3] Slavic Republics and Moldavia: Russian SFSR, Moscow, Ukraine, Belorussia, and Moldavia.
[4] Baltic Republics: Estonia, Latvia, and Lithuania.
[5] Central Asia: Kazakhstan, Kirghizia, Turkmenia, Tadzhikistan, and Uzbekistan.


*Table 22.* First Congress — Political Affiliation by Social Position[1]

| Social | Radicals | | | | Mediators | | | | Apparatchiki | | | | Pre-perestr. | | | | Total |
|---|---|---|---|---|---|---|---|---|---|---|---|---|---|---|---|---|---|
| | | | Left Indep. | | | | Centrists | | | | Right Indep. | | | | Unknown | | |
| | No. | % | No. | % | No. | % | No. | % | No. | % | No. | % | No. | % | No. | % | No. |
| Nomenklatura | 1 | (1.3) | 0 | -- | 18 | (19.8) | 19 | (28.3) | 17 | (38.6) | 0 | -- | 4 | (16.0) | 0 | -- | 59 |
| Cadres | 1 | (1.3) | 7 | (6.2) | 4 | (4.4) | 3 | (4.5) | 2 | (4.5) | 3 | (12.5) | 0 | -- | 0 | -- | 20 |
| Military | 0 | -- | 0 | -- | 1 | (1.1) | 4 | (6.0) | 0 | -- | 6 | (25.0) | 1 | (4.0) | 1 | (4.8) | 13 |
| Managers | 4 | (5.0) | 12 | (10.7) | 6 | (6.6) | 10 | (4.9) | 5 | (11.3) | 2 | (8.3) | 6 | (24.0) | 0 | -- | 45 |
| Intelligentsia | 44 | (55.0) | 46 | (41.1) | 37 | (40.6) | 13 | (19.4) | 9 | (20.4) | 4 | (16.6) | 2 | (8.0) | 1 | (4.8) | 156 |
| Technicians | 18 | (22.5) | 26 | (23.2) | 13 | (14.3) | 3 | (4.5) | 4 | (9.1) | 2 | (8.3) | 4 | (16.0) | 2 | (9.5) | 72 |
| Workers | 3 | (3.7) | 11 | (9.8) | 3 | (3.3) | 7 | (10.4) | 5 | (11.3) | 4 | (16.6) | 5 | (20.0) | 0 | -- | 38 |
| Others | 2 | (2.5) | 1 | (0.9) | 2 | (2.2) | 1 | (1.5) | 1 | (2.3) | 0 | -- | 2 | (8.0) | 0 | -- | 9 |
| Unknown | 7 | (8.7) | 9 | (8.0) | 7 | (7.7) | 7 | (10.4) | 1 | (2.3) | 3 | (12.5) | 1 | (4.0) | 17 | (80.9) | 52 |
| Total | 80 | (100) | 112 | (100) | 91 | (100) | 67 | (100) | 44 | (100) | 24 | (100) | 25 | (100) | 21 | (100) | 464 |

[1] Political affiliation measured by speeches to the First Congress. Only those deputies speaking at least once are included. Percentages are vertical--that is, showing proportions of those speaking from each political group rather than from each republic.

## Table 23. Second Congress — Political Affiliation by Social Position[1]

| Social | Radicals | Left Indep. | Mediators | Centrists | Apparatchiki | Right Indep. | Pre-perestr. | Unknown | Total[2] |
|---|---|---|---|---|---|---|---|---|---|
| | No. % | No. % | No. % | No. % | No. % | No. % | No. % | No. % | No. % |
| Nomenklatura | 1 (1.6) | 4 (4.9) | 19 (20.2) | 29 (43.9) | 27 (43.6) | 3 (15.0) | 3 (15.8) | 215 (11.7) | 301 (13.4) |
| Cadres | 1 (1.6) | 2 (2.4) | 6 (6.4) | 9 (13.6) | 4 (6.4) | 1 (5.0) | 1 (5.3) | 130 (7.1) | 154 (6.9) |
| Military | 2 (3.1) | 2 (2.4) | 1 (1.1) | 2 (3.0) | 5 (8.1) | 4 (20.0) | 0 -- | 75 (4.1) | 91 (4.1) |
| Managers | 9 (14.1) | 7 (8.5) | 10 (10.6) | 14 (21.2) | 8 (12.9) | 5 (25.0) | 5 (26.3) | 338 (18.4) | 396 (17.6) |
| Intelligentsia | 32 (50.0) | 34 (41.5) | 35 (37.2) | 3 (4.6) | 3 (4.8) | 2 (10.0) | 3 (15.8) | 274 (14.9) | 386 (17.2) |
| Technicians | 14 (21.9) | 26 (31.7) | 14 (14.9) | 4 (6.1) | 6 (9.7) | 2 (10.0) | 2 (10.5) | 296 (16.1) | 364 (16.2) |
| Workers | 5 (7.8) | 5 (6.1) | 6 (6.4) | 5 (7.6) | 6 (9.7) | 3 (15.0) | 5 (26.3) | 462 (25.1) | 497 (22.1) |
| Others | 0 -- | 2 (2.4) | 3 (3.2) | 0 -- | 3 (4.8) | 0 -- | 0 -- | 41 (2.2) | 49 (2.2) |
| Unknown | 0 -- | 0 -- | 0 -- | 0 -- | 0 -- | 0 -- | 0 -- | 7 (0.4) | 7 (0.3) |
| Total[3] | 64 (100) | 82 (100) | 94 (100) | 66 (100) | 62 (100) | 20 (100) | 19 (100) | 1838 (100) | 2245 (100) |

[1] Political affiliation measured by speeches to the Second Congress. Only those deputies speaking at least once are included. (Non-speakers and those not categorized are included in the "Unknown" column.) Percentages are vertical-- that is, showing proportions within political groups rather than within social positions.
[2] Total figures for some social positions differ from those given in Table 8. These changes result from shifts in social status experienced by deputies during the Congress.
[3] Totals are smaller than those in column 2 of Table 19 because here only deputies identified by name in the official records have been counted. (Table 19 includes speeches by unidentified deputies.)

## Table 24. Third Congress — Political Affiliation by Social Position[1]

| Social | Radicals | Left Indep. | Mediators | Centrists | Apparatchiki | Right Indep. | Pre-perestr. | Unknown | Total[2] |
|---|---|---|---|---|---|---|---|---|---|
| | No. % | No. % | No. % | No. % | No. % | No. % | No. % | No. % | No. % |
| Nomenklatura | 0 -- | 2 (4.3) | 13 (26.5) | 15 (35.7) | 7 (30.4) | 0 -- | 0 -- | 262 (12.9) | 299 (13.3) |
| Cadres | 1 (2.5) | 3 (6.5) | 3 (6.1) | 3 (7.1) | 1 (4.3) | 0 -- | 0 -- | 143 (7.1) | 154 (6.9) |
| Military | 0 -- | 1 (2.2) | 1 (2.0) | 4 (9.5) | 2 (8.7) | 5 (23.8) | 0 -- | 78 (3.9) | 91 (4.1) |
| Managers | 3 (7.5) | 1 (2.2) | 4 (8.2) | 7 (16.7) | 5 (21.7) | 6 (28.6) | 0 -- | 370 (18.3) | 396 (17.6) |
| Intelligentsia | 22 (55.0) | 26 (56.5) | 16 (32.6) | 8 (19.0) | 2 (8.7) | 2 (9.5) | 0 -- | 310 (15.3) | 386 (17.2) |
| Technicians | 9 (22.5) | 11 (23.9) | 8 (16.3) | 4 (9.5) | 2 (8.7) | 4 (19.0) | 1 (100) | 325 (16.1) | 364 (16.2) |
| Workers | 5 (12.5) | 2 (4.3) | 4 (8.2) | 1 (2.4) | 3 (13.0) | 4 (19.0) | 0 -- | 478 (23.6) | 497 (22.1) |
| Others | 0 -- | 0 -- | 0 -- | 0 -- | 1 (4.3) | 0 -- | 0 -- | 48 (2.4) | 49 (2.2) |
| Unknown | 0 -- | 0 -- | 0 -- | 0 -- | 0 -- | 0 -- | 0 -- | 9 (0.4) | 9 (0.3) |
| Total[3] | 40 (100) | 46 (100) | 49 (100) | 42 (100) | 23 (100) | 21 (100) | 1 (100) | 2023 (100) | 2245 (100) |

[1] Political affiliation measured by speeches to the Third Congress. Only those deputies speaking at least once are included. (Non-speakers and those not categorized are included in the "Unknown" column.) Percentages are vertical-- that is, showing proportions within political groups rather than within social positions.
[2] Total figures for some social positions differ from those given in Table 8. These changes result from shifts in social status experienced by deputies during the Congress.
[3] Totals are smaller than those in column 2 of Table 19 because here only deputies identified by name in the official records have been counted. (Table 19 includes speeches by unidentified deputies.)

*Table 25.* The Social Composition of Political Groups

Int = Intelligentsia
Tech = Technicians
Work = Workers
Oth = Other

Nom = *Nomenklatura*
Cad = Cadres
Mil = Military
Man = Managers

FIRST CONGRESS

Radicals

Int 55.0%

Tech 22.5%

Cad 1.3%
Work 3.7%

Oth 11.2%

Nom 1.3%

Man 5.0%

SECOND CONGRESS

Radicals

Int 50.0%

Tech 21.9%

Cad 1.6%
Work 7.8%

Mil 3.1%
Nom 1.6%

Man 14.1%

THIRD CONGRESS

Radicals

Int 55.0%

Tech 22.5%

Cad 2.5%
Work 12.5%

Man 7.5%

Left-wing Independents

Int 41.1%
Man 10.7%
Oth 8.9%
Tech 23.2%
Work 9.8%
Cad 6.2%

Left-wing Independents

Int 41.5%
Man 8.5%
Mll 2.4%
Nom 4.9%
Oth 2.4%
Tech 31.7%
Work 6.1%
Cad 2.4%

Left-wing Independents

Int 55.3%
Man 2.1%
Mll 2.1%
Nom 4.2%
Tech 25.5%
Work 4.2%
Cad 6.3%

Mediators

Int 40.6%
Man 6.6%
Mll 1.1%
Nom 19.8%
Oth 9.9%
Tech 14.3%
Work 3.3%
Cad 4.4%

Mediators

Int 37.2%
Man 10.6%
Mll 1.1%
Nom 20.2%
Oth 3.2%
Tech 14.9%
Work 6.4%
Cad 6.4%

Mediators

Int 32.7%
Man 8.2%
Mll 2.0%
Nom 26.5%
Tech 16.3%
Work 8.2%
Cad 6.1%

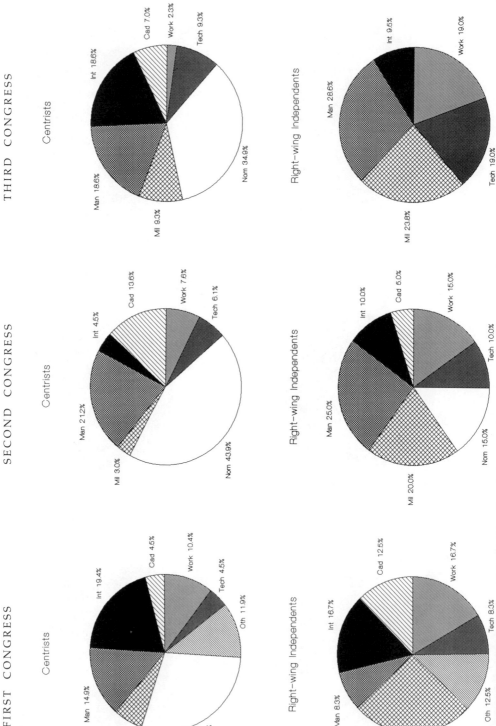

FIRST CONGRESS

SECOND CONGRESS

THIRD CONGRESS

Centrists

Centrists

Centrists

Right-wing Independents

Right-wing Independents

Right-wing Independents

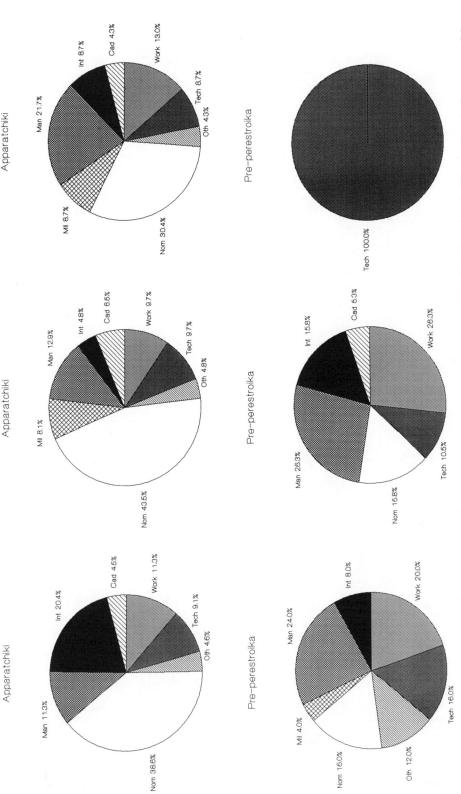

Apparatchiki

Cad 4.3%
Int 8.7%
Man 21.7%
Mil 8.7%
Nom 30.4%
Work 13.0%
Tech 8.7%
Oth 4.3%

Apparatchiki

Cad 6.5%
Int 4.8%
Man 12.9%
Mil 8.1%
Nom 43.5%
Work 9.7%
Tech 9.7%
Oth 4.8%

Apparatchiki

Cad 4.5%
Int 20.4%
Man 11.3%
Nom 38.6%
Work 11.3%
Tech 9.1%
Oth 4.6%

Pre-perestroika

Tech 100.0%

Pre-perestroika

Cad 5.3%
Int 15.8%
Man 26.3%
Nom 15.8%
Work 26.3%
Tech 10.5%

Pre-perestroika

Int 8.0%
Man 24.0%
Mil 4.0%
Nom 16.0%
Oth 12.0%
Tech 16.0%
Work 20.0%

Note on table 25: Figures are taken from tables 22, 23, and 24, but do not include deputies of unknown social position. Deputies who did not speak at the Congresses, and those whose speeches could not be categorized, have also been excluded.

## Table 26. First Congress — Political Profiles by Social Position[1]

| Social Position | Radicals % | Left Indep. % | Mediators % | Centrists % | Apparatchiki % | Right Indep. % | Pre-perestr. % | Unknown % | Total % |
|---|---|---|---|---|---|---|---|---|---|
| Nomenklatura | 1.7 | -- | 30.5 | 32.2 | 28.8 | -- | 6.8 | -- | 100 |
| Cadres | 5.0 | 35.0 | 20.0 | 15.0 | 10.0 | 15.0 | -- | -- | 100 |
| Military | -- | -- | 7.7 | 30.8 | -- | 46.2 | 7.7 | 7.7 | 100 |
| Managers | 8.9 | 26.7 | 13.3 | 22.2 | 11.1 | 4.4 | 13.3 | -- | 100 |
| Intelligentsia | 28.2 | 29.5 | 23.7 | 8.3 | 5.8 | 2.6 | 1.3 | 0.6 | 100 |
| Technicians | 25.0 | 36.1 | 18.0 | 4.2 | 5.6 | 2.8 | 5.6 | 2.8 | 100 |
| Workers | 7.9 | 28.9 | 7.9 | 18.4 | 13.1 | 10.5 | 13.1 | -- | 100 |
| Others | 22.2 | 11.1 | 22.2 | 11.1 | 11.1 | -- | 22.2 | -- | 100 |
| Unknown | 13.5 | 17.3 | 13.5 | 1.9 | 1.9 | 5.8 | 1.9 | 32.7 | 100 |

[1] Political affiliation measured by speeches to the First Congress. This table shows the relative proportion of speeches in each political group. Thus, a vocal deputy may be counted more than once. Percentages are horizontal--that is, showing proportions within social positions rather than within political affiliations.

## Table 27. Second Congress — Political Profiles by Social Position[1]

| Social Position | Radicals % | Left Indep. % | Mediators % | Centrists % | Apparatchiki % | Right Indep. % | Pre-perestr. % | Total % |
|---|---|---|---|---|---|---|---|---|
| Nomenklatura | 1.5 | 4.5 | 22.1 | 33.7 | 31.4 | 3.4 | 3.4 | 100 |
| Cadres | 4.2 | 8.3 | 25.0 | 37.5 | 16.7 | 4.2 | 4.2 | 100 |
| Military | 12.5 | 12.5 | 6.2 | 12.5 | 31.2 | 25.0 | -- | 100 |
| Managers | 15.5 | 12.0 | 17.2 | 24.1 | 13.8 | 8.6 | 8.6 | 100 |
| Intelligentsia | 28.6 | 30.3 | 31.2 | 2.7 | 2.7 | 1.8 | 2.7 | 100 |
| Technicians | 20.6 | 38.2 | 20.6 | 5.9 | 8.8 | 2.9 | 2.9 | 100 |
| Workers | 14.3 | 14.3 | 17.1 | 14.3 | 17.1 | 8.6 | 14.3 | 100 |
| Others | -- | 25.0 | 37.5 | -- | 37.5 | -- | -- | 100 |

[1] Political affiliation measured by speeches to the Second Congress by deputies identified by name. This table shows the relative proportion of speeches in each political group. Thus, a vocal deputy may be counted more than once. Percentages are horizontal--that is, showing proportions within social positions rather than within political affiliations.

## *Table 28.* Third Congress — Political Profiles by Social Position[1]

| Social Position | Radicals | Left Indep. | Mediators | Centrists | Apparatchiki | Right Indep. | Pre-perestr. | Total |
|---|---|---|---|---|---|---|---|---|
| | % | % | % | % | % | % | % | % |
| Nomenklatura | -- | 5.4 | 35.1 | 40.5 | 18.9 | -- | -- | 100 |
| Cadres | 9.1 | 27.3 | 27.3 | 27.3 | 9.1 | -- | -- | 100 |
| Military | -- | 7.7 | 7.7 | 30.8 | 15.4 | 38.5 | -- | 100 |
| Managers | 11.5 | 3.8 | 15.4 | 26.9 | 19.2 | 23.1 | -- | 100 |
| Intelligentsia | 28.9 | 34.2 | 21.0 | 10.5 | 2.6 | 2.6 | -- | 100 |
| Technicians | 23.1 | 28.2 | 20.5 | 10.3 | 5.1 | 10.3 | 2.6 | 100 |
| Workers | 26.3 | 10.5 | 21.0 | 5.3 | 15.8 | 21.0 | -- | 100 |
| Others | -- | -- | -- | -- | 100 | -- | -- | 100 |

[1] Political affiliation measured by speeches to the Third Congress by deputies identified by name. This table shows the relative proportion of speeches in each political group. Thus, a vocal deputy may be counted more than once. Percentages are horizontal--that is, showing proportions within social positions rather than within political affiliations.

*Table 29.* The Political Composition of Social Groups

Rad = Radicals
LI = Left-wing Independents
Med = Mediators
Cen = Centrists

RI = Right-wing Independents
App = *Apparatchiki*
Pre = Pre-*perestroika*

FIRST CONGRESS

SECOND CONGRESS

THIRD CONGRESS

Nomenklatura

App 28.8%

Rad 1.7%

Pre 6.8%

Med 30.5%

Cen 32.2%

Nomenklatura

App 31.4%

Rad 1.2%

RI 3.5%

Pre 3.5%

Med 22.1%

LI 4.7%

Cen 33.7%

Nomenklatura

App 18.9%

Med 35.1%

LI 5.4%

Cen 40.5%

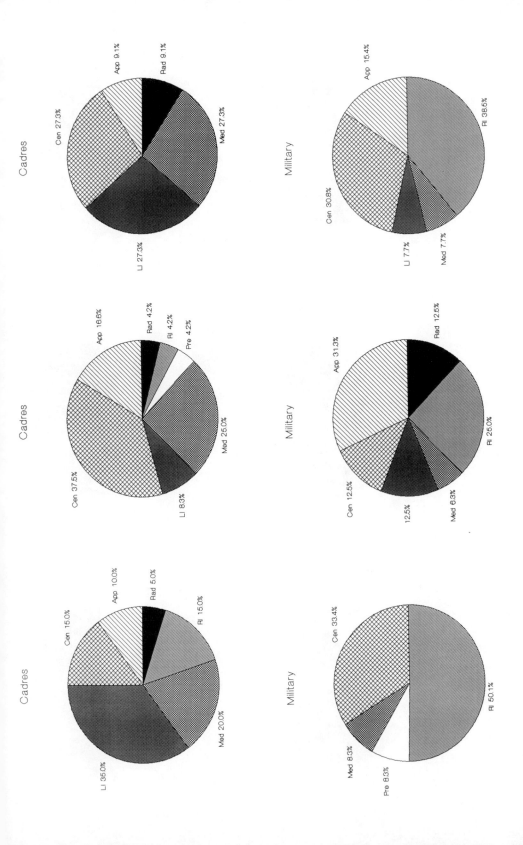

Cadres

Li 35.0%
Med 20.0%
Rl 15.0%
Rad 5.0%
App 10.0%
Cen 15.0%

Cadres

App 16.6%
Rad 4.2%
Rl 4.2%
Pre 4.2%
Med 25.0%
Li 8.3%
Cen 37.5%

Cadres

App 9.1%
Rad 9.1%
Med 27.3%
Li 27.3%
Cen 27.3%

Military

Rl 50.1%
Pre 8.3%
Med 8.3%
Cen 33.4%

Military

Rad 12.5%
Rl 26.0%
Med 6.3%
12.5%
Cen 12.5%
App 31.3%

Military

Rl 38.5%
Med 7.7%
Li 7.7%
Cen 30.8%
App 15.4%

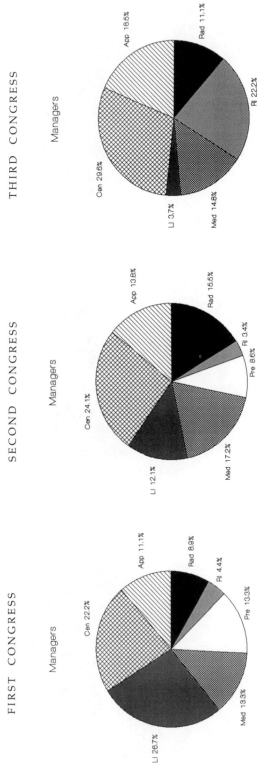
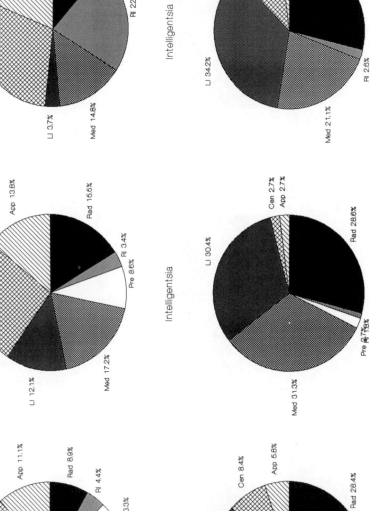

FIRST CONGRESS

SECOND CONGRESS

THIRD CONGRESS

Managers

Managers

Managers

Intelligentsia

Intelligentsia

Intelligentsia

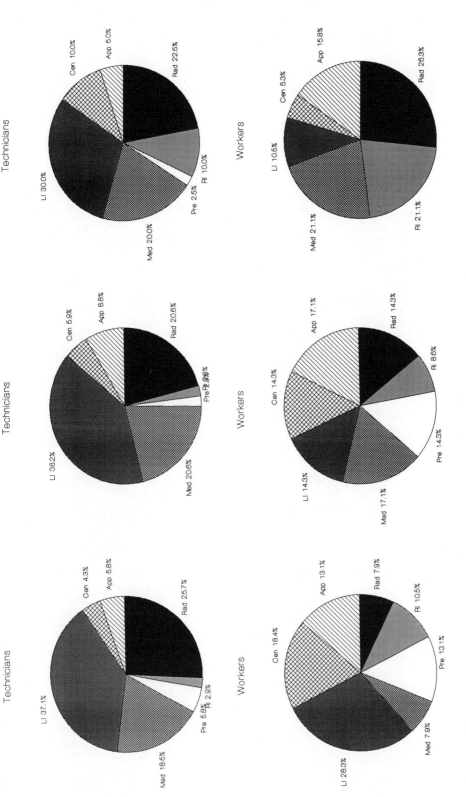

Technicians

Technicians

Technicians

Workers

Workers

Workers

Note on table 29: Figures are taken from tables 26, 27, and 28, but do not include deputies who did not speak at the Congresses, nor those whose speeches could not be categorized. Deputies of unknown social position and those classified as "Other" have also been excluded.

## *Table 30.* Important First Congress Votes

| Issue | For | Against | Abstain | Prop. 1 | Prop. 2 |
|---|---|---|---|---|---|
| 1) Agenda | Majority | 379 | 9 | -- | -- |
| 2) Stankevich for open roll-call | -- | -- | ? | 431 | Majority |
| 3) Alksnis against electoral irreg. in Lithuania | -- | -- | ? | 246 | Majority |
| 4) Obolenskii on self-nomination | 689 | 1415 | 33 | -- | -- |
| 5) Gorbachev for president | 2123 | 87 | 11 | -- | -- |
| 6) Cancel government decree of 28 June 1988 | 831 | 1261 | 30 | -- | -- |
| 7) Full-time deputy status | -- | -- | ? | 1419 | 636 |
| 8) Konovalov on state duties | 851 | 1130 | 47 | -- | -- |
| 9) Lukianov for first vice president | Majority | 179 | 137 | -- | -- |
| 10) Inquiry about Gdlian | Majority | 61 | 91 | -- | -- |
| 11) Constitutional Control Committee | Majority | 433 | 61 | -- | -- |
| 12) Kolbin for pres. of People's Control Committee | Majority | 252 | 138 | -- | -- |
| 13) Sukharev for General Prosecutor | Majority | 330 | 273 | -- | -- |
| 14) Obolenskii for Const. Control | 934 | 903 | 273 | -- | -- |
| 15) To exclude Samsonov from Const. Control | 555 | 1188 | 101 | -- | -- |
| 16) Evtushenko for Const. Control | 449 | Majority | ? | -- | -- |
| 17) Vlasov for Const. Control | 830 | 934 | ? | -- | -- |

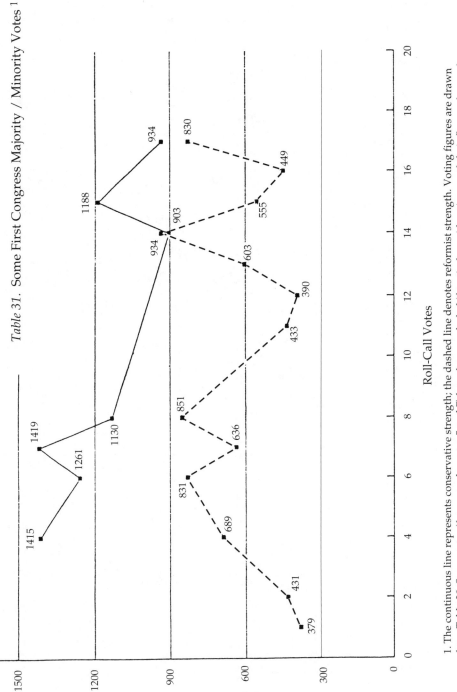

*Table 31.* Some First Congress Majority / Minority Votes [1]

Roll-Call Votes

Number of Deputies

1. The continuous line represents conservative strength; the dashed line denotes reformist strength. Voting figures are drawn from Table 30. Some votes (for example, votes 5 and 7) have been excluded if tactical considerations unduly influenced — and distorted — deputy behavior. Abstentions have been omitted, except in votes 12 and 13, where abstentions are counted as progressive because they helped secure the measure's defeat.

*Table 32.* Supreme Soviet Committees and Permanent Commissions

*Committees*

Agriculture and Food Supply.
    Chair: Arkadii Veprev (Sovkhoz director, Krasnoiarsk).

Foreign Affairs.
    Chair: Alexander Dzasokov (Former Party First Secretary,
    North Ossetian Autonomous Republic).

Veterans and Invalids.
    Chair: Nikolai Bosenko (President, RSFSR Union of War
    Veterans and Labour).

Building and Architecture.
    Chair: Boris Yeltsin (Former First Deputy President, State
    Building Committee).

Defense and State Security.
    Chair: Vladimir Lapygin (Director, Moscow scientific-
    industrial enterprise).

Ecology and Natural Resources.
    Chair: Salykov Kalymbek (Former Party First Secretary,
    Karakalpak Autonomous Republic).

Economic Reform.
    Chair: Valentin Vologzhin (Director of "Conveyor" factory,
    Lvov).

Glasnost, Civil Rights, and Citizen Complaints.
    Chair: Vladimir Foteev (Former Party First Secretary,
    Checheno-Ingush Autonomous Republic).

Legislation, Law, and Order.
    Chair: Sergei Alekseev (Director, Institute of Philosophy and
    Law, Siberian section, USSR Academy of Sciences).

Soviets and Local Administrative Development.
    Chair: Nikolai Pivovarov (Former President, Regional
    Executive Committee, Rostov).

Science, National Education, and Culture.
    Chair: Iurii Ryzhov (Rector, Moscow Aviation Institute).

Women, Family Protection, Maternity, and Childhood.
    Chair: Valentina Matveenko (Former Deputy President, City
    Executive Committee, Leningrad).

Youth.

    Chair: Valerii Tsybukh (Former First Secretary, Ukrainian
Komsomol).

*Permanent Commissions, Soviet of the Union*

Planning, Budget, and Finance.
    Chair: Viktor Kucherenko (Former President, Executive
Committee, Donetsk Region).

Industry, Energy, Factories, and Technology.
    Chair: Vladimir Kurtashin (Director, "Kriogenmash" union,
    Moscow region).

Labor, Prices, and Welfare.
    Chair: Nikolai Gritsenko (Rector, Higher School of Trade
    Unions).

Transport, Communication, and Information.
    Chair: Valentin Tetenov (First Deputy Chief, Railroad
    Department, Perm).

*Permanent Commissions, Soviet of Nationalities*

Consumer Goods, Commerce, and Services.
    Chair: Gennadi Kiselev (Former Party Second Secretary,
    Kirghizia).

Nationalities Policy and Interethnic Relations.
    Chair: Georgii Tarasevich (Former President, Belorussian
    Supreme Soviet).

Cultural Development, Linguistic and Historical Traditions, and
Protection of Historical Heritage.
    Chair: Chingiz Aitmatov (President, Kirghiz Union of
    Writers).

Republican and Regional Economic and Social Development.
    Chair: Eduard Vilkas (Director, Lithuanian Economic
    Institute).

**Table 33.** Second Congress Roll-Call Statistics by Political Affiliation as Measured by Second Congress Speeches

| Affiliation | | No. of Cases | Minimum | Maximum | Mean | Standard Deviation |
|---|---|---|---|---|---|---|
| Radicals | Votes | 64 | 3 | 23 | 19.48 | 5.19 |
| | Average | | -0.95 | 45.71 | 26.37 | 12.36 |
| Left-wing Indep. | Votes | 82 | 4 | 23 | 17.81 | 5.28 |
| | Average | | -20.44 | 52.50 | 14.56 | 18.35 |
| Mediators | Votes | 94 | 2 | 23 | 20.22 | 4.68 |
| | Average | | -26.09 | 47.00 | 1.92 | 14.84 |
| Centrists | Votes | 66 | 4 | 23 | 20.41 | 3.62 |
| | Average | | -27.33 | 25.71 | -8.31 | 10.17 |
| Apparatchiki | Votes | 62 | 6 | 23 | 20.94 | 3.19 |
| | Average | | -28.33 | 37.50 | -10.44 | 10.59 |
| Right-wing Indep. | Votes | 20 | 5 | 23 | 19.75 | 4.53 |
| | Average | | -17.73 | 16.09 | -2.22 | 9.51 |
| Pre-perestroika | Votes | 19 | 20 | 23 | 21.90 | 1.29 |
| | Average | | -19.50 | 29.55 | -6.46 | 13.30 |

```
                Political Spectrum by Group Mean Averages
Radicals                      +26.37
Left-wing Independents        +14.56
Mediators                      +1.92
Right-wing Independents        -2.22
Pre-perestroika                -6.46
Centrists                      -8.31
Apparatchiki                  -10.44
```

**Table 34.** Third Congress Roll-Call Statistics by Political Affiliation as Measured by Third Congress Speeches

| Affiliation | | No. of Cases | Minimum | Maximum | Mean | Standard Deviation |
|---|---|---|---|---|---|---|
| Radicals | Votes | 40 | 7 | 26 | 23.73 | 4.15 |
| | Average | | -10.00 | 31.54 | 15.72 | 8.85 |
| Left-wing Indep. | Votes | 46 | 0 | 26 | 22.20 | 7.52 |
| | Average | | -25.77 | 55.00 | 9.70 | 14.02 |
| Mediators | Votes | 49 | 18 | 26 | 24.94 | 1.84 |
| | Average | | -25.00 | 20.53 | 0.17 | 10.43 |
| Centrists | Votes | 42 | 0 | 26 | 24.64 | 4.30 |
| | Average | | -18.00 | 28.08 | -0.87 | 10.46 |
| Apparatchiki | Votes | 23 | 18 | 26 | 25.17 | 1.92 |
| | Average | | -16.92 | 10.77 | -5.05 | 7.88 |
| Right-wing Indep. | Votes | 21 | 7 | 26 | 23.05 | 5.60 |
| | Average | | -21.43 | 17.69 | 4.94 | 9.75 |
| Pre-perestroika | Votes | 1 | 26 | 26 | 26 | -- |
| | Average | | -5.77 | -5.77 | -5.77 | -- |

```
                Political Spectrum by Group Mean Averages
Radicals                      +15.72
Left-wing Independents         +9.70
Right-wing Independents        +4.94
Mediators                      +0.17
Centrists                      -0.87
Apparatchiki                   -5.05
Pre-perestroika                -5.77
```

*Table 35.* Second Congress Roll-Call Statistics by Means of Election [1]

| Affiliation | | No. of Cases | Minimum | Maximum | Mean | Standard Deviation |
|---|---|---|---|---|---|---|
| Social Organizations | Votes | 746 | 0 | 23 | 19.27 | 5.57 |
| | Average | | -40.00 | 60.00 | -4.02 | 15.21 |
| Electoral Districts | Votes | 1497 | 0 | 23 | 20.03 | 5.03 |
| | Average | | -50.00 | 70.00 | 2.75 | 17.22 |

[1] Does not include two deputies for whom means of election is unknown.

*Table 36.* Third Congress Roll-Call Statistics by Means of Election [1]

| Affiliation | | No. of Cases | Minimum | Maximum | Mean | Standard Deviation |
|---|---|---|---|---|---|---|
| Social Organizations | Votes | 747 | 0 | 26 | 22.83 | 7.48 |
| | Average | | -34.29 | 40.00 | 0.07 | 9.13 |
| Electoral Districts | Votes | 1496 | 0 | 26 | 22.76 | 7.33 |
| | Average | | -50.00 | 55.00 | 3.18 | 11.49 |

[1] Does not include two deputies for whom means of election is unknown.

## Table 37. Second Congress Roll-Call Statistics by Republic [1]

| Affiliation | | No. of Cases | Minimum | Maximum | Mean | Standard Deviation |
|---|---|---|---|---|---|---|
| Armenia | Votes | 53 | 0 | 23 | 18.15 | 6.08 |
| | Average | | -40.00 | 43.00 | 2.42 | 16.10 |
| Azerbaijan | Votes | 72 | 0 | 23 | 17.64 | 7.08 |
| | Average | | -37.78 | 34.00 | -6.09 | 11.92 |
| Georgia | Votes | 91 | 0 | 23 | 18.15 | 6.49 |
| | Average | | -21.54 | 44.00 | 8.37 | 12.19 |
| Russian SFSR | Votes | 900 | 0 | 23 | 21.22 | 3.67 |
| | Average | | -40.00 | 60.00 | 0.93 | 14.96 |
| Moscow | Votes | 195 | 0 | 23 | 17.30 | 6.57 |
| | Average | | -38.00 | 47.86 | -1.84 | 18.04 |
| Ukraine | Votes | 262 | 0 | 23 | 21.07 | 3.55 |
| | Average | | -23.64 | 45.71 | -1.24 | 14.13 |
| Belorussia | Votes | 94 | 0 | 23 | 21.15 | 4.01 |
| | Average | | -21.30 | 55.63 | -3.18 | 13.91 |
| Moldavia | Votes | 55 | 0 | 23 | 18.89 | 6.08 |
| | Average | | -18.26 | 29.55 | 3.17 | 12.08 |
| Estonia | Votes | 48 | 3 | 23 | 12.08 | 4.90 |
| | Average | | -12.50 | 52.27 | 25.75 | 15.43 |
| Latvia | Votes | 52 | 7 | 23 | 15.14 | 3.95 |
| | Average | | -18.26 | 54.00 | 19.04 | 18.25 |
| Lithuania | Votes | 58 | 0 | 23 | 8.31 | 5.66 |
| | Average | | -20.00 | 70.00 | 35.27 | 17.44 |
| Kazakhstan | Votes | 97 | 0 | 23 | 20.68 | 4.32 |
| | Average | | -50.00 | 31.82 | -8.64 | 14.39 |
| Kirghizia | Votes | 53 | 10 | 23 | 20.96 | 2.90 |
| | Average | | -27.33 | 26.82 | -10.15 | 10.05 |
| Turkmenia | Votes | 46 | 11 | 23 | 21.89 | 2.09 |
| | Average | | -22.17 | 37.00 | -7.90 | 10.94 |
| Tadzhikistan | Votes | 57 | 0 | 23 | 21.46 | 3.60 |
| | Average | | -20.87 | 22.61 | -8.96 | 8.29 |
| Uzbekistan | Votes | 110 | 8 | 23 | 20.56 | 3.31 |
| | Average | | -33.75 | 9.05 | -12.59 | 8.00 |
| Entire Congress | Votes | 2245 | 0 | 23 | 19.76 | 5.26 |
| | Average | | -50.00 | 70.00 | 0.50 | 16.87 |

*Political Spectrum by Republican Mean Averages*

1) Lithuania       +35.27
2) Estonia         +25.75
3) Latvia          +19.04
4) Georgia          +8.37
5) Moldavia         +3.17
6) Armenia          +2.42
7) Russian SFSR     +0.93
8) Ukraine          -1.24
9) Moscow           -1.84
10) Belorussia      -3.18
11) Azerbaijan      -6.09
12) Turkmenia       -7.90
13) Kazakhstan      -8.64
14) Tadzhikistan    -8.96
15) Kirghizia      -10.15
16) Uzbekistan     -12.59

---

[1] Republic is unknown for two deputies.

## *Table 38.* Third Congress Roll-Call Statistics by Republic [1]

| Affiliation | | No. of Cases | Minimum | Maximum | Mean | Standard Deviation |
|---|---|---|---|---|---|---|
| Armenia | Votes | 53 | 0 | 26 | 23.47 | 6.05 |
| | Average | | -12.31 | 21.15 | 5.34 | 8.06 |
| Azerbaijan | Votes | 72 | 0 | 26 | 21.86 | 8.15 |
| | Average | | -23.85 | 22.29 | -4.85 | 8.02 |
| Georgia | Votes | 91 | 0 | 26 | 19.08 | 9.47 |
| | Average | | -36.67 | 22.27 | -0.89 | 8.81 |
| Russian SFSR | Votes | 902 | 0 | 26 | 24.41 | 4.87 |
| | Average | | -34.23 | 48.33 | 3.39 | 11.18 |
| Moscow | Votes | 193 | 0 | 26 | 22.54 | 7.78 |
| | Average | | -34.29 | 33.82 | -1.29 | 10.48 |
| Ukraine | Votes | 262 | 0 | 26 | 24.23 | 5.03 |
| | Average | | -25.88 | 45.00 | 2.06 | 10.41 |
| Belorussia | Votes | 94 | 0 | 26 | 24.30 | 5.31 |
| | Average | | -13.46 | 23.46 | 3.44 | 7.88 |
| Moldavia | Votes | 55 | 0 | 26 | 23.04 | 6.81 |
| | Average | | -12.08 | 28.08 | 5.30 | 9.47 |
| Estonia | Votes | 48 | 0 | 26 | 9.25 | 10.41 |
| | Average | | -21.43 | 47.50 | 13.18 | 17.52 |
| Latvia | Votes | 52 | 0 | 26 | 18.19 | 9.28 |
| | Average | | -13.46 | 55.00 | 11.91 | 13.90 |
| Lithuania | Votes | 58 | 0 | 25 | 0.60 | 3.47 |
| | Average | | -50.00 | 10.00 | -0.60 | 6.67 |
| Kazakhstan | Votes | 97 | 0 | 26 | 23.97 | 5.62 |
| | Average | | -21.11 | 28.89 | 2.03 | 9.10 |
| Kirghizia | Votes | 53 | 0 | 26 | 24.11 | 5.40 |
| | Average | | -21.60 | 27.50 | -0.04 | 10.49 |
| Turkmenia | Votes | 46 | 22 | 26 | 25.63 | 0.90 |
| | Average | | -16.92 | 18.07 | -1.25 | 7.66 |
| Tadzhikistan | Votes | 56 | 0 | 26 | 25.27 | 3.52 |
| | Average | | -18.85 | 22.80 | -1.79 | 8.20 |
| Uzbekistan | Votes | 110 | 0 | 26 | 24.02 | 5.49 |
| | Average | | -15.20 | 22.73 | -2.17 | 7.14 |
| Entire Congress | Votes | 2245 | 0 | 26 | 22.79 | 7.38 |
| | Average | | -50.00 | 55.00 | 2.14 | 10.86 |

```
           Political Spectrum by Republican Mean Averages
 1) Estonia          +13.18
 2) Latvia           +11.91
 3) Armenia          +5.34
 4) Moldavia         +5.30
 5) Belorussia       +3.44
 6) Russian SFSR     +3.39
 7) Ukraine          +2.06
 8) Kazakhstan       +2.03
 9) Kirghizia        -0.04
10) Lithuania        -0.60
11) Georgia          -0.89
12) Turkmenia        -1.25
13) Moscow           -1.29
14) Tadzhikistan     -1.79
15) Uzbekistan       -2.17
16) Azerbaijan       -4.84
```

---

[1] Republic is unknown for three deputies.

## *Table 39.* Second Congress Roll-Call Statistics by Social Position

| Affiliation | | No. of Cases | Minimum | Maximum | Mean | Standard Deviation |
|---|---|---|---|---|---|---|
| *Nomenklatura* | Votes | 301 | 0 | 23 | 19.65 | 5.24 |
| | Average | | -50.00 | 45.71 | -9.38 | 12.89 |
| Cadres | Votes | 154 | 0 | 23 | 19.86 | 4.72 |
| | Average | | -35.00 | 59.00 | -1.71 | 16.45 |
| Military | Votes | 91 | 0 | 23 | 21.10 | 3.87 |
| | Average | | -23.64 | 38.64 | -5.05 | 14.47 |
| Managers | Votes | 396 | 0 | 23 | 20.46 | 4.35 |
| | Average | | -25.77 | 49.00 | -0.16 | 14.86 |
| Intelligentsia | Votes | 386 | 0 | 23 | 16.44 | 7.13 |
| | Average | | -40.00 | 70.00 | 11.26 | 19.64 |
| Technicians | Votes | 364 | 0 | 23 | 20.24 | 4.72 |
| | Average | | -38.00 | 55.83 | 5.23 | 17.20 |
| Workers | Votes | 497 | 0 | 23 | 21.29 | 3.46 |
| | Average | | -27.33 | 54.00 | -2.13 | 12.94 |
| Other | Votes | 49 | 0 | 23 | 19.17 | 5.22 |
| | Average | | -33.75 | 24.00 | -9.04 | 12.82 |
| Unknown | Votes | 7 | 0 | 23 | 14.57 | 10.31 |
| | Average | | -21.50 | 14.33 | -3.39 | 11.23 |

*Political Spectrum by Group Mean Averages*

| | |
|---|---|
| Intelligentsia | +11.26 |
| Technicians | +5.23 |
| Managers | -0.16 |
| Cadres | -1.71 |
| Workers | -2.13 |
| Military | -5.05 |
| Other | -9.03 |
| *Nomenklatura* | -9.38 |

## Table 40. Third Congress Roll-Call Statistics by Social Position

| Affiliation | | No. of Cases | Minimum | Maximum | Mean | Standard Deviation |
|---|---|---|---|---|---|---|
| Nomenklatura | Votes | 299 | 0 | 26 | 22.99 | 7.30 |
| | Average | | -34.29 | 47.50 | -5.75 | 9.05 |
| Cadres | Votes | 154 | 0 | 26 | 24.04 | 5.75 |
| | Average | | -20.39 | 30.00 | 0.47 | 9.53 |
| Military | Votes | 91 | 0 | 26 | 24.74 | 3.79 |
| | Average | | -29.23 | 26.82 | -1.28 | 11.76 |
| Managers | Votes | 396 | 0 | 26 | 23.66 | 6.02 |
| | Average | | -23.85 | 48.33 | 3.42 | 10.46 |
| Intelligentsia | Votes | 386 | 0 | 26 | 18.54 | 10.63 |
| | Average | | -50.00 | 55.00 | 5.56 | 11.32 |
| Technicians | Votes | 364 | 0 | 26 | 22.63 | 7.52 |
| | Average | | -23.85 | 40.00 | 5.62 | 10.79 |
| Workers | Votes | 497 | 0 | 26 | 24.55 | 4.52 |
| | Average | | -36.67 | 33.75 | 5.62 | 10.79 |
| Other | Votes | 49 | 0 | 26 | 23.27 | 6.47 |
| | Average | | -18.85 | 28.08 | -1.19 | 9.09 |
| Unknown | Votes | 9 | 23 | 26 | 24.89 | 1.05 |
| | Average | | -15.65 | -0.80 | -9.18 | 5.38 |

*Political Spectrum by Group Mean Averages*

| | |
|---|---|
| Technicians | +5.62 |
| Intelligentsia | +5.55 |
| Managers | +3.42 |
| Workers | +2.34 |
| Cadres | +0.47 |
| Other | -1.19 |
| Military | -1.28 |
| *Nomenklatura* | -5.75 |

## Table 41. Shifts in Political Affiliation of Speakers between First and Second Congresses [1]

| First Congress Affiliation | Radicals (%) | Mediators Left Indep. (%) | Mediators (%) | Centrists (%) | Apparat. (%) | Right Indep. (%) | Pre-perestr. (%) | Unknown | Total |
|---|---|---|---|---|---|---|---|---|---|
| Radicals (%) | 27 (60.0) (61.4) | 12 (29.3) (27.3) | 2 (4.9) (4.5) | 1 (5.3) (2.3) | 1 (6.2) (2.3) | 1 (10.0) (2.3) | -- -- -- | 30 | 74 |
| Left Indep. (%) | 13 (28.9) (29.5) | 17 (41.5) (38.6) | 10 (24.4) (22.3) | -- -- -- | 3 (18.7) (6.8) | 1 (10.0) (2.3) | -- -- -- | 56 | 100 |
| Mediators (%) | 3 (6.7) (7.5) | 6 (14.7) (15.0) | 26 (63.4) (65.0) | 4 (21.0) (10.0) | -- -- -- | -- -- -- | 1 (50.0) (2.5) | 41 | 81 |
| Centrists (%) | -- -- -- | 2 (4.9) (14.3) | 2 (4.9) (14.3) | 6 (31.6) (42.8) | 2 (12.5) (14.3) | 1 (10.0) (7.1) | 1 (50.0) (7.1) | 39 | 53 |
| Apparat. (%) | -- -- -- | 2 (4.9) (11.8) | -- -- -- | 7 (36.8) (41.1) | 7 (43.7) (41.1) | 1 (10.0) (5.3) | -- -- -- | 27 | 44 |
| Right Indep. (%) | 1 (2.2) (10.0) | 2 (4.9) (20.0) | -- -- -- | -- -- -- | 1 (6.2) (10.0) | 6 (60.0) (60.0) | -- -- -- | 11 | 21 |
| Pre-perestr. (%) | -- -- -- | -- -- -- | 1 (2.4) (25.0) | 1 (5.3) (25.0) | 2 (12.5) (50.0) | -- -- -- | -- -- -- | 18 | 22 |
| Unknown | 20 | 41 | 53 | 47 | 46 | 10 | 17 | 1616 | 1850 |
| *Total* | 64 | 82 | 94 | 66 | 62 | 20 | 19 | 1838 | 2245 |

[1] Percentages have been calculated only on identified deputies who spoke in both Congresses.

*Table 42.* Shifts in Political Affiliation of Speakers between Second and Third Congresses [1]

| Second Congress Affiliation | Radicals | Mediators | | | Apparat. | Pre-perestr. | | Unknown | Total |
| | | Left Indep. | | Centrists | | Right Indep. | | | |
| | Radicals (%) | Left Indep. (%) | Mediators (%) | Centrists (%) | Apparat. (%) | Right Indep. (%) | Pre-perestr. (%) | Unknown | Total |
|---|---|---|---|---|---|---|---|---|---|
| Radicals | 24 (80.0) | -- -- | 1 (3.8) | -- -- | -- -- | 2 (14.3) | -- -- | 36 | 63 |
| (%) | (88.9) | -- | (3.7) | -- | -- | (7.4) | -- | | |
| Left Indep. | 2 (6.7) | 20 (83.3) | 2 (7.6) | 1 (6.7) | -- -- | -- -- | -- -- | 57 | 82 |
| (%) | (8.0) | (80.0) | (8.0) | (4.0) | -- | -- | -- | | |
| Mediators | 4 (13.4) | 2 (8.3) | 20 (76.9) | -- -- | -- -- | 1 (7.1) | -- -- | 66 | 93 |
| (%) | (14.8) | (7.4) | (74.1) | -- | -- | (3.7) | -- | | |
| Centrists | -- -- | 1 (4.2) | 1 (3.8) | 11 (73.3) | -- -- | 3 (31.4) | -- -- | 50 | 66 |
| (%) | -- | (6.2) | (6.2) | (68.7) | -- | (18.6) | -- | | |
| Apparat. | -- -- | -- -- | 2 (7.6) | 1 (6.7) | 3 (60.0) | 1 (14.3) | -- -- | 55 | 62 |
| (%) | -- | -- | (28.6) | (14.3) | (42.8) | (14.3) | -- | | |
| Right Indep. | -- -- | -- -- | -- -- | 2 (13.4) | 1 (20.0) | 7 (50.0) | -- -- | 10 | 20 |
| (%) | -- | -- | -- | (20.0) | (10.0) | (70.0) | -- | | |
| Pre-perestr. | -- -- | 1 (4.2) | -- -- | -- -- | 1 (20.0) | -- -- | -- -- | 17 | 19 |
| (%) | -- | (50.0) | -- | -- | (50.0) | -- | -- | | |
| Unknown | 10 | 22 | 23 | 27 | 18 | 7 | 1 | 1732 | 1840 |
| Total | 40 | 46 | 49 | 42 | 23 | 21 | 1 | 2023 | 2245 |

[1] Percentages have been calculated only on identified deputies who spoke in both Congresses.

*Table 43.* Shifts in Political Affiliation of Speakers between First and Third Congresses [1]

| First Congress Affiliation | Radicals | Mediators | | | Apparat. | Pre-perestr. | | Unknown | Total |
| | | Left Indep. | | Centrists | | Right Indep. | | | |
| | Radicals (%) | Left Indep. (%) | Mediators (%) | Centrists (%) | Apparat. (%) | Right Indep. (%) | Pre-perestr. (%) | Unknown | Total |
|---|---|---|---|---|---|---|---|---|---|
| Radicals | 16 (55.2) | 8 (25.5) | -- -- | -- -- | -- -- | 1 (9.1) | -- -- | 49 | 74 |
| (%) | (64.0) | (32.0) | -- | -- | -- | (4.0) | -- | | |
| Left Indep. | 10 (34.5) | 18 (52.9) | 7 (28.0) | -- -- | -- -- | 3 (27.3) | -- -- | 62 | 100 |
| (%) | (26.3) | (47.4) | (18.4) | -- | -- | (7.9) | -- | | |
| Mediators | 3 (10.3) | 8 (25.5) | 14 (56.0) | 3 (17.6) | -- -- | 1 (9.1) | -- -- | 52 | 81 |
| (%) | (10.3) | (27.6) | (48.3) | (10.3) | -- | (3.4) | -- | | |
| Centrists | -- -- | -- -- | 4 (16.0) | 11 (64.7) | 2 (40.0) | -- -- | -- -- | 36 | 53 |
| (%) | -- | -- | (23.5) | (64.7) | (11.8) | -- | -- | | |
| Apparat. | -- -- | -- -- | -- -- | 2 (11.8) | 3 (60.0) | -- -- | -- -- | 39 | 44 |
| (%) | -- | -- | -- | (40.0) | (60.0) | -- | -- | | |
| Right Indep. | -- -- | -- -- | -- -- | -- -- | -- -- | 6 (54.5) | -- -- | 15 | 21 |
| (%) | -- | -- | -- | -- | -- | (100.) | -- | | |
| Pre-perestr. | -- -- | -- -- | -- -- | 1 (5.9) | -- -- | -- -- | -- -- | 21 | 22 |
| (%) | -- | -- | -- | (100.) | -- | -- | -- | | |
| Unknown | 11 | 12 | 24 | 25 | 18 | 10 | 1 | 1744 | 1845 |
| Total | 40 | 46 | 49 | 42 | 23 | 21 | 1 | 2023 | 2245 |

[1] Percentages have been calculated only on identified deputies who spoke in both Congresses.

## Table 44. Second Congress Roll-Call Vote Statistical Codings [1]

| Vote No.[2] | Total Voting | Majority (%) | "For" (Value) | (Coeff.) | "Against" (Value) | (Coeff.) | "Abstain" (Value) | (Coeff.) |
|---|---|---|---|---|---|---|---|---|
| 1 | 2119 | 56.34 | 867 (+10) | (5) | 1194 (−10) | (4) | 57 (−5) | (4) |
| 4 | 2081 | 76.93 | 1601 (−10) | (3) | 438 (+10) | (6) | 42 (+5) | (6) |
| 8 | 2006 | 83.59 | 1677 (+10) | (2) | 273 (−10) | (7) | 56 (−5) | (7) |
| 19 | 1885 | 92.30 | 1740 (−10) | (1) | 98 (+10) | (8) | 47 (+5) | (8) |
| 20 | 1902 | 70.97 | 1350 (−10) | (3) | 510 (+10) | (6) | 42 (−5) | (6) |
| 21 | 1888 | 55.66 | 773 (−10) | (5) | 1051 (+10) | (4) | 64 (+5) | (4) |
| 26 | 1995 | 76.79 | 1532 (−10) | (3) | 419 (+10) | (6) | 44 (+5) | (6) |
| 27 | 1985 | 77.17 | 389 (+10) | (6) | 1532 (−10) | (3) | 64 (+5) | (6) |
| 28 | 1982 | 85.01 | 199 (+10) | (7) | 1685 (−10) | (2) | 98 (+5) | (7) |
| 41 | 1932 | 55.79 | 1078 (−10) | (4) | 810 (+10) | (5) | 44 (+5) | (5) |
| 73 | 1917 | 82.05 | 1573 (−10) | (2) | 306 (+10) | (7) | 38 (+5) | (7) |
| 75 | 1928 | 87.44 | 1686 (−10) | (1) | 197 (+10) | (8) | 45 (+5) | (8) |
| 76 | 1921 | 65.74 | 520 (−10) | (5) | 1263 (+10) | (4) | 138 (+5) | (4) |
| 85 | 1927 | 88.06 | 1697 (−10) | (1) | 170 (+10) | (8) | 60 (+5) | (8) |
| 88 | 1942 | 67.61 | 1313 (−10) | (3) | 578 (+10) | (6) | 51 (+5) | (6) |
| 91 | 1889 | 91.90 | 1736 (+10) | (1) | 75 (−10) | (8) | 78 (+5) | (1) |
| 92 | 1886 | 87.80 | 1656 (−10) | (1) | 119 (+10) | (8) | 111 (+5) | (8) |
| 93 | 1879 | 87.22 | 1639 (−10) | (1) | 137 (+10) | (8) | 103 (+5) | (8) |
| 94 | 1878 | 87.69 | 1647 (−10) | (1) | 116 (+10) | (8) | 115 (+5) | (8) |
| 95 | 1876 | 93.97 | 1763 (+10) | (1) | 47 (−10) | (8) | 66 (+5) | (1) |
| 96 | 1879 | 95.98 | 1735 (+10) | (1) | 61 (−10) | (8) | 83 (+5) | (1) |
| 97 | 1897 | 80.17 | 306 (+10) | (7) | 1521 (−10) | (2) | 70 (−5) | (2) |
| 105 | 1783 | 87.26 | 1556 (+10) | (1) | 197 (−10) | (8) | 30 (−5) | (8) |

[1] Data source: *Vtoroi S''ezd Narodnykh Deputatov SSSR, Biulleteny, Izdanie Verkhovnogo Soveta SSSR* (Moscow, 1989). For an explanation of these codes, especially the values and coefficients, see the discussion of methodology in chapter 15.
[2] Indicates the number of the vote as given in the official Congress records.

## Table 45. Third Congress Roll-Call Vote Statistical Codings [1]

| Vote No.[2] | Total Voting | Majority (%) | "For" (Value) | (Coeff.) | "Against" (Value) | (Coeff.) | "Abstain" (Value) | (Coeff.) |
|---|---|---|---|---|---|---|---|---|
| 12 | 2011 | 90.3 | 1817 (−10) | (1) | 133 (+10) | (8) | 61 (+5) | (8) |
| 13 | 2009 | 88.7 | 1771 (−10) | (1) | 164 (+10) | (8) | 74 (+5) | (8) |
| 14 | 2012 | 53.0[3] | 1067 (+10) | (4) | 906 (−10) | (5) | 39 (−5) | (5) |
| 15 | 2001 | 67.1[3] | 1343 (+10) | (3) | 605 (−10) | (6) | 53 (−5) | (6) |
| 16 | 1966 | 76.5 | 349 (+10) | (6) | 1505 (−10) | (3) | 112 (−5) | (3) |
| 17 | 1987 | 71.9[3] | 1428 (+10) | (3) | 485 (−10) | (6) | 74 (−5) | (6) |
| 18 | 1972 | 83.2 | 266 (+10) | (7) | 1642 (−10) | (2) | 64 (−5) | (2) |
| 19 | 1989 | 94.7 | 1884 (+10) | (1) | 64 (−10) | (8) | 41 (−5) | (8) |
| 20 | 1974 | 66.0[3] | 1303 (+10) | (4) | 607 (−10) | (5) | 64 (−5) | (5) |
| 22 | 1977 | 85.7 | 1694 (−10) | (2) | 218 (+10) | (7) | 65 (+5) | (7) |
| 23 | 1977 | 86.9 | 1718 (−10) | (2) | 183 (+10) | (7) | 76 (+5) | (7) |
| 24 | 1966 | 94.8 | 1864 (+10) | (1) | 40 (−10) | (8) | 62 (+5) | (1) |
| 26 | 1987 | 64.6[3] | 1283 (−10) | (4) | 638 (+10) | (5) | 66 (+5) | (5) |
| 27 | 1982 | 62.5[3] | 1238 (−10) | (4) | 660 (+10) | (5) | 84 (+5) | (4) |
| 29 | 1965 | 63.7[3] | 1353 (+10) | (4) | 527 (−10) | (5) | 85 (−5) | (5) |
| 31 | 1961 | 44.4[4] | 871 (+10) | (5) | 930 (−10) | (4) | 160 (−5) | (4) |
| 32 | 1922 | 59.8 | 652 (+10) | (5) | 1153 (−10) | (4) | 117 (−5) | (4) |
| 33 | 1922 | 96.9 | 1862 (+10) | (1) | 35 (−10) | (8) | 25 (−5) | (8) |
| 34 | 1938 | 97.6 | 1892 (+10) | (1) | 26 (−10) | (8) | 20 (−5) | (8) |
| 35 | 1941 | 91.1 | 1769 (+10) | (1) | 127 (−10) | (8) | 45 (−5) | (8) |
| 36 | 1951 | 97.3 | 1838 (+10) | (1) | 37 (−10) | (8) | 16 (−5) | (8) |
| 37 | 1945 | 94.6 | 1840 (+10) | (1) | 63 (−10) | (8) | 42 (−5) | (8) |
| 38 | 1955 | 94.6 | 1849 (+10) | (1) | 84 (−10) | (8) | 22 (−5) | (8) |
| 39 | 1944 | 94.7 | 1894 (+10) | (1) | 12 (−10) | (8) | 38 (−5) | (8) |
| 41 | 1949 | 94.7 | 1805 (+10) | (1) | 108 (−10) | (8) | 36 (−5) | (8) |
| 43 | 1953 | 94.6 | 1849 (+10) | (1) | 66 (−10) | (8) | 38 (−5) | (8) |

[1] Data source: *Tretii Vneocherednoi S''ezd Narodnykh Deputatov SSSR, Biulleteny, Izdanie Verkhovnogo Soveta SSSR* (Moscow, 1990). For an explanation of these codes, especially the values and coefficients, see the discussion of methodology in chapter 15.
[2] Indicates the number of the vote as given in the official Congress records. Records for two other roll-call votes, numbers 42 and 44, were not available.
[3] Votes on constitutional questions in which a simple majority of those present was insufficient to secure passage. (A two-thirds majority of all deputies eligible to vote--even if not present--was required.)
[4] The large number of abstentions prevented a majority from emerging on vote 31. We hence utilized the same coefficients as for a majority between 50% and 66.6%, and treated deputies in the plurality of 930 as members of the majority.

## *Table 46.* Some Prominent Deputies

| Second Congress | | Third Congress | |
|---|---|---|---|
| No.[1]  Name (Affiliation)[2] | Average[3] | No.[1]  Name (Affiliation)[2] | Average[3] |
| 214 Belosertsev S.V. (Rad) | +44.13 | | |
| 295 Bunich P.G. (Rad) | +43.33 | 424 Gdlian T.Kh. (None) | +33.82 |
| 1816 Starovoitova G.V. (Rad) | +43.00 | 2189 Shchelkanov A.A. (Rad) | +28.80 |
| 275 Bocharov M.A. (None) | +41.92 | 142 Afanas'ev Iu.N. (Rad) | +28.09 |
| 424 Gdlian T.Kh. (Rad) | +33.00 | 214 Belsertsev S.V. (Rad) | +25.24 |
| 259 Boldyrev Iu.Iu. (LI) | +32.83 | 647 Emelianov A.M. (None) | +24.61 |
| 299 Burbulis G.Ia. (Rad) | +31.35 | 299 Burbulis G.Ia. (None) | +24.00 |
| 2189 Shchelkanov A.A. (Rad) | +30.65 | 2226 Iakovlev E.V. (None) | +21.43 |
| 1894 Tikhonov V.A. (None) | +28.33 | 1907 Travkin N.I. (Rad) | +21.15 |
| 142 Afanas'ev Iu.N. (Rad) | +27.22 | 1988 Khadzhiev S.N. (LI) | +20.83 |
| -------RADICAL MEAN AVERAGE | +26.37 | 1816 Starovoitova G.V. (Rad) | +20.00 |
| 644 Eltsin B.N. (Rad) | +23.75 | -------RADICAL MEAN AVERAGE | +15.72 |
| 1813 Stankevich S.B. (Med) | +18.26 | 1813 Stankevich S.B. (Rad) | +15.60 |
| 114 Arbatov G.A. (Med) | +16.96 | 259 Boldyrev Iu.Iu. (LI) | +13.85 |
| 1907 Travkin N.I. (Rad) | +16.96 | ----LEFT INDEP. MEAN AVERAGE | +9.70 |
| 933 Kogan E.V. (RI) | +14.74 | 75 Alksnis V.I. (RI) | +8.89 |
| ----LEFT INDEP. MEAN AVERAGE | +14.56 | 1834 Tikhonov V.A. (None) | +8.85 |
| 1988 Khadzhiev S.N. (None) | +14.54 | 351 Veprev A.F. (None) | +7.31 |
| 301 Burlatskii F.M. (Med) | +13.33 | 2238 Iarin V.A. (RI) | +5.58 |
| 1788 Sobchak A.A. (LI) | +13.04 | ---RIGHT INDEP. MEAN AVERAGE | +4.94 |
| 647 Emel'ianov A.M. (Rad) | +11.36 | 456 Golik V.A. (RI) | +3.85 |
| 2226 Iakovlev E.V. (None) | +10.00 | 1788 Sobchak A.A. (LI) | +3.85 |
| 1234 Medvedev R.A. (Med) | +8.09 | 1509 Petrushenko N.S. (RI) | +3.33 |
| 351 Veprev A.F. (Med) | +5.45 | -------CONGRESS MEAN AVERAGE | +2.14 |
| 2238 Iarin V.A. (RI) | +3.64 | -------MEDIATOR MEAN AVERAGE | +0.17 |
| 465 Gol'danskii V.I. (LI) | +3.18 | -------CENTRIST MEAN AVERAGE | -0.87 |
| -------MEDIATOR MEAN AVERAGE | +1.92 | 275 Bocharov M.A. (Rad) | -2.20 |
| 348 Velikhov E.P. (None) | +1.82 | 65 Alekseev S.S. (Med) | -2.40 |
| 436 Gidaspov B.V. (RI) | +1.00 | 266 Borovik G.A. (Cen) | -3.08 |
| -------CONGRESS MEAN AVERAGE | +0.50 | 465 Gol'danskii V.I. (LI) | -3.08 |
| 1650 Ryzhkov N.I. (Cen) | -0.91 | 1166 Makashov A.M. (RI) | -3.08 |
| 2014 Khmura V.V. (Cen) | -0.91 | 2223 Iakovlev A.N. (Med) | -3.08 |
| 266 Borovik G.A. (None) | -2.04 | 380 Vol'skii A.I. (Med) | -4.35 |
| ---RIGHT INDEP. MEAN AVERAGE | -2.22 | 933 Kogan E.V. (RI) | -4.71 |
| 75 Alksnis V.I. (RI) | -3.50 | 510 Gromov B.V. (None) | -4.81 |
| 753 Ivashko V.A. (App) | -3.70 | ----APPARATCHIK MEAN AVERAGE | -5.06 |
| 2223 Iakovlev A.N. (Med) | -5.00 | 753 Ivashko V.A. (Cen) | -5.77 |
| ---PRE-PERESTR. MEAN AVERAGE | -6.46 | ---PRE-PERESTR. MEAN AVERAGE | -5.77 |
| 257 Boldin V.I. (None) | -6.52 | 348 Velikhov E.P. (None) | -6.54 |
| 1166 Makashov A.M. (App) | -6.52 | 1387 Nishanov R.N. (Cen) | -6.54 |
| 1509 Petrushenko N.S. (RI) | -6.52 | 1943 Umalatova S.Z. (RI) | -6.54 |
| 65 Alekseev S.S. (None) | -7.73 | 2014 Khmura V.V. (None) | -7.31 |
| 380 Vol'skii A.I. (None) | -8.00 | 114 Arbatov G.A. (None) | -9.01 |
| -------CENTRIST MEAN AVERAGE | -8.31 | 148 Akhromeev S.F. (Cen) | -10.00 |
| 510 Gromov B.V. (App) | -10.00 | 295 Bunich P.G. (Rad) | -10.00 |
| ---APPARATCHIK MEAN AVERAGE | -10.44 | 301 Burlatskii F.M. (None) | -10.00 |
| 148 Akhromeev S.F. (Cen) | -11.30 | 436 Gidaspov B.V. (App) | -10.00 |
| 2082 Chermiaev A.S. (None) | -12.50 | 1122 Ligachev E.K. (None) | -10.00 |
| 344 Vezirov A.Kh. (None) | -12.86 | 2082 Cherniaev A.S. (None) | -10.00 |
| 456 Golik Iu.V. (Med) | -14.35 | 1030 Kriuchkov G.K. (None) | -11.80 |
| 160 Bagirov T.G. (None) | -15.24 | 474 Gorbachev M.S. (Med) | -12.80 |
| 1122 Ligachev E.K. (App) | -17.00 | 1650 Ryzhkov N.I. (Cen) | -13.46 |
| 1030 Kriuchkov G.K. (Med) | -18.26 | 160 Bagirov T.G. (None) | -16.40 |
| 1387 Nishanov R.N. (Cen) | -18.26 | 344 Vezirov A.Kh. (None) | -16.52 |
| 2234 Ianaev G.I. (App) | -18.57 | 1234 Medvedev R.A. (Med) | -16.92 |
| 474 Gorbachev M.S. (Med) | -18.64 | 2234 Ianaev G.I. (App) | -16.92 |
| 1147 Lukianov A.I. (Cen) | -18.64 | 1147 Lukianov A.I. (Cen) | -18.00 |
| 1943 Umalatova S.Z. (Cen) | -18.67 | 257 Boldin V.I. (None) | -34.23 |

[1] Deputy number used for referencing purposes in the statistical analysis. See "List of Deputies."
[2] Surname with initials as given in official Congress records. Affiliations identified through speeches to Congress. (Rad=Radical; LI=Left Independent; Med=Mediator; Cen=Centrist; RI=Right Independent; App=Apparatchik; Pre=Pre-perestroika; None=Did not speak or speech not classified.)
[3] Mean deputy score on roll-call votes. (Methodology as explained in text.)

# List of Deputies

## List of Deputies (in Russian alphabetical order)

**KEY:**

DEP (column 1): Deputy number, used for indexing purposes in the statistical analysis.

NAME (column 2): Deputy surname and initials, with any further essential identifying information given in the official Congress records.

REP (column 3): First three letters of each deputy's republic of origin. As in the text, Moscow is treated separately from the RSFSR.

| | | |
|---|---|---|
| Arm=Armenia | Kir=Kirghizia | Tad=Tadzhikistan |
| Aze=Azerbaijan | Lat=Latvia | Tur=Turkmenia |
| Bel=Belorussia | Lit=Lithuania | Ukr=Ukraine |
| Est=Estonia | Mol=Moldavia | Uzb=Uzbekistan |
| Geo=Georgia | Mos=Moscow | ?=Unknown |
| Kaz=Kazakhstan | Rus=Russian SFSR | |

ELEC (column 4): Means of election.
E=Elected          A=Appointed          ?=Unknown

SOC (column 5): Social origins, categories as elaborated in text.

| | |
|---|---|
| Nom=Nomenklatura | Int=Intelligentsia |
| Cad=Cadres | Tec=Technicians |
| Mil=Military | Wor=Workers |
| Man=Managers | Oth=Other |
| | ?=Unknown |

SPK1, SPK2, SPK3 (columns 6, 7, and 9, respectively): Political affiliation, as measured by speeches to the First (SPK1), Second (SPK2), and Third (SPK3) Congresses of People's Deputies.

Pre=Pre-perestroika          Med=Mediators
App=Apparatchiki             LI=Left Independent
RI=Right Independent         Rad=Radicals
Cen=Centrists
?=Not categorized or did not speak
.=Not in Congress (resigned or deceased before Congress began, or not elected until later Congress)

AVG2, AVG3 (columns 8 and 10, respectively): Mean deputy score on roll-call votes in Second (AVG2) and Third (AVG3) Congresses of People's Deputies. Methodology explained in text.
.=Missing value (not in Congress: resigned or deceased before Congress began, or not elected until later Congress)

| DEP | NAME | REP | ELEC | SOC | SPK1 | SPK2 | AVG2 | SPK3 | AVG3 |
|---|---|---|---|---|---|---|---|---|---|
| 1 | Aare Iu.I. | Est | E | Int | ? | ? | 35.417 | ? | 40.000 |
| 2 | Aasmiaye Kh.Iu. | Est | E | Tec | ? | ? | 37.500 | ? | 40.000 |
| 3 | Abakirov Ye. | Kir | A | Nom | ? | ? | -14.762 | ? | -7.917 |
| 3006 | Abalkin L.I. | Mos | A | Int | ? | . | . | . | . |
| 4 | Abasov K.A.K. | Aze | E | Man | ? | ? | -13.750 | ? | -6.538 |
| 5 | Abasov M.T. | Aze | E | Int | App | App | 4.643 | ? | 0.385 |
| 6 | Abbasov Ia.I. | Aze | E | Wor | ? | ? | -8.913 | ? | -11.731 |
| 7 | Abbasova Kh.Z. | Aze | E | Man | ? | ? | -6.000 | ? | -4.423 |
| 8 | Abdalova M.V. | Uzb | E | Wor | ? | App | -15.217 | ? | -5.600 |
| 9 | Abdimuratova Sh. | Uzb | E | Wor | ? | ? | -2.609 | ? | 0.000 |
| 10 | Abdulguseev M. | Rus | E | Wor | ? | ? | -12.857 | ? | 0.833 |
| 11 | Abdullaev I.A. | Aze | E | Wor | ? | ? | -5.682 | ? | -6.538 |
| 12 | Abdulmazhidova P.R. | Rus | E | Wor | ? | ? | -4.545 | ? | 0.000 |
| 13 | Abdurakhimov A. | Uzb | E | Tec | ? | ? | -7.143 | ? | -6.538 |
| 14 | Abdykarimov S. | Uzb | E | Wor | ? | ? | -4.706 | ? | -4.800 |
| 15 | Abzianidze G.S. | Geo | E | Nom | ? | ? | 11.500 | ? | 11.818 |
| 16 | Abiatari T.I. | Geo | E | Wor | ? | ? | 12.250 | ? | 5.417 |
| 17 | Ablameiko I.V. | Bel | A | Wor | ? | ? | 31.522 | ? | 17.692 |
| 18 | Aboev A.S. | Rus | E | Tec | ? | ? | -1.500 | ? | -22.308 |
| 19 | Abramovich M.T. | Bel | E | Wor | ? | ? | -1.500 | App | 7.885 |
| 20 | Abramian D.N. | Arm | A | Tec | ? | ? | -10.435 | Cen | -1.042 |
| 21 | Abramian Kh.B. | Arm | A | Int | ? | ? | -40.000 | ? | 2.273 |
| 22 | Abrashkina L.M. | Aze | E | Wor | ? | ? | -18.261 | ? | -20.385 |
| 23 | Abuladze T.E. | Geo | A | Int | Rad | LI | 14.737 | ? | 0.625 |
| 24 | Abutalipov Sh.A. | Rus | A | Tec | ? | ? | -6.522 | ? | 1.346 |
| 25 | Avaliani T.G. | Rus | E | Man | ? | ? | 11.389 | RI | 16.667 |
| 26 | Averintsev S.S. | Mos | A | Int | ? | ? | 47.857 | ? | 16.923 |
| 27 | Averkin V.N. | Rus | A | Tec | ? | ? | -15.000 | ? | -3.077 |
| 28 | Avotin' V.M. | Lat | E | Int | ? | ? | 42.000 | ? | 13.750 |
| 29 | Avtorkhanov S.Ye. | Rus | E | Cad | ? | ? | 2.667 | LI | 7.308 |
| 30 | Agapova N.I. | Uzb | A | Wor | ? | ? | -13.182 | ? | -6.538 |
| 31 | Agrba V.Z. | Geo | E | Tec | ? | LI | -1.500 | ? | 17.727 |
| 32 | Aguzarova S.B. | Rus | E | Wor | ? | ? | 7.826 | ? | -2.500 |
| 33 | Adamovich A.M. | Mos | A | Int | Rad | Rad | 6.923 | ? | 0.000 |
| 34 | Advadze V.S. | Geo | E | Man | ? | Rad | 20.476 | ? | 0.000 |
| 35 | Adleiba B.V. | Geo | E | Oth | ? | ? | -4.444 | ? | -10.800 |
| 36 | Adomaitis R.V. | Lit | A | Int | ? | ? | 39.583 | ? | 0.000 |
| 37 | Adylov V.T. | Uzb | A | Wor | ? | App | -11.053 | ? | -13.462 |
| 38 | Azarov V.Ia. | Mos | A | Oth | ? | ? | -13.043 | ? | -2.885 |
| 39 | Azarov S.I. | Ukr | A | Man | ? | Cen | -20.526 | ? | -6.538 |
| 40 | Azizbekova P.A. | Aze | E | Int | App | ? | 0.000 | ? | -18.889 |
| 41 | Azizova Z.A. | Aze | E | Wor | ? | ? | -14.091 | ? | -4.038 |
| 42 | Aidak A.P. | Rus | E | Man | LI | ? | -5.238 | ? | -7.083 |
| 43 | Aidamirov A.A. | Rus | E | Int | ? | ? | 3.500 | ? | 0.000 |
| 44 | Aipin E.D. | Rus | E | Int | ? | ? | 47.941 | LI | 10.192 |
| 45 | Aitmatov Ch. | Kir | A | Int | Med | Med | 12.000 | ? | 3.913 |
| 46 | Aitkhozhina N.A. | Kaz | A | Int | ? | ? | -6.429 | ? | 7.292 |
| 47 | Akaev A. | Kir | E | Int | ? | Med | 1.304 | Med | 3.846 |
| 48 | Akbarov Iu.T. | Uzb | E | Wor | Pre | App | -14.545 | ? | -5.962 |
| 49 | Akebaev Zh. | Kaz | A | Cad | ? | ? | -26.429 | ? | -5.769 |
| 50 | Akent'ev A.V. | Ukr | A | Oth | ? | ? | -8.182 | ? | 7.857 |
| 51 | Akimenko V.S. | Rus | A | Man | ? | ? | -14.348 | ? | 0.385 |
| 52 | Akmamedov G.M. | Tur | E | Wor | ? | ? | -0.909 | ? | -10.769 |
| 53 | Akmammedova S.M. | ? | ? | ? | ? | ? | 0.000 | ? | -4.583 |
| 54 | Akmatalieva U.K. | Kir | E | Wor | ? | ? | -11.364 | ? | 0.385 |
| 55 | Akmatov T. | Kir | E | Nom | ? | ? | -11.429 | ? | -6.538 |
| 56 | Akramov Ye.Kh. | Kir | E | Tec | ? | ? | 3.095 | ? | 7.308 |
| 57 | Akramova T.M. | Tad | E | Tec | ? | ? | 1.500 | ? | 14.000 |
| 58 | Aksenov V.I. | Rus | E | Wor | ? | ? | 1.304 | ? | 0.385 |
| 59 | Aksenov I.M. | Rus | A | Man | ? | Cen | -3.333 | ? | 2.800 |
| 60 | Aleksandrin V.G. | Rus | E | Tec | ? | ? | -0.909 | ? | 1.200 |
| 61 | Aleksankin A.V. | Rus | E | Tec | ? | ? | -14.348 | ? | -13.913 |
| 62 | Alekseev A.A. | Rus | E | Man | ? | ? | -0.769 | ? | 12.692 |
| 63 | Alekseev B.G. | Rus | E | Cad | ? | ? | 19.545 | Cen | 18.000 |
| 64 | Alekseev O.N. | Rus | E | Cad | ? | Med | 5.217 | ? | 19.600 |
| 65 | Alekseev S.S. | Rus | A | Int | LI | ? | -7.727 | Med | -2.400 |
| 66 | Alekseeva L.M. | Rus | A | Cad | ? | ? | -6.818 | ? | -8.889 |
| 67 | Alekseenko M.G. | Rus | E | Tec | ? | Med | 9.130 | ? | 2.400 |
| 68 | Aleskerova R.M. | Aze | E | Cad | ? | ? | -13.182 | ? | 0.385 |
| 69 | Aleshin E.P. | Rus | A | Int | ? | ? | -23.636 | ? | 0.000 |
| 70 | Alieva G.B. | Aze | E | Wor | ? | ? | -14.348 | ? | 0.588 |
| 71 | Aliluev N.I. | Rus | E | Wor | ? | ? | -6.522 | ? | -6.538 |
| 72 | Alimbetov I.A. | Uzb | E | Wor | ? | ? | -8.696 | ? | -8.800 |
| 73 | Alimov S. | Tad | E | Man | ? | ? | -4.783 | ? | 3.846 |
| 74 | Alimova Kh. | Uzb | A | Nom | ? | ? | -21.333 | ? | 0.000 |
| 75 | Alksnis V.I. | Lat | E | Mil | RI | RI | -3.500 | RI | 8.889 |
| 76 | Allamuradov B.A. | Uzb | E | Nom | ? | Cen | -7.692 | ? | -10.000 |
| 77 | Allakhverdieva M.K. | Aze | E | Wor | ? | ? | -17.273 | ? | -6.538 |
| 78 | Allaiarov R.A. | Tur | E | Man | Pre | ? | 1.304 | ? | 3.846 |
| 79 | Almazov V.A. | Rus | A | Tec | ? | ? | -2.609 | ? | 4.808 |
| 80 | Alferov Zh.I. | Rus | A | Int | Med | Med | 0.000 | ? | -11.923 |
| 81 | Alybekov A. | Kir | E | Wor | ? | ? | -18.261 | ? | -16.923 |

```
 82 Amaglobeli N.S.        Geo E Int ?    ?   16.957 ?     -3.077
 83 Amanbaev D.B.          Kir E Nom ?    Cen -18.261 ?   -16.000
 84 Amangel'dinova G.A.    Kaz A Tec Pre  ?  -14.348 ?      4.583
 85 Amanov A.M.            Aze E Wor ?    ?   -8.000 ?     -2.308
 86 Amanov T.              Uzb E Man ?    Pre -14.348 ?   -10.000
 87 Amanova M.B.           Tur A Int ?    ?  -10.435 ?      0.385
 88 Ambartsumian V.A.      Arm E Int App  ?    5.000 ?      4.800
 89 Ambartsumian S.A.      Arm E Int LI   LI  -7.647 ?     -1.200
 90 Amzarakov V.G.         Rus E Wor ?    ?   -0.909 ?      3.846
 91 Amonashvili Sh.A.      Geo A Man Med  ?   16.957 ?      7.308
 92 Amosov N.M.            Ukr E Tec ?    ?   13.333 ?      8.000
 93 Anan'ev A.A.           Mos A Int ?    ?   -2.826 ?     -2.115
 94 Angapov S.V.           Rus A Oth ?    ?  -21.818 ?     -8.462
 95 Angarkhaev A.L.        Rus E Int ?    ?   -1.500 ?      2.885
 96 Andreev A.E.           Bel A Cad ?    ?  -15.455 Cen    0.385
 97 Andreev Kh.G.          Mol E Man ?    ?   28.500 ?     12.500
 98 Andreev Iu.Ye.         Mos E Man Rad  Rad 37.619 ?      9.167
 99 Andreeva I.A.          Mos A Tec Cen  LI  -3.500 Med    3.846
100 Andronati S.A.         Ukr E Int ?    ?   -7.273 ?      4.615
101 Anisimov A.I.          Rus E Tec ?    ?    9.130 ?     10.769
102 Amisimova G.A.         Rus A Tec ?    ?   -4.130 ?      9.583
103 Amishchev V.P.         Uzb E Nom ?    ?  -12.273 ?      0.000
104 Annamukhamedov A.      Tur E Tec ?    ?   -2.609 ?     10.769
105 Annamukhamedov O.      Tur A Nom ?    App -19.048 ?     -6.538
106 Antanavichius K.A.     Lit E Int LI   LI  41.154 ?      0.000
107 Antanaitis V.V.        Lit E Int ?    LI  42.778 LI     0.000
108 Antifeev A.E.          Ukr E Man LI   LI   0.500 ?      2.105
109 Anufriev V.G.          Kaz E Nom ?    ?  -22.174 ?     -7.600
110 Anufriev G.P.          Ukr E Tec ?    ?   -1.500 ?     10.769
111 Anufrieva L.A.         Rus E Tec ?    ?   12.727 ?     34.038
112 Aparin I.V.            Rus E Nom LI   ?  -13.333 ?     -3.077
113 Apostol V.G.           Mol A Int ?    ?   14.348 ?     17.692
114 Arbatov G.A.           Mos A Int Med  Med 16.957 ?     -9.808
115 Ardzinba V.G.          Geo E Int LI   ?   22.778 LI    22.273
116 Aripdzhanov M.M.       Uzb E Nom ?    ?  -29.000 ?      0.200
117 Arslonov A.K.          Uzb E Wor ?    ?  -18.261 ?     -6.538
118 Artemenko G.I.         Bel E Wor ?    ?  -12.727 ?      3.750
119 Aruvald A.Ye.-Ye.      Est A Man ?    ?   20.625 ?     21.000
120 Arutiunian A.B.        Arm E Wor ?    ?  -12.500 ?      0.962
121 Arutiunian A.A.        Arm A Int LI   LI   8.913 ?      6.800
122 Arutiunian M.K.        Arm A Nom ?    ?  -15.217 ?      0.000
123 Arutiunian S.G.        Arm E Nom Med  Med -14.762 Med -10.000
124 Arutiunian Ye.T.       Arm E Wor LI   ?    6.154 ?     12.692
125 Arkhipov P.M.          Tur E Mil ?    ?   -6.522 ?     -6.538
126 Arkhipova I.K.         Mos A Int ?    ?   10.000 ?     -5.000
127 Arshba R.A.            Geo E Wor ?    ?   19.444 ?     19.130
128 Arystanbaev S.T.       Kaz E Int ?    ?   -2.609 ?      7.083
129 Asankulov D.           Kir E Mil ?    ?  -10.435 ?    -16.667
130 Askarov A.             Kir E Wor ?    ?  -15.909 ?     -3.077
131 Askarov Iu.A.          Uzb E Man ?    ?  -10.435 ?      3.846
132 Astaf'ev V.M.          Rus A Oth ?    ?   -2.609 ?      3.846
133 Astaf'ev V.P.          Rus A Int ?    ?  -21.429 ?      0.000
134 Astakhova M.M.         Rus A Tec ?    ?  -12.045 ?     11.538
135 Atadzhanov A.R.        Uzb E Nom ?    Cen -27.333 ?    -15.200
136 Ataev S.               Tur A Cad ?    ?  -10.476 ?      0.385
137 Atdaev Kh.             Tur E Wor App  ?   -1.667 ?     -3.600
138 Auel'bekov E.N.        Kaz E Nom ?    ?    1.304 ?      3.846
139 Aushev R.S.            Rus E Mil ?    ?    3.810 ?     10.769
140 Afanas'ev V.G.         Mos A Nom ?    ?   -6.667 ?     -2.800
141 Afanas'ev G.N.         Rus E Tec ?    Med 27.826 ?     18.200
142 Afanas'ev Iu.N.        Rus E Int Rad  Rad 27.222 Rad  28.095
143 Afanas'eva L.V.        Rus E Tec ?    ?   18.947 ?     24.615
144 Afonin V.G.            Rus E Nom ?    ?   -5.000 ?      4.800
145 Akhmedov O.A.          Aze E Wor ?    ?   -8.333 ?      0.385
146 Akhmedov R.            Uzb E Man ?    App -19.500 ?     -6.522
147 Akhmetova R.S.         Kaz E Tec ?    ?    2.727 ?      9.800
148 Akhromeev S.F.         Mol E Mil Cen  Cen -11.304 Cen -10.000
149 Akhunov P.A.           Uzb A Tec LI   ?    6.000 LI     7.500
150 Achilov A.             Tad E Man ?    ?  -10.435 ?      3.846
151 Aiubov N.              Tad E Man ?    ?  -10.435 ?      3.846
152 Aiapbergenov S.        Kaz E Wor ?    ?  -11.818 ?     -3.077
153 Babaev I.A.            Aze E Wor ?    ?  -12.045 ?    -14.423
154 Babanov T.B.           Kir E Man ?    ?  -21.538 ?      0.000
155 Babeshko V.A.          Rus A Int ?    LI -17.059 ?     -1.538
156 Babich V.M.            Ukr A Cad ?    ?  -15.333 ?      0.800
157 Babchenko N.I.         Ukr A Cad ?    ?   -3.684 ?     -6.818
158 Babynin G.V.           Rus E Tec ?    ?   19.565 ?      9.231
159 Bavula V.S.            Ukr E Wor ?    ?   -1.818 ?      7.308
160 Bagirov T.G.           Aze E Wor ?    ?  -15.238 ?    -16.400
161 Bagirova S.K.          Aze E Wor ?    ?   -5.682 ?     -8.462
162 Badalbaeva P.          Uzb A Tec ?    ?  -18.261 ?      0.000
163 Badamiants V.G.        Arm E Mil ?    ?  -17.619 ?     -1.200
164 Badzhelidze N.U.       Geo E Wor ?    ?    3.409 ?      4.200
165 Bazhanov N.N.          Mos A Tec ?    ?  -16.667 ?    -13.462
166 Bazarova R.A.          Tur E Nom Pre  Cen -22.174 Cen -10.000
```

| | | | | | | | | | |
|---|---|---|---|---|---|---|---|---|---|
| 167 | Baizhanov S.M. | Kaz | E | Nom | ? | ? | -18.261 | ? | -3.077 |
| 168 | Bairamova N.A. | Aze | E | Wor | ? | ? | -3.889 | ? | -6.538 |
| 169 | Bairamova N.N. | Rus | E | Wor | ? | ? | 0.000 | ? | -5.652 |
| 170 | Baklanov V.V. | Ukr | A | Wor | ? | ? | -12.273 | ? | -4.000 |
| 171 | Baklanov O.D. | Mos | A | Nom | ? | ? | -12.500 | ? | -20.385 |
| 172 | Bakradze A.V. | Geo | E | Int | ? | ? | 43.333 | ? | 0.000 |
| 173 | Bakulin V.I. | Rus | A | Wor | RI | ? | 2.273 | ? | -5.000 |
| 174 | Balaian Z.G. | Aze | E | Int | RI | ? | 18.929 | ? | 14.038 |
| 175 | Balenko A.G. | Rus | A | Tec | ? | ? | 19.130 | ? | 4.000 |
| 176 | Baleshev N.F. | Tur | E | Nom | ? | ? | -10.435 | ? | -6.538 |
| 177 | Baltaeva R. | Uzb | E | Tec | ? | ? | -12.727 | ? | -5.200 |
| 178 | Baluev V.G. | Bel | E | Mil | ? | ? | -18.261 | ? | -6.538 |
| 179 | Barabanov V.I. | Kir | E | Man | ? | ? | -11.364 | ? | 0.385 |
| 180 | Baravikas G.V. | Lit | A | Int | ? | ? | 25.500 | ? | 0.000 |
| 181 | Barannikova O.V. | Rus | A | Oth | ? | ? | 12.333 | ? | 21.923 |
| 182 | Baranov A.E. | Rus | A | Oth | ? | ? | -14.545 | ? | -3.600 |
| 183 | Baranov A.I. | Rus | A | Cad | ? | ? | -3.913 | ? | -3.654 |
| 184 | Baranova G.T. | Rus | A | Tec | ? | ? | -10.435 | ? | -12.308 |
| 185 | Baranovskii V.V. | Ukr | A | Oth | ? | ? | -2.609 | ? | 0.385 |
| 186 | Barashkov Iu.A. | Rus | E | Tec | Rad | ? | 4.000 | ? | 17.826 |
| 187 | Barbolova K.Zh. | Kaz | A | Wor | ? | ? | -15.455 | ? | -5.577 |
| 188 | Barsov A.I. | Rus | E | Wor | ? | ? | 2.500 | ? | -3.077 |
| 189 | Barusheva L.V. | Aze | E | Wor | Pre | ? | -13.636 | ? | -15.385 |
| 190 | Baryshnikov I.A. | Rus | A | Wor | ? | ? | -8.889 | ? | 15.000 |
| 191 | Baskova V.A. | Rus | A | Wor | ? | ? | -22.174 | ? | 1.346 |
| 192 | Batiashvili S.A. | Geo | E | Wor | ? | ? | 5.000 | ? | 5.870 |
| 193 | Batorov O.B. | Rus | E | Cad | ? | ? | 9.750 | ? | 5.577 |
| 194 | Batrachenko S.V. | Ukr | A | Cad | ? | ? | 28.478 | ? | 7.308 |
| 195 | Batynskaia L.I. | Rus | A | Int | ? | ? | 7.619 | ? | 0.000 |
| 196 | Batyshev S.Ia. | Mos | A | Int | ? | ? | -13.182 | LI | 9.200 |
| 197 | Bachinskii D.G. | Ukr | A | Tec | ? | ? | -15.217 | ? | 0.000 |
| 198 | Bashev N.A. | Rus | E | Man | ? | ? | -2.609 | ? | -6.400 |
| 199 | Bashirova L.M.G. | Aze | E | Wor | ? | ? | -2.955 | ? | -11.600 |
| 200 | Bashmakov E.F. | Kaz | E | Nom | ? | ? | -22.174 | ? | -6.538 |
| 201 | Begel'dinov T.Ia. | Kaz | A | Oth | ? | ? | -22.174 | ? | 3.600 |
| 202 | Bedulia V.L. | Bel | A | Man | Cen | ? | -18.261 | ? | -6.538 |
| 203 | Bezbakh Ia.Ia. | Ukr | E | Wor | LI | ? | 33.409 | ? | 3.846 |
| 204 | Beishekeeva Z. | Kir | A | Wor | App | ? | -14.091 | ? | -8.400 |
| 205 | Bekbosinov N.U. | Kaz | E | Man | ? | ? | -20.000 | ? | 2.400 |
| 206 | Bekbulatova G.I. | Uzb | E | Wor | ? | ? | -18.421 | ? | 3.846 |
| 207 | Bekishev A.D. | Rus | E | Wor | ? | ? | 7.826 | ? | 15.000 |
| 208 | Beknazarov S. | Tad | E | Nom | ? | ? | -6.522 | ? | -13.810 |
| 209 | Belenkov Iu.N. | Mos | A | Tec | ? | ? | -13.158 | ? | 5.417 |
| 210 | Belikov M.A. | Ukr | A | Int | ? | ? | 26.818 | ? | 0.000 |
| 211 | Belina A.V. | Rus | E | Tec | LI | ? | -0.952 | ? | 17.692 |
| 212 | Belov V.I. | Rus | A | Int | RI | RI | -12.000 | ? | -3.077 |
| 213 | Belogolov A.K. | Rus | E | Man | ? | ? | 33.333 | ? | 8.000 |
| 214 | Belozertsev S.V. | Rus | E | Int | Rad | Rad | 44.130 | Rad | 25.238 |
| 215 | Belous N.P. | Rus | E | Wor | ? | ? | 17.273 | ? | 21.304 |
| 216 | Beliaev V.N. | Mos | E | Int | ? | Rad | 36.739 | ? | 18.800 |
| 217 | Beliaev V.S. | Rus | E | Wor | ? | ? | 0.455 | ? | 7.200 |
| 218 | Beliaev S.V. | Rus | A | Mil | ? | ? | -10.435 | ? | 3.846 |
| 219 | Beliakov A.M. | Rus | E | Nom | ? | ? | -12.857 | ? | -13.462 |
| 220 | Beliakov O.S. | Rus | E | Nom | ? | ? | -10.435 | ? | -15.600 |
| 221 | Beliakova G.F. | Rus | A | Tec | ? | ? | 1.304 | ? | 7.692 |
| 222 | Berger A.V. | Kaz | E | Man | ? | ? | -10.435 | ? | 14.231 |
| 223 | Berdzenishvili M.I. | Geo | E | Oth | ? | ? | 12.826 | ? | 0.000 |
| 224 | Berezin A.I. | Rus | E | Nom | ? | ? | -14.348 | ? | -16.923 |
| 225 | Berezov V.A. | Lit | E | Nom | Med | ? | 43.333 | ? | 0.000 |
| 226 | Berikashvili V.G. | Geo | E | Wor | ? | ? | 19.091 | ? | 3.000 |
| 227 | Berko M.D. | Ukr | E | Man | ? | ? | -2.609 | ? | 7.308 |
| 228 | Bekh N.I. | Rus | E | Man | ? | Cen | -2.609 | ? | 14.231 |
| 229 | Bekhtereva N.P. | Rus | A | Int | Cen | ? | 60.000 | ? | -1.923 |
| 230 | Bigunets N.V. | Ukr | E | Tec | ? | ? | -8.000 | ? | 6.538 |
| 231 | Bikkenin N.B. | Mos | A | Int | ? | ? | 13.333 | ? | 7.200 |
| 232 | Biliukovich E.G. | Bel | E | Tec | ? | ? | 1.304 | ? | 7.200 |
| 233 | Bimbaev B.M. | Rus | E | Man | ? | ? | -2.045 | ? | 16.739 |
| 234 | Biriukov V.A. | Rus | E | Wor | Rad | ? | 6.818 | ? | 0.385 |
| 235 | Bichenov R.R. | Rus | E | Man | ? | ? | -5.625 | ? | -11.667 |
| 236 | Bichkauskas Ye.V. | Lit | E | Tec | Rad | LI | 47.500 | ? | 0.000 |
| 237 | Bisher I.O. | Lat | E | Int | LI | LI | 18.000 | LI | 13.333 |
| 238 | Biiushkin S.N. | Rus | A | Wor | ? | Med | 13.333 | ? | 5.385 |
| 239 | Blaev B.Kh. | Rus | E | Man | ? | ? | -17.273 | ? | -10.000 |
| 240 | Blazhievskii B.V. | Geo | E | Man | ? | ? | -11.304 | ? | -11.538 |
| 241 | Bliznov L.E. | Rus | E | Wor | ? | ? | 1.304 | App | 7.308 |
| 242 | Blinova A.A. | Rus | A | Cad | ? | ? | -9.524 | ? | 0.385 |
| 243 | Blokhin Iu.V. | Mol | E | Tec | ? | Cen | 3.636 | RI | 7.200 |
| 244 | Blums G.V. | Lat | A | Man | ? | ? | 6.875 | ? | 10.600 |
| 245 | Bobadzhanov M. | Tad | A | Oth | ? | ? | -13.636 | ? | -18.846 |
| 246 | Bobrik B.F. | Rus | E | Man | ? | Pre | -6.522 | ? | -3.600 |
| 247 | Bobritskii N.G. | Bel | E | Man | ? | Rad | 34.048 | ? | 10.769 |
| 248 | Bobyleva E.F. | Rus | A | Tec | ? | ? | -18.261 | Pre | -5.769 |
| 249 | Bogdanov I.M. | Rus | E | Tec | ? | ? | 25.455 | ? | 10.769 |
| 250 | Bogdanov R.G. | Rus | E | Tec | ? | ? | -10.435 | ? | -7.200 |
| 251 | Bogomolov O.T. | Mos | E | Int | LI | ? | 28.333 | ? | 9.808 |

| | | | | | | | | |
|---|---|---|---|---|---|---|---|---|
| 252 | Bogomolov Iu.A. | Rus | E | Man | ? | ? | 1.304 | ? | -1.923 |
| 253 | Boztaev K.B. | Kaz | E | Nom | ? | ? | -22.174 | ? | -3.077 |
| 254 | Boiko A.N. | Ukr | E | Int | LI | Rad | 15.217 | ? | 0.000 |
| 255 | Boikov S.V. | Rus | E | Wor | ? | ? | 29.130 | ? | 10.769 |
| 256 | Bokuchava N.T. | Geo | A | Tec | ? | ? | 1.304 | ? | -6.000 |
| 257 | Boldin V.I. | Rus | E | Nom | ? | ? | -6.522 | ? | -34.231 |
| 258 | Boldyrev I.S. | Rus | E | Nom | ? | ? | -15.714 | ? | -10.000 |
| 259 | Boldyrev Iu.Iu. | Rus | E | Tec | LI | LI | 32.826 | LI | 13.846 |
| 260 | Bol'basov V.S. | Bel | A | Int | ? | ? | 26.750 | ? | 17.692 |
| 261 | Bondarenko B.V. | Ukr | E | Tec | ? | ? | 17.391 | ? | 19.200 |
| 262 | Borisov A.S. | Rus | E | Int | ? | ? | 21.364 | ? | 14.231 |
| 263 | Borisovskii V.Z. | Ukr | E | Nom | ? | ? | -10.435 | ? | 0.385 |
| 264 | Borisiuk N.P. | Rus | A | Wor | ? | ? | -8.182 | ? | -5.385 |
| 265 | Borkovets V.I. | Rus | E | Wor | Cen | ? | -0.952 | ? | 1.200 |
| 266 | Borovik G.A. | Mos | A | Int | Cen | ? | -2.045 | Cen | -3.077 |
| 267 | Borovikov G.G. | Rus | E | Wor | Rad | ? | 13.261 | ? | 22.333 |
| 268 | Borovkov V.A. | Rus | A | Wor | Cen | ? | -5.909 | ? | -4.615 |
| 269 | Borodin N.V. | Rus | A | Man | ? | ? | -16.522 | ? | -6.538 |
| 270 | Borodin O.P. | Rus | E | Int | Rad | ? | 22.826 | ? | 17.083 |
| 271 | Borodin Iu.I. | Rus | A | Int | ? | Cen | -10.500 | ? | -20.769 |
| 272 | Borodulin A.V. | Rus | E | Wor | ? | ? | -2.609 | Cen | 10.800 |
| 273 | Bosenko N.V. | Mos | A | Oth | ? | LI | -15.000 | ? | -5.769 |
| 274 | Botandaev I.N. | Rus | E | Wor | ? | ? | -1.087 | ? | 3.846 |
| 275 | Bocharov M.A. | Mos | E | Man | ? | ? | 41.923 | Rad | -2.200 |
| 276 | Bochkov O.A. | Rus | E | Mil | ? | ? | 1.304 | ? | 18.846 |
| 277 | Boiars Iu.R. | Lat | E | Int | LI | LI | 17.647 | LI | 55.000 |
| 278 | Bragin A.S. | Rus | A | Cad | ? | ? | 5.217 | ? | 14.231 |
| 279 | Bragish D.P. | Mol | E | Nom | ? | ? | -8.696 | ? | 4.800 |
| 280 | Brazauskas A.-M. K. | Lit | E | Nom | Med | Med | 43.333 | ? | 0.000 |
| 281 | Bratun' R.A. | Ukr | E | Int | Med | LI | 21.667 | ? | 20.455 |
| 282 | Braun A.G. | Kaz | E | Nom | ? | ? | -18.261 | ? | 2.000 |
| 283 | Bredikis Iu.Iu. | Lit | A | Tec | Med | ? | 20.000 | ? | 0.000 |
| 284 | Bresis V.-Ye. G. | Lat | E | Nom | Med | Med | 14.000 | ? | 14.808 |
| 285 | Breurosh B.S. | Ukr | E | Wor | ? | ? | -10.435 | ? | 5.417 |
| 286 | Britvin N.V. | Tad | E | Mil | ? | ? | -14.348 | ? | -10.000 |
| 287 | Brovkin V.M. | Rus | E | Man | ? | ? | 14.565 | ? | 7.308 |
| 288 | Brodavskii A.P. | Lit | E | Man | ? | ? | 5.217 | ? | 0.000 |
| 289 | Bronshtein M.L. | Est | E | Int | ? | LI | 17.917 | LI | 11.250 |
| 290 | Bruss A.P. | Lat | A | Tec | ? | ? | 13.077 | ? | 14.423 |
| 291 | Briukhanova N.V. | Rus | A | Tec | ? | ? | -5.909 | ? | 6.667 |
| 292 | Buachidze T.P. | Geo | E | Cad | ? | LI | 15.217 | LI | 3.846 |
| 293 | Buburuz P.D. | Mol | E | Oth | ? | ? | 24.000 | ? | 18.333 |
| 294 | Bulatov V.K. | Rus | A | Tec | ? | ? | 31.667 | ? | 22.955 |
| 295 | Bunich P.G. | Mos | A | Int | Rad | Rad | 43.333 | Rad | -10.000 |
| 296 | Buravov G.V. | Rus | E | Wor | ? | ? | -0.435 | ? | 15.200 |
| 297 | Buraev I.Z. | Rus | E | Wor | ? | ? | -2.174 | ? | 12.500 |
| 298 | Burachas A.I. | Lit | E | Int | LI | ? | 70.000 | ? | 0.000 |
| 299 | Burbulis G.Ye. | Rus | E | Man | Rad | Rad | 31.364 | ? | 24.000 |
| 300 | Burduzhan V.V. | Mol | A | Man | ? | ? | 11.316 | ? | 10.769 |
| 301 | Burlatskii F.M. | Mos | A | Int | Med | Med | 13.333 | ? | -10.000 |
| 302 | Burskii V.I. | Bel | E | Nom | ? | ? | -14.348 | ? | -3.600 |
| 303 | Burtsev M.P. | Rus | E | Man | ? | ? | 17.500 | ? | 20.476 |
| 304 | Burykh Iu.E. | Ukr | E | Tec | LI | ? | 24.118 | ? | 7.308 |
| 305 | Bushuev V.V. | Rus | A | Int | LI | App | -9.565 | ? | -8.846 |
| 306 | Bykanov P.I. | Rus | A | Wor | ? | ? | -2.273 | ? | 10.769 |
| 307 | Bykov V.V. | Bel | A | Int | ? | ? | 55.625 | ? | 0.000 |
| 308 | Bykov G.V. | Rus | E | Wor | RI | ? | 9.130 | ? | -0.800 |
| 309 | Bykov R.A. | Mos | A | Int | LI | ? | 0.000 | Med | -14.231 |
| 310 | Bykovskikh N.G. | Rus | A | Wor | ? | ? | -15.455 | App | -1.200 |
| 311 | Biazyrova V.T. | Rus | E | Tec | ? | ? | -6.522 | ? | 0.625 |
| 312 | Biakova L.S. | Rus | A | Wor | ? | ? | -6.522 | ? | 7.308 |
| 313 | Vavakin L.V. | Mos | A | Int | ? | ? | 5.217 | ? | 3.846 |
| 314 | Vagin M.G. | Rus | A | Man | ? | ? | -13.684 | ? | -6.538 |
| 315 | Vagris Ia.Ia. | Lat | E | Nom | ? | ? | 12.353 | ? | 7.826 |
| 316 | Vaishvila Z.Z. | Lit | E | Tec | LI | ? | 55.833 | ? | 0.000 |
| 317 | Vakarchuk I.A. | Ukr | E | Int | ? | ? | 23.750 | ? | 30.000 |
| 318 | Valeeva Z.S. | Rus | A | Wor | ? | ? | -10.435 | ? | -8.000 |
| 319 | Valentinov L.F. | Rus | E | Wor | ? | ? | 25.588 | LI | 11.154 |
| 320 | Valov V.A. | Rus | E | Man | ? | ? | -2.609 | RI | 3.846 |
| 321 | Vanag Ia.Ia. | Lat | E | Nom | ? | ? | 42.857 | ? | 0.000 |
| 322 | Vardanian R.P. | Arm | E | Man | ? | ? | -11.250 | ? | 7.800 |
| 323 | Vare V.I. | Est | A | Int | ? | ? | 20.000 | ? | 8.333 |
| 324 | Varek T.K. | Est | A | Man | ? | ? | 33.000 | ? | 40.000 |
| 325 | Varennikov V.I. | Rus | E | Mil | ? | App | -18.261 | ? | -20.385 |
| 326 | Varzhin E.D. | Rus | E | Tec | ? | ? | -2.609 | ? | -9.167 |
| 327 | Vasilenko M.F. | Kir | E | Cad | ? | Pre | -14.348 | ? | -13.462 |
| 328 | Vasilets A.N. | Ukr | E | Wor | ? | ? | 3.913 | ? | 11.600 |
| 329 | Vasil'ev B.G. | Rus | E | Man | ? | ? | -1.364 | ? | 17.692 |
| 330 | Vasil'ev B.L. | Mos | A | Int | Rad | ? | 26.818 | ? | 1.200 |
| 331 | Vasil'ev I.A. | Rus | A | Int | ? | ? | 0.000 | ? | -6.538 |
| 332 | Vasil'ev I.V. | Rus | A | Mil | ? | ? | -15.000 | ? | -0.192 |
| 333 | Vasil'ev K.S. | Rus | E | Tec | ? | ? | -6.522 | ? | 3.846 |
| 334 | Vasil'ev S.V. | Rus | E | Int | ? | ? | 8.158 | ? | 21.600 |
| 335 | Vasil'eva S.G. | Kaz | E | Tec | ? | LI | 31.667 | ? | 17.692 |
| 336 | Vasil'chuk N.P. | Ukr | A | Man | ? | ? | -18.261 | ? | -6.538 |

| # | Name | | | | | | | | |
|---|---|---|---|---|---|---|---|---|---|
| 337 | Vasnetsov A.V. | Mos | A | Int | ? | ? | 0.000 | ? | -6.538 |
| 338 | Vas'ko N.P. | Kaz | E | Man | ? | ? | -11.818 | ? | 4.808 |
| 339 | Vakhidov V. | Tad | E | Nom | ? | ? | -10.500 | ? | 0.385 |
| 340 | Vakhitov F.M. | Rus | E | Man | ? | ? | -8.000 | ? | -10.800 |
| 341 | Vdovkin N.I. | Rus | E | Tec | ? | ? | 5.217 | ? | 7.308 |
| 342 | Veden'kina Z.A. | Rus | A | Wor | ? | ? | -14.348 | ? | -4.400 |
| 343 | Vedmid' A.P. | Ukr | A | Man | ? | ? | -13.810 | ? | -8.400 |
| 344 | Vezirov A.-R. Kh. | Aze | E | Nom | App | ? | -12.857 | ? | -16.522 |
| 345 | Vezirova S.M. | Aze | E | Wor | ? | ? | -10.476 | ? | -4.800 |
| 346 | Veiser L.M. | Kaz | A | Cad | RI | ? | -11.000 | ? | 7.308 |
| 347 | Velikonis V.P. | Lit | E | Man | ? | ? | 43.333 | ? | 0.000 |
| 348 | Velikhov E.P. | Mos | A | Int | Med | ? | 1.818 | ? | -6.538 |
| 349 | Venglovskaia V.S. | Ukr | E | Wor | ? | ? | -3.824 | ? | -10.000 |
| 350 | Venediktov D.D. | Mos | A | Cad | ? | App | -15.455 | ? | -6.346 |
| 351 | Veprev A.F. | Rus | E | Man | ? | Med | 5.455 | ? | 7.308 |
| 352 | Vertebnyi I.A. | Ukr | A | Man | ? | ? | -12.857 | ? | 10.769 |
| 353 | Vershedenko A.M. | Ukr | A | Wor | ? | ? | -14.348 | ? | 3.846 |
| 354 | Vidiker V.I. | Kaz | E | Man | ? | ? | -15.217 | ? | 10.769 |
| 355 | Vieru G.P. | Mol | E | Int | ? | ? | 0.000 | ? | 18.125 |
| 356 | Vizniuk V.P. | Ukr | E | Wor | ? | ? | -2.609 | ? | 7.308 |
| 357 | Viktorovich A.A. | Bel | E | Wor | ? | Rad | 1.304 | ? | 6.957 |
| 358 | Vilkas Ye.I. | Lit | E | Int | ? | ? | 0.000 | ? | 0.000 |
| 359 | Vilkova M.S. | Rus | A | Wor | ? | ? | -13.043 | ? | 3.846 |
| 360 | Viltsans A.P. | Lat | A | Int | ? | LI | 43.500 | ? | 18.269 |
| 361 | Vindizhev A.Kh. | Rus | E | Wor | ? | ? | 1.304 | ? | 14.231 |
| 362 | Vinnik A.Ia. | Ukr | E | Nom | ? | ? | -3.696 | ? | 0.000 |
| 363 | Visakavichius M.Iu. | Lit | E | Wor | ? | ? | 54.000 | ? | 0.000 |
| 364 | Vladislavlev A.P. | Mos | A | Int | ? | Med | 1.429 | ? | -6.538 |
| 365 | Vlazneva M.I. | Rus | E | Wor | ? | ? | -2.609 | ? | -6.538 |
| 366 | Vlasenko A.A. | Rus | E | Nom | ? | ? | -19.524 | Cen | -11.667 |
| 367 | Vlasov A.V. | Rus | E | Nom | ? | Cen | -14.348 | ? | -3.600 |
| 368 | Vlasov Iu.P. | Mos | E | Int | Rad | ? | 36.667 | ? | 0.000 |
| 369 | Vnebrachnyi I.S. | Rus | E | Wor | ? | ? | 1.304 | ? | 3.846 |
| 370 | Voblikov V.A. | Rus | E | Cad | Cen | ? | 23.696 | ? | 14.231 |
| 371 | Voistrochenko A.F. | Rus | E | Nom | ? | ? | -14.348 | ? | -6.818 |
| 372 | Volkov V.A. | Rus | E | Cad | ? | ? | 21.087 | Rad | 18.462 |
| 373 | Volgzhin V.M. | Ukr | A | Man | ? | LI | -13.182 | ? | -0.577 |
| 374 | Volodin B.M. | Rus | E | Nom | ? | ? | -14.348 | ? | -3.077 |
| 375 | Volodichev V.V. | Rus | E | Wor | ? | ? | 9.048 | ? | 0.962 |
| 376 | Volod'ko A.A. | Bel | A | Man | ? | ? | -6.522 | ? | 4.375 |
| 377 | Volokha P.F. | Ukr | E | Man | ? | ? | -9.524 | ? | -10.000 |
| 378 | Voloshin A.V. | Rus | E | Wor | ? | ? | -6.522 | ? | -20.192 |
| 379 | Voloshkina L.F. | Rus | E | Tec | ? | ? | 1.818 | ? | 17.692 |
| 380 | Vol'skii A.I. | Aze | E | Nom | Med | ? | -8.000 | Med | -4.348 |
| 381 | Vooglaid Iu.V. | Est | E | Tec | ? | ? | 44.091 | ? | 20.000 |
| 382 | Vorob'ev A.I. | Mos | A | Tec | ? | ? | 16.136 | ? | 11.667 |
| 383 | Vorob'ev N.N. | Rus | A | Cad | ? | ? | 4.091 | ? | 3.846 |
| 384 | Vorob'ev Ye.A. | Ukr | E | Mil | ? | ? | -2.609 | ? | 8.800 |
| 385 | Vorob'eva A.N. | Rus | A | Wor | ? | ? | -10.435 | ? | 1.154 |
| 386 | Voronezhtsev Iu.I. | Bel | E | Int | ? | ? | 13.043 | Cen | 17.692 |
| 387 | Voronina L.M. | Ukr | E | Wor | ? | ? | -20.870 | ? | -11.731 |
| 388 | Voronina R.G. | Rus | A | Wor | Pre | ? | -14.348 | ? | -12.800 |
| 389 | Voronov S.I. | Rus | A | Wor | ? | ? | -6.522 | ? | -5.833 |
| 390 | Voronov Iu.P. | Mos | A | Int | ? | Med | -2.609 | ? | -4.808 |
| 391 | Vorontsov A.E. | Rus | A | Man | ? | ? | -6.522 | ? | -2.308 |
| 3015 | Vorontsov N.N. | Mos | A | Int | LI | . | . | | . |
| 392 | Vorontsov S.A. | Rus | E | Man | ? | ? | -14.348 | ? | -7.308 |
| 393 | Vorotnikov V.I. | Rus | E | Nom | App | Cen | -10.455 | Cen | -16.923 |
| 394 | Voskanian G.M. | Arm | E | Nom | ? | ? | -18.261 | ? | -3.077 |
| 395 | Voskoboinikov V.I. | Rus | E | Wor | LI | ? | 40.000 | RI | 17.308 |
| 396 | Vostrukhov O.V. | Rus | A | Tec | ? | ? | 7.826 | ? | 3.846 |
| 397 | Vuichitskii A.S. | Ukr | E | Man | ? | ? | -10.435 | ? | -7.200 |
| 398 | Vul'fson M.G. | Lat | E | Tec | ? | LI | 26.333 | ? | 8.611 |
| 399 | Vyucheiskii A.I. | Rus | E | Tec | ? | ? | 9.565 | ? | 11.600 |
| 400 | Viali A.I. | Est | E | Cad | ? | ? | 31.875 | ? | 30.000 |
| 401 | Vialais V.I. | Est | E | Nom | ? | ? | 27.500 | ? | -1.600 |
| 402 | Viatkina G.I. | Bel | E | Man | ? | ? | 18.333 | ? | 15.000 |
| 403 | Gabitova M.G. | Rus | A | Cad | ? | ? | -6.522 | ? | 0.769 |
| 404 | Gabrielian V.M. | Aze | E | Cad | ? | ? | 10.652 | ? | -2.600 |
| 405 | Gabrusev S.A. | Bel | E | Man | LI | Rad | 16.957 | ? | 17.692 |
| 406 | Gavrilov A.P. | Rus | E | Int | ? | ? | 26.739 | ? | 16.000 |
| 407 | Gagloev A.S. | Rus | A | Wor | ? | ? | -12.500 | ? | -30.769 |
| 408 | Gadzhiev M.N. | Aze | A | Wor | ? | ? | -9.444 | ? | -7.500 |
| 409 | Gaer E.A. | Rus | E | Int | Rad | ? | 27.143 | ? | 14.231 |
| 410 | Gazenko O.G. | Mos | A | Int | ? | ? | 19.524 | ? | 11.154 |
| 411 | Gaida M.M. | Ukr | E | Mil | ? | ? | 37.500 | ? | 26.818 |
| 412 | Gaiduchenia S.N. | Ukr | A | Wor | ? | ? | -16.522 | ? | 3.846 |
| 413 | Galoian G.A. | Arm | E | Nom | ? | ? | -18.333 | Cen | -1.200 |
| 414 | Galstian S.S. | Arm | E | Man | ? | ? | 14.412 | ? | 17.115 |
| 415 | Gamzatov R.G. | Rus | E | Int | ? | ? | -16.429 | ? | -1.600 |
| 416 | Gamkrelidze T.V. | Geo | E | Int | Rad | ? | 44.000 | ? | 0.000 |
| 417 | Gams Ye.S. | Rus | E | Mil | ? | ? | -5.238 | ? | 17.692 |
| 418 | Gaponov-Grekhov A.V. | Rus | A | Int | ? | ? | 24.737 | ? | 13.600 |
| 419 | Gasanova Sh.M. | Aze | E | Man | ? | ? | -18.261 | ? | -10.000 |
| 420 | Gausknekht Iu.G. | Rus | E | Wor | ? | ? | 9.130 | ? | 7.308 |

| # | Name | Reg | | Occ | | | Val1 | | Val2 |
|---|---|---|---|---|---|---|---|---|---|
| 421 | Gashper M.A. | Mol | A | Wor | ? | ? | 5.455 | ? | 11.600 |
| 422 | Gvenetagze A.D. | Geo | E | Tec | ? | ? | 16.957 | ? | -1.739 |
| 423 | Gvozdev V.M. | Rus | A | Wor | App | ? | -10.652 | ? | 3.846 |
| 424 | Gdlian T.Kh. | Mos | E | Tec | Rad | Rad | 33.000 | ? | 33.824 |
| 425 | Geda S.Z.Z. | Lit | E | Int | ? | ? | 43.333 | ? | 0.000 |
| 426 | Gezhin K.G. | Rus | A | Wor | ? | Med | -6.522 | ? | 1.154 |
| 427 | Geiba Ia.A. | Lat | E | Cad | ? | ? | 6.071 | ? | 3.333 |
| 428 | Gel'man A.I. | Mos | A | Int | ? | ? | 31.667 | ? | 18.000 |
| 429 | Genzialis B.K. | Lit | E | Int | ? | ? | 43.333 | ? | -50.000 |
| 430 | Genchev A.A. | Rus | E | Tec | ? | ? | 15.000 | ? | 23.333 |
| 431 | Gerzanich M.V. | Ukr | E | Tec | ? | ? | -3.158 | ? | 7.727 |
| 432 | German D.A. | Rus | A | Int | ? | ? | -0.556 | ? | 7.308 |
| 433 | German N.F. | Ukr | E | Wor | ? | ? | 4.348 | ? | 7.115 |
| 434 | Germel' S.V. | Bel | A | Wor | ? | ? | -17.000 | ? | 0.000 |
| 435 | Gibadullin M.R. | Rus | A | Wor | ? | ? | 7.273 | ? | 9.167 |
| 436 | Gidaspov B.V. | Rus | E | Nom | Cen | RI | 1.000 | App | -10.000 |
| 437 | Gidirim G.P. | Mol | E | Tec | ? | ? | 21.000 | ? | 11.538 |
| 438 | Gilalzade D.G. | Aze | E | Wor | ? | ? | 0.000 | ? | -5.952 |
| 439 | Gil' Ia.Ia. | Ukr | E | Tec | ? | ? | 3.158 | ? | 12.200 |
| 440 | Ginzburg V.L. | Mos | A | Int | LI | ? | 4.211 | Med | -0.962 |
| 441 | Girenko A.N. | Ukr | E | Nom | ? | ? | -16.667 | ? | -4.167 |
| 442 | Giro V.A. | Tad | E | Tec | Cen | ? | -2.609 | App | 10.769 |
| 443 | Giiasova P.G. | Aze | E | Wor | ? | ? | -18.261 | ? | -2.692 |
| 444 | Glavatskikh M.V. | Rus | E | Wor | ? | ? | 6.136 | ? | 4.615 |
| 445 | Glazkov N.S. | Mos | E | Wor | ? | ? | 12.500 | ? | 6.731 |
| 446 | Glazunov A.N. | Rus | E | Tec | ? | ? | 16.316 | ? | -3.077 |
| 447 | Glazunov V.I. | Rus | A | Man | ? | ? | -7.273 | ? | -13.462 |
| 448 | Glazunov I.F. | Tad | E | Man | ? | ? | -6.522 | ? | 3.846 |
| 449 | Gnatiuk V.V. | Ukr | E | Tec | ? | ? | -18.261 | ? | -3.846 |
| 450 | Gninenko Iu.I. | Kaz | E | Tec | ? | ? | -7.391 | Med | 10.769 |
| 451 | Govorov V.L. | Rus | E | Mil | ? | ? | -14.545 | ? | -16.923 |
| 452 | Gogeshvili A.R. | Geo | E | Wor | ? | ? | 15.217 | ? | 0.962 |
| 453 | Gogua A.N. | Geo | E | Int | ? | ? | 11.364 | ? | 14.400 |
| 454 | Godzhaeva S.A. | Aze | E | Wor | ? | ? | 0.000 | ? | 0.000 |
| 455 | Golev A.V. | Rus | E | Tec | ? | ? | -6.522 | Med | -6.875 |
| 456 | Golik Iu.V. | Rus | E | Int | LI | Med | -14.348 | Med | 3.846 |
| 457 | Golov I.A. | Rus | A | Man | ? | ? | -14.348 | ? | -13.462 |
| 458 | Golovin S.P. | Rus | E | Wor | LI | ? | 1.304 | ? | 0.000 |
| 459 | Golovlev E.L. | Rus | E | Int | LI | Rad | 16.818 | ? | 14.091 |
| 460 | Golovnev V.E. | Bel | E | Mil | ? | ? | 1.304 | ? | 1.346 |
| 461 | Golovnitskii L.N. | Rus | A | Int | ? | ? | 0.000 | ? | 3.846 |
| 462 | Golubeva V.N. | Rus | A | Man | ? | Med | -6.522 | ? | -3.077 |
| 463 | Golubkov G.N. | Est | E | Man | ? | ? | 19.333 | ? | 12.647 |
| 464 | Golushko N.M. | Ukr | E | Mil | ? | ? | -8.095 | ? | 2.600 |
| 465 | Gol'danskii V.I. | Mos | A | Int | Med | LI | 3.182 | LI | -3.077 |
| 466 | Goliakov A.I. | Mos | A | Cad | ? | ? | -21.538 | ? | -8.000 |
| 467 | Gontar V.A. | Ukr | A | Man | LI | Med | 1.304 | ? | -2.115 |
| 468 | Gonchar A.N. | Rus | A | Mil | ? | ? | -18.261 | ? | -10.000 |
| 469 | Gonchar A.T. | Ukr | A | Int | ? | ? | 24.783 | ? | 0.000 |
| 470 | Goncharik V.I. | Bel | A | Nom | ? | ? | -10.435 | ? | -6.538 |
| 471 | Goncharov V.V. | Ukr | E | Cad | LI | Rad | 16.136 | Med | 5.577 |
| 472 | Gorbatko V.V. | Mos | A | Mil | ? | ? | -16.667 | ? | -21.111 |
| 473 | Gorbachev A.G. | Rus | E | Man | ? | ? | 8.571 | ? | 12.692 |
| 474 | Gorbachev M.S. | Mos | A | Nom | Med | Med | -18.636 | Med | -12.800 |
| 475 | Gorbenko A.P. | Ukr | E | Wor | ? | ? | -8.636 | ? | 10.769 |
| 476 | Gorbunov A.V. | Lat | E | Nom | Med | LI | 12.222 | LI | 10.652 |
| 477 | Gorbunov G.N. | Rus | E | Man | ? | ? | 0.000 | ? | 0.000 |
| 478 | Gorbunov Iu.G. | Kir | E | Man | ? | ? | -10.435 | ? | 2.500 |
| 479 | Gordeev V.S. | Rus | A | Man | ? | ? | 10.526 | ? | 12.692 |
| 480 | Gordeev I.D. | Rus | E | Man | ? | ? | -16.364 | ? | -1.304 |
| 481 | Gordeeva V.I. | Rus | A | Man | ? | ? | -20.000 | ? | -3.077 |
| 482 | Gorelkina V.A. | Rus | A | Cad | ? | ? | 12.609 | ? | 3.333 |
| 483 | Gorelovskii I.I. | Aze | E | Mil | ? | ? | -18.261 | ? | -23.846 |
| 484 | Gorinov T.I. | Rus | A | Oth | Pre | ? | -26.818 | ? | -6.538 |
| 485 | Gorinchei V.V. | Mol | E | Man | ? | ? | 16.957 | ? | 12.308 |
| 486 | Gorlov G.K. | Rus | A | Man | ? | Pre | -19.500 | App | -10.000 |
| 487 | Gorozhaninov Iu.I. | Rus | E | Man | ? | ? | 20.870 | ? | 7.308 |
| 488 | Gorokhov V.A. | Rus | E | Oth | ? | ? | 1.304 | ? | 7.500 |
| 489 | Gorshkov L.A. | Rus | E | Nom | ? | ? | -1.905 | ? | 7.200 |
| 490 | Gorynin I.V. | Rus | A | Tec | ? | Med | 0.000 | ? | -8.462 |
| 491 | Grakhovskii A.A. | Bel | E | Nom | Cen | ? | -10.435 | ? | -10.000 |
| 492 | Grachev N.P. | Rus | E | Man | ? | ? | -10.435 | ? | -2.400 |
| 493 | Gracheva G.P. | Rus | A | Man | ? | ? | -14.348 | ? | -3.077 |
| 494 | Grebneva T.F. | Rus | A | Tec | ? | ? | -0.870 | ? | -1.000 |
| 495 | Gretsov S.N. | Rus | A | Wor | ? | ? | -17.273 | ? | -7.500 |
| 496 | Grib A.V. | Ukr | E | Wor | ? | ? | 5.217 | ? | 16.346 |
| 497 | Grigor'ev V.V. (401) | Rus | E | Man | ? | ? | 5.217 | ? | 3.846 |
| 498 | Grigor'ev V.V. (80) | Bel | E | Nom | | App | -11.905 | ? | 3.846 |
| 499 | Grigor'ev F.G. | Rus | E | Tec | ? | ? | -5.000 | Cen | 14.231 |
| 500 | Grigorian A.G. | Arm | A | Int | LI | LI | -6.190 | ? | 4.600 |
| 501 | Grigorian V.S. | Aze | E | Cad | Rad | ? | 10.000 | ? | 22.292 |
| 502 | Grigorian N.A. | Arm | E | Cad | ? | ? | -7.143 | ? | -0.200 |
| 503 | Grinovskis Ye.Ia. | Lat | E | Tec | ? | ? | 23.571 | ? | 37.778 |
| 504 | Grintsov I.G. | Ukr | E | Nom | ? | ? | -16.522 | ? | -3.077 |
| 505 | Grintsenko N.N. | Mos | A | Cad | ? | Cen | -13.182 | ? | -10.000 |

| | | | | | | | | | |
|---|---|---|---|---|---|---|---|---|---|
| 506 | Grishchenko P.S. | Rus | E | Nom | ? | ? | -18.261 | ? | -10.000 |
| 507 | Grishchenkov G.Z. | Bel | A | Man | ? | ? | -10.435 | ? | -3.846 |
| 508 | Grishchuk V.P. | Ukr | E | Int | Med | Rad | 17.391 | ? | 12.308 |
| 509 | Grozdev S.V. | Mol | E | Cad | ? | ? | 0.000 | ? | 10.000 |
| 510 | Gromov B.V. | Ukr | E | Mil | ? | App | -10.000 | ? | -4.808 |
| 511 | Bromov B.F. | Rus | A | Wor | ? | ? | -10.435 | ? | -7.200 |
| 512 | Gromov V.I. | Rus | A | Wor | ? | ? | -14.348 | ? | -3.077 |
| 513 | Gromiak R.T. | Ukr | E | Int | ? | ? | -2.609 | ? | 21.923 |
| 514 | Gross V.I. | Rus | E | Man | ? | ? | -8.182 | ? | 8.077 |
| 515 | Grossu S.K. | Mol | E | Nom | ? | ? | -3.500 | ? | -6.538 |
| 516 | Grudinina A.K. | Rus | E | Tec | ? | ? | -10.435 | ? | -10.000 |
| 517 | Grudinina S.V. | Kaz | E | Wor | ? | ? | -15.217 | ? | 8.077 |
| 518 | Gruzdov I.P. | Rus | A | Man | ? | ? | -6.000 | ? | -3.077 |
| 519 | Gryezhdieru A.G. | Mol | E | Int | ? | Pre | 29.545 | ? | 28.077 |
| 520 | Griazin I.N. | Est | E | Int | Med | Med | 30.455 | ? | 39.167 |
| 521 | Gubarev V.A. | Rus | E | Man | ? | ? | 14.348 | ? | 21.923 |
| 522 | Gubin V.A. | Rus | A | Tec | ? | LI | 8.261 | ? | 5.192 |
| 523 | Guguchiia D.I. | Geo | A | Man | ? | ? | 9.048 | ? | 1.500 |
| 524 | Gudaitis R.V. | Lit | E | Int | LI | ? | 42.500 | ? | 0.000 |
| 525 | Gudzhabidze A.V. | Geo | E | Man | ? | ? | 23.043 | ? | -11.500 |
| 526 | Gudilina V.G. | Rus | E | Tec | ? | ? | 11.304 | ? | 10.833 |
| 527 | Gudushauri O.N. | Geo | E | Tec | ? | ? | 21.957 | ? | -9.412 |
| 528 | Gukasov Ye.K. | Kaz | E | Nom | ? | Cen | -16.667 | ? | -8.462 |
| 529 | Gulamov R. | Uzb | A | Oth | ? | ? | -33.750 | ? | -3.077 |
| 530 | Gulii V.V. | Rus | E | Int | Rad | ? | 32.381 | ? | 23.000 |
| 531 | Gulova Z.S. | Tad | A | Wor | ? | App | -16.190 | ? | -3.077 |
| 532 | Gul'chenko I.M. | Kaz | E | Tec | ? | ? | 17.692 | ? | 28.889 |
| 533 | Guliaev Iu.V. | Mos | A | Int | ? | ? | -7.273 | ? | -5.769 |
| 534 | Gumbaridze G.G. | Geo | E | Nom | Med | Med | -4.000 | LI | -25.769 |
| 535 | Gumennaia Z.L. | Rus | A | Wor | ? | ? | -3.684 | ? | 5.800 |
| 536 | Gummyev O. | Tur | E | Wor | ? | ? | -2.609 | ? | -3.000 |
| 537 | Gundogdyev Ia.P. | Tur | E | Cad | ? | ? | -6.591 | ? | -0.200 |
| 538 | Gurenko S.I. | Ukr | E | Nom | ? | ? | -12.727 | ? | -6.538 |
| 539 | Guruleva N.G. | Rus | A | Wor | ? | ? | 0.000 | ? | 0.000 |
| 540 | Gusev V.V. | Rus | E | Nom | ? | ? | 1.304 | ? | -6.538 |
| 541 | Gustov V.V. | Rus | A | Wor | Med | ? | 22.727 | ? | 8.846 |
| 542 | Gus'kova L.M. | Rus | A | Cad | ? | App | -28.333 | ? | -3.846 |
| 543 | Gutskalov N.I. | Rus | A | Tec | ? | ? | -6.522 | ? | 16.000 |
| 544 | Dabizha N.T. | Mol | E | Int | ? | ? | 20.870 | LI | 19.583 |
| 545 | Davituliani V.V. | Rus | E | Tec | ? | Rad | 45.227 | ? | 15.417 |
| 546 | Davliatov S.I. | Tad | E | Wor | ? | ? | -1.429 | ? | 7.308 |
| 547 | Davranov N. | Uzb | E | Tec | ? | ? | -16.364 | ? | -6.538 |
| 548 | Davronov A. | Uzb | E | Wor | ? | ? | -15.000 | ? | -3.077 |
| 549 | Dadamian B.V. | Aze | E | Man | LI | ? | 34.000 | RI | 10.000 |
| 550 | Dadov Kh.A. | Rus | E | Wor | ? | ? | -18.261 | ? | 8.400 |
| 551 | Dambaev D.B. | Rus | E | Man | ? | ? | -3.500 | ? | -3.077 |
| 552 | Dambis A.A. | Lat | A | Wor | ? | Rad | 15.313 | ? | 18.182 |
| 553 | Danzberg A.K. | Lat | E | Man | ? | LI | 24.615 | ? | 14.583 |
| 554 | Danilenko A.S. | Ukr | A | Man | ? | ? | 0.909 | ? | 3.846 |
| 555 | Danilov V.M. | Rus | E | Wor | ? | ? | 11.429 | ? | 17.692 |
| 556 | Danilov V.N. | Ukr | E | Wor | ? | ? | 1.304 | ? | 3.846 |
| 557 | Danilov L.I. | Rus | A | Tec | ? | ? | -10.435 | ? | -7.000 |
| 558 | Danilov S.N. | Rus | E | Wor | ? | ? | 8.261 | ? | 16.154 |
| 559 | Danilova L.A. | Rus | E | Tec | ? | ? | -4.545 | ? | 0.000 |
| 560 | Daniliuk I.V. | Ukr | E | Man | ? | ? | -10.435 | ? | -7.400 |
| 561 | Daniliuk N.N. | Rus | E | Nom | ? | Cen | -7.727 | ? | 0.000 |
| 562 | Darsigov M.Iu. | Rus | E | Wor | ? | ? | -20.000 | ? | -10.833 |
| 563 | Degaeva A.M. | Rus | E | Wor | ? | ? | -0.435 | ? | 7.308 |
| 564 | Degtiarev M.P. | Bel | E | Wor | ? | ? | -6.522 | ? | 0.000 |
| 565 | Dedeneva N.N. | Rus | A | Wor | ? | Pre | -2.609 | ? | 3.846 |
| 566 | Dediukhin L.S. | Rus | A | Tec | ? | ? | -14.348 | ? | 0.385 |
| 567 | Demakov N.A. | Rus | E | Tec | ? | ? | 19.130 | ? | 17.692 |
| 568 | Dementei N.I. | Bel | A | Nom | ? | Med | -14.348 | Med | -13.462 |
| 569 | Demidov A.I. | Rus | E | Tec | Rad | App | 3.158 | ? | 7.308 |
| 570 | Demidov G.I. | Rus | E | Tec | ? | App | 1.304 | ? | -3.077 |
| 571 | Demidov M.V. | Rus | E | Cad | ? | ? | 0.909 | ? | -1.200 |
| 572 | Demin A.B. | Rus | E | Mil | ? | ? | 9.130 | ? | 11.000 |
| 573 | Demurchieva F.M. | Geo | E | Wor | ? | ? | -11.250 | ? | 0.385 |
| 574 | Demchenko F.M. | Ukr | E | Wor | ? | ? | -10.435 | ? | 0.000 |
| 575 | Demchuk A.D. | Ukr | A | Tec | ? | ? | -14.348 | ? | -5.385 |
| 576 | Demchuk M.I. | Bel | A | Nom | ? | ? | -8.043 | ? | 7.308 |
| 577 | Denisenko A.G. | Ukr | A | Man | ? | ? | -6.522 | ? | -6.538 |
| 578 | Denisov A.A. | Rus | E | Int | ? | ? | 9.130 | ? | 4.423 |
| 579 | Denisov V.I. | Rus | E | Man | ? | ? | -6.522 | ? | 7.308 |
| 580 | Denisov N.P. | Rus | A | Wor | ? | ? | 16.739 | ? | 3.846 |
| 581 | Derevianko B.F. | Ukr | E | Int | LI | ? | 3.478 | ? | 3.654 |
| 582 | Desiatov V.M. | Rus | E | Man | ? | LI | 6.364 | Rad | 14.231 |
| 583 | Dzhanasbaev A.T. | Kaz | E | Wor | ? | ? | -17.391 | ? | -8.077 |
| 584 | Dzharimov A.A. | Rus | E | Nom | ? | App | -10.435 | App | -3.077 |
| 585 | Dzhafarov V.D. | Aze | E | Cad | App | ? | -35.000 | ? | -8.421 |
| 586 | Dzhimov M. Sh. | Rus | A | Wor | ? | ? | -12.826 | ? | 18.077 |
| 587 | Dzhoraev K. | Tur | E | Wor | ? | ? | -2.609 | ? | 4.423 |
| 588 | Dzhumagulov A. | Kir | E | Nom | ? | Cen | -21.364 | ? | -5.600 |
| 589 | Dzhumatova M.D. | Kaz | A | Tec | ? | ? | -18.261 | ? | -3.077 |
| 590 | Dzhunaidov I. | Tad | E | Tec | ? | ? | -10.435 | ? | -9.038 |

```
591 Dzhusoity N.G.           Geo E Int ?    ?    13.043 ?     -2.000
592 Dzasokhov A.S.           Rus E Nom Cen  Med  -6.522 Med -25.000
593 Dzidzariia V.V.          Geo E Wor ?    ?     0.000 ?     -7.647
594 Dikul' V.I.              Mos E Tec ?    ?     3.889 Cen    8.077
595 Dikusarov V.G.           Ukr E Nom ?    ?   -14.348 ?      0.833
596 Dilekov Kh.              Tur E Wor ?    ?    -9.783 ?      9.808
597 Dikhtiar' A.D.           Geo E Wor ?    ?    24.565 ?      0.385
598 Dmitriev A.A.            Rus E Wor ?    ?    -7.500 ?     -0.400
599 Dmitriev V.V.            Rus E Wor ?    ?    -6.522 ?      1.154
600 Dmitriev N.G.            Rus A Int Med  ?    -3.500 Cen   -2.000
601 Dmitrieva V.D.           Rus A Wor ?    ?    -9.545 ?      0.000
602 Dobrovol'skaia T.N.      Rus A Cad ?    ?   -14.348 ?    -10.000
603 Dobrovol'skii A.I.       Bel E Tec Med  ?    17.391 ?     23.462
604 Dobrotoliubov V.M.       Kir E Tec ?    ?    -2.609 ?      3.846
605 Dovlatian F.V.           Arm E Int Rad  ?    -7.692 ?     -3.864
606 Doga E.D.                Mol E Int ?    ?    12.368 ?     15.200
607 Dolganov A.V.            Rus E Man ?    ?   -10.435 ?    -10.800
608 Dondup M.V.              Rus E Tec ?    ?   -18.182 ?     -6.538
609 Donchak Ia.A.            Kaz E Wor ?    ?   -18.261 ?      7.308
610 Donchenko Iu.A.          Ukr E Wor ?    ?    11.364 ?      8.077
611 Doronina Z.N.            Rus E Tec ?    ?     1.304 ?      0.385
612 Dorokhov I.V.            Rus E Nom ?    ?   -12.727 App -10.000
613 Druzhinina L.N.          Kir A Wor ?    ?   -17.273 ?      0.000
614 Druz' P.A.               Rus A Oth ?    ?   -14.348 ?      7.308
615 Drunina Iu.V.            Mos A Int ?    ?    11.333 Med    3.333
616 Drutsye I.P.             Mol E Int LI   ?    20.000 ?     18.333
617 Dubko A.I.               Bel A Man App  Cen  -7.692 ?     -2.200
618 Dubnikov V.D.            Rus E Man ?    ?    13.095 ?     20.417
619 Dubovitskii G.A.         Rus E Wor ?    ?    -2.273 ?      0.000
620 Dudko T.N.               Bel A Cad ?    ?   -10.000 ?      2.308
621 Dumbravan M.G.           Mol E Man ?    ?    15.682 ?      7.308
622 Dumitrash I.P.           Mol A Cad ?    ?    -8.824 ?     -4.600
623 Dusmatov A.              Tad A Cad ?    ?   -10.435 ?      0.385
624 Dygai G.G.               Mol A Oth ?    ?   -17.778 ?     -5.263
625 Dylevich G.P.            Bel A Cad ?    ?   -14.091 ?     -1.200
626 Dyiakov I.N.             Rus E Nom ?    App -14.000 ?      3.846
627 Dyiachenko A.N.          Mol E Man ?    ?     6.739 ?      5.600
628 Diusembaev V.            Kaz E Wor RI   ?    10.455 ?     10.769
629 Diusov L.L.              Bel E Wor ?    ?   -14.348 ?     14.231
630 Diadenko N.S.            Ukr A Cad ?    RI  -17.727 ?     -2.400
631 Evtukh V.G.              Bel E Nom ?    ?   -18.261 ?     -6.400
632 Evtushenko E.A.          Ukr E Int LI   LI   22.222 ?     13.000
633 Evtushkov M.G.           Rus E Man ?    ?    34.348 ?      4.615
634 Egizekova A.N.           Kaz E Wor ?    ?   -18.261 ?      3.600
635 Egorov O.M.              Rus A Wor ?    ?    11.250 ?      0.385
636 Egorova I.A.             Rus A Tec Med  ?    -6.190 ?      3.600
637 Egorshin V.V.            Rus E Wor ?    ?     1.304 ?      7.308
638 Ezhelev A.S.             Rus A Int ?    ?    12.857 ?      7.308
639 Ezhikov-Babakhanov E.G.  Kaz E Nom ?    ?    -5.909 ?     -2.917
640 Elagin V.F.              Rus E Wor ?    LI   13.333 ?      3.846
641 Eliseev A.S.             Mos A Tec ?    ?    19.783 LI     3.654
642 Eliseev E.A.             Rus E Nom ?    Cen -18.500 ?    -21.111
643 Elistratov E.N.          Rus A Wor ?    ?    -5.217 ?      3.846
644 El'tsin B.N.             Mos E Nom Rad  Rad  23.750 ?      0.000
645 El'chenko Iu.N.          Ukr E Nom ?    ?   -14.348 ?    -10.000
646 Emel'ianenkov A.F.       Rus E Int Rad  ?    13.261 ?     12.885
647 Emel'ianov A.M.          Mos E Int Rad  Rad  11.364 ?     24.615
648 Emel'ianov P.E.          Rus E Tec ?    ?    -6.522 ?    -13.462
649 Enokian G.A.             Arm E Man LI   ?    -0.870 ?      3.846
650 Enshakov Ye.V.           Rus A Cad ?    ?   -10.435 ?    -10.000
651 Eraliev Zh.              Kaz E Man ?    ?    -7.391 ?      7.200
652 Eraliev T.E.             Kaz A Int ?    ?   -14.545 ?     10.000
653 Erelina V.K.             Rus E Tec ?    ?     5.217 ?     -3.077
654 Eremei G.I.              Mol E Nom ?    Med  -9.545 ?     -6.538
655 Eremenko S.F.            Rus E Tec ?    Rad  40.435 ?     22.692
656 Ermakov V.F.             Mos A Man ?    ?   -15.000 ?    -10.000
657 Ermakov N.V.             Rus E Tec ?    ?    -6.522 ?    -10.000
658 Ermilov N.K.             Rus E Man ?    ?   -10.000 Cen    6.250
659 Ermolaev G.M.            Rus E Man ?    ?     1.304 ?      3.846
660 Erokhin V.A.             Ukr E Mil ?    ?    13.043 ?     17.692
661 Erokhin V.L.             Rus E Tec ?    ?     5.217 ?      7.308
662 Erokhovets I.Ia.         Bel A Wor ?    Cen -18.636 ?     -3.846
663 Eseikin N.V.             Rus E Wor Pre  ?   -13.182 ?     -2.000
664 Etylen V.M.              Rus E Int ?    Med  -2.609 ?     -2.083
665 Efimov A.N.              Mos A Mil ?    ?   -19.048 ?    -18.000
666 Efimov A.S.              Uzb E Nom ?    ?   -17.000 ?     -3.846
667 Efimov V.G.              Rus E Tec ?    ?     2.174 ?      3.846
668 Efimov N.V.              Rus E Wor ?    ?    17.500 ?     -6.538
669 Efremov A.G.             Rus E Man ?    ?   -12.273 ?     14.231
670 Efremov O.N.             Mos A Int ?    ?     9.706 ?     -3.077
671 Zhakselekov Ye.          Kaz A Nom ?    Pre -17.000 ?     -7.885
672 Zhanybekov Sh.Zh.        Kaz A Cad ?    ?   -14.000 App -13.600
673 Zhgeriia I.A.            Geo E Wor ?    ?    17.273 ?    -10.556
674 Zhdakaev I.A.            Rus E Wor ?    ?    26.364 ?     21.154
```

```
675 Zhdanov A.G.            Mol E Cad ?     Cen  -6.522 ?    -12.083
676 Zhivotov A.A.           Rus E Man ?     ?   -14.348 ?     -3.077
677 Zhigulin A.S.           Kaz E Nom ?     ?   -27.333 ?    -20.385
678 Zhigunova L.T.          Rus E Tec ?     ?     1.304 ?    -13.462
679 Zhitkov O.A.            Rus E Wor ?     ?    -2.609 ?      4.615
680 Zhonkuvvatova R.N.      Uzb E Wor ?     ?   -20.455 ?     -8.077
681 Zhuk A.V.               Rus A Int ?     ?    22.381 ?     14.231
682 Zhukov A.A.             Rus A Wor ?     ?   -11.087 ?     -1.923
683 Zhukova T.P.            Rus A Tec Cen ?     35.000 ?     12.917
684 Zhukovskaia L.L.        Bel A Man ?     ?   -10.455 ?      0.000
685 Zhurabaeva T.           Uzb E Tec ?     ?   -18.500 ?    -12.308
686 Zhuravlev A.G.          Bel E Tec LI  Rad  16.591 ?     10.769
687 Zabrodin I.A.           Ukr E Nom ?     ?    -1.176 ?     -0.652
688 Zavizion O.V.           Rus A Man ?     ?   -25.769 ?     -4.615
689 Zagainov E.A.           Rus E Tec ?     ?   -12.727 ?     -3.077
690 Zadoia N.K.             Ukr E Nom ?     ?   -14.348 ?    -10.000
691 Zadyrko V.I.            Ukr E Man ?    Rad  -0.952 ?     11.667
692 Zaikov L.N.             Mos A Nom ?     ?   -18.182 ?    -13.462
693 Zainalkhanov D.G.       Rus E Wor ?     ?     4.545 ?      9.200
694 Zakarian V.Z.           Arm E Wor ?     ?     4.722 ?      7.500
695 Zakis Iu.R.             Lat E Int ?     ?    15.357 ?     14.091
696 Zaletskas K.V.          Lit E Nom ?     ?    43.333 ?      0.000
697 Zalikhanov M.Ch.        Rus E Int App Cen  -9.091 ?     -2.000
698 Zalomai V.A.            Bel E Nom ?    App -14.348 ?      3.077
699 Zalygin S.P.            Mos A Int LI    ?     0.000 LI   -12.308
700 Zamaniagra M.F.         Mol A Wor ?     ?    -7.273 ?      3.846
701 Zanokha A.I.            Kir E Man ?     ?    -5.000 ?    -16.923
702 Zarin' I.A.             Lat A Int ?     ?    17.000 ?      3.929
703 Zaslavskaia\T.I.        Mos A Int Rad Rad   3.636 ?      0.000
704 Zaslavskii I.I.         Mos E Tec Rad Rad  19.444 Rad   16.600
705 Zakhaev L.              Rus E Tec ?     ?   -10.435 ?     -3.077
706 Zakharenko A.A.         Ukr E Tec ?     ?     1.304 LI   10.200
707 Zakharov A.A.           Rus E Wor ?     ?    21.087 ?     33.750
708 Zakharov V.A.           Rus E Nom ?     ?   -10.435 ?    -11.600
709 Zakarov V.V.            Ukr E Tec ?     ?    28.409 ?     21.154
710 Zakharov M.A.           Mos A Int ?     ?    10.000 ?     14.400
711 Zakharova G.I.          Rus E Tec ?     ?    -2.609 ?     -4.783
712 Zakharchenko V.F.       Ukr E Wor ?     ?    -6.667 ?     -2.000
713 Zbykovskii I.I.         Ukr E Man ?    Cen   0.435 ?      0.385
714 Zverev V.V.             Ukr E Wor ?     ?     1.304 ?      9.231
715 Zvonov S.N.             Rus A Man LI    ?    21.087 ?     13.654
716 Zgerskaia A.A.          Ukr E Int Rad Rad  12.727 ?     26.731
717 Zelenovskii A.A.        Bel E Nom ?     ?   -15.217 ?     -2.885
718 Zelinskii I.P.          Ukr E Int ?     ?     1.304 ?     10.769
719 Zemskova A.V.           Rus A Tec ?     ?     3.636 RI    7.308
720 Zen'ko M.F.             Rus E Wor ?     ?     8.913 ?     28.800
721 Ziatdinov N.Z.          Rus A Man ?     ?    -2.609 ?     13.913
722 Zoidze N.T.             Geo E Wor ?     ?     4.000 ?      1.600
723 Zokirov M.Z.            Uzb A Cad ?     ?    -4.318 ?      5.000
724 Zolotareva L.A.         Rus A Oth ?     ?   -13.810 ?    -12.000
725 Zolotkov A.A.           Rus E Tec ?     ?     4.348 ?     13.200
726 Zolotukhin V.P.         Uzb E Int LI    ?     7.222 ?      5.577
727 Zol'nikov F.F.          Arm E Tec ?     ?   -26.087 ?    -12.308
728 Zorina V.S.             Geo E Wor ?     ?     8.000 ?     -9.474
729 Zubanov V.A.            Ukr E Cad LI    ?     3.182 ?     11.667
730 Zubkov V.N.             Rus E Tec LI  Rad  41.000 ?     16.957
731 Zubov I.I.              Rus A Cad ?     ?   -18.261 ?    -10.000
732 Zubov Iu.I.             Rus E Man ?     ?   -16.667 ?      7.083
733 Zuikov V.P.             Rus A Int ?     ?     5.217 ?     15.000
734 Zumakulova T.M.         Rus A Int ?     ?     0.000 ?    -11.923
735 Zukhbaia O.G.           Geo E Wor ?     ?     3.684 ?      1.667
736 Zykova L.V.             Rus A Wor ?     ?   -21.579 ?    -16.250
737 Ibragimbekov R.M.I.     Aze E Int ?     ?    12.813 ?      0.000
738 Ibragimov G.R.          Aze A Wor ?    Med  -3.864 ?      0.385
739 Ibragimov M.A.          Aze E Int Pre ?      0.000 ?      0.000
740 Ibragimov M.I.          Uzb E Nom ?    Cen  -6.364 Cen  -10.800
741 Ibraeva K.              Kaz E Wor ?     ?   -17.143 ?      0.000
742 Ibraimova R.B.          Kir A Cad ?     ?   -10.500 ?      4.600
743 Ivanenko N.I.           Rus E Wor ?     ?   -23.636 ?      2.083
744 Ivanov V.B.             Rus E Int ?     ?     0.000 ?     12.692
745 Ivanov V.V. (482)       Ukr E Wor ?     ?    22.273 Med  17.692
746 Ivanov V.V. (AN)        Mos A Int Med ?     11.429 ?      5.882
747 Ivanov V.P.             Rus E Mil ?    RI   -3.636 Cen  -3.077
748 Ivanov Vik.V. (potreb.) Rus A Wor ?     ?     3.000 ?     14.231
749 Ivanov Viach.V. (potreb.)Rus A Man ?    ?    -6.522 ?      8.077
750 Ivanov K.E.             Rus E Man ?     ?     1.304 ?     10.833
751 Ivanov N.V.             Rus E Tec Rad Rad  38.750 Rad    4.000
752 Ivans D.Ye.             Lat E Int Rad ?     29.545 ?      0.000
753 Ivashko V.A.            Ukr A Nom ?    App  -3.696 Cen  -5.769
754 Ivchenko I.M.           Rus E Wor ?     ?     1.304 ?     12.400
755 Igitian G.S.            Arm A Int Rad LI   33.333 LI    12.500
756 Ignatov S.V.            Rus E Man ?     ?    29.783 ?     20.962
757 Ignatovich N.I.         Bel E Tec ?     ?    21.000 ?     13.077
758 Ignat'ev I.G.           Rus E Cad ?     ?     1.304 ?     -3.077
```

| # | Name | | | | | | | | |
|---|---|---|---|---|---|---|---|---|---|
| 759 | Igrunov N.S. | Bel | E | Nom | ? | ? | -15.217 | ? | 0.577 |
| 760 | Igumnov O.A. | Kir | E | Tec | ? | ? | 5.909 | ? | 17.692 |
| 761 | Izvekov S.M. | Mos | A | Int | ? | ? | 0.000 | ? | 0.000 |
| 762 | Izmodenov A.K. | Rus | E | Nom | LI | ? | 29.750 | ? | 14.583 |
| 763 | Ikaev G.D. | Rus | E | Cad | ? | ? | -20.000 | ? | -3.462 |
| 764 | Ikramov A.S. | Uzb | E | Nom | ? | ? | -18.235 | ? | -1.923 |
| 765 | Ikramova M. | Uzb | E | Wor | ? | ? | -19.545 | ? | 3.846 |
| 766 | Ilakov A.V. | Rus | E | Cad | ? | ? | 3.636 | ? | -3.077 |
| 767 | Ilamanov D. | Tur | E | Wor | ? | ? | -6.667 | ? | 1.346 |
| 768 | Ilizarov G.A. | Rus | A | Tec | ? | ? | -7.647 | ? | -9.231 |
| 769 | Il'in A.N. | Rus | E | Nom | ? | ? | -10.870 | ? | -6.400 |
| 770 | Il'in V.M. | Rus | E | Man | ? | ? | 20.870 | ? | 21.154 |
| 771 | Inkens Ye.Ye. | Lat | E | Int | LI | LI | 20.833 | LI | 21.000 |
| 772 | Inochkin A.M. | Rus | A | Wor | ? | ? | -18.261 | ? | 0.385 |
| 773 | Iovlev D.M. | Mos | A | Wor | ? | ? | -3.478 | ? | 9.231 |
| 774 | Irgashev A.K. | Uzb | E | Man | ? | App | -14.348 | Cen | -6.538 |
| 775 | Isaev G.I. | Aze | E | Nom | Pre | ? | 0.000 | ? | -7.200 |
| 776 | Isaev Iu.A. | Rus | E | Man | ? | ? | -6.522 | ? | 7.308 |
| 777 | Isaeva A.I. | Ukr | A | Wor | ? | ? | -6.842 | ? | 0.385 |
| 778 | Isakadze L.A. | Mos | A | Int | ? | ? | 40.833 | ? | 0.000 |
| 779 | Isakov B.S. | Kir | E | Tec | ? | ? | -18.261 | ? | -10.000 |
| 780 | Isakov I.I. | Kir | E | Wor | ? | ? | 1.176 | ? | 2.885 |
| 781 | Iskakov K.D. | Kir | E | Wor | ? | ? | -7.273 | ? | -0.385 |
| 782 | Kskakova B.S. | Kaz | E | Tec | ? | ? | -15.652 | ? | -4.615 |
| 783 | Iskaliev N. | Kaz | E | Nom | ? | ? | -20.652 | ? | -9.167 |
| 784 | Iskandarov I.N. | Uzb | E | Man | ? | ? | -15.263 | ? | -7.200 |
| 785 | Iskander F.A. | Geo | E | Int | ? | ? | 0.000 | ? | 15.000 |
| 786 | Ismailov T.K. | Aze | E | Man | ? | RI | -3.500 | Cen | -7.200 |
| 787 | Iskhaki Iu.B. | Tad | E | Tec | ? | Med | -10.435 | ? | -3.077 |
| 788 | Ishanov Kh. | Tur | E | Tec | ? | ? | -5.455 | ? | 0.962 |
| 789 | Ishin A.Ia. | Rus | A | Cad | ? | ? | -6.522 | ? | -4.800 |
| 790 | Iorga L.A. | Mol | E | Tec | ? | LI | 20.682 | ? | 0.000 |
| 791 | Iotsas A.P. | Lit | A | Man | ? | ? | 23.000 | ? | 0.000 |
| 792 | Kabakov V.S. | Rus | E | Int | ? | ? | 12.632 | ? | 10.769 |
| 793 | Kabanov E.N. | Rus | A | Tec | ? | ? | -10.000 | ? | 0.000 |
| 794 | Kabasin G.S. | Rus | E | Nom | ? | ? | -14.348 | ? | -20.385 |
| 795 | Kavun V.M. | Ukr | E | Nom | ? | ? | -1.667 | ? | 0.192 |
| 796 | Kadannikov V.V. | Rus | E | Man | ? | Cen | -2.273 | ? | 17.692 |
| 797 | Kadyrov G.Kh. | Uzb | E | Nom | ? | ? | -18.261 | ? | -10.000 |
| 798 | Kazakov V.I. | Rus | E | Nom | ? | ? | -18.261 | ? | -10.000 |
| 799 | Kazakova T.D. | Uzb | E | Tec | Pre | ? | -22.500 | ? | -11.200 |
| 800 | Kazamarov A.A. | Mos | E | Man | ? | ? | 11.875 | ? | 26.087 |
| 801 | Kazannik A.I. | Rus | E | Int | Rad | Rad | 40.652 | Rad | 7.917 |
| 802 | Kazarezov V.V. | Rus | E | Nom | Med | ? | -2.609 | ? | 0.385 |
| 803 | Kazarin A.A. | Rus | A | Wor | ? | ? | 0.000 | ? | 14.231 |
| 804 | Kazachenko P.P. | Rus | E | Man | ? | ? | -2.609 | ? | 12.200 |
| 805 | Kaznin Iu.F. | Rus | E | Int | ? | ? | 18.864 | Rad | 21.600 |
| 806 | Kaz'min G.P. | Rus | E | Nom | ? | ? | -7.609 | ? | -1.200 |
| 807 | Kaipbergenov T. | Uzb | E | Int | LI | LI | -20.435 | LI | -8.000 |
| 808 | Kaira N.I. | Ukr | E | Man | ? | ? | 1.304 | ? | 0.962 |
| 809 | Kakadzhikov Ch. | Tur | E | Wor | ? | ? | -6.522 | ? | 3.846 |
| 810 | Kakaras G.I.A. | Lit | E | Int | LI | ? | 33.333 | ? | 0.000 |
| 811 | Kalandarov A.O. | Uzb | A | Man | ? | ? | -14.762 | ? | -9.038 |
| 812 | Kalandarov B. | Uzb | E | Wor | ? | ? | -10.455 | ? | -10.000 |
| 813 | Kalachev L.M. | Rus | A | Tec | ? | ? | 9.130 | ? | 12.000 |
| 814 | Kalachik V.M. | Bel | E | Man | ? | ? | -13.478 | ? | 0.385 |
| 815 | Kalashnikov V.I. | Rus | E | Nom | ? | ? | -13.810 | ? | 0.000 |
| 816 | Kalashnikov V.Ia. | Rus | E | Man | ? | ? | -6.364 | ? | -6.538 |
| 817 | Kalashnikov S.F. | Bel | A | Cad | LI | ? | -8.000 | ? | 6.154 |
| 818 | Kalamullina R.M. | Rus | E | Wor | ? | ? | -10.000 | ? | 0.000 |
| 819 | Kalin I.P. | Mol | E | Nom | ? | ? | -14.348 | ? | -3.077 |
| 820 | Kalinin N.V. | Mos | A | Mil | ? | ? | -8.000 | ? | -1.600 |
| 821 | Kalinichenko A.I. | Ukr | E | Wor | ? | ? | -2.609 | ? | 1.538 |
| 822 | Kalinchenko V.M. | Rus | E | Tec | ? | ? | 15.000 | ? | 10.769 |
| 823 | Kalish V.N. | Ukr | A | Wor | App | ? | -2.609 | ? | -6.400 |
| 824 | Kallas S.U. | Est | E | Int | ? | ? | 13.333 | ? | 0.000 |
| 825 | Kalmykov A.N. | Rus | A | Wor | ? | ? | -7.826 | ? | -10.000 |
| 826 | Kalmykov Iu.Kh. | Rus | E | Tec | ? | Med | -14.348 | Med | -3.077 |
| 827 | Kalnyn'sh A.A. | Lat | E | Tec | ? | LI | 8.667 | ? | 28.571 |
| 828 | Kaliagin S.B. | Rus | E | Man | LI | Rad | 28.913 | Rad | 16.154 |
| 829 | Kamenshchikova G.N. | Rus | E | Tec | ? | ? | 4.348 | ? | 7.308 |
| 830 | Kanarovskaia A.M. | Mol | E | Man | ? | ? | -10.435 | Cen | 0.385 |
| 831 | Kangliev A.Ia. | Rus | E | Wor | ? | ? | -6.522 | ? | 2.400 |
| 832 | Kandaurov S.N. | Rus | E | Wor | ? | ? | 5.217 | ? | 5.962 |
| 833 | Kanibalotskii V.I. | Rus | E | Man | ? | ? | -6.522 | ? | -10.000 |
| 834 | Kanin V.I. | Rus | A | Wor | ? | ? | -14.348 | ? | -16.923 |
| 835 | Kanoatov M. | Tad | E | Int | ? | ? | -5.867 | ? | 3.846 |
| 836 | Kanovich Ia.S. | Lit | E | Int | LI | ? | 30.000 | ? | 0.000 |
| 837 | Kanchaveli Sh.Sh. | Geo | E | Wor | ? | ? | 19.545 | ? | -8.043 |
| 838 | Kanchukoeva R.Kh. | Rus | E | Tec | ? | ? | 1.304 | ? | 1.154 |
| 839 | Kapitsa M.S. | Mos | A | Int | ? | ? | -20.952 | ? | -10.000 |
| 840 | Kapto A.S. | Mos | A | Nom | ? | App | -18.261 | ? | -9.038 |
| 841 | Kapustin A.V. | Rus | A | Cad | ? | ? | -12.826 | ? | -1.154 |
| 842 | Kara-sal D.B. | Rus | E | Man | ? | ? | -1.429 | ? | -10.000 |

| | | | | | | | | | |
|---|---|---|---|---|---|---|---|---|---|
| 843 | Karaganov S.V. | Rus | A | Tec | App | ? | 1.304 | ? | 10.400 |
| 844 | Karasev V.I. | Ukr | E | Tec | LI | Rad | 31.087 | ? | 0.769 |
| 845 | Karaulov A.O. | Rus | E | Tec | ? | ? | 4.130 | ? | 13.846 |
| 846 | Karepin V.E. | Rus | E | Wor | ? | ? | 5.217 | ? | 12.083 |
| 847 | Karieva B.R. | Uzb | A | Int | ? | LI | -12.105 | ? | 1.875 |
| 848 | Karimberdieva N.S. | Uzb | A | Wor | ? | ? | -18.261 | ? | -4.423 |
| 849 | Karimov D.Kh. | Tad | E | Nom | ? | Cen | -5.000 | ? | -6.538 |
| 850 | Karimov I.A. | Uzb | E | Nom | ? | ? | -12.609 | ? | -6.538 |
| 851 | Karimov Kh.Kh. | Tad | A | Int | ? | ? | -18.182 | ? | -4.800 |
| 852 | Karlov N.V. | Mos | A | Int | ? | Med | -15.000 | ? | 1.346 |
| 853 | Karmanovskii V.E. | Rus | E | Man | App | ? | 23.913 | ? | 48.333 |
| 854 | Karpenko V.F. | Rus | E | Wor | ? | ? | 1.304 | ? | 21.154 |
| 855 | Karpenko M.I. | Bel | A | Int | ? | ? | -15.909 | ? | 0.000 |
| 856 | Karpenko N.I. | Bel | E | Tec | ? | ? | -14.348 | ? | -6.538 |
| 857 | Karpenko S.Iu. | Ukr | A | Tec | ? | ? | 1.304 | ? | 10.769 |
| 858 | Karpov A.E. | Mos | A | Int | Med | ? | -17.143 | ? | 0.000 |
| 859 | Karpov V.V. | Mos | A | Int | App | ? | -13.333 | ? | -3.077 |
| 860 | Karpochev V.A. | Rus | E | Man | ? | ? | 0.435 | ? | -7.200 |
| 861 | Kartashov L.L. | Rus | E | Int | ? | ? | 9.130 | ? | 5.769 |
| 862 | Kariagin V.Ia. | Tad | E | Tec | ? | ? | 17.826 | ? | 14.808 |
| 863 | Kariakin Iu.F. | Mos | A | Int | Rad | Rad | 10.000 | ? | 0.000 |
| 864 | Kasymova K.M. | Uzb | E | Wor | ? | ? | -12.826 | ? | -3.846 |
| 865 | Kas'ian V.V. | Rus | E | Tec | ? | ? | -18.261 | ? | 0.192 |
| 866 | Kas'ian N.A. | Ukr | A | Tec | Pre | ? | -19.500 | ? | -2.115 |
| 867 | Kas'ianov A.V. | Ukr | E | Nom | ? | ? | -6.522 | ? | -3.077 |
| 868 | Kas'ianov A.F. | Ukr | A | Man | ? | ? | 2.727 | ? | -4.792 |
| 869 | Kataev A. | Tad | E | Tec | ? | ? | -10.435 | ? | -6.538 |
| 870 | Katilevskii S.M. | Ukr | E | Nom | ? | Med | -2.609 | ? | -3.077 |
| 871 | Katolikov A.A. | Rus | A | Tec | ? | ? | 1.000 | ? | 7.308 |
| 872 | Katorgin B.I. | Rus | E | Tec | ? | ? | 2.727 | ? | 21.154 |
| 873 | Katrinich V.A. | Mol | E | Wor | ? | ? | 1.364 | ? | 12.083 |
| 874 | Kauls A.Ye. | Lat | E | Man | ? | ? | 6.667 | ? | 11.400 |
| 875 | Kafarova Ye.M. | Aze | E | Nom | ? | ? | -5.909 | Cen | -13.462 |
| 876 | Kakhirov K.Z. | Rus | E | Wor | ? | ? | 1.818 | ? | 5.769 |
| 877 | Kakhn Iu.Kh. | Est | A | Int | ? | ? | 25.769 | ? | 0.000 |
| 878 | Kachalovskii E.V. | Ukr | E | Nom | ? | ? | -18.261 | ? | -10.000 |
| 879 | Kashauskas S.F. | Lit | E | Int | ? | ? | 57.857 | ? | 0.000 |
| 880 | Kashnikov N.I. | Rus | E | Tec | Rad | LI | 22.619 | LI | 3.750 |
| 881 | Kashperko V.K. | Bel | E | Wor | ? | App | -10.435 | ? | -6.538 |
| 882 | Kaiumova T.I. | Uzb | E | Tec | Pre | ? | -11.304 | ? | -2.000 |
| 883 | Kvaratskhelia G.Sh. | Geo | A | Int | ? | ? | 27.500 | ? | 0.000 |
| 884 | Kebich V.F. | Bel | E | Nom | ? | ? | -10.476 | ? | 0.000 |
| 885 | Kezbers I.Ia. | Lat | E | Nom | Med | LI | 20.000 | ? | 0.000 |
| 886 | Kemova T.N. | Rus | E | Wor | ? | ? | -22.174 | ? | -10.000 |
| 887 | Kenesbaeva K.K. | Kaz | A | Wor | ? | ? | -18.261 | ? | -3.077 |
| 888 | Kerimbekov T.A. | Kir | E | Wor | ? | ? | -3.500 | ? | -10.000 |
| 889 | Kerimov D.A.A. | Aze | E | Int | Cen | Med | -1.087 | ? | -7.895 |
| 890 | Kiisk K.K. | Est | A | Int | ? | ? | 12.333 | ? | 0.000 |
| 891 | Kiknadze Sh.D. | Geo | A | Cad | ? | ? | -9.091 | ? | -8.000 |
| 892 | Kim E.U. | Rus | E | Int | Med | Med | -6.522 | RI | -3.600 |
| 893 | Kimketov P.D. | Rus | E | Wor | ? | ? | -18.261 | ? | -3.077 |
| 894 | Kirakosian A.B. | Arm | A | Wor | ? | ? | 18.913 | ? | 8.654 |
| 895 | Kirgizbaeva T.B. | Uzb | A | Wor | ? | ? | -18.261 | ? | -10.800 |
| 896 | Kirilenko N.A. | Rus | E | Tec | ? | ? | 5.476 | ? | 29.375 |
| 897 | Kirillov V.I. | Rus | E | Int | LI | Rad | 42.667 | Rad | 12.115 |
| 898 | Kiriiak N.P. | Mol | A | Cad | Pre | ? | -16.111 | ? | 0.000 |
| 899 | Kiselev A.A. | Rus | E | Nom | ? | ? | 17.500 | ? | 9.200 |
| 900 | Kiselev V.N. | Rus | E | Tec | Rad | ? | 7.174 | LI | 17.692 |
| 901 | Kiseleva G.N. | Kir | E | Nom | ? | ? | -14.286 | ? | -8.846 |
| 902 | Kiseleva V.A. | Bel | E | Wor | Cen | ? | -2.609 | ? | 5.962 |
| 903 | Kisin V.I. | Mos | A | Tec | ? | ? | -6.111 | ? | 5.577 |
| 904 | Kislitsyn V.A. | Rus | E | Man | App | ? | 5.217 | ? | 3.846 |
| 905 | Kistanov A.T. | Kaz | A | Tec | ? | ? | -14.348 | ? | -10.000 |
| 906 | Kiiamov N.V. | Rus | E | Man | ? | ? | -14.545 | ? | 8.077 |
| 907 | Klautsen A.P. | Lat | E | Nom | ? | App | -17.273 | ? | -13.462 |
| 908 | Klepikov A.F. | Uzb | E | Nom | ? | ? | -22.174 | ? | -6.538 |
| 909 | Klepikov M.I. | Rus | A | Wor | ? | ? | -22.174 | ? | -3.077 |
| 910 | Klepikov Iu.N. | Rus | A | Int | ? | ? | 26.000 | ? | 14.808 |
| 911 | Kletskov L.G. | Bel | E | Nom | ? | ? | 0.000 | ? | 3.846 |
| 912 | Klibik V.S. | Lat | A | Cad | ? | ? | -1.739 | ? | 3.846 |
| 913 | Klikunene V.S. | Lit | A | Nom | ? | ? | 16.333 | ? | 0.000 |
| 914 | Klimentova L.A. | Rus | A | Cad | ? | ? | -14.348 | ? | 10.800 |
| 915 | Klimov M.V. | Rus | E | Tec | ? | ? | 6.087 | ? | 0.385 |
| 916 | Klimova G.N. | Rus | E | Wor | ? | ? | -6.522 | ? | 3.846 |
| 917 | Klimuk P.I. | Rus | A | Mil | ? | ? | -7.647 | ? | 5.417 |
| 918 | Klishchuk P.M. | Kaz | E | Wor | ? | ? | -12.941 | ? | -6.538 |
| 919 | Klokov V.I. | Ukr | A | Int | RI | ? | -18.261 | ? | 8.077 |
| 920 | Klochkov I.F. | Rus | A | Cad | ? | App | -19.545 | ? | 0.385 |
| 921 | Klumbis Ye.L. | Lit | E | Tec | ? | ? | 43.000 | ? | 0.000 |
| 922 | Klushin O.G. | Est | E | Man | ? | ? | -2.609 | ? | 7.308 |
| 923 | Kliukin V.V. | Rus | E | Tec | ? | ? | 20.870 | ? | 17.692 |
| 924 | Kniazev N.T. | Kaz | E | Nom | App | App | -27.333 | ? | -10.800 |
| 925 | Kniazev Iu.I. | Rus | A | Cad | ? | ? | -22.500 | ? | -7.400 |
| 926 | Kobaliia L.N. | Geo | E | Wor | ? | ? | 7.778 | ? | 3.462 |

```
 927 Koberidze V.G.       Geo A Cad ?   ?    -6.522 ?    -6.538
 928 Kobzon I.D.          Mos A Oth Med Med  -5.526 ?    -7.200
 929 Kovalev V.G.         Rus E Wor ?   ?    -6.522 ?     7.308
 930 Kovalev V.N.         Rus E Tec ?   LI  -14.348 ?    -5.577
 931 Kovalev M.V.         Bel E Nom ?   Cen -15.455 ?    -6.538
 932 Kovalevskii E.M.     Bel A Int ?   ?     5.217 ?     8.000
 933 Kogan E.V.           Est E Tec RI  RI   14.737 RI   -4.706
 934 Kodyrov B.K.         Tad E Wor ?   ?   -20.870 ?     7.885
 935 Kozhauov Zh.         Kaz A Wor ?   ?   -14.348 ?    -6.538
 936 Kozhakhmetov I.      Kaz A Man ?   ?   -21.333 ?    -6.538
 937 Kozhedub I.N.        Mos A Mil ?   ?     0.000 App  -6.538
 938 Kozachko A.V.        Rus E Cad ?   ?    -6.667 ?   -16.923
 939 Kozik A.M.           Bel A Tec ?   ?   -12.727 ?    -3.077
 940 Kozin Ye.G.          Ukr E Tec ?   LI   42.273 ?    13.043
 941 Kozlov A.A.          Rus E Tec ?   ?    21.000 ?    18.000
 942 Kozlov V.V.          Rus E Man ?   ?    -2.609 ?     7.308
 943 Kozyrev N.K.         Ukr E Tec ?   Cen  13.500 Med  11.600
 944 Kokarev M.A.         Rus E Wor ?   ?    13.913 ?    10.769
 945 Kolbeshkin A.E.      Rus A Wor ?   ?   -14.348 ?   -16.923
 946 Kolbin G.V.          Kaz E Nom Cen ?   -50.000 Cen -13.462
 947 Kolesnik A.I.        Rus E Wor ?   ?    -7.391 ?     1.346
 948 Kolesnik N.D.        Rus E Man ?   ?   -10.455 ?     5.600
 949 Kolesnikov V.I.      Rus E Tec LI  Med   7.619 ?    18.958
 950 Kolesnikov S.I.      Rus E Int LI  ?     8.913 ?     1.731
 951 Kolinichenko A.N.    Rus E Mil ?   ?   -10.435 ?   -21.600
 952 Kolodesnikov A.S.    Rus A Mil ?   LI   -2.778 ?     0.000
 953 Kolomiets Iu.A.      Ukr E Nom ?   ?   -10.435 ?     0.385
 954 Kolotov V.I.         Rus E Int LI  ?    24.545 LI   28.077
 955 Kolnakova N.Z.       Arm E Wor ?   ?    -9.773 ?     1.154
 956 Kol'tsov Iu.A.       Ukr E Mil Cen ?    28.696 ?    14.231
 957 Kol'chukova N.M.     Rus A Man ?   ?   -17.727 ?     0.385
 958 Komarov G.A.         Kir E Tec ?   ?     1.304 ?     0.385
 959 Komarov Iu.T.        Rus E Man ?   ?     1.304 App -11.667
 960 Kondratenko N.I.     Rus E Nom ?   RI  -11.500 ?     2.500
 961 Kondrat'ev A.I.      Rus E Nom ?   ?   -10.455 ?   -10.000
 962 Konev S.I.           Ukr E Tec LI  ?    40.625 ?    11.739
 963 Konovalov A.I.       Rus E Int LI  ?    19.474 ?    18.462
 964 Konovalov V.P.       Rus E Wor ?   ?     1.304 ?    -3.077
 965 Kononenko L.A.       Ukr A Wor ?   ?     5.217 ?    14.231
 966 Konoplev G.P.        Lit E Cad ?   ?    35.714 ?     0.000
 967 Kontselidze M.R.     Geo E Wor ?   ?    14.474 ?    -2.500
 968 Kon'kov P.I.         Rus A Oth ?   ?    -8.000 ?    -6.538
 969 Kopylova A.V.        Rus E Tec ?   ?   -18.261 ?   -23.846
 970 Kopysov N.M.         Rus E Wor ?   ?    11.250 ?    12.692
 971 Korbutov I.I.        Bel E Mil ?   ?   -14.348 ?    -8.000
 972 Kordiiak E.K.        Tur E Wor ?   ?    20.870 ?     1.154
 973 Korenev A.A.         Rus A Wor ?   ?     2.273 ?    -6.731
 974 Korneva S.I.         Ukr A Man ?   ?     5.217 ?    11.458
 975 Korneenko V.N.       Bel E Tec LI  Rad  25.000 ?    21.200
 976 Kornienko A.I.       Ukr E Nom ?   ?   -16.522 ?    -3.077
 977 Korobkin V.V.        Rus E Tec ?   ?    32.609 ?    17.692
 978 Korobtsev V.P.       Rus A Oth ?   ?   -11.739 ?    -6.538
 979 Koroviatskii V.V.    Rus A Wor ?   ?   -18.261 ?   -10.000
 980 Koromyslov G.F.      Mos A Tec ?   ?    -5.455 ?     0.000
 981 Korostelev A.F.      Rus E Tec ?   ?   -10.435 ?   -10.000
 982 Korotich V.A.        Ukr E Int ?   ?    24.091 ?    11.200
 983 Korotkin V.I.        Bel E Wor ?   ?     1.818 ?    10.000
 984 Korshunov A.A.       Uzb A Wor Med Cen -10.870 LI    7.308
 985 Korshunov A.I.       Ukr E Wor ?   ?     5.217 ?     3.846
 986 Koriugin N.N.        Rus E Tec LI  LI   18.636 ?    17.692
 987 Kosarchuk V.P.       Mol E Tec ?   ?     0.909 ?     7.308
 988 Kostenetskaia M.G.   Lat E Int ?   ?    35.833 ?    18.200
 989 Kostenko A.I.        Bel E Mil ?   ?   -18.261 ?    -3.077
 990 Kostenko V.I.        Rus E Tec ?   ?     1.304 ?     4.615
 991 Kosteniuk A.G.       Rus E Nom Med ?   -18.261 ?    -3.077
 992 Kostishin N.A.       Mol E Wor ?   ?     0.000 ?     3.846
 993 Kosygin V.V.         Rus E Int ?   ?    18.636 ?     5.385
 994 Kotik V.D.           Rus E Wor ?   ?     9.130 ?    10.769
 995 Kotlovtsev N.N.      Mos A Mil ?   ?   -15.909 ?    -6.538
 996 Kotliakov V.M.       Mos A Int LI  ?    25.652 ?    23.462
 997 Kotov Iu.S.          Rus E Int ?   ?    25.870 ?    22.500
 998 Kochetov K.A.        Rus E Mil ?   ?     1.304 ?    -2.083
 999 Kochmuradov G.Ia.    Tur E Wor ?   ?    -5.000 ?    -5.769
1000 Koshlakov G.V.       Tad E Nom App Cen -14.348 ?    -3.077
1001 Kravets V.A.         Ukr E Nom ?   ?    -6.818 ?   -10.217
1002 Kravtsov N.I.        Kaz E Man ?   ?    13.043 ?     5.833
1003 Kravchenko G.I.      Rus E Wor Pre ?    -1.364 ?    -0.455
1004 Kravchenko K.F.      Rus A Oth ?   ?   -18.261 ?     0.385
1005 Kravchenko L.P.      Mos A Nom App ?   -12.857 ?    -6.538
1006 Kravchenko N.V.      Rus A Cad ?   ?    -7.273 ?   -20.385
1007 Kraiko A.N.          Mos E Tec Rad LI   -8.000 LI    4.808
1008 Krasil'nikov Iu.G.   Rus E Man ?   ?    38.750 ?    24.615
1009 Krasnova L.M.        Rus A Tec ?   ?    -4.444 ?     0.000
1010 Krasnokutskii B.I.   Rus E Man ?   ?     5.217 ?    10.769
1011 Kraft Iu.A.          Est E Man ?   ?    17.308 ?    17.000
```

```
1012 Kreshtak V.I.        Kaz E Wor ?     ?  -4.762 ?    -2.308
1013 Krivenko V.M.        Ukr A Cad ?     ? -14.348 ?    -2.115
1014 Krivov G.I.          Rus E Man ?     ? -10.435 ?     0.385
1015 Krivorotov V.I.      Ukr A Man ?     ?  -5.238 ?     0.385
1016 Krivoruchko E.V.     Kaz A Wor ?     ?   1.818 ?     0.385
1017 Krikunova O.I.       Uzb E Tec ?     ?  -7.174 ?     1.538
1018 Krishevich V.P.      Ukr E Wor ?     ?  -0.952 ?    -7.200
1019 Krotkov I.M.         Rus E Wor ?     ?   3.913 ?     2.308
1020 Kruglov A.T.         Rus E Tec LI  App  37.500 Med  20.526
1021 Krumin' V.M.         Lat A Cad ?     ? -16.818 ?    -3.077
1022 Krutov A.N.          Rus E Int ?   Rad  18.636 ?    17.692
1023 Kruchina N.E.        Rus E Nom ?     ? -18.261 ?    -3.077
1024 Kryzhanovskii D.P.   Kaz E Wor ?     ?   1.304 ?     3.846
1025 Kryzhkov B.V.        Rus E Tec Rad Cen  25.714 RI    3.600
1026 Krylova Z.P.         Mos A Int ?   Med -22.857 ?     4.808
1027 Kryshkin A.M.        Kaz E Wor ?     ?  18.000 ?     7.200
1028 Kriuchenkova N.A.    Rus E Tec ?   Pre -13.182 ?   -10.800
1029 Kriuchkov V.I.       Rus E Man ?     ?   9.091 ?     3.846
1030 Kriuchkov G.K.       Ukr E Nom ?   Med -18.261 ?   -11.800
1031 Kubdasheva K.        Kaz E Tec ?     ? -10.435 ?     0.000
1032 Kubilius I.P.        Lit E Int ?     ?  55.000 ?     0.000
1033 Kublashvili V.V.     Geo E Wor ?     ?  25.500 ?    -3.158
1034 Kugul'tinov D.N.     Rus E Int Med Med -14.348 Med -10.417
1035 Kudarauskas S.I.     Lit E Tec ?     ?  25.000 ?     0.000
1036 Kudrin L.S.          Rus E Wor ?     ?  43.333 ?    30.800
1037 Kudriavtsev A.P.     Mos A Int ?   Med   5.500 ?    10.800
1038 Kudriavtsev V.N.     Mos A Int Med ?    0.000 Med  -1.200
1039 Kuznetsov V.P.       Kaz A Wor ?     ?   1.579 ?     3.846
1040 Kuznetsov L.A.       Rus A Int ?   Med   0.909 Med  10.962
1041 Kuzovlev A.T.        Rus A Man ?     ? -20.000 ?    -3.077
1042 Kuzubov V.F.         Rus E Tec ?     ?  28.696 ?    -6.538
1043 Kuz'min A.N.         Mos E Int ?     ?  28.696 ?    17.200
1044 Kuz'min P.I.         Bel E Man ?     ?  -6.522 ?    -5.200
1045 Kuz'min F.M.         Lat E Mil ?     ? -18.182 ?   -10.000
1046 Kukain R.A.          Lat E Int ?     ?  19.474 ?     0.000
1047 Kukushkin N.T.       Rus E Man ?     ?  -8.636 ?    -0.800
1048 Kulagin V.K.         Rus E Man ?     ?   4.348 ?    20.208
1049 Kulakova R.G.        Rus A Cad ?     ?  -8.095 ?    -4.583
1050 Kuldyshev M.S.       Kir E Wor ?     ? -11.304 ?    -5.577
1051 Kuleshov A.A.        Rus E Nom ?   Cen   5.217 ?     0.385
1052 Kulibaev A.A.        Kaz E Nom ?     ? -14.348 ?    -5.385
1053 Kuliev A.G.          Aze A Tec App ? -14.167 ?    -6.538
1054 Kuliev S.O.          Rus E Man ?     ?   3.182 ?    10.000
3001 Kulik G.V.           Rus E ?     .     .       .  ?  -15.652
1055 Kulikov V.G.         Mos A Mil ?     ? -15.333 Cen -10.000
1056 Kulikov E.A.         Rus E Man ?     ?  -1.905 ?   -10.000
1057 Kulikov F.M.         Rus E Nom ?     ?  -9.091 ?   -13.462
1058 Kulikov Ia.P.        Ukr A Tec ?   Pre -18.261 ?     0.385
1059 Kul'matov R.S.       Kir E Nom ?     ?  -7.895 ?   -10.000
1060 Kupin A.D.           Rus E Wor ?     ? -18.261 ?    -3.000
1061 Kupliauskene Iu.I.   Lit E Cad ?     ?  50.000 ?     0.000
1062 Kuptsov V.A.         Rus E Nom ?     ?  -6.522 ?   -10.000
1063 Kurashvili Z.G.      Geo E Wor ?     ?  31.818 ?   -36.667
1064 Kurbanov S.U.        Tad A Int ?     ?  -9.000 ?     9.167
1065 Kurbanov Kh.         Uzb E Wor ?     ? -26.364 ?    -6.538
1066 Kurbanova A.         Tur A Wor ?     ?  -8.913 ?   -10.769
1067 Kurdiumov G.L.       Lat E Man ?     ?   7.500 Med  11.400
1068 Kurilenko V.T.       Ukr E Wor ?     ? -14.348 ?   -16.923
1069 Kurochka G.M.        Rus E Cad LI    ?  13.043 ?    -3.077
1070 Kurtashin V.E.       Rus A Man ?     ?  -6.522 ?     9.200
3002 Kustarev N.P.        Rus A Wor  .     .       .  ?   -9.038
1071 Kutashov N.A.        Est E Tec ?     ?   3.913 ?     2.000
1072 Kutepov E.A.         Rus E Man ?     ?  13.043 ?    14.231
1073 Kutuzov P.P.         Rus E Man ?     ?  -6.522 ?     0.385
1074 Kukhar' I.I.         Rus A Man Cen Cen -15.333 ?   -10.000
1075 Kutsenko N.A.        Ukr E Tec Med Rad  45.714 Rad   6.364
1076 Kucharova M.         Uzb E Wor ?     ?  -9.333 ?    -9.091
1077 Kucheiko A.P.        Bel E Wor ?     ? -14.348 ?     4.808
1078 Kucher V.N.          Rus A Int ?    RI  16.087 ?     9.800
1079 Kucherenko V.G.      Ukr E Nom ?     ?  -4.762 ?    -6.538
1080 Kucherskii N.I.      Uzb E Man ?     ?  -2.273 ?    -5.200
1081 Kuchinskas L.-A.A.   Lit A Int ?     ?   0.000 ?     0.000
1082 Kushnerenko M.M.     Ukr E Nom ?   App  -6.522 ?    -1.538
1083 Kushchenko E.P.      Ukr E Wor ?     ? -11.429 ?    -7.083
1084 Kiabin T.R.          Est E Int ?     ?  50.625 ?     0.000
1085 Kiazimova Z.G.       Aze E Wor ?     ?  -1.250 ?   -10.000
1086 Laak T.Kh.           Est E Nom ?     ?  35.000 ?    40.000
1087 Labunov V.A.         Bel E Int ?     ? -10.000 ?     3.846
3007 Laverov N.P.         Kir E Int ?     .       .  .     .
1088 Lavrenishina V.A.    Rus E Tec ?     ?   9.130 ?    17.083
1089 Lavrent'ev A.P.      Rus E Man ?     ?  -3.478 ?    11.346
1090 Lavrov K.Iu.         Rus A Int ?    LI   9.130 ?     6.731
1091 Lavrov S.B.          Rus A Int ?     ?  13.043 ?     3.846
1092 Lazarev V.N.         Rus E Wor ?     ?   3.333 ?     5.000
1093 Lazarenko V.N.       Rus E Tec ?   App  -8.636 ?    -3.077
```

| | | | | | | | |
|---|---|---|---|---|---|---|---|
| 1094 | Lakman T.Ia. | Kir E Man ? | ? | -5.455 | ? | 2.917 |
| 1095 | Landsbergis V.V. | Lit E Int Rad LI | 52.500 | ? | 0.000 |
| 1096 | Lapkin V.A. | Rus E Man ? | ? | 1.053 | ? | 9.200 |
| 1097 | Laptev I.D. | Mos A Int ? | ? | -3.333 | ? | -3.077 |
| 1098 | Lapshov B.M. | Rus E Man ? | ? | 26.364 | ? | 28.261 |
| 1099 | Lapygin V.L. | Rus E Man ? | ? | -11.429 | ? | -16.923 |
| 1100 | Larionov V.P. | Rus A Int Med Med | 0.909 | ? | 8.400 |
| 1101 | Lasuta E.P. | Bel E Tec ? | ? | 8.261 | ? | 8.077 |
| 1102 | Laurinkus M.M. | Lit E Int ? | ? | 47.500 | ? | 0.000 |
| 1103 | Lauristin M.I. | Est E Int Rad LI | 36.875 | ? | 0.000 |
| 1104 | Laurushas V.A. | Lit A Int ? | ? | 34.333 | ? | 0.000 |
| 1105 | Lautsis U.V. | Lat A Cad ? | ? | 32.500 | ? | 24.615 |
| 1106 | Lashchenov S.Ia. | Tad E Man ? | ? | 0.000 | ? | 3.846 |
| 1107 | Lashchin P.K. | Rus E Wor ? | ? | -18.261 | ? | 3.462 |
| 1108 | Laius A.-Iu.P. | Lit A Cad ? | ? | 34.000 | ? | 0.000 |
| 1109 | Lebedev A.T. | Rus A Oth ? | ? | -13.810 | ? | -4.737 |
| 1110 | Levakin V.A. | Rus E Man ? | ? | 1.304 | ? | -13.462 |
| 1111 | Levashev A.V. | Rus E Tec Rad LI | 20.667 | ? | 15.769 |
| 1112 | Levitskas V.Iu. | Lit A Man ? | ? | 30.000 | ? | 0.000 |
| 1113 | Levykin Iu.A. | Rus E Int LI | ? | 20.250 Rad | 21.600 |
| 1114 | Lezhenko G.F. | Ukr E Wor ? | ? | -19.545 | ? | -3.077 |
| 1115 | Lezhnev M.A. | Rus E Man LI | ? | 36.364 | ? | 17.692 |
| 1116 | Leksin N.S. | Rus A Oth ? | ? | -14.348 | ? | 3.846 |
| 1117 | Lemesheva N.V. | Bel A Man ? | Cen | -11.304 | ? | -0.769 |
| 1118 | Leonchev V.A. | Rus E Wor LI | ? | -2.174 | ? | 17.115 |
| 1119 | Leskin D.T. | Bel E Tec ? | ? | 0.435 | ? | 10.800 |
| 1120 | Lesnichenko V.E. | Rus E Nom ? | ? | -22.174 | ? | -10.000 |
| 1121 | Lesiuk Ia.S. | Ukr A Cad ? | ? | -2.381 | ? | 6.154 |
| 1122 | Ligachev E.K. | Mos A Nom ? | App | -17.000 | ? | -10.000 |
| 1123 | Lizichev A.D. | Mos A Mil Cen ? | -17.500 | ? | -10.000 |
| 1124 | Lippmaa Ye.T. | Est E Int Med LI | 48.667 | ? | 20.000 |
| 1125 | Lisitskii V.I. | Ukr E Man ? | ? | 5.217 Cen | 11.346 |
| 1126 | Lisichkin G.S. | Mos A Int ? | ? | -1.364 | ? | 0.200 |
| 1127 | Lisichii D.V. | Ukr E Wor ? | ? | 5.217 | ? | 10.800 |
| 1128 | Lisov N.I. | Rus A Man ? | ? | -14.348 | ? | -13.462 |
| 1129 | Litvinov V.V. | Rus E Man ? | ? | 9.130 | ? | 10.769 |
| 1130 | Litvinov I.A. | Rus A Oth ? | ? | -9.091 | ? | -3.077 |
| 1131 | Litvintsev Iu.I. | Rus E Nom ? | ? | -10.435 | ? | -13.462 |
| 1132 | Litvintseva G.N. | Rus E Wor ? | ? | 1.304 | ? | -6.538 |
| 1133 | Likhanov A.A. | Mos A Int Cen ? | -17.857 | ? | -4.615 |
| 1134 | Likhachev D.S. | Rus A Int LI LI | -12.000 Med | 9.200 |
| 1135 | Litskevich M.N. | Rus A Wor ? | ? | -6.522 | ? | 7.083 |
| 1136 | Lobov V.N. | Kaz E Mil ? | ? | -18.261 | ? | -0.400 |
| 1137 | Lobov O.I. | Arm E Nom ? | Med | -0.952 | ? | -4.231 |
| 1138 | Logeiko A.V. | Rus E Tec ? | ? | 25.455 | ? | 21.600 |
| 1139 | Logunov V.A. | Mos E Int Rad Rad | 25.000 Rad | 23.600 |
| 1140 | Lokotupin V.I. | Kaz E Nom ? | ? | -13.750 | ? | 3.846 |
| 1141 | Lopatin V.N. | Rus E Mil ? | ? | 18.182 LI | 14.231 |
| 1142 | Lochmelis A.A. | Lat E Man ? | ? | 35.000 | ? | 24.706 |
| 1143 | Lubenchenko K.D. | Rus E Int Med Med | 1.667 LI | 13.200 |
| 1144 | Lukin V.P. | Rus E Wor Cen ? | -0.455 | ? | 7.308 |
| 1145 | Lukkoev Iu.P. | Rus A Wor ? | ? | -2.609 | ? | -6.538 |
| 1146 | Luk'ianenko O.F. | Ukr E Tec ? | ? | 0.000 | ? | 0.000 |
| 1147 | Luk'ianov A.I. | Mos A Nom Cen Cen | -18.636 Cen | -18.000 |
| 1148 | Luk'ianov A.S. | Rus E Tec ? | ? | 1.304 | ? | 14.400 |
| 1149 | Lunev V.A. | Mos A Wor ? | ? | -4.783 | ? | 6.667 |
| 1150 | Lun'kov D.A. | Rus A Int ? | ? | 15.263 | ? | 17.692 |
| 1151 | Lutsans Ia.P. | Lat E Man ? | LI | 27.778 | ? | 30.000 |
| 1152 | Lutsik I.A. | Rus A Man ? | ? | -18.421 | ? | -15.600 |
| 1153 | Luchenok I.M. | Bel A Int ? | ? | -12.000 | ? | 7.000 |
| 1154 | Luchinskii P.K. | Tad E Nom ? | ? | -13.056 | ? | 0.385 |
| 1155 | Lushev P.G. | Mos A Mil ? | ? | -14.762 | ? | 0.385 |
| 1156 | Lushnikov V.P. | Rus E Wor ? | ? | 21.000 | ? | 14.231 |
| 1157 | Lushchikov S.G. | Rus E Cad ? | ? | 13.043 | ? | -3.077 |
| 1158 | Lyzo I.S. | Est A Cad ? | ? | -4.118 | ? | -6.538 |
| 1159 | Magomadov L.D. | Rus E Cad ? | Cen | -4.762 | ? | 0.385 |
| 1160 | Magomedov G.M. | Rus E Cad ? | Cen | 5.500 | ? | -3.077 |
| 1161 | Magomedov S.A. | Rus A Wor ? | ? | -13.333 | ? | 6.800 |
| 1162 | Made T.R. | Est E Tec ? | ? | 50.714 | ? | 40.000 |
| 1163 | Madiiarova K. | Uzb A Man ? | ? | -10.435 | ? | -9.231 |
| 1164 | Mazurov K.T. | Mos A Nom Cen ? | 0.000 | . | . |
| 1165 | Maiboroda V.A. | Rus E Wor ? | ? | 19.130 | ? | 14.231 |
| 1166 | Makashov A.M. | Rus E Mil ? | App | -6.522 RI | -3.077 |
| 1167 | Maksimov V.N. | Rus E Wor ? | ? | 20.870 | ? | -3.600 |
| 1168 | Maksimov Iu.P. | Rus E Mil ? | ? | -10.435 | ? | -13.462 |
| 1169 | Malikova L.A. | Rus A Man ? | ? | -9.500 | ? | 1.154 |
| 1170 | Malmygin A.A. | Rus E Tec ? | ? | 13.043 | ? | 17.692 |
| 1171 | Malofeev A.A. | Bel E Nom ? | ? | -16.739 | ? | -4.615 |
| 1172 | Malykova E.K. | Mos A Wor ? | LI | 5.682 | ? | 0.000 |
| 1173 | Malykovskaia V.M. | Rus E Wor ? | ? | -6.522 | ? | 3.846 |
| 1174 | Malytsev E.D. | Rus A Int ? | LI | 24.783 | ? | 21.154 |
| 1175 | Malytsev I.I. | Mos A Wor ? | ? | -16.667 | ? | -12.308 |
| 1176 | Maliuta O.L. | Ukr E Tec ? | ? | -11.053 | ? | -0.800 |
| 1177 | Mamarasulov S. | Uzb E Nom ? | ? | -15.000 | ? | 0.000 |
| 1178 | Mambetov A.M. | Uzb A Int Cen ? | -2.609 | ? | 22.727 |
| 1179 | Mamedov A.M. | Aze A Man ? | ? | -19.545 | ? | 3.846 |

```
1180 Mamedov V.G.           Aze E Cad App ?   -18.261 ?   -16.923
1181 Mamedov M.R.           Aze E Nom App ?   -37.778 ?   -13.462
1182 Mamedov R.D.           Aze E Wor ?     ?   -6.522 ?    -9.200
1183 Mamedov S.F.           Aze E Nom ?   App -18.261 ?    -6.538
1184 Mamedov F.A.           Aze E Tec ?     ?   -2.273 ?     0.000
1185 Mamedov Ye.P.          Aze A Wor ?     ?   18.500 ?     7.308
1186 Mamonov A.G.           Ukr A Wor ?     ?  -13.043 ?     3.846
1187 Manaenkov Iu.A.        Rus E Nom App Cen -17.000 ?   -13.462
1188 Manonov Kh.            Tad E Man ?     ?   -6.190 ?     0.385
1189 Mansurov R.Kh.         Rus E Wor ?     ?   16.957 ?    16.400
1190 Manyko N.M.            Tad E Wor ?   Med  -7.955 .        .
1191 Mamiakin S.I.          Mos A Nom ?     ?  -18.261 ?   -16.923
1192 Margarian S.M.         Arm E Tec ?     ?   13.810 ?    17.500
1193 Margvelashvili P.I.    Geo E Int ?     ?   40.909 ?     0.000
1194 Mares'ev A.P.          Mos A Cad ?     ?  -30.000 ?   -10.000
1195 Marinichev Iu.M.       Rus A Man Med ?  -11.818 ?    17.692
1196 Markar'iants V.S.      Arm E Nom ?     ?  -26.087 ?   -10.000
1197 Markevich A.L.         Rus E Man ?   Med  24.091 ?    21.600
1198 Markin N.A.            Kaz E Tec ?     ?    9.130 ?    21.538
1199 Markov O.I.            Rus E Wor ?     ?   15.000 ?     3.846
1200 Marmilov A.N.          Rus E Man ?     ?   -2.609 ?     7.308
1201 Martinaitis M.-T.I.    Lit E Int ?     ?   44.000 ?     0.000
1202 Martirosian V.A.       Ukr E Mil RI Rad 13.043 RI  14.231
1203 Martynov F.N.          Rus E Man ?     ?   12.857 ?     0.000
1204 Martsinkliavichius Iu.M. Lit A Int ?   ?   43.333 ?     0.000
1205 Marchenko G.A.         Rus E Tec ?     ?    9.130 ?    26.400
1206 Marchuk G.I.           Mos A Int ?     ?  -35.000 ?   -10.000
1207 Masaliev A.M.          Kir E Nom App App -13.636 App  -6.538
1208 Masel'skii A.S.        Ukr E Nom ?     ?  -10.500 ?     3.846
1209 Maslakova A.P.         Rus E Wor ?     ?   -2.609 ?     0.000
1210 Maslii M.D.            Ukr A Tec ?     ?    2.857 ?     8.800
1211 Maslin V.P.            Mos A Cad ?     ?  -13.810 ?    -8.750
1212 Masol V.A.             Ukr E Nom App App -10.750 ?     4.808
1213 Mas'ko G.I.            Bel A Tec ?     ?  -15.909 ?    -3.077
1214 Matveev E.I.           Rus E Wor ?     ?   14.091 ?    14.231
3008 Matveev Iu.G.          Ukr E Nom ?     .        .        .
1215 Matveichuk S.I.        Ukr E Wor ?     ?   -2.609 ?    12.885
1216 Matvievskii I.S.       Ukr E Tec ?     ?    1.304 ?    -6.538
1217 Matvienko V.I.         Rus A Nom ?    LI -13.043 ?    -3.077
1218 Mateushuk Z.K.         Bel E Tec ?     ?   -2.143 ?     2.500
1219 Matiiko L.T.           Ukr E Wor ?     ?   -3.000 ?    -6.538
1220 Matkovski D.L.         Mol E Int ?     ?    0.000 ?     0.000
1221 Matiukha V.N.          Rus E Wor ?    RI   9.130 ?    21.154
1222 Matiukhin L.I.         Rus E Man ?   Pre  -8.636 ?   -10.000
1223 Mukhammedzhumaeva O.A. ?  ? ? ?   ?    0.000 ?    -4.800
1224 Makhanov T.            Uzb E Tec ?     ?  -14.545 ?    -3.333
1225 Makharashvili B.D.     Geo E Nom ?     ?   -1.842 ?    -7.273
1226 Makhkamov K.           Tad E Nom Cen ?  -11.000 Cen -10.800
1227 Makhmudov U.N.         Uzb A Wor ?     ?  -15.263 ?     0.385
1228 Machavariani M.I.      Geo E Int ?     ?   12.500 ?     0.000
1229 Mashbashev I.Sh.       Rus E Int ?     ?  -10.435 App  -3.077
1230 Mgaloblishvili N.M.    Geo A Int ?     ?   15.250 ?    -0.200
1231 Mgeladze G.D.          Geo E Nom ?   Med  16.000 ?    16.429
1232 Medvedev V.A.          Mos A Nom Med ?  -19.500 Med -15.200
1233 Medvedev N.N.          Lit E Tec Rad LI  41.250 LI   0.000
1234 Medvedev R.A.          Mos E Int Med Med  8.095 Med -16.923
1235 Medvedev S.A. (718)    Kir E Man ?   App -15.909 ?    11.800
1236 Medvedev S.A. (151)    Kaz E Nom ?     ?  -22.174 ?   -16.923
1237 Medeubekov K.U.        Kaz A Int ?     ?  -11.765 ?    -8.846
1238 Medikov V.Ia.          Rus E Tec ?     ?   24.565 ?    19.615
1239 Mezhelaitis Ye.B.      Lit A Int ?     ?    0.000 ?     0.000
1240 Mezentsev A.M.         Kaz E Wor ?     ?  -22.174 ?    -3.077
1241 Melekhin S.T.          Rus A Wor Cen LI  -7.000 ?     6.000
1242 Meliev A.              Uzb A Wor ?     ?    8.913 ?    19.615
1243 Melikov A.D.           Aze E Int ?     ?   -0.455 ?     7.000
1244 Mel'nik K.A.           Mol A Man ?   Cen -18.261 ?    -5.556
1245 Mel'nikov A.I. (46)    Rus E Wor ?     ?    1.304 ?     0.385
1246 Mel'nikov A.I. (210)   Rus E Wor ?     ?    0.000 ?     4.808
1247 Mel'nikov B.I.         Rus E Nom ?     ?    0.000 .        .
1248 Mel'nikov V.P.         Rus E Nom Cen Cen  -2.609 Cen   8.462
1249 Melyeev K.             Tur E Tec ?     ?  -14.348 ?    -8.462
1250 Memanishvili O.A.      Geo E Wor ?     ?    1.087 ?    -1.000
1251 Mendybaev M.S.         Kaz A Nom ?     ?  -26.364 ?    -1.923
1252 Menteshashvili T.N.    Geo E Nom ?     ?    4.348 ?     0.200
1253 Men'shatov A.D.        Rus E Man ?    LI   2.667 ?    14.231
1254 Men'shikov V.V.        Mos A Cad ?     ?  -14.348 ?     7.308
1255 Mergenov E.T.          Kaz A Int ?     ?   20.455 ?    14.200
1256 Merkulov I.A.          Rus E Man ?     ?  -15.000 ?    10.800
1257 Mesiats V.K.           Rus E Nom ?   App  -0.870 ?   -10.000
1258 Metonidze G.A.         Geo E Wor ?     ?    7.143 ?     0.000
1259 Mekheda M.I.           Ukr A Oth ?     ?  -18.261 App  -8.889
1260 Meshalkin E.N.         Rus A Int App ?  -21.667 ?   -19.200
1261 Meshcheriakov Iu.A.    Kaz E Nom ?   Med -26.087 ?     1.154
1262 Mikiver M.A.           Est E Int ?     ?   46.250 ?     0.000
1263 Militenko S.A.         Rus E Tec ?     ?   -6.522 ?     0.385
1264 Milkin A.V.            Kaz E Nom ?     ?    0.000 ?     0.000
```

```
1265 Miloserdnyi A.K.      Bel E Man ?    ?    -0.500 ?    -6.538
1266 Miliutin A.S.         Rus E Tec ?    ?     1.304 ?    14.231
1267 Minaev V.F.           Rus E Tec ?    LI    9.130 ?     3.600
1268 Minasbekian M.S.      Arm E Nom Med Med  12.857 Med  17.500
1269 Minzhurenko A.V.      Rus E Int Rad Rad  36.739 ?    14.231
1270 Minin V.M.           Rus A Tec ?    ?    40.476 ?    10.769
1271 Minnullin T.A.        Rus E Int Med  ?    20.000 Med   8.750
1272 Miralieva Ye.M.       Rus E Wor ?    ?    -6.364 ?    -3.846
1273 Mirgaziamov M.P.      Rus E Nom ?    Cen   3.333 ?     3.333
1274 Mirzabekov A.M        Rus E Nom ?    ?     1.818 ?    -6.667
1275 Mirzoev R.Z.          Tad E Cad ?    ?   -14.545 ?   -11.923
1276 Mirzoian M.A.         Arm A Cad ?    ?     8.947 ?     0.000
1277 Mirzoian Ye.M.        Arm A Int ?    ?    -1.053 ?     4.400
1278 Mirkadirov M.         Kaz E Wor ?    ?   -13.182 ?     0.385
1279 Mirkasymov M.M.       Uzb E Nom ?    Cen -18.261 ?   -13.462
1280 Mironenko V.I.        Mos A Nom Cen  ?   -11.111 Med   6.600
1281 Mironov N.S.          Mos E Man ?    ?    -7.826 ?     7.885
1282 Mironova D.S.         Rus A Wor ?    App  -2.609 ?     0.385
1283 Mironova S.L.         Rus E Tec ?    ?    -2.609 ?    -7.826
1284 Miroshin B.V.         Rus E Cad LI   ?     5.217 ?     3.846
1285 Miroshnik V.M.        Kaz E Mil ?    ?   -22.174 ?     7.391
1286 Mirrakhimov M.M.      Kir E Tec ?    ?     4.783 ?    12.308
1287 Mirkhalikov T.        Tad E Nom ?    ?   -15.217 ?   -16.923
1288 Misrikhanov K.Z.      Rus E Wor ?    ?    13.043 ?    11.600
1289 Misuna I.I.           Rus E Wor ?    ?    22.955 ?    23.846
1290 Mitalene O.A.         Lit A Tec ?    ?    37.857 ?     0.000
1291 Mitin B.S.            Mos A Int Med  ?   -16.471 ?    -6.538
1292 Mitin V.S.            Rus E Tec ?    ?    34.565 ?    14.231
1293 Mikhailov V.M.        Rus E Mil ?    ?   -18.261 ?   -16.923
1294 Mikhailova L.I.       Rus E Tec ?    ?    -1.739 ?    -0.192
1295 Mikhedov F.F.         Rus E Wor ?    ?    -5.455 ?     8.077
1296 Mikheev M.A.          Rus E Wor App  ?     5.217 ?     7.308
1297 Mitskis A.M.          Lit E Tec ?    ?    43.333 ?     0.000
1298 Mishuk S.M.           Ukr E Wor ?    ?    -3.158 ?    17.692
1299 Mkrtumian G.T.        Arm E Man ?    ?    12.826 ?     0.800
1300 Mkrtchian M.L.        Arm A Cad ?    ?   -18.500 ?     1.667
1301 Mnatsakanian B.G.     Arm A Cad ?    ?    13.182 ?     0.600
1302 Mogilievets Iu.K.     Tur E Nom ?    ?   -15.000 ?     0.385
1303 Moiseev A.Mil         Mos A Mil ?    Cen -21.333 Cen  -6.538
1304 Moiseev N.A.          Rus E Mil ?    ?   -14.348 ?    -9.412
1305 Mokanu A.A.           Mol E Nom Cen  ?    -5.652 ?     0.000
1306 Moldobaev A.T.        Kir E Wor ?    Pre -10.909 ?    12.308
1307 Moldobasanov K.M.     Kir A Int ?    ?    -5.385 ?    14.583
1308 Mollaniiazov K.       Tur A Wor ?    ?   -13.182 ?    10.769
1309 Molotkov N.V.         Rus E Wor ?    LI   19.565 ?    21.154
1310 Momotova T.V.         Bel E Man Cen  ?     1.304 ?     5.962
1311 Mongo M.I.            Rus E Cad Med Cen  -1.818 ?    -3.077
1312 Moroz D.V.            Ukr E Man ?    ?     1.304 ?    10.769
1313 Morozov I.S.          Mol E Mil ?    ?   -14.348 ?   -10.000
1314 Moskalenko G.S.       Ukr E Wor ?    ?   -17.619 ?   -13.462
1315 Moskalik M.N.         Ukr A Wor ?    ?     5.652 ?     3.462
3009 Mostovoi P.I.          Ukr E Man ?    .      .    .      .
1316 Moteka K.V.           Lit E Tec ?    ?    37.083 ?     0.000
1317 Motornyi D.K.         Ukr A Man ?    ?    -3.182 ?    -3.077
1318 Moshniaga T.V.        Mol E Tec Med  ?    13.889 LI   17.692
1319 Muzafarov S.B.        Aze E Wor ?    ?    -6.364 ?     0.417
1320 Mukishev V.Zh.        Kaz E Wor ?    ?   -10.435 ?     0.000
1321 Muntian M.I.          Mol A Oth ?    Med  10.000 ?     8.125
1322 Muravko M.M.          Bel E Man ?    ?     2.000 ?    10.769
1323 Muradian V.A.         Arm E Wor ?    ?     6.364 ?    21.154
1324 Muradian N.G.         Arm E Cad ?    ?    12.000 ?    -1.538
1325 Murashev A.N.         Mos E Int LI   Rad  38.824 Rad  10.192
1326 Murashov V.K.         Rus E Wor ?    ?    14.286 ?    10.769
1327 Musaeva G.Ye.         Aze E Wor ?    ?    -8.947 ?    -3.077
1328 Mutalibov A.N.        Aze E Nom Cen App -19.231 ?   -16.731
1329 Mukhabatova S.Kh.     Tad E Wor ?    ?   -15.455 ?   -16.923
1330 Mukhamedzhanov B.G.   Kaz A Int ?    ?    13.478 ?     0.000
1331 Mukhametzianov A.K.   Rus E Man ?    ?    -0.667 ?    -0.962
1332 Mukhametzianov M.T.   Rus A Man ?    ?     2.727 ?     0.385
1333 Mukhammad-Iusuf M.-S. Uzb E Int Cen  ?   -13.333 ?    -6.579
1334 Mukhidinov Kh.I.      Tad E Tec ?    ?   -14.348 ?     0.385
1335 Mukhtarov A.G.        Uzb A Int App  ?   -20.625 ?    -3.600
1336 Mukhtarov L.I.        Aze E Wor ?    ?    -6.522 ?    -3.077
1337 Mkhitarian R.E.       Arm E Man ?    ?    16.316 ?     0.385
1338 Myl'nikov A.A.        Rus A Int ?    Pre  -3.000 ?    -4.400
1339 Myl'nikov V.V.        Ukr A Oth ?    ?   -14.348 ?    -6.538
1340 Mysnichenko V.P.      Ukr E Nom ?    ?   -18.261 ?    -3.077
1341 Miakota A.S.          Ukr E Nom ?    ?   -20.455 ?   -16.800
1342 Nabieva Iu.           Uzb A Wor ?    ?   -27.333 ?    -2.115
1343 Navruzov Sh.          Tad E Wor ?    ?   -18.636 ?     0.385
1344 Nagiev R.Sh.          Aze E Wor ?    ?    -3.333 ?   -22.045
1345 Nadeliuev V.I.        Rus E Man ?    ?     1.304 ?    14.231
1346 Nazarbaev N.A.        Kaz E Nom Med Med -18.261 Med -18.800
1347 Nazarenko A.F.        Ukr E Tec ?    ?    23.214 ?    16.957
1348 Nazarov I.A.          Rus A Cad Med  ?    -2.609 ?     2.308
```

```
1349 Nazarov T.           Tad E Nom ?     App -20.500 ?     -13.462
1350 Nazarian S.E.        Arm A Man ?     ?     5.789 ?       9.600
1351 Naidenov N.A.        Rus A Wor ?     ?    18.750 ?       1.346
1352 Namazova A.A.        Aze A Tec ?     ?   -10.435 ?       0.000
1353 Napalkov N.P.        Rus A Int ?     ?     0.000 ?     -10.000
1354 Narmatov B.Y.        Kir E Wor ?     ?   -19.545 ?     -21.600
1355 Nasennik V.N.        Ukr E Wor ?     ?    -2.609 ?       4.615
1356 Nasonov A.F.         Rus E Man ?     ?     3.636 ?       4.423
3003 Naumov N.F.          ?   A ?   .     .         . ?     -14.400
1357 Naumov S.Ia.         Rus E Man ?     Pre  26.500 ?      25.200
1358 Nevolin S.I.         Rus E Tec ?     ?    -5.882 ?      16.346
1359 Negmatulloev S.Kh.   Tad E Int Pre   ?   -12.500 ?      -6.538
1360 Nedzhko M.I.         Rus A Tec ?     ?     9.130 ?      18.400
1361 Neelov Iu.V.         Rus E Cad ?     ?    13.182 ?      21.154
1362 Neiland N.V.         Lat E Nom ?     ?    45.714 ?       7.115
1363 Nemkova L.G.         Mos A Tec ?     ?   -17.727 ?     -18.889
1364 Nemtsev E.I.         Rus E Wor ?     ?   -10.435 ?       0.000
1365 Nesterenko E.E.      Mos A Int ?     ?     0.000 ?       0.000
1366 Nesterenko S.M.      Tur E Nom ?     App -10.435 ?     -10.000
1367 Neumyvakin A.Ia.     Mos A Oth LI    App -14.737 ?       0.000
1368 Nefedov O.M.         Mos A Int ?     ?   -16.591 ?      -5.577
1369 Neff Ye.M.           Kaz E Wor ?     ?   -14.348 ?      -1.667
1370 Nekhaevskii A.P.     Ukr E Nom ?     ?   -18.261 ?     -10.000
1371 Nechaev K.V.         Mos A Int Cen   ?   -14.762 ?       4.783
1372 Nechetnaia N.P.      Rus E Wor ?     ?   -11.818 ?       0.385
1373 Nivalov N.N.         Ukr E Nom ?     ?    -3.333 ?       0.385
1374 Nikanorov I.A.       Rus A Wor ?     ?   -22.174 ?     -13.462
3010 Nikitin V.V.         Rus E Nom ?     .         . ?          .
1375 Nikitin R.I.         Rus E Man ?     ?   -12.941 ?      -6.538
1376 Nikishin N.P.        Ukr A Wor ?     ?   -12.174 ?       0.385
1377 Nikolaev A.A.        Rus E Man ?     ?   -14.091 ?      -4.800
1378 Nikolaev V.V.        Rus E Tec ?     ?     3.000 ?       0.385
1379 Nikolaenko A.F.      Ukr E Tec ?     ?    -4.545 ?      -6.538
1380 Nikolaichuk V.F.     Rus E Man ?     Rad  31.818 ?      20.400
1381 Nikol'skii B.V.      Geo E Nom ?     ?    -2.609 ?     -16.923
1382 Nikol'skii B.N.      Rus E Int LI    ?    20.909 LI     -1.875
1383 Nikonov A.A.         Mos A Int ?     ?   -20.909 ?      -2.308
1384 Nikonov V.P.         Mos A Nom ?     ?   -14.348 ?     -10.000
1385 Nimbuev Ts.          Rus E Man ?     ?    33.333 ?      20.667
1386 Ninnas T.A.          Est E Man ?     ?    23.846 ?      11.304
1387 Nishanov R.N.        Uzb E Nom Cen   Cen -18.261 Cen    -6.538
1388 Niiazov D.Ia.        Tur A Wor ?     ?    -5.909 ?      14.231
1389 Niiazov S.A.         Tur E Nom Cen   Pre  -6.522 ?     -10.000
1390 Novikov V.M.         Rus E Man ?     ?     1.304 ?       6.400
1391 Novikov G.F.         Rus E Tec ?     ?    28.696 Rad    20.833
1392 Novikov E.F.         Rus A Man ?     ?   -11.429 ?       0.385
1393 Novikov I.G.         Ukr A Wor ?     ?    20.000 ?       4.348
1394 Novozhilov G.V.      Mos A Man ?     Med -13.182 ?      -1.200
1395 Novotnyi S.I.        Rus E Man Cen   ?    -2.609 ?       7.308
1396 Nozdria V.A.         Ukr E Wor ?     ?    14.667 ?      17.692
1397 Norikhin V.A.        Rus A Wor ?     ?     4.286 ?      15.000
1398 Noroian A.G.         Arm E Wor ?     ?    21.957 ?      12.500
1399 Nosov V.P.           Rus E Tec Rad   Med  -5.000 ?     -10.000
1400 Nosov K.G.           Ukr E Man Pre   Med  21.739 ?       7.400
1401 Nugis Iu.I.          Est E Man ?     ?    49.000 ?      45.000
1402 Nuzhnyi B.P.         Rus E Man ?     ?   -12.381 ?      -3.077
1403 Nurm Kh.Ye.          Est E Tec ?     ?    35.000 ?      27.500
1404 Nyrkov A.I.          Rus E Man ?     ?    -2.609 ?      -0.769
1405 Niuksha K.I.         Lat A Wor ?     ?     4.545 ?      15.192
1406 Obolenskii A.M.      Rus E Tec Rad   Rad  24.750 Rad    31.538
1407 Oborin A.V.          Rus E Tec Cen   ?    -3.182 ?       7.308
1408 Oborok K.M.          Mol E Cad ?     ?    17.778 ?       9.808
1409 Obraz V.S.           Ukr A Oth Pre   App -18.261 ?      -6.800
1410 Obraztsov I.F.       Rus A Nom ?     ?   -15.455 ?       5.600
1411 Ovezgel'dyev O.      Tur E Int ?     ?    -5.000 Cen     6.818
1412 Ovchinnikov A.I.     Uzb E Mil ?     App -18.261 ?      -6.538
1413 Ovchinnikov A.N.     Rus E Man ?     ?    -1.136 Cen     7.308
1414 Ovchinnikov V.P.     Rus E Man ?     ?    13.043 ?       3.846
1415 Oganesian M.V.       Geo E Wor ?     ?     0.435 ?      -0.556
1416 Oganesian R.G.       Arm E Tec ?     ?    23.913 ?       9.600
1417 Oganesian S.V.       Arm E Wor ?     ?    15.000 ?       7.308
1418 Oganesian Ye.S.      Arm E Int ?     ?    21.053 ?       4.318
1419 Ogarok V.I.          Uzb E Nom ?     Cen -23.636 ?     -13.462
1420 Odzhiev R.K.         Tad A Man LI    Med -11.250 ?       0.000
1421 Ozolas R.A.          Lit E Int ?     ?    31.667 ?       0.000
1422 Ozolinysh L.A.       Lat E Tec ?     ?    32.500 ?      13.846
1423 Okeev T.O.           Kir A Int ?     ?    -6.522 ?      10.208
1424 Oleinik B.I.         Ukr A Int Med   ?    -5.000 ?       0.000
1425 Olekas Iu.Iu.        Lit E Int LI    Med  47.000 ?       0.000
1426 Omelichev B.A.       Tur E Mil ?     ?   -16.818 ?      -6.538
1427 Omel'ianenko K.S.    Ukr E Man ?     ?   -10.435 ?      -3.077
1428 Oplanchuk B.Ia.      Tad E Man ?     ?   -14.348 ?      -6.538
1429 Opolinskii V.A.      Ukr A Wor ?     ?     1.304 ?      10.769
1430 Oragvelidze R.T.     Geo A Wor ?     ?     8.478 ?      -9.600
1431 Orazbaev A.          Uzb E Wor ?     ?    -3.636 ?       3.846
```

| | | | | | | | | | |
|---|---|---|---|---|---|---|---|---|---|
| 1432 | Orazberdiev A. | Tur | E | Cad | ? | ? | -11.053 | ? | -16.923 |
| 1433 | Orazliev M. | Tur | E | Wor | ? | ? | -3.500 | Med | -3.077 |
| 1434 | Orazmuradova O.M. | Tur | E | Tec | ? | ? | -14.348 | ? | 0.000 |
| 1435 | Orazov K.M. | Tur | E | Nom | ? | ? | 0.000 | ? | -6.538 |
| 1436 | Orekhov A.P. | Rus | E | Cad | ? | ? | -2.609 | ? | 3.846 |
| 1437 | Oripov A. | Uzb | E | Int | ? | ? | -16.316 | ? | -13.462 |
| 1438 | Orlik M.A. | Ukr | A | Nom | ? | ? | -13.182 | ? | -1.000 |
| 1439 | Orlov A.K. | Rus | E | Cad | ? | Cen | -3.500 | ? | -3.077 |
| 1440 | Orlov V.M. | Rus | E | Man | ? | ? | 12.000 | ? | 3.600 |
| 1441 | Orozova U.Sh. | Kir | A | Int | ? | ? | -14.348 | ? | -2.115 |
| 1442 | Orunbekova B.M. | Kir | E | Wor | ? | ? | -15.217 | ? | 0.385 |
| 1443 | Osipov A.K. | Rus | E | Cad | ? | ? | -2.609 | ? | -0.417 |
| 1444 | Osipov V.V. | Mol | E | Mil | ? | ? | -10.500 | ? | -10.800 |
| 1445 | Osipov P.D. | Rus | E | Cad | ? | ? | 23.913 | ? | 17.692 |
| 1446 | Osip'ian Iu.A. | Mos | A | Int | Med | ? | 0.526 | Med | 0.385 |
| 1447 | Ostrozhinskii V.E. | Ukr | E | Nom | ? | ? | -6.522 | ? | -7.292 |
| 1448 | Ostroukhov V.A. | Rus | A | Cad | Med | Med | -2.609 | ? | 6.923 |
| 1449 | Os'kin A.D. | Rus | E | Man | ? | ? | 32.250 | ? | 18.462 |
| 1450 | Otarashvili G.Z. | Geo | E | Wor | ? | ? | 5.500 | ? | -12.308 |
| 1451 | Otsason R.A. | Est | E | Nom | ? | ? | 30.000 | ? | 36.667 |
| 1452 | Ochirov V.M. | Rus | E | Wor | ? | ? | -8.182 | ? | 10.769 |
| 1453 | Ochirov V.N. | Rus | E | Mil | RI | LI | -6.842 | ? | 10.800 |
| 1454 | Oiun V.O. | Rus | E | Man | ? | ? | -13.182 | ? | -10.000 |
| 1455 | Pavlevich I.B. | Ukr | E | Tec | ? | ? | 14.130 | ? | 14.400 |
| 1456 | Pavlenko V.P. | Rus | E | Man | ? | ? | -17.273 | ? | -16.923 |
| 1457 | Pavlenko L.I. | Ukr | E | Nom | ? | ? | -10.000 | ? | -10.800 |
| 1458 | Pavliashvili Z.A. | Geo | E | Wor | ? | ? | 7.750 | ? | 0.833 |
| 1459 | Pavlii A.A. | Ukr | A | Cad | ? | ? | -15.000 | ? | 0.000 |
| 1460 | Pavlov A.V. | Rus | E | Wor | ? | Rad | 31.087 | Rad | 13.913 |
| 1461 | Pavlov A.S. | Uzb | E | Nom | ? | ? | -10.435 | ? | -13.462 |
| 1462 | Pavlov V.A. | Rus | A | Wor | ? | ? | 0.435 | ? | 12.391 |
| 1463 | Pavlychko D.V. | Ukr | E | Int | . | Rad | 12.273 | ? | 24.167 |
| 1464 | Paiziev D. | Kaz | E | Wor | ? | ? | -18.261 | ? | 3.182 |
| 1465 | Paishchikov V.V. | Rus | A | Cad | ? | ? | -18.261 | ? | -13.462 |
| 1466 | Palagniuk B.T. | Mol | E | Man | ? | ? | -2.609 | ? | -10.000 |
| 1467 | Paldzhian V.A. | Arm | E | Int | ? | ? | 0.000 | ? | 0.000 |
| 1468 | Pallaev G. | Tad | E | Nom | ? | Cen | -7.727 | ? | -8.400 |
| 1469 | Paltyshev N.N. | Ukr | A | Tec | ? | ? | -17.778 | ? | -3.800 |
| 1470 | Pal' O.M. | Kaz | E | Man | ? | ? | -19.545 | ? | 0.000 |
| 1471 | Pal'm V.A. | Est | E | Int | Rad | Rad | 20.000 | Rad | 18.571 |
| 1472 | Pal'chin S.Ia. | Rus | E | Man | ? | ? | 19.348 | ? | 8.077 |
| 1473 | Pamfilova Ye.A. | Mos | A | Cad | ? | App | 23.889 | Med | 10.769 |
| 3011 | Panasenko T.I. | Ukr | E | Nom | ? | . | . | . | . |
| 1474 | Panov I.M. | Mos | A | Int | ? | ? | -6.190 | ? | -3.077 |
| 1475 | Panov N.N. | Rus | E | Wor | ? | Rad | 22.826 | Rad | 16.154 |
| 1476 | Panteleev N.V. | Rus | A | Wor | ? | ? | -3.077 | ? | 7.308 |
| 1477 | Pantykin V.P. | Rus | E | Man | ? | ? | 1.818 | ? | 8.077 |
| 1478 | Panchenko Ye.A. | Ukr | A | Tec | ? | ? | -7.609 | ? | 6.346 |
| 1479 | Paplevchenkov I.M. | Rus | A | Man | ? | ? | -6.522 | ? | -6.538 |
| 1480 | Parachev V.P. | Rus | E | Man | ? | ? | -2.609 | ? | -3.077 |
| 1481 | Parubok E.N. | Ukr | A | Wor | ? | ? | -14.545 | ? | -10.000 |
| 1482 | Parusnikov V.A. | Rus | A | Wor | ? | ? | 16.957 | ? | 5.577 |
| 1483 | Pastorov I.I. | Rus | E | Man | ? | ? | 5.217 | ? | 0.000 |
| 1484 | Patiashvili D.I. | Geo | E | Oth | Cen | ? | 0.000 | ? | 0.000 |
| 1485 | Paton B.E. | Ukr | A | Int | Med | Med | -6.522 | ? | -1.200 |
| 1486 | Patrakhin A.A. | Kir | E | Tec | ? | ? | 5.217 | ? | 16.000 |
| 1487 | Pauls R.V. | Lat | E | Int | ? | ? | 28.571 | ? | 0.000 |
| 1488 | Patsaliuk M.P. | Ukr | A | Man | ? | ? | -2.609 | ? | 0.385 |
| 1489 | Patsatsiia O.A. | Geo | E | Man | ? | ? | -4.615 | ? | 11.176 |
| 1490 | Pasha-zade A.G. | Aze | E | Int | ? | ? | -5.000 | ? | 5.417 |
| 1491 | Pashaly M.K. | Mol | E | Man | ? | ? | -5.263 | ? | -6.538 |
| 1492 | Pashian S.A. | Arm | E | Wor | ? | ? | 4.000 | ? | 18.269 |
| 1493 | Pegar'kov N.G. | Rus | A | Man | ? | ? | -25.263 | ? | -15.385 |
| 1494 | Peniagin A.N. | Rus | E | Wor | ? | ? | 24.375 | ? | 18.889 |
| 1495 | Perelygina L.F. | Ukr | A | Cad | ? | ? | 3.409 | ? | 12.692 |
| 1496 | Pershilin K.G. | Rus | A | Man | ? | ? | -10.435 | ? | -10.000 |
| 1497 | Pershin A.L. | Uzb | E | Wor | ? | ? | 7.273 | ? | 7.727 |
| 1498 | Peters Ia.Ia. | Lat | E | Int | Rad | ? | 33.846 | ? | 7.174 |
| 1499 | Petkevich Z.S. | Lat | E | Cad | ? | ? | 4.000 | ? | 10.769 |
| 1500 | Petkel' V.V. | Tad | E | Mil | ? | ? | -18.261 | ? | -3.077 |
| 1501 | Petrakov N.Ia. | Mos | A | Int | ? | Med | 7.778 | ? | -3.077 |
| 1502 | Petrenko A.F. | Rus | E | Man | ? | ? | 16.957 | ? | 3.846 |
| 1503 | Petrov A.P. (400) | Rus | E | Nom | ? | ? | -15.455 | ? | -9.167 |
| 1504 | Petrov A.P. (Soiuz komp.) | Rus | A | Int | ? | ? | 16.957 | ? | 0.000 |
| 1505 | Petrov N.N. | Rus | E | Man | ? | ? | 1.304 | ? | 12.400 |
| 1506 | Petrova L.N. | Rus | A | Man | ? | ? | -13.636 | ? | -8.400 |
| 1507 | Petrova R.A. | Rus | A | Cad | ? | ? | -18.636 | ? | -6.538 |
| 1508 | Petropavlovskii V.S. | Rus | E | Tec | Med | Med | 15.455 | ? | 8.077 |
| 3012 | Petrukovich A.S. | Ukr | A | Wor | ? | . | . | . | . |
| 1509 | Petrushenko N.S. | Kaz | E | Mil | RI | RI | -6.522 | RI | 3.333 |
| 1510 | Pivovarov N.D. | Rus | E | Nom | ? | ? | -10.435 | ? | 3.846 |
| 1511 | Pilipets I.N. | Ukr | A | Man | ? | ? | -17.000 | ? | -1.200 |
| 1512 | Pil'nikov S.V. | Rus | E | Tec | ? | Med | -6.522 | Med | 0.385 |
| 1513 | Pirnazarov R. | Tur | E | Tec | ? | ? | 13.043 | ? | 18.077 |
| 1514 | Pirov M. | Tad | E | Tec | ? | ? | -9.565 | ? | 3.846 |

```
1515 Pirtskhalaishvili Z.G.   Geo E Wor ?     ?      9.688 ?    -3.500
1516 Piriazeva N.M.           Rus E Wor ?     ?      1.304 ?    -3.077
1517 Pisanets V.A.            Ukr E Wor ?     ?    -16.304 ?    -9.167
1518 Pisarenko V.A.           Rus E Mil Med ?        1.818 ?    16.400
1519 Piskunovich G.P.         Bel E Wor ?     ?     -9.091 ?     7.308
1520 Pichuzhkin M.S.          Ukr E Nom ?     ?     -7.273 ?   -10.000
1521 Plamadiala A.A.          Mol A Tec ?     ?     -1.364 ?    15.714
1522 Platon S.I.              Mol E Cad ?     ?     -2.609 ?    10.769
1523 Platonov V.P.            Bel A Int ?     ?      2.647 ?     2.500
1524 Platonov Iu.P.           Mos A Int Med ?       -8.095 ?     0.385
1525 Pletenetskii D.E.        Rus E Man ?     ?      9.130 ?    10.769
1526 Plekhanov A.N.           Rus E Nom ?     ?    -10.435 ?   -16.923
1527 Plotnieks A.A.           Lat E Int Rad LI     33.529 LI    55.000
1528 Plotnikov A.L.           Rus A Wor LI    Med   24.783 Rad   16.000
1529 Pliutinskii V.A.         Ukr A Man ?     ?    -18.636 ?   -13.462
1530 Pogorelov V.G.           Ukr E Man ?     ?    -10.435 ?     3.846
1531 Pogosian G.A.            Aze E Oth Rad ?        5.714 ?     0.385
1532 Podberezskii G.N.        Bel E Man Med Med    -2.609 Med    3.077
1533 Podziruk V.S.            Rus E Mil ?     ?     16.190 App  10.000
1534 Podobaev S.A.            Bel E Man ?     ?     -2.609 ?     0.385
1535 Podol'skii E.M.          Rus E Nom ?     ?    -26.087 ?   -12.400
1536 Podolianina E.I.         Ukr A Man ?     ?    -18.261 App -16.923
1537 Pozharskii B.I.          Rus A Cad ?     ?     -4.783 ?    -8.462
1538 Pokrovskii B.A.          Mos A Int ?     ?     -4.118 ?     9.600
1539 Pokrovskii V.I.          Mos A Int ?     ?      1.304 ?     3.846
1540 Polikarpov N.A.          Rus E Man Pre ?       -2.609 ?     3.846
1541 Polikarpov N.P.          Rus E Man ?     ?      0.435 ?     3.846
1542 Polozkov I.K.            Rus E Nom ?     ?    -16.364 App  -3.077
1543 Poltoranin M.N.          Mos A Int Rad Rad    20.652 ?    19.615
1544 Poluyektov A.S.          Rus E Tec ?     ?     25.682 ?    28.077
1545 Poluyektova T.A.         Rus E Man ?     ?     32.391 ?     3.333
1546 Polianichko V.P.         Aze E Nom App ?       -2.609 ?    -6.538
1547 Polianskaia P.A.         Rus A Wor ?     Pre  -10.435 ?    -3.077
1548 Poliachenko M.N.         Rus E Tec ?     ?     20.870 ?    14.231
1549 Pometun G.K.             Ukr A Tec ?     ?    -22.174 ?    -9.231
1550 Ponomarev A.F.           Rus E Nom ?     ?    -18.095 ?   -10.000
1551 Ponomarev V.M.           Rus A Wor ?     ?      5.217 ?    -0.417
1552 Ponomarenko L.V.         Ukr A Tec ?     ?     -3.810 ?   -10.000
1553 Popadiuk S.A.            Ukr E Wor ?     ?     -2.609 ?    14.231
1554 Popov V.A.               Rus E Tec ?     ?     -0.909 ?    -4.615
1555 Popov G.Kh.              Mos A Int Rad Rad    35.952 Rad   18.889
1556 Popov N.I.               Aze E Mil ?     ?      1.304 ?     0.385
1557 Popov F.V.               Rus E Nom ?     ?    -18.261 ?    -9.231
1558 Popov Iu.V.              Rus E Int ?     LI     5.000 ?     2.500
1559 Popova N.V.              Mos A Oth ?     ?    -13.810 ?   -11.600
1560 Portnov G.A.             Rus E Wor ?     ?     26.957 ?     3.269
1561 Posibeev G.A.            Rus E Nom Cen ?       -4.706 Cen  -6.538
1562 Postnikov V.I.           Rus A Man ?     ?    -21.429 ?     0.870
1563 Postnikov S.I.           Bel E Mil ?     ?     -2.609 ?   -10.000
1564 Postoronko I.G.          Ukr E Nom ?     ?     -6.522 ?     8.077
1565 Potapov A.S.             Mos A Int ?     ?     -7.391 ?     0.385
1566 Potapov V.I.             Rus E Nom ?     Med   -6.522 ?     0.000
1567 Pokhitailo E.D.          Rus E Nom ?     ?     -7.813 ?    -8.462
1568 Pokhla V.P.              Est E Int ?     ?     42.143 ?     0.000
1569 Pokhodnia G.S.           Rus A Tec ?     ?    -16.818 App -10.000
1570 Poshkus B.I.             Lit A Int ?     ?     50.000 ?    10.000
1571 Pribylova N.N.           Rus A Tec ?     LI    -0.952 ?    -3.600
1572 Priimachenko N.I.        Ukr E Nom ?     ?    -10.769 ?   -10.000
1573 Primakov E.M.            Mos A Nom Med Med   -14.375 Med   -6.538
1574 Prikhod'ko E.S.          Ukr A Man ?     ?    -17.000 ?    -1.538
1575 Prikhod'ko Z.S.          Ukr A Cad ?     ?    -19.130 ?    -9.800
1576 Prishchepa P.K.          Ukr E ?     .   ?     -7.619 ?   -13.462
1577 Prokopchuk B.V.          Rus E Cad ?     ?      5.217 ?    14.231
1578 Prokop'ev Iu.N.          Rus E Nom ?     ?     -4.545 App  -6.538
1579 Prokushev V.I.           Rus E Int ?     ?     11.053 LI    8.571
1580 Pronin G.V.              Rus E Wor ?     ?      9.130 Med  10.769
1581 Prudnikov I.V.           Rus E Tec ?     ?     35.556 ?    16.923
1582 Prunskene K.D.P.         Lit E Man LI    ?     43.333 ?     0.000
1583 Prusak M.M.              Rus A Man ?     ?     18.810 ?    18.462
1584 Pugo B.K.                Mos A Nom ?     ?    -14.348 ?    -3.077
1585 Pupkevich T.K.           Est E Wor ?     Pre  -12.500 ?    -2.083
1586 Pukhova Z.P.             Mos A Nom Med ?      -14.348 ?    -5.000
1587 Pfeifer A.G.             Rus A Wor ?     ?     11.333 ?     7.308
1588 Pchelka N.F.             Rus A Wor ?     ?     -2.609 ?    17.692
1589 Pshenichnikov V.K.       Mol E Nom ?     ?     -2.609 ?    -8.400
1590 Pylin B.F.               Rus E Mil RI    ?     20.870 ?    14.231
1591 Pyndyk G.V.              Ukr E Wor ?     ?      1.304 ?     3.846
1592 P'iankov B.E.            Rus E Mil ?     ?      5.217 ?   -13.462
1593 P'iankov P.P.            Rus E Wor ?     ?     16.957 ?     4.423
1594 Radzhabaliev T.          Tad E Man ?     ?    -10.435 ?    -1.600
1595 Radzhabov R.R.           Tad E Tec ?     ?    -11.304 ?     3.654
1596 Razbivnaia G.A.          Rus A Cad ?     ?     -2.381 ?    -1.600
1597 Razuvaeva G.P.           Rus E Wor ?     ?    -13.684 ?     3.333
1598 Razumovskii V.G.         Mos A Int ?     ?    -10.435 ?     0.000
1599 Razumovskii G.P.         Mos A Nom ?     ?    -20.000 ?    -6.538
```

| 1600 | Raig I.Kh. | Est | E | Int | ? | ? | 25.556 | ? | 0.000 |
|------|------------|-----|---|-----|---|---|--------|---|-------|
| 1601 | Ramanauskas V.A. | Lit | A | Man | ? | ? | 10.000 | ? | 0.000 |
| 1602 | Rasputin V.G. | Rus | A | Int | RI | ? | -6.316 | ? | -3.077 |
| 1603 | Rastrogina N.A. | Tur | E | Wor | ? | ? | -2.381 | ? | 3.846 |
| 1604 | Raud I.P. | Est | A | Int | ? | ? | 13.333 | ? | 9.167 |
| 1605 | Rakhimov A. | Uzb | A | Man | ? | ? | -19.545 | ? | -13.462 |
| 1606 | Rakhimov M.G. | Rus | E | Man | ? | ? | -6.522 | ? | -3.600 |
| 1607 | Rakhimova B.F. | Tad | A | Nom | ? | Cen | -19.500 | ? | -10.000 |
| 1608 | Rakhimova D.S. | Kaz | A | Cad | ? | ? | -10.435 | ? | 3.846 |
| 1609 | Rakhimova S.Kh. | Uzb | A | Wor | ? | ? | -25.238 | ? | -6.538 |
| 1610 | Rakhmadiev E. | Kaz | E | Int | ? | ? | -0.769 | ? | 18.333 |
| 1611 | Rakhmankulova T. | Uzb | E | Wor | ? | ? | -19.545 | ? | 5.417 |
| 1612 | Rakhmanov B. | Uzb | A | Wor | ? | ? | -15.556 | ? | 3.600 |
| 1613 | Rakhmanova M.N. | Rus | A | Tec | Med | ? | -16.250 | ? | 0.385 |
| 1614 | Rakhmatullin M.Z. | Rus | E | Wor | ? | ? | -10.435 | ? | -2.917 |
| 1615 | Rebane K.K. | Est | A | Int | ? | ? | 17.500 | ? | 0.000 |
| 1616 | Revenko G.I. | Ukr | E | Nom | ? | Cen | -4.211 | ? | 3.846 |
| 3013 | Revnitsev V.I. | Rus | A | Man | Cen | . | . | . | . |
| 1617 | Reznik A.I. | Ukr | A | Man | ? | ? | -13.182 | ? | -3.600 |
| 1618 | Reish B.Ye. | Kaz | E | Tec | ? | ? | -2.609 | ? | 2.917 |
| 1619 | Rekus V.M. | Rus | A | Man | ? | ? | -14.545 | ? | -6.538 |
| 1620 | Reshetnikov A.V. | Rus | E | Tec | ? | ? | 0.455 | ? | 1.923 |
| 1621 | Reshetnikova A.S. | Ukr | E | Tec | ? | ? | -10.455 | ? | -6.818 |
| 1622 | Reshetova N.Iu. | Rus | A | Tec | ? | ? | -2.273 | ? | 1.923 |
| 1623 | Rzaev A.R. | Aze | E | Int | ? | ? | -1.429 | ? | 0.000 |
| 1624 | Rzaev F.O. | Aze | E | Wor | ? | ? | -0.909 | ? | 0.000 |
| 1625 | Ridiger A.M. | Rus | A | Int | LI | Med | -10.435 | ? | 1.400 |
| 1626 | Rogatin B.N. | Mos | A | Cad | ? | ? | -14.348 | ? | -6.538 |
| 1627 | Rogozhina V.A. | Rus | A | Int | ? | LI | -12.826 | ? | 0.000 |
| 1628 | Rodionov I.N. | Geo | E | Mil | RI | ? | -5.909 | ? | -10.800 |
| 1629 | Rozanov E.G. | Mos | A | Int | ? | ? | -15.455 | ? | 7.308 |
| 1630 | Romazan I.Kh. | Rus | A | Man | ? | ? | -13.158 | ? | -6.400 |
| 1631 | Romazanov K.Z. | Kaz | A | Wor | ? | ? | -8.636 | ? | 14.038 |
| 1632 | Romanenko V.D. | Ukr | A | Int | Cen | ? | -3.571 | Med | 10.000 |
| 1633 | Romanov V.I. | Rus | A | Cad | ? | Cen | 15.000 | ? | 17.692 |
| 1634 | Romanov V.F. | Rus | E | Int | Cen | ? | -6.522 | Cen | -6.538 |
| 1635 | Romanov G.N. | Rus | E | Wor | ? | ? | 29.048 | Med | 11.667 |
| 1636 | Romanov Iu.V. | Rus | A | Cad | ? | ? | 18.667 | ? | 16.600 |
| 1637 | Rotar' S.A. | Mol | A | Wor | ? | ? | 14.091 | ? | 7.308 |
| 1638 | Rubiks A.P. | Lat | E | Nom | ? | App | -18.261 | ? | -10.000 |
| 1639 | Rugin R.P. | Rus | E | Int | ? | Med | 6.471 | ? | 16.346 |
| 1640 | Ruzhitskii A.A. | Ukr | E | Nom | ? | ? | -9.048 | ? | -19.348 |
| 1641 | Rusanov A.I. | Rus | A | Int | ? | ? | 19.783 | ? | 28.077 |
| 1642 | Russkikh V.G. | Rus | E | Wor | ? | ? | 37.250 | ? | 24.615 |
| 1643 | Russu G.S. | Mol | E | Tec | ? | ? | 4.211 | ? | 8.077 |
| 1644 | Russu I.N. | Mol | E | Cad | ? | ? | -1.905 | ? | 1.200 |
| 1645 | Rustamova Z.K. | Uzb | A | Tec | Med | ? | -17.143 | ? | -2.500 |
| 1646 | Ruchkin A.S. | Rus | E | Man | ? | ? | -10.435 | ? | -14.400 |
| 1647 | Rybakov V.I. | Rus | E | Wor | ? | ? | 5.217 | ? | 14.231 |
| 1648 | Rybianchenko L.I. | Rus | A | Man | ? | ? | -11.304 | ? | 2.885 |
| 1649 | Ryzhikov M.B. | Mos | A | Nom | ? | ? | -14.348 | ? | -10.000 |
| 1650 | Ryzhkov N.I. | Mos | A | Nom | Med | Cen | -0.909 | Cen | -13.462 |
| 1651 | Ryzhov A.A. | Rus | E | Tec | ? | ? | -7.273 | ? | -2.083 |
| 1652 | Ryzhov Iu.A. | Mos | E | Int | ? | Rad | 32.750 | Rad | 10.769 |
| 1653 | Rynka A.A. | Ukr | E | Cad | ? | ? | 2.941 | ? | 0.385 |
| 1654 | Rychin E.S. | Mos | A | Man | ? | ? | -6.522 | ? | -3.077 |
| 1655 | Riuitel' A.F. | Est | E | Nom | ? | ? | 15.833 | ? | 47.500 |
| 1656 | Riumin V.V. | Mos | A | Man | ? | ? | 10.652 | ? | 0.000 |
| 1657 | Riabkov V.M. | Rus | E | Tec | ? | App | -6.522 | ? | -5.000 |
| 1658 | Riabtsov B.I. | Rus | E | Wor | ? | ? | 1.304 | ? | 20.870 |
| 1659 | Riabchenko S.M. | Ukr | E | Tec | Med | Rad | 22.391 | Rad | 11.154 |
| 1660 | Riazanova G.I. | Rus | A | Tec | ? | ? | 20.909 | ? | 12.917 |
| 1661 | Saar V.A. | Est | A | Wor | ? | ? | 22.667 | ? | -6.000 |
| 1662 | Sabirov A.G. | Uzb | E | Tec | ? | ? | -14.348 | ? | 14.231 |
| 1663 | Sabirova N. | Uzb | E | Wor | ? | ? | -18.261 | ? | 6.538 |
| 1664 | Savinova E.I. | Rus | E | Tec | ? | ? | 5.217 | ? | 7.308 |
| 1665 | Savinykh V.P. | Rus | E | Int | ? | ? | 1.818 | ? | 0.000 |
| 1666 | Savisaar Ye.Ye. | Est | E | Man | ? | Rad | 43.333 | ? | 0.000 |
| 1667 | Savitskaia S.E. | Mos | A | Tec | ? | ? | 1.522 | ? | -2.381 |
| 1668 | Savitskii M.A. | Bel | A | Int | ? | ? | 13.333 | ? | 17.143 |
| 1669 | Savkov V.A. | Ukr | A | Tec | ? | ? | -6.522 | ? | 7.308 |
| 1670 | Savostina Z.S. | Rus | A | Tec | ? | ? | -22.174 | ? | 7.308 |
| 1671 | Savostiuk O.M. | Mos | A | Int | LI | ? | -8.000 | Rad | 4.808 |
| 1672 | Savchenko N.V. | Rus | A | Man | Pre | ? | -10.000 | ? | 11.400 |
| 1673 | Sagaandai G.S. | Rus | A | Tec | ? | ? | -7.273 | ? | -6.538 |
| 1674 | Sagdeev R.Z. | Mos | A | Int | Rad | ? | 38.929 | ? | 0.000 |
| 1675 | Sagdiev M.R. | Kaz | E | Nom | ? | ? | -17.000 | ? | 0.385 |
| 1676 | Sadygova N.Sh. | Aze | E | Tec | ? | ? | -4.545 | ? | -0.600 |
| 1677 | Sazonov N.S. | Rus | E | Cad | LI | ? | 36.875 | LI | 0.000 |
| 1678 | Sazonova Z.V. | Rus | E | Wor | ? | ? | -7.273 | ? | 0.000 |
| 1679 | Saidov K.M. | Uzb | E | Cad | ? | Med | 0.909 | ? | 10.769 |
| 1680 | Saidaliev S. | Tad | A | Wor | ? | ? | -10.435 | ? | -2.308 |
| 1681 | Saidakhmedov I.M. | Uzb | E | Tec | ? | ? | 1.000 | ? | 3.846 |
| 1682 | Saifitdinova M. | Uzb | A | Man | ? | ? | -10.500 | ? | -2.308 |
| 1683 | Sakandelidze I.B. | Geo | E | Wor | ? | ? | 6.739 | ? | 2.400 |

| | | | | | | | | | |
|---|---|---|---|---|---|---|---|---|---|
| 1684 | Salaev Ye.Iu. | Aze | E | Int | ? | Med | 7.619 | Med | -1.053 |
| 1685 | Salakhian G.S. | Arm | E | Wor | ? | ? | -6.818 | ? | 3.846 |
| 1686 | Salimov A.Kh. | Aze | A | Man | ? | ? | -7.955 | ? | -6.538 |
| 1687 | Salikhov M. | Tad | E | Cad | ? | ? | -10.435 | ? | -4.808 |
| 1688 | Saltykov N.P. | Rus | A | Wor | ? | ? | -14.348 | ? | -10.000 |
| 1689 | Salukvadze R.G. | Geo | E | Tec | ? | ? | 11.905 | ? | 3.846 |
| 1690 | Salykov K.S. | Uzb | E | Nom | ? | ? | -10.000 | ? | -7.000 |
| 1691 | Samaev P.L. | Rus | E | Man | ? | ? | -1.136 | ? | 15.600 |
| 1692 | Samarin V.I. | Rus | E | Int | Med | Med | 10.455 | Rad | 8.333 |
| 1693 | Samedova G.S. | Aze | E | Wor | ? | ? | -3.409 | ? | -3.077 |
| 1694 | Samilyk N.I. | Ukr | E | Nom | ? | ? | -6.522 | ? | -10.800 |
| 1695 | Samoilov A.I. | Ukr | E | Wor | ? | ? | 1.304 | ? | 12.885 |
| 1696 | Samoilov I.D. | Rus | A | Tec | ? | ? | -13.636 | ? | -16.000 |
| 1697 | Samolichenko I.I. | Rus | A | Man | ? | ? | -6.190 | ? | -7.200 |
| 1698 | Samoplavskii V.I. | Ukr | E | Nom | ? | ? | -5.238 | ? | -10.000 |
| 1699 | Samsonov A.S. | Mos | E | Man | App | RI | -10.000 | ? | 0.385 |
| 1700 | Samsonov N.A. | Rus | E | Wor | ? | ? | 1.304 | ? | 10.769 |
| 1701 | Samsonov Iu.G. | Rus | E | Nom | ? | RI | -10.435 | ? | -10.000 |
| 1702 | Sanduliak L.I. | Ukr | E | Int | LI | Med | 13.043 | Rad | 25.200 |
| 1703 | Sandurskii B.F. | Rus | E | Man | ? | App | -15.455 | ? | -3.600 |
| 1704 | Sanchat A.S. | Rus | E | Cad | ? | ? | -6.000 | ? | -14.038 |
| 1705 | Saparov Kh. | Tur | E | Wor | ? | ? | -14.348 | ? | 3.846 |
| 1706 | Sapegin A.A. | Rus | E | Wor | ? | ? | -2.609 | ? | -3.077 |
| 1707 | Saprykin A.B. | Rus | A | Wor | ? | ? | 2.143 | ? | -5.385 |
| 1708 | Saraev S.B. | Rus | E | Wor | ? | ? | 5.909 | Rad | 17.826 |
| 1709 | Sarakaev A.T. | Rus | E | Man | ? | ? | -11.364 | ? | 4.615 |
| 1710 | Sarkisian S.A. | Arm | E | Oth | Rad | ? | 22.692 | ? | 5.417 |
| 1711 | Sarsenov M.A. | Uzb | E | Man | ? | Cen | -0.435 | ? | -5.200 |
| 1712 | Sarsenov U. | Kaz | A | Man | ? | ? | -15.455 | ? | 2.000 |
| 1713 | Sarychev A.I. | Rus | E | Man | ? | ? | -3.478 | ? | 6.250 |
| 1714 | Satin B.F. | Uzb | E | Nom | ? | ? | -15.217 | ? | -10.577 |
| 1715 | Satybaldiev R.A. | Kir | E | Tec | ? | Cen | -7.826 | ? | 16.346 |
| 1716 | Saunin A.N. | Ukr | E | Tec | LI | LI | 20.250 | ? | 7.500 |
| 1717 | Safarov B.S. | Tad | E | Tec | ? | ? | -5.652 | ? | -2.308 |
| 1718 | Safarov I. | Tad | A | Man | ? | ? | -9.545 | ? | 0.385 |
| 1719 | Safarov Iu.O. | Uzb | E | Wor | ? | ? | -15.263 | ? | 0.385 |
| 1720 | Safarova R.N. | Aze | E | Wor | ? | ? | -5.000 | ? | -4.400 |
| 1721 | Safieva G. | Tad | A | Int | ? | ? | 10.500 | ? | -2.600 |
| 1722 | Safin M.M. | Rus | E | Man | ? | ? | 1.905 | ? | 4.615 |
| 1723 | Safiullin M.G. | Rus | A | Wor | ? | Cen | -2.174 | ? | -2.308 |
| 1724 | Safiullin R.F. | Rus | A | Man | ? | ? | -17.273 | Med | -10.652 |
| 1725 | Safonov A.K. | Kaz | E | Man | Cen | ? | 23.182 | Cen | 1.000 |
| 3000 | Sakharov A.D. | Mos | A | Int | Rad | Rad | 43.333 | . | . |
| 1726 | Sbitnev A.M. | Ukr | E | Wor | ? | ? | 1.304 | ? | -6.538 |
| 1727 | Svatkovskii V.V. | Rus | A | Man | ? | ? | -13.636 | ? | 7.308 |
| 1728 | Svid G.S. | Rus | A | Man | ? | ? | -18.261 | App | -8.571 |
| 1729 | Sebentsov A.E. | Mos | E | Tec | Rad | ? | 3.043 | Rad | 8.400 |
| 1730 | Sevriukov V.V. | Ukr | A | Cad | Cen | ? | -13.810 | ? | -0.769 |
| 3014 | Seitkulieva O.A. | Tur | E | Wor | ? | . | . | . | . |
| 1731 | Sekacheva R.I. | Rus | A | Wor | ? | ? | -18.261 | ? | -13.600 |
| 1732 | Seleznev A.I. | Rus | E | Nom | App | ? | -2.500 | ? | -6.957 |
| 1733 | Seleznev I.S. | Rus | A | Man | ? | ? | 6.000 | ? | 10.769 |
| 1734 | Seleznev S.V. | Rus | E | Tec | ? | ? | 24.783 | ? | 19.773 |
| 1735 | Selimov N. | Tur | E | Cad | ? | ? | -22.174 | ? | -8.800 |
| 1736 | Semenikhin A.V. | Kaz | E | Wor | ? | ? | 10.000 | ? | 7.308 |
| 1737 | Semenko V.I. | Rus | A | Tec | ? | Med | -6.522 | ? | -10.000 |
| 1738 | Semenov V.A. | Ukr | E | Int | ? | ? | 16.364 | ? | 4.615 |
| 1739 | Semenov V.M. (560) | Bel | E | Nom | App | Cen | -16.000 | Cen | 0.385 |
| 1740 | Semonov V.M. (523) | Rus | E | Mil | ? | ? | -18.182 | ? | -18.000 |
| 1741 | Semonova G.V. | Mos | A | Int | ? | ? | -30.000 | ? | 0.000 |
| 1742 | Semonova G.I. | Rus | E | Man | ? | ? | 3.750 | ? | 19.130 |
| 1743 | Semonova N.M. | Rus | A | Wor | ? | ? | -2.609 | ? | 8.077 |
| 1744 | Semukha V.I. | Bel | A | Cad | ? | ? | -21.304 | ? | 5.833 |
| 1745 | Sergienko V.I. | Rus | E | Nom | Cen | ? | -6.522 | ? | -3.077 |
| 1746 | Serdiukovskaia G.N. | Mos | A | Tec | ? | ? | -29.000 | ? | 6.042 |
| 1747 | Seredkin V.S. | Rus | E | Man | ? | ? | 14.737 | ? | -10.000 |
| 1748 | Setkin Iu.B. | Rus | E | Oth | ? | Med | 19.412 | ? | 28.077 |
| 1749 | Sefershaev F. | Uzb | E | Wor | ? | ? | -16.087 | ? | 0.192 |
| 1750 | Sidor I.N. | Ukr | A | Tec | ? | ? | -8.667 | Med | 4.583 |
| 1751 | Sidoreiko V.L. | Rus | A | Wor | ? | ? | 9.130 | ? | 5.962 |
| 1752 | Sidorenko V.D. | Ukr | A | Int | ? | LI | 8.000 | ? | 19.808 |
| 1753 | Sidorov A.A. | Rus | A | Oth | App | LI | -5.238 | ? | -1.346 |
| 1754 | Sidorov V.P. | Rus | E | Wor | ? | ? | -10.455 | ? | -12.500 |
| 1755 | Sidorchuk T.V. | Ukr | E | Wor | ? | ? | 5.652 | ? | 7.692 |
| 1756 | Silant'ev A.P. | Mos | A | Mil | ? | ? | -13.889 | ? | 9.200 |
| 1757 | Simvolokov V.V. | Ukr | E | Tec | ? | ? | 19.091 | ? | 18.800 |
| 1758 | Simonov M.P. | Mos | A | Man | ? | ? | -8.947 | ? | -5.455 |
| 1759 | Simonov S.B. | Rus | E | Wor | ? | ? | -6.522 | ? | 3.846 |
| 1760 | Simonian V.V. | Arm | E | Wor | ? | ? | 14.737 | ? | 11.346 |
| 1761 | Simonian K.A. | Arm | E | Int | ? | ? | 0.000 | ? | 0.000 |
| 1762 | Sinel'nikov V.M. | Ukr | E | Wor | ? | Pre | 1.304 | ? | -3.077 |
| 1763 | Siradze V.M. | Geo | E | Nom | ? | ? | 7.857 | ? | 3.636 |
| 1764 | Sirman V.V. | Ukr | E | Wor | ? | ? | -18.261 | ? | -20.385 |
| 1765 | Sitnikov A.P. | Rus | A | Oth | ? | ? | -14.348 | ? | -3.077 |
| 1766 | Skakun G.F. | Bel | A | Wor | ? | ? | -18.571 | ? | 5.417 |

```
1767 Skarulis R.I.           Lit A Tec ?    ?    29.286 ?     0.000
1768 Skvortsov V.V.          Rus E Tec ?    ?     5.217 ?    18.462
1769 Skiba I.I.              Mos A Nom ?    ?   -10.435 ?   -10.000
1770 Skokov V.V.             Ukr E Mil ?    ?   -18.261 ?    -6.538
1771 Skokov Iu.V.            Mos E Man ?   Cen  -3.333 ?     0.962
1772 Skrobuk I.I.            Bel E Mil ?    ?    -7.955 ?     3.333
1773 Skudra V.Ia.            Lat E Nom ?   LI   24.000 ?     8.600
1774 Skulme D.O.             Lat A Int ?    ?    36.667 ?    15.000
1775 Sleptsov S.E.           Rus A Wor ?    ?     9.565 ?     8.077
1776 Sliun'kov N.N.          Mos A Nom ?   App -13.684 ?   -34.286
1777 Smailova K.             Kir E Tec ?    ?   -22.000 ?     7.708
1778 Smailis A.Iu.           Lit E Tec Med  ?    28.571 ?     0.000
1779 Smirnov V.S.            Rus E Mil ?    ?    36.522 ?    24.615
1780 Smirnov D.G.            Ukr E Man LI   ?    26.957 ?     8.077
1781 Smolina Z.P.            Rus A Cad ?    ?    -8.000 ?   -11.600
1782 Smorodin I.M.           Rus E Wor ?    ?    19.348 ?    15.000
1783 Smyk N.M.               Rus A Wor ?    ?   -10.000 ?    -3.077
1784 Snegur M.I.             Mol E Nom ?   App   2.500 ?     0.000
1785 Sobolev V.V.            Rus E Wor ?    ?   -14.348 ?    -5.385
1786 Sobolev V.M.            Rus E Man ?    ?     0.000 ?     6.346
1787 Sobolev V.P.            Lat E Nom ?    ?   -14.211 ?    -8.462
1788 Sobchak A.A.            Rus E Int Rad LI   13.043 LI    3.846
1789 Sozinov A.A.            Ukr A Int ?    ?    -5.263 ?     0.385
1790 Sokolov A.A. (164)      Rus E Nom Cen  ?   -13.810 ?   -13.462
1791 Sokolov A.A. (207)      Rus E Int ?    ?    44.348 Cen  13.269
1792 Sokolov V.I.            Rus E Tec ?    ?    -5.455 ?     5.200
1793 Sokolov E.E.            Bel E Nom App  ?   -11.429 ?   -13.462
1794 Sokolov Iu.I.           Rus E Tec ?    ?     7.826 ?     7.308
1795 Sokolova Iu.Iu.         Mos A Mil ?    ?   -10.435 ?    -5.600
1796 Solntsev R.Kh.          Rus E Int LI   ?    14.286 LI   10.769
1797 Solov'ev Iu.B.          Mos A Int LI   ?   -12.353 ?     2.400
1798 Solodilov Iu.I.         Rus E Tec ?   App  -6.522 ?     8.800
1799 Soltanov B.             Tur A Wor ?    ?   -14.348 ?     2.800
1800 Sopyev M.               Tur A Man ?    ?   -22.174 ?   -11.923
1801 Sorokin A.A.            Kaz E Wor ?    ?     5.217 ?    10.385
1802 Sorokin A.I.            Mos A Mil ?    ?   -15.455 ?   -14.400
1803 Sorokin I.V.            Rus E Tec LI   LI   25.588 LI   -1.154
1804 Sorokin M.I.            Rus E Mil ?    ?   -18.261 ?   -10.000
1805 Sorochik Iu.Iu.         Ukr E Cad ?    ?    18.409 ?    21.905
1806 Soskovets O.N.          Kaz E Man ?   Cen   9.091 ?     8.200
1807 Sotnikov N.I.           Rus E Man ?    ?   -10.476 ?    13.846
1808 Spanderashvili T.M.     Geo E Wor ?    ?    16.000 ?     6.346
1809 Spasskii I.D.           Rus A Man ?    ?     6.316 ?    -3.077
1810 Spiridonov M.V.         Rus A Man Pre  ?   -11.579 ?   -23.846
3004 Spiridonov Iu.A.        Rus E Nom .    .      .    ?   -11.600
1811 Stadmik V.Ia.           Rus E Tec ?   LI   30.000 Rad  17.692
1812 Stakviliavichius M.I.   Lit E Tec ?   LI   30.000 ?     0.000
1813 Stankevich S.B.         Mos E Int Rad Med  18.261 Rad  15.600
1814 Stankovich E.F.         Ukr A Int ?    ?    23.810 ?     0.000
1815 Starovoitov V.K.        Bel A Man Cen  ?    -7.273 ?     0.385
1816 Starovoitova G.V.       Arm E Int Rad Rad  43.000 Rad  20.000
1817 Starodubtsev V.A.       Rus A Man LI   ?    -1.765 ?    16.800
1818 Starodubtsev D.A.       Rus E Man ?    ?   -16.667 ?     7.200
1819 Starostina T.A.         Mos A Tec ?   Med  10.909 ?    -3.077
1820 Statuliavichius V.A.    Lit E Int Med  ?    18.000 ?     0.000
1821 Stel'mashonok V.I.      Bel A Int ?    ?    16.957 ?    14.231
1822 Stepanenko A.V.         Bel A Int ?    ?    13.043 ?    13.200
1823 Stepanov V.N.           Rus E Man RI  App -11.364 ?     3.600
1824 Stepanova G.Samb.       Rus E Tec ?    ?     3.913 ?     8.077
1825 Stepanova G.S.          Rus A Man ?    ?   -12.500 ?   -10.000
1826 Stepnadze T.S.          Geo E Wor ?    ?     0.227 ?     2.083
1827 Stefanenko I.D.         Rus A Oth Cen  ?   -10.435 ?   -13.462
1828 Stipakov E.G.           Rus E Tec ?    ?     9.524 ?    14.400
1829 Stolbunov V.K.          Kaz E Man ?    ?    19.130 ?    12.308
1830 Stoumova G.I.           Rus E Man Med  ?   -11.429 ?    10.833
1831 Strautin' I.F.          Lat A Man ?    ?    32.000 ?    27.059
1832 Strelavin S.V.          Rus E Man ?    ?     4.091 ?     3.846
1833 Strelkov A.I.           Rus E Wor ?    ?    11.739 ?    22.600
1834 Stroev E.S.             Rus E Nom Cen  ?   -14.000 ?   -27.308
1835 Strukov N.A.            Rus E Tec Rad RI   14.286 ?     0.385
1836 Studenikin M.Ia.        Mos A Tec ?    ?   -38.000 ?    -3.600
1837 Supin Iu.B.             Mos A Cad ?    ?   -12.273 ?   -13.462
1838 Stupina E.D.            Rus E Tec ?    ?     5.217 ?     3.600
1839 Subbi O.I.              Est A Int ?    ?    20.938 ?    29.000
1840 Subbotina O.G.          Rus E Tec ?    ?    -4.545 ?     0.000
1841 Sulakshin S.S.          Rus E Int Med Med  32.273 ?    11.667
1842 Suleimenov O.O.         Kaz E Int LI   ?     2.222 LI    2.400
1843 Sultangazin U.M.        Kaz E Int ?   Med -14.348 ?     4.808
1844 Sumarokov I.A.          Rus E Man ?    ?    -2.609 ?     3.846
1845 Suntsov S.D.            Rus E Man ?    ?    14.091 ?   -20.400
1846 Suprunov L.Ia.          Rus A Cad ?    ?   -11.304 ?    -3.077
1847 Surkov M.S.             Arm E Mil ?   RI   -2.609 RI    0.385
1848 Surmanidze Ts.O.        Geo E Wor ?    ?    15.217 ?     0.385
1849 Sukharev A.Ia.          Rus E Nom Cen App -16.667 ?    -5.625
1850 Sukhinin V.Iu.          Rus E Wor ?    ?   -10.435 ?    -3.077
```

| | | | | | | | | |
|---|---|---|---|---|---|---|---|---|
| 1851 | Sukhov L.I. | Ukr | E | Wor | LI | RI | -3.077 | RI | 14.583 |
| 1852 | Sukhorukov D.S. | Ukr | E | Mil | ? | ? | -23.636 | ? | -15.600 |
| 1853 | Sushko B.I. | Ukr | A | Wor | ? | ? | -6.087 | ? | 7.692 |
| 1854 | Sadykov U. | Kir | E | Nom | ? | ? | -19.375 | ? | -3.600 |
| 1855 | Syrgii A.A. | Mol | E | Man | ? | ? | -2.500 | ? | 6.250 |
| 1856 | Sysoev V.A. | Rus | A | Cad | ? | ? | -19.545 | ? | -8.000 |
| 1857 | Sysoev V.S. | Mos | A | Cad | ? | ? | -14.348 | ? | -17.885 |
| 1858 | Sychev N.Ia. | Mos | A | Oth | ? | ? | -28.333 | ? | -8.462 |
| 1859 | Sychev Iu.P. | Rus | E | Mil | ? | ? | 8.696 | ? | 11.538 |
| 1860 | Taabaldiev Ye. | Kir | E | Wor | ? | ? | -27.333 | ? | -7.200 |
| 1861 | Tabeev F.A. | Rus | E | Nom | ? | ? | -10.435 | ? | -10.000 |
| 1862 | Tabukashvili R.Sh. | Geo | E | Tec | Rad | ? | 0.000 | ? | 0.000 |
| 1863 | Tavkhelidze A.N. | Geo | E | Int | Rad | ? | 19.722 | ? | 0.000 |
| 1864 | Tagandurdyev B. | Tur | E | Nom | ? | ? | -18.261 | ? | 0.000 |
| 1865 | Tazhimuratova A. | Uzb | E | Tec | ? | ? | -2.609 | ? | 5.000 |
| 1866 | Talanchuk P.M. | Ukr | E | Int | ? | ? | 16.957 | ? | 17.692 |
| 1867 | Talashin I.S. | Rus | E | Tec | ? | ? | 9.130 | ? | 10.769 |
| 1868 | Tamberg Ye.M. | Est | A | Int | ? | ? | 38.667 | ? | 0.000 |
| 1869 | Tapanian S.M. | Arm | A | Wor | ? | ? | -2.609 | ? | 17.692 |
| 1870 | Tarazevich G.S. | Bel | E | Nom | Cen | Cen | -1.250 | ? | -2.115 |
| 1871 | Taranov I.T. | Rus | E | Nom | ? | ? | -22.727 | ? | -10.000 |
| 1872 | Tarasov A.P. | Rus | E | Tec | ? | ? | -8.000 | ? | 4.615 |
| 1873 | Tarasov I.S. | Ukr | A | Cad | ? | ? | -10.000 | ? | -1.200 |
| 1874 | Tarnavskii G.S. | Bel | E | Nom | ? | ? | -13.810 | Med | -3.889 |
| 1875 | Tatarchuk V.I. | Rus | A | Man | ? | ? | 16.957 | ? | 12.115 |
| 1876 | Tatarchuk N.F. | Rus | E | Nom | ? | ? | -10.435 | ? | -6.538 |
| 1877 | Tashev S.M. | Tur | E | Tec | ? | ? | 37.000 | ? | 14.231 |
| 1878 | Tedeev L.R. | Geo | E | Wor | ? | ? | -2.174 | ? | 0.400 |
| 1879 | Telegin B.L. | Rus | A | Cad | ? | ? | 13.043 | ? | 2.308 |
| 1880 | Telezin A.F. | Ukr | E | Wor | ? | ? | 12.391 | ? | 1.346 |
| 1881 | Temirbaev V.B. | Kaz | E | Nom | ? | ? | -20.909 | ? | 0.385 |
| 1882 | Temnogrudova Z.S. | Rus | A | Tec | ? | ? | -2.778 | ? | 0.000 |
| 1883 | Ten R.L. | Kir | E | Man | ? | ? | -0.556 | ? | 14.783 |
| 1884 | Terekhova Ye.I. | Rus | E | Man | ? | ? | -8.095 | ? | 0.385 |
| 1885 | Tereshkova V.V. | Mos | A | Nom | ? | ? | -14.348 | ? | -11.923 |
| 1886 | Terniuk N.Ye. | Ukr | E | Tec | Med | ? | 7.895 | ? | 14.231 |
| 1887 | Tertyshnyi E.A. | Rus | E | Man | ? | ? | -8.636 | ? | 0.000 |
| 1888 | Tetenov V.A. | Rus | E | Man | ? | ? | 3.333 | ? | 2.083 |
| 1889 | Tileubaeva K.T. | Kaz | E | Wor | ? | ? | -18.500 | ? | 0.385 |
| 1890 | Timashova N.I. | Rus | A | Oth | Pre | ? | -15.263 | ? | 5.909 |
| 1891 | Timchenko V.M. | Rus | E | Wor | ? | ? | 20.870 | ? | 7.308 |
| 1892 | Timchenko M.A. | Rus | E | Man | ? | ? | 5.217 | ? | 10.769 |
| 1893 | Tikhonenkov Ye.P. | Ukr | E | Tec | ? | ? | 21.304 | ? | 7.308 |
| 1894 | Tikhonov V.A. | Mos | A | Int | ? | ? | 28.333 | ? | 8.846 |
| 1895 | Tikhonov G.I. | Tad | E | Tec | ? | ? | -6.522 | ? | -11.923 |
| 1896 | Tikhonovich I.S. | Lit | E | Int | ? | LI | -5.652 | Cen | 5.200 |
| 3005 | Tkalenko N.I. | Ukr | A | Int | . | . | ? | 7.200 |
| 1897 | Tkachev Z.N. | Bel | E | Tec | Med | ? | -0.952 | ? | 5.000 |
| 1898 | Tkachenko S.N. | Kaz | E | Tec | ? | ? | 20.227 | ? | 17.115 |
| 1899 | Tkachuk V.M. | Ukr | E | Man | ? | ? | 29.318 | ? | 19.800 |
| 1900 | Tkemaladze G.A. | Geo | E | Cad | ? | ? | 9.000 | ? | 10.870 |
| 1901 | Tlostanov V.K. | Rus | E | Int | ? | Med | -10.435 | ? | -10.000 |
| 1902 | Tozik L.A. | Bel | A | Wor | ? | ? | -11.739 | ? | 2.400 |
| 1903 | Tolpezhnikov V.F. | Lat | E | Tec | Rad | LI | 41.538 | ? | 24.118 |
| 1904 | Tolstoukhov I.A. | Rus | E | Nom | ? | App | -18.261 | ? | -3.077 |
| 1905 | Tomkus V.P. | Lit | E | Int | Rad | ? | 62.500 | ? | 0.000 |
| 1906 | Toome I.Kh. | Est | E | Nom | Med | ? | 16.667 | ? | 0.000 |
| 1907 | Travkin N.I. | Rus | E | Int | ? | Rad | 16.957 | Rad | 21.154 |
| 1908 | Tret'iak I.M. | Mos | A | Mil | ? | ? | -21.538 | ? | -13.462 |
| 1909 | Trefilov V.I. | Ukr | A | Int | ? | ? | -17.000 | ? | -25.882 |
| 1910 | Troitskii A.Ia. | Rus | A | Tec | App | ? | -6.522 | ? | 1.600 |
| 1911 | Trofimov A.V. | Rus | E | Man | ? | ? | 0.455 | ? | 20.962 |
| 1912 | Trofimov V.I. | Rus | E | Tec | ? | ? | 23.571 | Cen | 28.077 |
| 1913 | Trokhimets M.A. | Ukr | A | Wor | ? | ? | 9.091 | ? | 3.846 |
| 1914 | Trubilin N.T. | Mos | A | Nom | ? | Med | -18.261 | ? | -13.462 |
| 1915 | Trubin A.A. | Rus | A | Wor | ? | ? | 7.609 | ? | 14.231 |
| 1916 | Trudoliubov A.I. | Rus | A | Man | Cen | ? | -6.522 | ? | 14.231 |
| 1917 | Tubolets I.I. | Bel | A | Wor | ? | ? | -2.609 | ? | 8.400 |
| 1918 | Tuzov V.N. | Mos | A | Cad | ? | ? | -14.348 | ? | -13.462 |
| 1919 | Tumetova M.M. | Kaz | E | Wor | ? | ? | -14.348 | ? | 10.800 |
| 1920 | Tupolev A.A. | Mos | A | Man | ? | ? | -11.364 | ? | -10.000 |
| 1921 | Turabov G.S. | Aze | E | Int | ? | ? | 24.583 | ? | -10.000 |
| 1922 | Turaeva M. | Uzb | E | Wor | ? | ? | -5.000 | ? | 3.462 |
| 1923 | Turganbaev D.T. | Uzb | E | Wor | ? | ? | -4.524 | ? | 5.800 |
| 1924 | Turenko V.S. | Kaz | E | Tec | ? | ? | 31.818 | LI | 10.769 |
| 1925 | Turysov K. | Mos | A | Nom | ? | Cen | -19.375 | ? | -10.417 |
| 1926 | Tutov N.D. | Rus | E | Mil | ? | Rad | 37.368 | ? | 17.200 |
| 1927 | Tukhtabaev A.T. | Uzb | E | Wor | ? | ? | -4.348 | ? | 6.538 |
| 1928 | Tkhor A.I. | Ukr | A | Wor | App | ? | -2.609 | ? | -3.913 |
| 1929 | Tyminskii G.A. | Ukr | E | Man | ? | ? | -10.435 | ? | -8.077 |
| 1930 | Tynspoeg G.A. | Est | E | Nom | ? | ? | 12.727 | ? | 11.000 |
| 1931 | Tyugu Ye.Kh. | Est | A | Int | ? | LI | 20.417 | ? | 0.000 |
| 1932 | Tiulebekov K.Kh. | Kaz | E | Nom | ? | ? | -11.579 | ? | -21.111 |
| 1933 | Tiuliandin A.D. | Mos | A | Cad | ? | ? | -15.238 | ? | -3.077 |
| 1934 | Tiupa S.V. | Ukr | E | Man | ? | ? | 20.476 | ? | 7.885 |

| | | | | | | | | |
|---|---|---|---|---|---|---|---|---|
| 1935 | Tiurina T.V. | Rus | E | Tec | ? | ? | 3.913 | ? | 9.583 |
| 1936 | Tiutriumov A.M. | Rus | A | Cad | ? | ? | 14.375 | ? | 17.692 |
| 1937 | Ubaidullaeva R.A. | Uzb | A | Int | Med | Pre | -11.905 | LI | 1.400 |
| 1938 | Uvarov A.I. | Rus | A | Mil | ? | ? | 19.348 | ? | 10.962 |
| 1939 | Ugarov B.S. | Mos | A | Int | ? | ? | -6.667 | ? | 0.385 |
| 1940 | Udalov A.V. | Rus | E | Man | ? | RI | -4.545 | ? | 10.769 |
| 1941 | Ulasevich E.G. | Bel | E | Wor | ? | ? | -2.609 | ? | 3.846 |
| 1942 | Ul'ianov M.A. | Rus | A | Int | ? | ? | -4.545 | ? | 0.000 |
| 1943 | Umalatova S.Z. | Rus | A | Wor | ? | Cen | -18.667 | RI | -6.538 |
| 1944 | Umarkhodzhaev M.I. | Uzb | E | Int | App | App | -12.727 | ? | 5.625 |
| 1945 | Umerenkov A.M. | Rus | E | Man | ? | ? | -2.609 | ? | 14.400 |
| 1946 | Uoka K.K. | Lit | E | Wor | ? | LI | 41.071 | ? | 0.000 |
| 1947 | Urvant V.N. | Ukr | E | Mil | ? | ? | 9.130 | ? | 7.308 |
| 1948 | Usenbekov K.U. | Kir | A | Oth | ? | ? | -17.895 | ? | -10.000 |
| 1949 | Usilina N.A. | Rus | E | Tec | ? | ? | -13.182 | ? | -10.000 |
| 1950 | Usichenko I.I. | Ukr | A | Cad | ? | ? | -10.435 | ? | -6.346 |
| 1951 | Usmanov G.I. | Rus | E | Nom | ? | ? | -6.522 | ? | -17.000 |
| 1952 | Usmanov R.K. | Uzb | E | Tec | ? | ? | -6.522 | ? | 2.000 |
| 1953 | Usian S.V. | Arm | E | Tec | ? | ? | 13.250 | ? | 18.043 |
| 1954 | Utkin V.F. | Ukr | A | Man | ? | ? | 0.000 | Med | 4.583 |
| 1955 | Ushakov V.S. | Rus | E | Wor | ? | ? | -10.500 | ? | 7.308 |
| 1956 | Fazletdinov M.G. | Rus | A | Man | ? | ? | -11.364 | ? | 0.385 |
| 1957 | Falin V.M. | Mos | A | Nom | ? | ? | -15.455 | Med | -6.538 |
| 1958 | Falin M.I. | Rus | A | Oth | ? | ? | -14.348 | ? | -0.962 |
| 1959 | Fal'k P.P. | Rus | E | Mil | Cen | ? | 38.636 | ? | 13.269 |
| 1960 | Fargiev Kh.A. | Rus | E | Tec | LI | Med | 15.000 | ? | 0.000 |
| 1961 | Fatullaev M. | Tad | E | Tec | ? | ? | -10.909 | ? | 3.846 |
| 1962 | Fedirko P.S. | Mos | A | Nom | ? | ? | -15.455 | ? | -10.800 |
| 1963 | Fedoriv R.N. | Ukr | E | Int | ? | ? | 14.130 | ? | 45.000 |
| 1964 | Fedorov A.P. | Uzb | E | Man | ? | ? | -6.522 | ? | 0.385 |
| 1965 | Fedorov N.V. | Rus | E | Int | LI | ? | 37.059 | LI | 27.708 |
| 1966 | Fedorov S.N. | Mos | A | Man | LI | Med | 22.813 | ? | 0.385 |
| 1967 | Fedotova V.I. | Mos | A | Int | ? | ? | -21.500 | ? | -13.462 |
| 1968 | Fediashin V.I. | Rus | E | Man | ? | RI | -10.455 | ? | -1.667 |
| 1969 | Fes'kov N.S. | Bel | E | Tec | ? | ? | -0.909 | ? | -0.200 |
| 1970 | Filippov V.P. | Rus | E | Tec | App | LI | 13.043 | ? | 0.385 |
| 1971 | Filippova V.G. | Rus | A | Man | ? | ? | -18.261 | ? | 3.077 |
| 1972 | Filonov G.N. | Mos | A | Int | ? | ? | -14.706 | ? | -10.000 |
| 1973 | Fil'shin G.I. | Rus | E | Int | Rad | Rad | 21.000 | Rad | 28.800 |
| 1974 | Finogenov V.V. | Rus | A | Wor | ? | ? | -6.250 | ? | 7.500 |
| 1975 | Firsov A.V. | Mos | E | Oth | ? | ? | 11.364 | ? | 10.417 |
| 1976 | Fisinin V.I. | Rus | A | Man | ? | App | 5.500 | ? | 4.800 |
| 1977 | Fokin V.P. | Ukr | E | Nom | ? | ? | -5.000 | ? | -1.250 |
| 1978 | Fomenko V.L. | Bel | E | Tec | LI | LI | 9.130 | LI | 14.808 |
| 1979 | Fomenko G.I. | Rus | A | Int | ? | ? | -1.500 | ? | -3.077 |
| 1980 | Fomin V.I. | Rus | E | Wor | ? | ? | -9.524 | ? | 2.000 |
| 1981 | Fominykh V.N. | Kaz | E | Wor | ? | ? | 9.130 | ? | 13.800 |
| 1982 | Foteev V.K. | Rus | E | Nom | ? | ? | -6.522 | ? | 0.000 |
| 1983 | Frolov I.T. | Ukr | E | Nom | ? | ? | -17.000 | ? | -20.385 |
| 1984 | Frolov K.V. | Mos | A | Int | ? | ? | -4.667 | ? | -3.077 |
| 1985 | Fuzhenko I.V. | Uzb | E | Mil | ? | ? | -7.619 | ? | 3.600 |
| 1986 | F'iuk I.V. | Est | E | Int | ? | LI | 52.273 | ? | 0.000 |
| 1987 | Khabibullin R.Kh. | Rus | E | Nom | ? | Pre | -10.435 | ? | -10.000 |
| 1988 | Khadzhiev S.N. | Rus | E | Man | LI | ? | 14.545 | LI | 20.833 |
| 1989 | Khadipash Iu.R. | Rus | E | Wor | ? | ? | -11.364 | ? | 2.500 |
| 1990 | Khadyrkye I.D. | Mol | E | Cad | ? | Med | 11.667 | ? | 3.846 |
| 1991 | Khaeev I. | Tad | E | Nom | ? | ? | -2.609 | ? | -6.538 |
| 1992 | Khaknazarov S. | Uzb | E | Wor | ? | ? | -10.000 | ? | 1.818 |
| 1993 | Khalilov S.Kh. | Rus | A | Tec | ? | ? | -11.905 | ? | -2.400 |
| 1994 | Khalilova S.M. | Aze | A | Wor | ? | ? | -9.091 | ? | -4.167 |
| 1995 | Khalimov I. | Tad | E | Nom | ? | ? | -17.727 | ? | -10.000 |
| 1996 | Khallik K.S. | Est | E | Int | Rad | ? | 20.385 | ? | 16.731 |
| 1997 | Khandzhian G.S. | Arm | E | Int | ? | ? | 19.000 | ? | 11.800 |
| 1998 | Khanzadian S.N. | Arm | E | Int | ? | ? | 18.750 | ? | 13.913 |
| 1999 | Kharitonov V.F. | Rus | E | Man | ? | Cen | -6.522 | ? | 11.538 |
| 2000 | Kharif S.L. | Rus | E | Man | ? | ? | 36.364 | ? | 14.400 |
| 2001 | Kharchenko G.P. | Ukr | E | Nom | ? | ? | -1.750 | ? | -10.800 |
| 2002 | Kharchenko K.A. | Rus | E | Mil | ? | Med | 16.957 | Med | 10.769 |
| 2003 | Kharchuk B.I. | Ukr | A | Mil | ? | ? | -10.435 | ? | -3.846 |
| 2004 | Khaug A.V. | Est | E | Tec | ? | ? | 28.333 | ? | 40.000 |
| 2005 | Khachatrian V.Kh. | Arm | E | Wor | ? | ? | 0.000 | ? | 14.231 |
| 2006 | Khachirov I.A. | Rus | E | Man | ? | ? | -15.294 | ? | -0.870 |
| 2007 | Khashimov A. | Tad | E | Man | ? | ? | -4.565 | ? | 1.923 |
| 2008 | Khvorov A.I. | Rus | E | Tec | ? | Med | -6.522 | ? | 0.000 |
| 2009 | Khitron P.A. | Rus | E | Man | ? | ? | 9.091 | ? | 25.263 |
| 2010 | Khitrun L.I. | Rus | E | Nom | ? | ? | -20.500 | ? | -14.400 |
| 2011 | Klebtsov K.A. | Bel | E | Wor | ? | ? | -10.435 | ? | 0.000 |
| 2012 | Kloponina I.V. | Ukr | E | Wor | ? | ? | -8.500 | ? | -4.783 |
| 2013 | Khmel' V.P. | Rus | A | Wor | Cen | ? | 5.217 | ? | 12.000 |
| 2014 | Khmura V.V. | Rus | E | Cad | App | Cen | -0.909 | ? | -7.308 |
| 2015 | Khodzhakov O. | Tur | E | Nom | ? | ? | -21.818 | Cen | -7.500 |
| 2016 | Khodzhamuradov A. | Tur | E | Nom | ? | ? | -20.455 | ? | -4.167 |
| 2017 | Khodyrev G.M. | Rus | E | Nom | Med | ? | -5.455 | ? | -6.538 |
| 2018 | Kohamkhanova N.Kh. | Rus | E | Wor | ? | ? | 1.304 | ? | 13.462 |
| 2019 | Kholboeva Z.A. | Tad | A | Wor | ? | ? | -14.348 | ? | 0.385 |

| | | | | | | | | | |
|---|---|---|---|---|---|---|---|---|---|
| 2020 | Khomeniuk A.P. | Rus | E | Tec | ? | ? | -25.714 | ? | -13.600 |
| 2021 | Khomiakov A.A. | Rus | E | Nom | ? | ? | -16.316 | ? | -16.000 |
| 2022 | Khomiakov A.I. | Rus | E | Man | ? | ? | 6.667 | ? | -1.923 |
| 2023 | Khorol'skaia N.I. | Ukr | E | Wor | ? | ? | -6.522 | ? | -10.000 |
| 2024 | Khokhlov A.F. | Rus | E | Int | ? | ? | -4.118 | ? | 5.833 |
| 2025 | Khrennikov T.N. | Mos | A | Int | ? | ? | -9.412 | ? | -3.077 |
| 2026 | Khripunov N.F. | Rus | E | Man | ? | ? | 5.217 | ? | 3.846 |
| 2027 | Khubaev V.A. | Geo | E | Wor | ? | ? | 8.182 | ? | -3.077 |
| 2028 | Khubiev Kh.N. | Kir | E | Man | ? | ? | -13.000 | ? | 8.889 |
| 2029 | Khugaeva D.V. | Geo | E | Man | ? | ? | 5.500 | ? | -14.583 |
| 2030 | Khudaerov P. | Uzb | E | Man | ? | ? | -4.348 | ? | 10.800 |
| 2031 | Khudaibergenova R.M. | Uzb | E | Nom | ? | ? | -7.826 | ? | -7.308 |
| 2032 | Khudonazarov D. | Tad | E | Int | LI | ? | 22.609 | ? | 22.800 |
| 2033 | Khudiakov R.M. | Rus | A | Tec | ? | ? | -6.000 | ? | 3.750 |
| 2034 | Khuzhamuratova S.I. | Uzb | E | Tec | ? | ? | -8.000 | ? | 3.333 |
| 2035 | Khurtsiia M.V. | Geo | A | Wor | ? | ? | 10.294 | ? | -7.400 |
| 2036 | Khusanbaev M.A. | Tad | E | Wor | ? | ? | -11.364 | ? | -3.077 |
| 2037 | Khusanov A.U. | Uzb | E | Int | App | ? | -5.789 | ? | -3.600 |
| 2038 | Tsavro Iu.S. | Ukr | E | Tec | ? | ? | 5.652 | ? | 7.308 |
| 2039 | Tsalko A.V. | Rus | E | Mil | ? | ? | 13.043 | ? | 11.154 |
| 2040 | Tsarevskii A.L. | Ukr | A | Wor | ? | ? | 5.217 | ? | 14.231 |
| 2041 | Tsarenko A.M. | Ukr | E | Man | ? | ? | -15.909 | ? | -3.077 |
| 2042 | Tsereteli Z.K. | Geo | A | Int | ? | ? | 0.227 | ? | 6.600 |
| 2043 | Tsigel'nikov A.S. | Rus | A | Man | ? | ? | 13.478 | ? | 16.000 |
| 2044 | Tsintsadze S.F. | Geo | A | Int | ? | ? | -6.389 | ? | -4.423 |
| 2045 | Tsirulis A.Ia. | Lat | E | Int | LI | ? | 36.333 | ? | 8.478 |
| 2046 | Tso V.I. | Uzb | E | Man | ? | ? | 9.048 | ? | 1.905 |
| 2047 | Tsoi K.N. | Rus | E | Tec | ? | ? | -6.522 | ? | 7.708 |
| 2048 | Tsybukh V.I. | Ukr | E | Nom | ? | Med | -18.182 | ? | -10.000 |
| 2049 | Tsyganov V.I. | Rus | A | Cad | ? | ? | -3.182 | ? | 6.042 |
| 2050 | Tsykalo R.I. | Rus | E | Cad | ? | ? | 19.348 | ? | 11.818 |
| 2051 | Tsypliaev S.A. | Rus | A | Int | Med | LI | 28.696 | LI | -3.654 |
| 2052 | Tsyrenov Zh.Ts. | Rus | E | Wor | ? | ? | -2.273 | ? | 4.615 |
| 2053 | Tsyu N.A. | Mol | E | Nom | ? | ? | -3.333 | ? | -3.600 |
| 2054 | Tsiurupa V.A. | Mos | E | Tec | ? | ? | 6.304 | ? | 3.846 |
| 2055 | Chabanov A.I. | Ukr | E | Man | Med | ? | -7.727 | ? | -19.200 |
| 2056 | Chaenkov V.A. | Rus | A | Oth | ? | ? | -14.348 | ? | 0.000 |
| 2057 | Chaika K.F. | Ukr | A | Tec | ? | ? | -9.524 | ? | -10.000 |
| 2058 | Chausova E.V. | Rus | A | Wor | ? | ? | -18.182 | ? | 7.308 |
| 2059 | Chebanu D.P. | Mol | E | Wor | ? | ? | 5.000 | ? | 10.769 |
| 2060 | Chebotar' B.P. | Mol | E | Man | ? | ? | 9.130 | ? | 10.800 |
| 2061 | Chebrikov V.M. | Mos | A | Nom | ? | ? | -35.000 | ? | -13.462 |
| 2062 | Chekov N.V. | Mos | A | Mil | ? | ? | -14.615 | ? | -12.800 |
| 2063 | Chekolis A.Iu.Iu. | Lit | E | Int | ? | ? | -20.000 | ? | 0.000 |
| 2064 | Chelyshev V.A. | Ukr | E | Int | LI | Rad | 23.500 | Rad | 2.692 |
| 2065 | Chemodanov Iu.M. | Rus | A | Tec | Med | ? | 9.130 | ? | 17.692 |
| 2066 | Chentsov N.I. | Ukr | E | Wor | ? | ? | 7.632 | ? | 8.654 |
| 2067 | Chepanis A.K. | Lat | E | Nom | ? | ? | 26.667 | ? | 0.000 |
| 2068 | Chepelev N.M. | Kir | E | ? | . | ? | -21.500 | ? | -10.000 |
| 2069 | Chepurnaia M.A. | Ukr | E | Tec | ? | ? | -10.000 | ? | -2.308 |
| 2070 | Chervonopiskii S.V. | Ukr | A | Cad | RI | ? | -11.667 | ? | -10.000 |
| 2071 | Cherednichenko F.G. | Rus | E | Man | ? | ? | -18.261 | ? | 3.846 |
| 2072 | Cherepovich V.A. | Ukr | E | Cad | ? | Cen | 5.217 | ? | 5.385 |
| 2073 | Cherkasova A.F. | Rus | A | Wor | ? | ? | -6.522 | ? | 10.769 |
| 2074 | Cherkeziia O.E. | Geo | E | ? | ? | ? | 1.522 | ? | -0.800 |
| 2075 | Chernavin B.N. | Aze | E | Mil | ? | App | -6.522 | ? | 1.600 |
| 2076 | Chernenko V.T. | Rus | E | Wor | ? | ? | -13.636 | ? | -6.538 |
| 2077 | Chernichenko Iu.D. | Mos | E | Int | Rad | ? | 9.474 | ? | 8.400 |
| 2078 | Chernykh A.G. | Rus | E | Man | ? | ? | 11.739 | RI | 17.692 |
| 2079 | Chernykh G.A. | Rus | E | Tec | ? | ? | 11.000 | ? | -6.538 |
| 2080 | Chernyshev O.V. | Bel | A | Tec | Rad | ? | 12.000 | ? | 8.333 |
| 2081 | Chernyshova L.P. | Rus | A | Wor | ? | ? | -15.909 | ? | -3.846 |
| 2082 | Cherniaev A.S. | Mos | A | Nom | ? | ? | -12.500 | ? | -10.000 |
| 2083 | Cherniaev N.F. | Rus | E | Wor | ? | ? | -6.522 | ? | 7.308 |
| 2084 | Cherniak V.K. | Ukr | E | Int | ? | ? | 33.478 | ? | 26.458 |
| 2085 | Chetberova M.G. | Aze | E | Wor | ? | ? | -8.947 | ? | -3.077 |
| 2086 | Chekhoev A.G. | Geo | E | Nom | ? | ? | -16.667 | ? | -14.400 |
| 2087 | Chigogidze G.E. | Geo | E | Nom | ? | ? | 5.526 | ? | 7.778 |
| 2088 | Chizhov A.A. | Rus | E | Man | ? | ? | 1.304 | ? | 7.308 |
| 2089 | Chiladze O.I. | Geo | A | Int | ? | ? | 0.000 | ? | 0.000 |
| 2090 | Chilaia E.G. | Geo | E | Tec | ? | ? | -1.364 | ? | 0.000 |
| 2091 | Chilebaev T.B. | Kir | A | Man | ? | ? | -16.957 | ? | 1.538 |
| 2092 | Chimpoi M.I. | Mol | E | Int | Rad | ? | 8.889 | ? | 13.600 |
| 2093 | Chitiia E.G. | Geo | E | Wor | ? | ? | 3.182 | ? | 4.167 |
| 2094 | Chichik Iu.M. | Rus | E | Man | ? | ? | 1.304 | ? | 3.846 |
| 2095 | Chobanu I.K. | Mol | A | Int | ? | ? | 9.130 | ? | 14.231 |
| 2096 | Cholokian K.S. | Geo | E | Wor | ? | ? | -9.524 | ? | -5.385 |
| 2097 | Chursina P.M. | Kaz | A | Wor | ? | Cen | -12.500 | ? | 11.389 |
| 2098 | Chukhraev A.M. | Rus | E | Tec | ? | ? | 5.909 | ? | -5.962 |
| 2099 | Chkheidze Z.A. | Geo | E | ? | ? | ? | 14.333 | ? | -5.417 |
| 2100 | Chkheidze T.N. | Geo | A | Int | ? | ? | 13.250 | ? | 2.500 |
| 2101 | Chiapas V.I. | Lit | E | Tec | ? | ? | 40.909 | ? | 0.000 |
| 2102 | Shabalin G.G. | Rus | E | Man | ? | ? | 9.130 | ? | 3.846 |
| 2103 | Shabanov V.M. | Ukr | E | Mil | ? | ? | -2.609 | ? | 3.846 |
| 2104 | Shabanov T.Kh. | Rus | E | Wor | ? | ? | -10.435 | ? | -3.077 |

```
2105  Shagiev Kh.Kh.         Rus E Man ?       ?   -11.364 ?    -3.077
2106  Shaidulin M.I.         Rus A Oth ?       ?   -22.174 ?     0.385
2107  Shaimiev M.Sh.         Rus E ?    .      ?   -10.435 ?   -13.462
2108  Shaklycheva D.         Tur E Wor ?       ?    -6.522 ?    -3.077
2109  Shalaev S.A.           Mos A Nom ?     App -11.364 ?     1.154
2110  Shalyev A.B.           Tur A Wor ?       ?   -13.636 ?    -3.077
2111  Shamanadze Sh.N.       Geo A Int ?       ?    18.750 ?     0.000
2112  Shamba T.M.            Geo E Cad Cen ?    -15.625 Cen   0.000
2113  Shamiladze V.M.        Geo E Int ?       ?    14.348 ?     0.000
2114  Shamin N.V.            Rus A Tec ?       ?     5.000 ?     0.000
2115  Shamikhin A.M.         Lat A Cad ?       ?   -14.545 ?    -5.000
2116  Shamshev I.B.          Rus E Int Rad Rad  39.783 ?    10.769
2117  Shamyrbekov K.I.       Kir A Wor ?       ?   -23.636 ?    11.522
2118  Shapovalenko V.A.      Rus E Tec Rad Rad  35.000 Rad  15.750
2119  Shapulin N.P.          Rus E Wor ?       ?   -18.095 ?    -2.885
2120  Shapkhaev S.G.         Rus E Tec ?     Rad  31.304 ?    21.154
2121  Sharaev L.G.           Ukr E Nom ?     Cen  -6.522 ?    -3.846
2122  Sharin L.V.            Rus E Nom ?       ?    -9.333 ?     0.385
2123  Sharipov Iu.K.         Rus E Man Med ?     -5.714 ?     0.000
2124  Sharipova F.           Uzb E Man ?       ?   -13.182 ?    -3.077
2125  Sharonov A.V.          Rus A Cad Med ?      9.412 ?    10.769
2126  Sharyi G.I.            Ukr A Man ?       ?    -9.333 ?    -9.231
2127  Shatornyi S.I.         Rus E Man ?       ?    -4.545 ?     6.731
2128  Shatrovenko Iu.N.      Ukr A Mil ?       ?    -0.952 ?     0.000
2129  Shakhanov M.           Kaz E Int LI      ?    14.737 ?    13.269
2130  Shakhnazarov G.Kh.     Mos A Nom ?       ?     0.000 ?    -2.500
2131  Shashkov N.V.          Rus E Man ?       ?    -2.609 ?     7.308
2132  Shvets A.M.            Ukr A Cad ?       ?   -15.000 ?     3.846
2133  Shevliuga V.Ia.        Rus E Wor LI      ?     1.304 ?     7.308
2134  Shevchenko A.F.        Rus A Man ?       ?   -18.261 ?   -10.800
2135  Shevchenko V.A.        Ukr E Nom ?       ?   -18.261 ?    -5.769
2136  Shevchenko V.I.        Ukr E Wor ?       ?    -2.609 ?    -5.000
2137  Shevchenko V.S.        Ukr E Nom App   App  -2.000 ?   -10.800
2138  Sheiko A.V.            Ukr E Tec ?       ?     1.905 ?     3.846
2139  Shein E.V.             Rus A Tec ?       ?    13.043 ?     7.308
2140  Shelistov N.M.         Rus E Tec ?       ?    -6.522 ?   -14.615
2141  Shelukhin Iu.S.        Rus E Tec ?     Med  -2.609 ?     3.846
2142  Shengelaia Ye.N.       Geo A Int Rad ?     10.652 ?    -2.917
2143  Shenin O.S.            Rus E Nom ?     App -11.364 ?   -13.462
2144  Sherali L.             Tad E Int ?       ?     5.000 ?     2.400
2145  Sheraliev A.           Uzb E Tec ?       ?   -15.455 ?     0.385
2146  Shergaziev M.          Uzb E Man ?       ?   -23.333 ?     5.000
2147  Shet'ko P.V.           Bel A Cad RI     LI   10.238 ?    10.192
2148  Shekhovtsov V.A.       Rus E Int ?      LI    3.636 ?    12.800
2149  Shibik N.A.            Ukr A Int ?       ?   -14.545 ?   -12.059
2150  Shinelev V.V.          Rus E Tec ?       ?     7.857 ?    10.769
2151  Shinkaruk V.I.         Ukr A Int ?       ?     1.304 ?     7.308
2152  Shinkevich I.A.        Mos A Cad ?     Med  -6.522 ?     0.385
2153  Shinkuba B.V.          Geo E Int ?       ?   -21.538 ?   -10.800
2154  Shipit'ko G.I.         Kir E Int ?       ?    26.818 ?    27.500
2155  Shirokopoias A.D.      Rus A Cad ?       ?   -10.435 ?     0.385
2156  Shirshin G.Ch.         Rus E Nom ?       ?   -16.957 ?   -16.400
2157  Shishov A.A.           Rus A Oth ?     App -10.435 ?   -10.000
2158  Shishov V.A.           Rus E Man ?     App   1.304 ?     0.000
2159  Shishov E.I.           Kaz E Man ?       ?     5.217 ?     3.846
2160  Shkanakin V.G.         Uzb E Mil ?       ?    -6.522 ?     5.962
2161  Shkol'nik L.B.         Rus E Cad ?       ?    59.000 ?    22.083
2162  Shlifer L.I.           Ukr A Man ?       ?   -11.304 ?    -6.538
2163  Shlichite Z.L.         Lit E Tec ?       ?    42.500 ?     0.000
2164  Shliakota V.V.         Lat E Man ?       ?    31.786 ?    19.423
2165  Shmal' Iu.Ia.          Rus E Man ?       ?     0.000 ?     5.577
2166  Shmelev N.P.           Mos A Int Rad ?      3.000 LI    0.000
2167  Shmonina T.N.          Rus A Tec ?       ?     7.609 ?    -5.000
2168  Shmot'ev V.I.          Rus E Wor ?       ?    34.091 ?    19.167
2169  Shniukas D.Iu.         Lit A Int ?       ?    43.333 ?     0.000
2170  Shopanaev K.A.         Kaz E Wor ?       ?    -2.609 ?    16.600
2171  Shorokhov V.N.         Rus A Man ?     App  -6.522 ?    -3.600
2172  Shoiubov Z.G.          Aze E Tec ?       ?   -32.500 ?     0.000
2173  Shtepo V.I.            Rus A Man ?       ?   -10.000 ?     2.609
2174  Shtoik G.G.            Kaz A Man ?     Med  -7.391 ?     3.077
2175  Shubin V.A.            Rus A Wor ?       ?   -15.000 ?   -13.462
2176  Shubin B.I.            Rus A Oth ?       ?    -6.522 ?     7.308
2177  Shuvalov S.G.          Mos A Oth ?       ?   -18.261 ?   -12.692
2178  Shushin A.S.           Rus A Wor ?       ?    -1.364 ?     3.846
2179  Shul'gin I.I.          Rus A Mil ?       ?    -3.478 ?    11.538
2180  Shul'deshova V.A.      Rus A Wor ?       ?     6.522 ?    21.154
2181  Shuliak V.K.           Ukr E Man ?       ?    10.000 ?     3.846
2182  Shundeev I.N.          Rus E Man ?       ?    17.500 ?    19.400
2183  Shust A.A.             Ukr A Man ?       ?   -19.524 ?    -5.769
2184  Shustko L.S.           Rus E Mil ?       ?    -6.522 ?   -29.231
2185  Shushkevich S.S.       Bel E Int LI      ?     7.609 Rad  14.808
2186  Shchapov Iu.S.         Rus E Man ?       ?    -1.500 ?    10.769
2187  Shchedrin R.K.         Mos A Int Med Med  40.000 ?     0.000
2188  Shchekochikhin Iu.P.   Ukr E Int .       ?    37.250 ?    12.917
2189  Shchelkanov A.A.       Rus E Wor LI     Rad  30.652 Rad  28.800
```

| | | | | | | | | | |
|---|---|---|---|---|---|---|---|---|---|
| 2190 | Shchelkonogov A.A. | Rus | E | Man | ? | ? | 1.304 | RI | 14.231 |
| 2191 | Shchepanovskii A.M. | Ukr | A | Man | ? | ? | -9.545 | ? | -15.962 |
| 2192 | Shcherbak Iu.N. | Ukr | E | Int | ? | Rad | 10.455 | ? | 24.800 |
| 2193 | Shcherbakov V.P. | Mos | A | Cad | App | ? | -12.500 | ? | -6.400 |
| 2194 | Shcherbina M.E. | Bel | A | Wor | ? | ? | -6.522 | ? | 3.913 |
| 2195 | Shcherbitskii V.V. | Ukr | E | Nom | ? | ? | 0.000 | . | . |
| 2196 | Yegnatashvili K.G. | Geo | E | Wor | ? | ? | 0.000 | ? | 0.000 |
| 2197 | Yezizov A. | Tur | E | Wor | ? | ? | -18.261 | ? | 0.385 |
| 2198 | Yeizan A.V. | Lat | E | Tec | Med | ? | 34.286 | ? | 15.600 |
| 2199 | Yemiridze G.Kh. | Geo | E | Nom | ? | ? | 2.500 | ? | 4.545 |
| 2200 | Yengver N.N. | Rus | E | Int | ? | Rad | 5.000 | RI | -1.731 |
| 2201 | Yergashev B.M. | Uzb | A | Man | ? | ? | -12.273 | ? | 10.385 |
| 2202 | Yergeshov A.Ye. | Kir | E | Wor | ? | ? | -18.261 | ? | -5.000 |
| 2203 | Yesambaev M.A. | Rus | E | Int | ? | ? | -40.000 | ? | 0.385 |
| 2204 | Yesirgapov A.D. | Uzb | E | Wor | ? | ? | -11.364 | ? | -3.077 |
| 2205 | Yeshpai A.Ia. | Mos | A | Int | Med | ? | 13.000 | ? | 3.214 |
| 2206 | Iudin V.D. | Rus | E | Tec | LI | LI | 13.043 | ? | 0.962 |
| 2207 | Iudov A.E. | Rus | E | Tec | ? | ? | 23.261 | ? | 21.154 |
| 2208 | Iuzeliunas Iu.A. | Lit | E | Int | ? | ? | 34.667 | ? | 0.000 |
| 2209 | Iuldashev Sh.M. | Uzb | E | Nom | ? | ? | -18.235 | ? | 0.000 |
| 2210 | Iulin B.E. | Rus | A | Man | ? | ? | 1.818 | ? | 5.600 |
| 2211 | Iuniaev P.A. | Rus | E | Man | ? | ? | 7.500 | ? | 11.538 |
| 2212 | Iusupov A.K. | Kir | E | Wor | ? | ? | -12.857 | ? | 3.654 |
| 2213 | Iusupov M.Iu. | Rus | E | Nom | ? | ? | -11.364 | ? | -13.462 |
| 2214 | Iusupov Ye.Iu. | Uzb | A | Int | App | ? | -21.333 | App | -3.077 |
| 2215 | Iablokov A.V. | Mos | A | Int | Rad | Rad | 30.294 | ? | 23.269 |
| 2216 | Iablonko N.V. | Rus | E | Man | ? | LI | 0.217 | ? | 4.800 |
| 2217 | Iavorivskii V.A. | Ukr | E | Int | Rad | ? | 17.391 | Rad | 27.083 |
| 2218 | Iagmyrov G. | Tur | E | Wor | ? | ? | -6.522 | ? | -6.000 |
| 2219 | Iagnyshev V.M. | Rus | E | Cad | ? | ? | -2.609 | ? | -2.308 |
| 2220 | Iadgarov D.S. | Uzb | E | Nom | ? | ? | -10.435 | ? | -10.800 |
| 2221 | Iazdurdieva R. | Uzb | A | Wor | ? | ? | -13.636 | ? | -6.538 |
| 2222 | Iakimenko A.N. | Ukr | E | Man | ? | ? | 1.304 | ? | 4.583 |
| 2223 | Iakovlev A.N. | Mos | A | Nom | ? | Med | -5.000 | Med | -3.077 |
| 2224 | Iakovlev A.M. | Mos | A | Int | Med | Cen | -10.000 | Cen | 1.200 |
| 2225 | Iakovlev Al'b. M. | Mos | A | Cad | ? | Med | -13.529 | Med | -13.462 |
| 2226 | Iakovlev E.V. | Mos | A | Int | LI | ? | 10.000 | ? | 21.429 |
| 2227 | Iakovlev M.M. | Rus | E | Tec | ? | ? | -5.455 | ? | 15.789 |
| 2228 | Iakubov A. | Uzb | A | Int | Med | ? | -6.500 | ? | -0.962 |
| 2229 | Iakubov Iu.R. | Uzb | E | Man | ? | ? | -14.348 | ? | -2.400 |
| 2230 | Iakutis V.S. | Rus | E | Wor | ? | ? | -8.000 | ? | -10.000 |
| 2231 | Iakushin I.N. | Rus | E | Man | ? | ? | 10.000 | ? | 3.846 |
| 2232 | Iakushkin V.V. | Bel | E | Tec | RI | ? | 7.045 | ? | 13.077 |
| 2233 | Ialakas P.M. | Est | E | Cad | ? | ? | 36.875 | ? | -6.250 |
| 2234 | Ianaev G.I. | Mos | A | Nom | App | App | -18.571 | App | -16.923 |
| 2235 | Ianeks Iu.A. | Lat | E | Cad | ? | ? | 54.000 | ? | 0.000 |
| 2236 | Ianenko A.P. | Rus | E | Int | Med | Med | 6.087 | Med | 0.000 |
| 2237 | Ianshin A.L. | Mos | A | Int | ? | Med | 6.000 | ? | 0.000 |
| 2238 | Iarin V.A. | Rus | E | Wor | RI | RI | 3.636 | RI | 5.577 |
| 2239 | Iarovaia O.L. | Rus | E | Wor | ? | ? | -10.435 | ? | 0.385 |
| 2240 | Iarovoi V.I. | Est | E | Man | RI | RI | -3.684 | RI | -21.429 |
| 2241 | Iaroshenko V.N. | Mos | E | Man | ? | ? | 27.895 | ? | 28.077 |
| 2242 | Iastrebov A.Z. | Rus | E | Man | Rad | ? | 26.136 | ? | 20.208 |
| 2243 | Iastrebtsov S.V. | Ukr | E | Mil | ? | ? | -6.154 | ? | -3.077 |
| 2244 | Iashin S.A. | Rus | E | Wor | ? | ? | 0.435 | ? | 8.077 |

# INDEX

UNIVERSITY PRESS OF NEW ENGLAND publishes books under its own imprint and is the publisher for Brandeis University Press, Brown University Press, University of Connecticut, Dartmouth College, Middlebury College Press, University of New Hampshire, University of Rhode Island, Tufts University, University of Vermont, and Wesleyan University Press.

GIULIETTO CHIESA is the Moscow correspondent for the Italian newspaper *la Stampa*. The author of several books on the Soviet Union, his *Time of Change* (coauthored with Roy Medvedev) appeared in 1990. The winner of the 1988 Milan Prize, awarded annually to the best Italian foreign correspondent, he spent the academic year 1989–1990 as a Fellow of the Woodrow Wilson Center in Washington, D.C.

DOUGLAS TAYLOR NORTHROP, a doctoral candidate in Soviet and modern European history at Stanford University, collaborated on the expanded edition of *Transition to Democracy*. A *summa cum laude* graduate and valedictorian of Williams College in Massachusetts, he spent the years 1989–1991 in England, where he earned a Starred First in history at Emmanuel College, Cambridge University.

Library of Congress Cataloging-in-Publication Data

Chiesa, Giulietto, 1940–
Transition to democracy : political change in the Soviet Union, 1987–1991 / Giulietto Chiesa with Douglas Taylor Northrop.
    p.   cm. — (The Nelson A. Rockefeller series in social science and public policy)
    Includes bibliographical references.
    ISBN 0–87451–614–5. — ISBN 0–87451–615–3 (pbk.)
1. Soviet Union. S''ezd Narodnykh Deputatov.   2. Soviet Union.
Verkhovnyĭ Sovet.    3. Soviet Union — Politics and government —
1985–1991.   I. Northrop, Douglas Taylor.   II. Title.   III. Series.
JN6554.C64   1993
947.085'4—dc20          92–56901

∞